NEW LEADERSHIP DNA

DEVELOPING ENLIGHTENED LEADERS

ISBN-13: 978-1478213031

ISBN-10: 1478213035

Cover design by Nicci Hattingh from Monarchy TV
Website: http://www.thisismonarchy.tv; email: nicci@thisismonarchy.tv
Editing by Copy-Writing: Quality Writing and Editing Services
Website: http://www.copy-writing.co.za;
email: david.barraclough@copy-writing.co.za
Graphics by Gerhard Snyman
Website: http://www.gerart.co.za; email: info@gerart.co.za

Published by:
Currency Communications. (Pty. Ltd.)
Johannesburg. South Africa.

For e-books see our websites
http://www.brendahattinghshop.co.za
Email: info@newsuccessdna.com

To order additional copies of this book, contact:
Currency Communications. (Pty. Ltd.)
Website: www.newsuccessdna.com
Email: info@newsuccessdna.com
For paperbacks see leading book stores
Or see Amazon books. www.amazon.com

NEW LEADERSHIP DNA

DEVELOPING ENLIGHTENED LEADERS

BRENDA HATTINGH   PH.D.

Published by:

Currency Communications International

Johannesburg, South Africa.

This book is dedicated to my children.
With Love. Mx

Guidance

"Two roads diverged in the woods.
I took the road less travelled
and that has made all the difference"

Robert Frost –
The road less travelled

INTRODUCTION

The large black leather wingback chair provided a safe haven as I scrambled up and found a comfortable place by nestling in the one corner. This was only one of the daunting challenges facing a six year old on her fist day at school. The major challenge was the apartheid system in a country like South Africa that in effect, affected everyone. Coming from a home with an Afrikaans father, English mother, and with a Zulu nanny called Favi, didn't work in my favour. The school principal was very reluctant to enroll me as a grade one pupil in an Afrikaans school. My father, however, convinced him to give me a chance. Not only was I small and felt very insignificant, I was also overwhelmed and very afraid. The principal, Mr Boshoff, was however very kind, and his warm smile put me at ease.

While the details of my entry into school were discussed, I glanced around the office, catching glimpses of all the trophies and medals neatly displayed in oak cabinets, and photos of all the school's best academic students, athletes and leaders hanging on the walls. Everyone looked so prestigious, accomplished and celebrated. I wondered what it would take to one day see one of my trophies displayed in the same way. Little did I know that this was the beginning, not only of my school career, but also of my journey as a leader in the making.

At a deep subconscious level I knew that in order to be accepted into this particular society, I needed to make my mark. However, at the age of six nobody knows about egos, power games and destructive programmes. All I knew was that if you do well, you get accepted; if not, you get rejected. My grandmother, Ma, kept on asking me 'Why do you work so hard to fit in, if you were born to stand out?' I didn't understand her then. Today, I know everyone has a time and place to fill.

We were all born to fit into the bigger picture and stand out as our own unique, authentic self. Little did I realise then, that leadership is all about discovering your authentic self and making your unique mark on life, while helping others to do the same. I only learnt later that authentic success and leadership have nothing to do with power, accolades, positions and possessions. Authentic leadership is all about becoming a catalyst for movement, change, transformation and transcendence. The question regarding whether leaders are born or bred was also answered. Leaders *are* born *and* bred. In essence we are all leaders as we all have the unique potential and an ability to influence others while making our mark on the fabric of society. I now know that leadership development and training are all about learning to make your mark as your authentic self, and helping others to do the same.

The challenges over the weeks and months in grade one grew more daunting, as children beat me up, and bullied and teased me about being an English 'redneck' and about me having a Zulu nanny. Although I remained still and endured it all, anger started rising from within. The silent scream of 'I'll show you!' became my silent motto. Fortunately my wonderful grade one teacher, Ms Wolmerans, opened the doors to new self expression. She taught me to draw.

One morning, amidst all these depressing challenges, Ms Wolmerans took me to the principal's office with one of my drawings. She explained to him how gifted I was, and that he should allow me to continue at the school. He agreed. Walking back to the classroom she stopped and bent down on one knee. Looking me straight in the eyes she said: 'You will be very successful in life, my dear. Don't believe anything else'. My whole life changed at that moment.

Although I was very confused and didn't understand what was going on at home, within social structures, the church, or with regards to the political situation, I believed Ms Wolmerans with all my heart, and had all my faith in her as only a child can have. It resonated deeply within my soul, and carried me through many a dark night. To me she was an angel from heaven and had given me a gift - a deep understanding that nothing is at it seems, and that anything is possible. I experienced a deep love and peace by just being in her class and in her presence.

Unknowingly she fulfilled her purpose on Earth - she introduced me to the truth! She not only motivated me to do my best in everything - I was also inspired to move beyond traditional beliefs, values, structures, and social programming. This continues to this day. Although I have worked very hard and experienced many hardships, this truth has always been alive in my heart - driving me forward to never give in or give up. I learned to listen to my heart, set high standards, and focussed on my goals, whilst turning every stumbling block into a stepping stone. I honour the legacy of that first teacher in my life.

I now know why her influence lasted more than half a century. Ms Wolmerans was successfully living the *Theoplexus* - the place 'love' meets a confused, lost, afraid, little six year-old girl. She unknowingly placed my feet securely on the path towards authentic success. On that special day she ignited a whole new awareness - a whole New Success DNA in me - by just being her authentic self: 'love in action'. Looking back, I realise that this is what true success is all about. Now we are being called and challenged to follow the example.

I have come to realise that the legacy we leave is not measured by the monetary value of our estate. A legacy is the kind of mark we place on the fabric of life. Success is the quality of the influence we have, and the stamp we leave on the hearts, minds and souls of others. Success has nothing to do with the earthly possessions or positions we have or hold - but rather relates to value, meaning and purpose. Success is not about what we are acquiring and accomplishing, but about discovering who we are and the quality of person we are becoming in the process.

During this early time in grade one, I consciously started to take control of my little life. I was focused and chose to do everything I did as best I could, at that time. I believed that this was the only way I could stay out of trouble. Working and studying diligently, taking music lessons, exercising, and playing my heart out on the sport fields, gave me a great sense of satisfaction. Anger and pain turned into a positive energy propelling me forward. However, it also had another positive spinoff. Academically I excelled and on the sports field I became a star athlete and a South African basketball player. Jeers turned to cheers. Pupils started to look up to me, teachers placed me in the foreground, while trophies started to line the shelves and photos appeared on the walls. The bullying stopped and the teasing became less. Everything went quiet. The tables were turned. I had become a leader in every respect.

School years followed one after the other, with one accomplishment after the other that included South African colors' for basketball. As captain of the basketball team, tennis team, athletic team, receiving academic awards, and becoming head girl of a large high school - placed the proverbial cherry on the cake. This continued into tertiary education. Not only did I play for the university basketball team, but I also excelled academically. A long and arduous academic career took me through various disciplines. It was as if I was constantly looking for something more. I also found that my insight and mindset differed from my peers. It was a challenge to integrate a wider perspective into the fixed mindset of the South African apartheid system. It was a question of adapt or die. I couldn't do either.

Silently, I continued my research on change, transformation and success, on my own. I knew that the system had to change and that many an old paradigm thinker would be left out in the cold. During the early 1990s I developed a holistic, integrated approach to leadership and management. By this time it was obvious that our academic leaders were not yet open to holistic thinking. I decided to present academic papers in Europe and Egypt, and received standing ovations. Back in South Africa the climate was dark and depressing, and fear reigned. Everyone was clutching to what they had. People told me I was 'crazy'. However, five companies with very enlightened leaders saw the value of a whole new leadership and training paradigm, and we started to prepare these companies for the changes that were inevitable.

By 1994 the whole political situation in the country had changed, and when the ANC under the leadership of President Nelson Mandela took over, these companies and their personnel were prepared, ready and waiting for a new season to begin. For this work they nominated me for the Professional Business Woman Year Award. This is an accomplishment that I deeply value, not because of the accolades, but because of the truth found in the saying: 'nothing is as powerful as an idea for which the time has arrived'. Miracles happen when preparation and opportunity meet. Now we are once again at the brink of the next wave of radical change and a dimensional shift. Leadership positions are bound to change as well.

We all get placed in difficult, uncomfortable and often very painful positions. These experiences make you either bitter or better. You also learn that a breakdown and a breakthrough are exactly at the same place. It is just a question of personal choice. You can go down the low road of resistance, anger, hate, resentment, self-pity, blaming, revenge and shaming. However, this all leads to self-destruction. On the other hand, you can vent your pain and anger in a constructive way, get up, get out, and move on. This is called forgiveness. Authentic leaders never come from a space or resonance of revenge, but of forgiveness[1].

I have always taken my leadership roles very seriously, as I know how difficult it is to be in such positions. Accomplishment too comes with a downside, as other less accomplished people feel threatened and become jealous and nasty. Looking back, I realise that you cannot please everyone. At the same time, we have the challenge to stay authentic and true to the self. In order to get to this level, every authentic leader will go through their 'desert' experience.

The desert experience

My desert experience took place about twelve years ago. After a motor accident in which three neck vertebrae were fractured, I knew I had to get up and get out of an old outworn mindset and comfort zone. I had to take back my authentic power, and Power Intelligence was born. I learnt that in order to take back your power, you first need to let go. This proved to be a long and arduous journey of letting go, cutting cords, re-identifying, and literally being re-born. This journey is not for the faint hearted. This is the journey of the 'dark night of the soul'.

After my accident and subsequent divorce, and with the moving and cutting of the cords of my old life and all it entailed, I started to enter into a whole new way of living. It felt as if I was a space shuttle on a mission to some faraway destination. The first step was to muster up all my courage and energy and leave the world as we know it, behind. This proved to be a challenging stage, as everyone wanted to know what was wrong and why I was retracting. It felt as if I had to defy the laws of gravity, just like a space shuttle needs to break free from the gravitational pull of Earth. This struggle to cut free was very difficult as you keep on questioning your motives and even your sanity. Slowly the external physical world ceased to have any power over me - I saw it from a new perspective as an illusion, and it ceased to exist for me. I was on a journey into the unknown.

At the same time, all unresolved issues bubbled to the surface and had to be contended with one by one. I consciously decided to assist this process and spent much time in silence, in order to understand what I needed to do. I learnt that I had to get my guidance from above, and direction from within. This led me back to my old schools and places of bullying and abuse. Here, in little personal ceremonies, I let go of all negativity and reclaimed that part of self that was fragmented and stuck in a time warp. At the same time, I visited places and people who had had a positive influence in my life, and I celebrated that uplifting influence.

I found Ms Wolmerans, at the age of close to ninety, in the frail care centre of a home for the elderly in White River. She didn't remember my name, but she remembered a little six year old who, she said, had crawled into her heart. I celebrated her legacy in my life. It took almost three years to complete this process, and many incidents still crop up to this day. They do, however, hold no power over me, and I am totally detached from my previous life and all the people in it.

The next phase proved to be still more daunting. Not only did I need to let go of everyone in my life, but I also moved and left all my physical possessions behind. During this stage it felt as if I was spending time behind the Moon. I was on the dark side of the Moon where it is cold, devoid of any light, lonely and very, very scary. Here I needed to face all my fears and inner demons. Here you get confronted with the worst part of self, as well as all the negative, self-defeating programmes we use in order to survive. Initial attempts to get out of this phase failed. All doors had closed. I had nothing, only my authentic self. I was on a path deeper into the darkness of what felt like hell - the absence of light. The struggle to survive emotionally, mentally, physically and spiritually, was all consuming. At the same time, I had a choice to have a breakdown or a breakthrough.

I chose the breakthrough, as a breakdown was not an option. I thought of the four boys who were on this journey with me, and who were looking to me to me as an example of how to cope in difficult circumstances and for guidance and direction. I had to show them the way, and in the process I first needed to 'go the way'. Keeping them in mind, I made conscious choices to move forward and upward. By this time I was so deeply involved in this journey and the challenge to understand it all, that I started to write it all down - not only for myself, but also, hopefully, for the use of my children as well. They were with me every step of the way, as they accepted financial responsibility for my basic needs - leaving me free to do the research and to write these books. I learnt that in this 'dark night of the soul' experience, you get stripped of everything. Not only are you stripped of everything physical, consciously or unconsciously you also take the 'vow' of poverty and chastity. It takes a sincere decision to abandon the importance of money and sex and consciously harness this energy in order to take you into higher dimensions and deeper understanding. I became aware of how we mindlessly we abuse this part of our lives and our life force and how powerful you can become once you learn to master the self. At the same time you begin to resonate at a higher level.

For more than seven years I have not had anything of my own. I left all financial responsibilities to the boys. Up until recently I did not buy one item of new clothing, and appreciated everything that I still had. All social contacts faded and then died away. My diet consisted of very basic foods. When there was no money for food, I saw it as a time for 'fasting and praying'. The universe provided me with everything I needed - that was just the bare minimum. In essence, this is all we truly need. I became aware how we get caught up in ego-driven wants, while the truth is that we can be happy when our basic needs are met. I learnt to appreciate everything that came my way, and became aware that 'less is more'.

My neurophysiology started to become hyper-sensitive. I could intuitively see, hear and know what the following steps should be. I met spiritual masters and other master leaders at higher dimensions - who have guided my path and have channeled most of this information. I also met René, a highly evolved Lady Master, and she has guided me diligently through every step[2]. My connection to new frequencies and higher dimensions became my whole life, and I was living on a whole new resonance while still being in my earthly body. I also learnt how fragile these physical 'containers' we inhabit on Earth, actually are.

As I became more tuned in, the downloads from the quantum universe became more frequent, and my body reacted violently to the higher energy. It was then that I realised why I was such a good athlete. The energy was never meant to be devoted to sport alone. My sport career had prepared me physically for this specific journey. If it had not happened - making me very fit for my age of sixty-two, I know that I would have physically died. My blood pressure went up to 190/120, my eyes couldn't focus, fillings in my teeth fell out of the upper jaw, and my whole body was in a constant arthritis-like pain, while the ringing in my ears was distracting. Severe headaches in my frontal lobes proved to be part of the awakening process, and as my understanding grew, this strange set of circumstances I found myself in, started to make sense. Yes, nothing is as it seems.

Only after reading through the manuscript of *New Success DNA* once again, did I come to realise that my DNA was awakening. I was genuinely on the path of enlightenment! It all suddenly came together. Enlightenment is not some fancy word to be used and abused, at will. This is what it is really like, and everyone including our new leaders will go through this process in their own time and own manner, as well.

My boys became worried and insisted on visits to specialists like ophthalmologists, physicians, ear specialists, and the like. Deep down I, however, knew there was nothing physically wrong with me. I knew, had clarity and certainty, that I was going through a rebirthing process. With this understanding I settled down and aided the process as best I could by detoxing body, mind soul and spirit. I let go of the struggle to survive, and began to enjoy the process.

I was happy and fulfilled in my new life

The most important stage was writing these books. I knew that nothing would change for me until the three books, *New Success DNA*, *Power Intelligence* and *New Leadership DNA*, were complete. The other books: *Life - Stumbling block or stepping stone* and the Afrikaans translation *Lewe - las of lus,* were written as a distraction from the very difficult academic and spiritual information in the other books. In the end another book *Power tools for Power People* was also completed before the end of 2012.

One of the most difficult challenges of the dark night of the soul, is of course being alone and the associated loneliness. It wasn't until I learnt the deep value of being alone that I grew to accept and enjoy my solitude. Looking back, it would have been so easy to escape this process by accepting the marriage proposals I received during this time as an easy-way-out option. However, I learnt that everyone deserves nothing less than the best. I couldn't give my best to any person or relationships at that time, and it would have been wrong to have taken an 'easy option'. Once you understand this principle, you also learn not to settle for the good, or even the second best. We all deserve nothing less than the best.

This 'desert experience' also included a visit to the Shamans in Peru.

The journey up the mountain

The long journey to meet the shamans in the Andes of Peru included a flight to Lima, a charter flight to Cusco, a bus ride up the mountain, and a journey further by foot. There were nine of us in this group of professional seekers, that included two medical doctors, a chemist, a herbalist, a psychologist/life coach (me), and a few others. We all wanted the answers to the same question. How did these shamans develop the power to heal the sick and master the elements? This turned out to be a path of self-discovery.

As the oxygen levels were very low, the air was thin, and breathing was laboured. The heavy backpacks we were hauling up the mountain became heavier with every step. Breathing was a mission, as most of us were not acclimatised. We had ignored the instruction to chew cocoa leaves at least a week before the time, and who would think of having Black Forest cake for breakfast? This proved to be a mistake.

Slowly we left the world behind, as we zigg-zagged up the face of the mountain - keeping to the small path. The higher we went the denser the mist became, until we couldn't see anymore. Stumbling along mechanically, whilst keeping to the path, kept us all going at a steady pace. When we stopped to rest, a few of us decided to leave some of our backpacks behind, in order to make the journey bearable. Slowly the mist began to lift, and the visibility increased the higher we climbed, until we came out into the open. We were on top of the world - looking down on creation! It was here that I learnt about the path of enlightenment and authentic leadership.

Once settled in and rested, the Shaman explained that life is like climbing up the mountain. Below in the valleys, on the lower ego planes of physicality, we have the clouded perceptions of the mindless masses and all this entails. Here we also find the ego-driven leaders of the masses who share the common clouded vision and perceptions. The challenge is, that as you choose to make your way up the mountain, you also need to let go of these lower ego attractions. You need to travel light!

At a stage you get to a cloud mass, or the veil of amnesia. The journey is not easy, as many people are not acclimatised. You have a choice to return and go back, or you can let go of the little baggage your still have left, and continue up the narrow mountain path. At one point you break through the mist and you begin to see the light! Here you 'plant your light' as a beacon, while making your mark for others to follow. This is the path of enlightenment and leadership.

In a personal session with the shaman, I asked about the role of religion. Coming from a traditional Christian background, I had been warned against new age philosophies and other religions which are going to lead you to 'hell'. However, I wanted to know for myself. He explained that all the spiritual masters, like Jesus, Buddha and others, were also souls who chose the path of enlightenment. Once they reached the top, they stayed become one with and identified with their authentic self and are 'anointed with light' or 'christed'. They are now the Christed ones.

A Master like Jesus Christ was prepared to make the journey down the mountain again, out of love, in order to mark the path back for the intoxicated masses down in the swamps of life. Religion and its teachings are just different paths up the mountain of enlightenment. The aim of all primary religions is enlightenment. This does not mean that religious leaders and/or leading academics are also enlightened, as many of them are still stuck on the lower planes of clouded perceptions, contaminated mindsets, ego-driven ways and unsound principles.

Enlightened leaders are people who have chosen to show the way up the mountain of enlightenment. Success is now about who you are becoming on the journey of life, and how far you can ascend up the mountain. The lower ego trappings of possessions and positions are left behind with the mindless masses living in despair. We, however, currently do not have the capacity to stay connected on this high level frequency for very long while still in a physical body, and we need to sometimes descend to a more comfortable level, with more 'oxygen'.

The shaman explained that down in the Amazon valleys of Peru and Mexico, there are drug dealers and cocaine producers manufacturing the poison of the soul. The higher you climb, the less susceptible we become to these trappings of the lower ego-driven existence. It is also well known that the cocoa plant has medicinal properties, and is revered as a holy plant in Peru. The only way we were able to maintain our pace up the mountain was to constantly chew cocoa leaves. The cocaine distributors and cocoa leaf distributors provide a service to the masses. The one takes you back to the morasses of life. The other takes you up the mountain of enlightenment. We also find leaders that can take us in both directions. It is our choice who we will follow.

Beating the odds

As the years passed, a solid foundation of beating the odds, standing my ground, overcoming obstacles, and doing my best, became a way of life. Although my training included a long academic career, it was the lessons from the school of 'hard-knocks' that have been the most significant. Here I found my authentic self, and learnt about the truth behind success and New Success DNA. I also found my inner guidance, and my inner GPS. New Leadership DNA was born. People wanted to know how I got to this place, and many started to follow the progress. Now many are joining in and asking for more. The books are the result of these requests.

Then, a few weeks ago, there was the sudden awakening to the fact that the journey of the dark night was over. I needed to get back onto the marketplace and bring this new information to the awakening masses. This awareness filled me with dismay and utter shock. I was so comfortable in my current situation, that to return to the open marketplace was the furthest thought in my mind. I felt that after all this hard work, it would be insane to want to return to an insane world. If people wanted access to this information, it was available on the internet and in all the leading bookstores. Why did I need to get up and get out - once again?

My idea of service was to sit silently by my computer, whilst writing my story down for others who might be interested in the journey of life and enlightenment. However, this wasn't meant to be. On this committed journey up the mountain of truth, nothing is ever as it seems. There is always something better and more rewarding and fulfilling waiting around every corner. Just when you think you have arrived - it is time to depart again. At the time you least expect it, opportunity knocks on your door. This is happening now.

While writing this introduction, so much has changed in just a few short days. Everything that initially seemed as insurmountable problems, have now been resolved. So many doors have opened in just a matter of days.

About the books

- *New Success DNA – What you should know and how to activate it*
- *New Leadership DNA – What everyone should know about leaders and leadership*
- *Power Intelligence - Mastering your Miracle Mind*
- *Life - stumbling block or stepping stone?*
- *Power tools for Power People*

These five books started off as one book many years ago. Over time, the vast body of information became too much for one book, and I have placed it into different volumes. Although there is an overlapping of fundamental scientific and spiritual information, each book covers a specific topic. The concepts *New Success DNA*, *New Leadership DNA*, and *Power Intelligence*, link and interlink with each other and the greater information network and spiritual matrix.

Some chapters are repeated in the different books as summarised versions of the main chapters. I also made a point not to read the latest research on leadership and leadership development, but allowed the book *New Leadership DNA* to evolve in its own time and in its own way. I am astounded by what has emerged from this process. I have become aware that I didn't write this book – the book wrote itself through me. I only became the silent observer. I also learnt that from the beginning of time – we all have been programmed to be leaders and make our mark. We have the authority to take dominion – it is encoded into our DNA. At the same time I learnt that it is the quality of our influence and presence that makes the difference and not necessarily our positions and possessions. All this work that includes these new concepts – is meant to help us find our way home. I believe that am only instrumental in producing this work at this stage. Nothing is or ever was of my own choice or of my own making.

The books were written, not only to gain more clarity for myself, but also to make this new information accessible to my children. Already they have started to read the books and we have lengthy discussions on various topics. At the same time I know that different people all over will be drawn to this information when the time is right. The hope is that the information contained in these books will inspire further spiritual growth, authentic self-discovery, purpose and meaning. It is therefore with deep gratitude that I share this all with you - my friends on this journey.

The books are meant to provide a new mindset for those now awakening to a new consciousness. How you choose to give meaning and value to the content and to colour it, is your personal choice. The research was done over a long period, and I am grateful to those who went before, who opened the way, and who left a legacy that we can build on. The references and bibliography at the end refer you to their original work, for further study. A short index is included in order to give easy access to some topics, while a glossary gives a short explanation of the terminology used in the text. Words have no meaning without understanding. Understanding and a comprehensive vocabulary go hand in hand. The glossary is to provide meaning and context for terms used, and this will hopefully broaden understanding. The hope is that the glossary in this book will not only bring deeper knowing, but also some colour to the reading - as it did to the writing.

Concerning the editing: We had to make a decision regarding the use of capital letters with certain words such as source/Source, spirit/Spirit; love/Love, light/Light or masters/Masters. I have total faith in David's expertise, and trust his personal and inner guidance. I therefore left the decisions to him. Typically, with a few exceptions, only proper nouns, and the names of places and people, are capitalised. Single quotes are often used to assign importance to words. Every reader, based on his/her beliefs or life path, will have different ideas about which words warrant capitalisation. In David's own words: "I have taken out reference to capital letters as it would be in conflict with my editing. It is better to be dispassionate about the importance of things - after all you are not preaching to the converted in this book".

Different topics in these books have already initiated various discussions. Many awakening individuals are now revisiting old concepts of spirituality, incarnation, reincarnation, life, death, miracles, multi-dimensions, higher beings, the soul, psychology, religion, our cosmos, and many others. My hope is that this will continue, as no work is ever complete, and we will never arrive at a point of complete understanding. I am sure that many more topics will open up as we go along.

I dedicate all these books to my children: PW, Liezl, Delarey, Nicci, Reinhardt, Andaleen, Zander and Francois, and my grandchildren Divan and Dané, and all those souls still to join our family. Not only has our biological family grown, but so has our spiritual family, with whom we share the same spiritual DNA.

Thank you to all!

Brenda Hattingh

WITH GRATITUDE

I want to convey my deepest love and gratitude to my children, and also to all who have supported me and this endeavour in many ways and over many years.

To Gerhardt Snyman, a refined and gifted artist, my deepest thanks for the graphics and lengthy discussions about our discoveries. My thanks also go to Jo-Anne Vorster for her personal interpretation of various concepts that she put into sketches. This all added a new colour the process.

To Nicci Hattingh, who never hesitates to create something new, my deepest appreciation for the cover design that speaks louder than words. We are but a shadow of who we can be! To Zander Hattingh who put the finishing touches to the cover and who also never hesitates to do what he needs to do, with his special creativity, flair and grace.

My appreciation goes to the publishers, Currency Communications (Pty.Ltd.) in Johannesburg for their professional attention given to this book and all the other books as well.

And to David Barraclough who edited all work of all the books – my deepest appreciation for your fine focus, insight and attention to detail. Your commitment to making the editing part of your personal spiritual journey has placed a personal stamp of excellence on this work – something I will always be deeply grateful for. Also my deepest gratitude goes to Mark Mattson and his contribution in securing the standard of editing as part of the 'team'.

The path of preparing this manuscript presented many personal and technological challenges along the way. In the end it all took commitment, perseverance and a conscious standard of excellence of everyone involved, to get it this level. In the process none of us were left untouched and unchanged. I believe it all formed part of our spiritual progress and initiation – and we also became friends.

You all walked the extra mile and I know you will all be equally blessed.

To everyone, known and unknown, who have made different contributions in different conscious and unconscious ways - you have had a defining influence on the quality on this work and on the path of my life – my humble gratitude and appreciation.

My deepest gratitude goes to all the teachers, mentors, guiding forces and Masters who invested in me, my life and my personal success process. I am forever humbled by the constant teaching, guidance, support, protection and unconditional love.

At the same time, I am deeply grateful for the knowing and understanding that life is part of a divine appointment, and it inspires me to continue ...

Thank you, from my heart – to your hearts ...

Brenda Hattingh

October 2012
Pretoria
South Africa

oooOooo

CONTENTS

CHAPTER 1

HISTORY OF LEADERS AND LEADERSHIP

Introduction

Leadership is about influencing the direction of movement and change, whilst affecting the quality of the lives of others. We all have a conscious or unconscious power to directly or indirectly affect other people's lives. This means that everyone, at some or other stage, takes on an influential or leadership role, and makes an impact or gives direction. The only things that differ are the levels of influence and the quality and quantity of impact that we have. Different levels of influence and leadership[3] are determined by different levels of consciousness and awareness. In essence, we all have influence - we are all leaders!

Levels of awareness differ between different people, communities, companies, organisations, political parties, religious groups, communities, and even countries. People support the pace-setters, way-showers or leaders who resonate with their personal level of consciousness and understanding. When we start to awake, we become mindful, our awareness expands, and the quality of our influence changes. As we access new levels of awareness, we consciously and unconsciously resonate at a higher level or frequency. This means our direction, movement and our choice of leaders and leadership styles, will necessarily also change.

An authentic leader is a positive 'change agent'. Everyone could therefore be a 'leader' at some or other level. The film *Pay it forward* with Haley Joel Osment in the lead role, is a clear and heartwarming confirmation of this powerful force that changes lives. The powerful message of this story of a young boy and the power of compassion and of 'paying it forward', has had widespread impact. It is the direct opposite of the destructive force of revenge and 'paying it back'. In leadership training circles especially, these two major approaches to life, leadership and living, have become prevalent.

Our personal influence only differs according to the time, place, people, methods and purpose of interaction with others. For most of our history, the masses have accepted leadership and guidance from designated leaders and 'important others'. They gave their power of responsible decision-making over to the leaders of the time. This placed the power to change and create quality living in the hands of a select few.

While many leaders have consciously accepted this positive responsibility on behalf of the masses, others have abused this power and served only themselves and their select few. These 'select few' have become very powerful and rich. However, a rising of human consciousness is currently taking place, as an expansion of human awareness and personal responsibility. The definitions of life, quality living and success are changing at an escalating pace. People are coming to realize that a New Success DNA is emerging[4]. As the concepts of 'success' and 'leadership' have always been closely interrelated, it means that a New Leadership DNA is emerging as well.

In order to safely undertake this transition into a whole new paradigm or mindset, we will all need to grow in our understanding of the fundamentals of authentic leaders and leadership. We are becoming mindful of the importance of our own influence and personal role in selecting and supporting the right leaders. These are the people who will secure our safe transition into the next level of success, prosperity and quality living.

Leadership is not for the selected few any more. We all have an important role to play in this important process of change, transformation and transition.

This is what this book is all about.

In order to grow in our understanding of leadership, the role of leaders, and our personal role as well, we can take some leadership lessons from history.

Background

Different authors have discussed different aspects of the history and evolution of leadership.[5] Helen Eckman says that "Ever since more than two people have been on the planet there have been discussions about leadership"[6]. Many state that the study of leadership can be dated back to Plato, Sun Tzu and Machiavelli. However, throughout history we find leadership training in different forms. In Greek mythology, Odysseus[7] placed his friend Mentor[8] in charge of his son Telemachus, when he, Odysseus, left for the Trojan War. Mentor guarded over, whilst teaching and advising Telemachus, in the ways and wisdoms of the world. Currently leadership training in the form of 'mentoring and coaching' has in fact become one of the fastest growing professions[9].

Sun Tzu and his well-known book *The art of war*[10], has provided many a leadership and management enthusiast with valuable guidance and information in our current-day situation. However, this line of thought is mostly prevalent to the warrior nature - especially to the male psyche. This reflects the subconscious acceptance that leadership was mainly for men although Sun Tzu included women .

Today the concept of 'leadership' has taken on a broader approach, and has become one of the fastest growing fields of contemporary academic studies over the last 60 years[11]. The awareness of the important role we all play in identifying, choosing and developing leaders has grown, and a personal consciousness has particularly escalated over the last two decades. People are starting to think independently for themselves.

However, the nature and place of formal leadership training within the academic world was initially met with confusion. This was because leadership spans many disciplines that include the social sciences, politics, financial and business contexts, religion, psychology, philosophy, business administration, and others. Today, at all levels, undergraduate through doctoral, an increasing number of colleges and universities have begun developing not only individual courses, but also entire degree programmes specifically devoted to the study of leadership[12].

During this time, different authors have provided different views[13] and leadership theories. These theories include The Great Man Theory, Trait Theory, Group Theory, Situational Theory, Behaviour Theory, Contingency Theory, Excellence Theory, and many more. This body of work, also provides different definitions of leaders and leadership, that include: "The process of social influence in which one person can enlist the aid and support of others in the accomplishment of a common task"[14]. Hollander & Julian suggested the definition "The presence of a particular influence relationship between two or more persons"[15]. Over recent decades, many other definitions of leadership and leadership theories have also emerged[16].

After all these contributions, the important question is:

> *What makes this book on leadership, different to any other book on leadership?*

This book has a specific point of view that has not yet adequately been covered. This includes:

- Asking the question: By what/whose authority are leaders chosen, trained or developed?
- Reviewing the connection between leadership, success, the quality of influence, personal power and DNA.
- Understanding how and where leaders find *their* guidance.
- Identifying the role of DNA and life activation played in the training of leaders in the past
- Outlining the role that DNA healing, activation and utilisation will play in new leader identification and the development of new leadership training programmes in the future.

We first question we need to ask:

> *How do leaders receive their authority to take the lead and to rule?*

Leadership and authority

Leaders are invested with power to make decisions that influence the lives of others. They receive this power of authority in different ways. According to Max Weber's[17] classification of authority, we find *traditional authority, charismatic authority and rational-legal authority.* Weber noted that in history these types of authority and/or domination are always found in combinations. However, domination always has to do with 'power over people'. With our current expansion of consciousness, many people are awakening and reclaiming their personal power. They will therefore no longer condone domination and dictatorship in any form. Leadership is now moving away from 'power over people' - to 'releasing power within people'. It has therefore become important to understand the true meaning of 'authority', the essence of authentic leadership, and the original source of authority, first.

The word 'authority' comes from Latin '*auctor*' meaning, 'author', that refers to someone who can write - write a law, script, or set guidelines. In short, it refers to a 'pathfinder' or 'mapmaker'. An authentic leader is a person with the *ability to create, grow, increase,* and someone *who obtains divine favour* - someone with the *ability to shine.* This refers to a person or group invested with authority and the power and right to write and enforce rules, or give orders. Authentic leaders are people who have influence and make their mark on the fabric of life. As we all have this ability, we all have a leadership role to play.

We find individuals or groups with official or unofficial authority[18] that includes:

- **Traditional authority**

In *traditional authority*, the legitimacy of the authority comes from cultural, religious or political traditions. Here we find traditional leaders, healers, priests, shamans as 'tribalists', who are committed to the protection, growth and development of their specific traditions, teachings and the norms and values of their 'tribe'.

- **Charismatic authority**

Charismatic authority derives from the personality and leadership qualities of the individual. This is someone who can influence others - by their mere presence and charisma.

- **Rational-legal authority**

With *rational-legal authority*, we find that a person is invested with power that is bureaucratically and legally attached to their position[19]. However, there is a higher, more powerful source of authority that Weber did not consider – namely universal or divine authority - an inner 'calling'.

- **Universal authority**

This is a level, a person, or group, receiving a higher 'calling'[20]. Today we find a new quality of leader, with a New Leadership DNA coming forward to take over the lead from those with outworn mindsets, values and direction. These are individuals and groups who have heard the 'calling' to secure the quantum leap to the next phase of human existence and quality living. This calling is not only meant for a select few - it is a calling meant for all of us. We are now moving beyond tribal, charismatic or political-legal authority. A new era of *'higher calling leadership'* is emerging. It is encoded into our DNA.

A leader like President Nelson Mandela, reflects all of these kinds of authority. First, he operated as a 'tribalist' securing the values, wants and needs of his culture, and his political party, the ANC. Once he was released from prison, he implemented a broader view that included the welfare of everyone. His authority as President of South Africa was from a bureaucratic-legal position, while his charismatic personality earned him worldwide acclaim.

However, deep down, most people revere him for his wisdom and leadership that could only have been given him by universal, divine authority. President Nelson Mandela has honoured his higher calling, and has set the bar very high for other leaders, especially in Africa, to follow.

In our quest to come to a deeper understanding of authentic leadership and the emerging New Leadership DNA, we necessarily need to revisit our initial leaders, and ask:

> *Under whose authority were the first leaders appointed? How were the first leaders identified, developed and placed in their leadership positions? What was the initial purpose of leaders and their leadership positions?*

In order to find answers to these questions, we need to go back to the creation of human kind.

Humankind and their leaders

There are various interpretations of the creation of *Homo sapiens*[21], 'humans' or Adam[22] - deriving from different viewpoints. According to various records - 'gods of the time' were the only inhabitants of Earth. It is stated that some of the 'gods' came down from heaven[23] and had children with the humans - giving rise to 'demi-gods', semi-gods, or half-human/half-god. Human beings were in service of their gods, fulfilling their goals, visions, and aspirations. The gods and demi-gods of the multitheistic religions of the time however, brought little comfort to their people. They were constantly in conflict with each other and warred with other gods in order to secure and maintain their supremacy[24].

Sumerian depictions engraved on stone cylinders[25], show hominids[26] standing on two feet, mingling with animals. In some circles, they are known as *Homo erectus*. Then 'suddenly', measured in the evolutionary time it takes for species to evolve, the first known and fully documented *Homo sapiens* civilisation sprang up in the land of Sumer – the biblical Shine'ar[27]. It 'suddenly' appeared all at once, some six thousand years ago, and gave Humankind almost every component that is today part of 'higher civilisation'[28].

In Sumer, in the Near East or Mesopotamia, we find just about the 'firsts' of everything - the first wheel, kilns[29], medicine, pharmacists, musicians, dancers, artisans, craftsmen, merchants, brick-makers, law codes, judges, weights and measures, mathematicians, astrologers and observatories. Not only were their written language, scrolls, art and treasures uncovered, their high-rise temples and palaces contained libraries with priceless information concerning their modern civilisation, religion, social structures, the people and their gods. At the pinnacle of this blossoming civilisation, we find kings and priests - the leaders of the time.

From these ancient texts, we learn that the gods were in total control. Who these gods were and where they came from, differed from group to group, and region to region. During this time, a 'bloodline' was of cardinal importance in the hierarchy of leaders and leadership. Over centuries, volumes have been written about leadership, bloodlines and DNA, and various contributions are still being made today[30].

Initial authority was granted by the gods/God to certain individuals, priests, shamans or spiritual leaders, who were authorised to represent the gods/God with the people. They had the ability to communicate directly with the gods or God. Their purpose was to function as intercessors between the gods, who presided at higher realms, and the people at a lower physical reality. There were different priests for different gods in the multitheistic religions. Although much is known about the empires of Babylon and Assyria from archaeological excavations, it was found that at a certain time, people started asking for one single god Yahweh. Monotheism was born. This occurred in the time of Enoch[31].

There is a biblical assertion that Kingship began with "a mighty hunter by the grace of Yahweh," named Nimrod[32]. The initial speculation of royal capitals and advanced civilisation have now been put to rest with the finding of these 'mythical' cities and the excavation of monuments, sculptures, artwork and treasures, depicting these kings and their royal capitals.

From everything that has up and till now been excavated from these ancient sites, it is evident that these royal capitals were authentic. These cultures really existed and what was once seen as just myth, has now become part of our human history. Many of these artifacts and treasures can now be seen in major museums around the world.

Different 'gods' - different leaders

This short history gave rise to two different levels of collective human consciousness. On the one hand, we find a multitheistic approach of various gods, their appointed representatives, leaders and supporters. On the other hand, we find a monotheistic view of a single God, Yahweh, and his hand-picked and appointed representatives, leaders and supporters. From history, we find that these two groups were opposing forces, and usually in conflict.

Many authors have researched the multitheistic view and documented different deities that range from the ancient Greek Gods, the pharaohs of Egypt, deities in Africa, India, Native Americans of Northern America, the Far East or Southern Americas. There are even speculations about intergalactic visitors from the planet Nibiru[33]. According to these writings, the deities ruled over Earth and all the humans on it. People were subservient to their specific god, presiding over their specific land.

Within the multitheistic view, leaders were chosen according to their commitment to their god, and their securing the demi-god bloodline. These individuals were crowned as kings on the premises that they were of a semi-god bloodline. Here physical genetic hereditary played an important role. Many marriages between humans and gods/demi-gods were arranged, while battles and wars were fought in order to maintain the 'royal bloodline' and secure leadership positions. This history is depicted in hieroglyphs of the pharaohs, as found in the National Museum in Cairo, Egypt, and other museums in Europe.

From a monotheistic view, there is only God, Yahweh - one God, the Creator, Central Sun, Source of all life that spans various dimensions of life and existence[34]. Here reality is defined as multidimensional - as physical, etheric and spiritual realities. The hereditary factor includes a spiritual DNA factor that scientists now have termed the God Gene[35]. This latest finding, that spirituality is encoded into our DNA, has opened a whole new approach to the social sciences, psychology, education, theology, business science and leadership development.

Diverse versions relating to the creation of the first humans, and the alternation between a plural *Elohim* (deities) and a single *Yahweh,* initially caused widespread confusion. However, various archaeological discoveries have increasingly validated the biblical record, and data concerning the tales of Creation, the Deluge and Noah's ark, the Patriarchs and the Exodus. Much of the disbelief and skepticism has now been muted and countered. In an ever-receding order - from the near past to the earlier times, farther and farther back through historical times, to prehistoric times - significant evidence has been uncovered. Texts written on clay tablets or papyrus, and inscriptions carved on stone walls or monuments, have resurrected the kingdoms, kings, events and cities documented in the Bible[36]. To many, what once was history and just hearsay has now become reality.

Divine encounters are the ultimate of human experience, perhaps because they were also the very first human experience. For when God created man, man met God at the very moment of being created[37]. In the 'Garden of Eden', as we know today, refers to the higher level of consciousness and spiritual awareness. God spoke directly to the first human beings, instructing them regarding their nourishment. It is accepted that Adam[38] could communicate with his Creator face-to-face, and that people could directly receive messages and guidance.

With the analogy of the 'Fall of Adam and Eve', humanity became disconnected, lived on a lower level of consciousness, and the direct communication became forgotten. Only a select few still maintained this connection, and an open spiritual communication channel to higher dimensions.

This description of the 'fall from grace' of human kind can be understood from different viewpoints. The main thread of the message, however, is when we are connected to the higher spiritual dimension, the one, the creator, or whatever your term for a higher power or deity may be - the higher the level of conscious is, the more access we have to direct communication and information from the universal matrix or God. Here our multidimensional DNA plays an important role.

This means that by getting reconnected while healing and activating our initial spiritual DNA, we can access higher levels of guidance and prosperity.

When people are disconnected, they resonate at a lower level and access lower levels of information. The lower the awareness, the more physical, earthbound people then become. Scientists previously defined these 'disconnections' as 'junk genes' in our DNA. Today scientists, such as Nowak, are causing a stir while making us aware of the many treasures just waiting to be mined from our 'junk genes'[39].

During these ancient multitheistic times, leaders had to provide proof of their 'bloodline'. Every possible method was used to secure the position of certain leaders. Treachery, murder, corruption and violating the laws were just a few methods used. Various pharaohs of Egypt, proclaimed themselves as 'gods' in order to secure their power positions. A hierarchy of command was employed, although the pharaoh was the foremost servant of the gods, and he never completely surrendered his sacerdotal role to the priests appointed to be his every day substitutes. While the pharaoh wielded great power over his people, it was not absolute, although in theory there could be no rightful opposition.

Kings on the other hand, always acted in political contexts, wooed power groups for their support, and tried to neutralise the influence of their opponents. Most people could be bought with gifts of power or possessions, and pharaohs lavished favours on the social groups, which could help them achieve their political aims: the military high command, the priesthood and the scribal elite[40].

During monotheistic times, leaders were called upon and appointed by God, Yahweh. They were anointed in their position as representatives and messengers from God on Earth. The persons chosen for these positions were evolved people and souls who would fulfill their spiritual calling and commission, to ensure prosperity for their people on Earth – as in heaven.

The appointment of leaders while receiving their guidance from the gods or God, has always been interconnected and inseparable. The purpose of leaders and leadership positions, has therefore always been a means to an end - fulfilling the will of the gods/God or higher mind/universal mind, for the people on Earth. Leaders were appointed to be of service to their god or God, and the people. Leadership positions and the accompanying power, were always meant to be a means to an end, and never a self-serving end in itself. Some of the historic leaders, who embraced their leadership role in this manner, were Pharaoh Akhenaten and King Solomon.

Akhenaten and King Solomon

The reign of Pharaoh Akhenaten with Queen Nefertiti and their son Tutankhamen was fraught with immense difficulties[41]. This couple caused a dramatic political upheaval when they stripped the manipulative priesthood of their authority, introduced a monotheistic religion and concentrated the idea of Divinity on a force emanating from the universal Light or Sun, rather than on individual god-beings.

The people were taught the truth about their spiritual connection to the One – the Godhead. From the modern world, especially from a Western and Middle-Eastern perspective, it is looked to Ancient Egypt as the beginning, because it was against the backdrop of this political climate that our current world religions developed. As such, it is because the ancient Osirian teachings were spread in an organised manner that they these teachings may be regarded as the first 'religion' on Earth. It was these already ancient teachings, all subsequent religions were based on. This ancient spiritual information teaches the Divine Truth of the Universe as constant loving and available to all. Here Spiritual Truth is defined as the expression of Divine Intelligence on Earth.

By returning to these original teachings, Akhenaten affected widespread, massive change in Egypt in a very short period of time. For a while corruption was curbed and Light was returned to Earth once more. However, the changes it brought were not always popular. The manner, in which the temples of this couple were defiled, defaced and destroyed after their reign; reflect the war between the Light and the dark. Although the end of the Egyptian Era came in 30BC, the struggle between these opposing forces of truth and corruption, light and dark, continue still to this day.

In Hebrew history, Solomon became the king of Israel because God had told David, that Saul's heirs would not follow him to the throne[42]. Thus, Solomon became king, although there was no clear precedent for his succession. Solomon's rise met with widespread

38

approval from the people, although David's officials were slow to accept the new king.

According to the chronology[43], Solomon was about 20 years old when he was crowned. He assumed leadership of Israel at a time of great material and spiritual prosperity. During his 40-year reign from 970 to 930 B.C., he expanded his kingdom until it covered about 50,000 square miles. After being crowned as king, Solomon immediately brought sacrifices to Yahweh, who appeared to the new king and asked him, "What shall I give thee?" Solomon asked for an understanding heart, in order to judge the people of Israel and the ability to tell good from evil. Yahweh not only granted Solomon's request, but he also promised him riches and honour if he would walk in the steps of his father, David[44].

Solomon's 40-year reign as king of the Hebrew people is a puzzle[45]. In his early years, he was both noble and humble - undoubtedly one of the best rulers of his day. Although he was surrounded by wealth and luxury as a young man, he seemed to be a person of honour and integrity. He was the first king in Israel who was the son of a king. The glory of his empire was a reflection of his own royal tastes, which he satisfied through a shrewd and successful foreign policy.

Unfortunately, Solomon was not strong enough to withstand the temptations that go with a long life of power and luxury. His contribution to the nation of Israel is figured largely in material terms. He made Jerusalem one of the most beautiful cities of the ancient world, and he will always be remembered as a great builder.

The tragedy is that after the building of the temple, Solomon did very little to promote the spiritual and religious life of his people. At the same time, his over-indulgence in women, money, luxury and the power it brings, caused him to divert from his initial path. Not only did this cause the disintegration of his empire, the Temple of Solomon was put to ruin as well[46]. The questions that now arise are:

> *What methods did Solomon use to train his leaders?*
> *How appropriate are these training methods for the*
> *leadership challenges we are facing today? What*
> *should we learn from his downfall?*

The first leadership training

Solomon organised Israel much as David had done, but he enlarged and expanded his government. He divided the country into 12 districts, each of which was responsible for providing the court with regular supplies, and with a supply officer in charge of each district. Over time, Solomon's court reached a standard of luxury that had never existed in Israel's history.

During this time, Solomon's fame as a man of deep wisdom and sound leadership principles, spread to surrounding and even warring lands. It is documented that leaders came from afar to hear Solomon speak, while the Queen of Sheba came to test his wisdom. During these speeches, King Solomon answered all questions with ease. The Queen of Sheba later confessed that she had underestimated him when she saw the extent of his empire and the vastness of his knowledge[47].

Although King Solomon's 'training' of the leaders of foreign countries was widely known, very little was documented about his 'in-house' selection, choice and training of appointed leaders and his representatives in influential positions. The reason can be found in the secrecy of his 'methods'. Although Solomon did not hesitate to impart his deep universal wisdoms to his neighbours and even his enemies, the methods, skills and tools were kept secret. In scientific terms today, we would say that he was open to share universal wisdoms or the 'theory'. The practical implementation, skills and tools and other important information, were only imparted to those who had undergone initiations in the 'mystery schools'[48].

The questions are:

> *What are 'mystery schools'? What have these*
> *schools got to do with leadership training?*

Mystery Schools

It is in our nature to constantly be on a quest to discover more about the deeper workings of the self, reality and spirituality. Initially it was the mystery schools[49] found in Egypt, Israel, the Middle and Far East, that held this knowledge. We find the same concept in the ancient cultures of Southern and Northern America. These schools had the function to protect closely-held spiritual wisdoms and teachings that have been preserved for the benefit of all of humanity. Many of these traditions are also found in ancient cultures that include the Incas of Peru, Mayans, African Americans and cultures of Africa. This information is passed down from teacher to student through the oral tradition and in an unbroken lineage of physical initiation.

Mystery schools exist because of a spiritual approach to life itself that produces so many mysteries. This includes the cycle of life and death, love, birth, who and what is God, as well as the workings of the universe. At this level, all mystery schools have the same fundamental spiritual information. However, the interpretation and application thereof could differ only according to one of two priorities. On the one hand, we find the use of these powers to the benefit of all while ensuring the quality of life. On the other hand, these wisdoms can be abused when applied for the benefit of the ego and the selected ego-driven individuals and/or groups. The conflict between these two perspectives of power can be found in the visit of Moses to pharoah, and the transforming of the staff into a snake[50].

Teachings at the mystery schools include various, now known, topics like the axiom 'As above - so below'. The mystery school teachings believe that everything which exists in the physical must first be created in the spirit, and everything physical has its counterpart in the etheric, quantum and spiritual realities. Today science has confirmed these ancient wisdoms. Throughout their tradition, the mystery schools have spoken of the Great Work[51], which is defined as *the unification of the body, mind and soul with the Spirit*. This unification is the ultimate transformation of the self into one's highest potential being or 'higher self' - an exalted state of divine awareness and consciousness. In short, mystery schools can be viewed as ancient spiritual 'universities'.

Today we have academic and scientific institutes that provide us with a deeper understanding of reality, human nature, and our place and functioning on different levels. Like our regular academic institutes, students first needed to be approved and accepted before they were permitted to enter and gain access to these teachings and wisdoms.

Here the leaders of the time were trained and prepared for their important and influential roles.

The teachings and tools handed down, lead the seeker towards the evolution and awakening of the soul, and to the reclaiming of one's spiritual self. It is also taught that this 'spiritual self' is not out there somewhere, but within our inner being and encoded into our DNA.

According to teachings in the mystery schools, if there are 12 strands of physical DNA, there are also 12 corresponding strands of spiritual DNA. Any activation of life, therefore, must include the physical, as well as our multidimensional or spiritual DNA. These wisdoms have now become part of our traditional scientific and academic world, and various research projects already focus on the connection between spirituality and our DNA[52].

One of the deepest mysteries is the mystery of the self or 'higher self'; therefore, the ancient decree of 'know thyself'[53]. The schools' deeper teachings help us answer questions such as: Who am I? What am I? Where do I come from? Where am I going and why? What is my purpose? The teachings of the mystery schools contain the innermost knowledge of life and wisdom.

There was a time when we used to live by these teachings and think and act according to certain ways of mystery. Various shamanic societies around the globe also understood and taught these wisdoms. However, this way of life was 'lost' to the masses in the Middle Ages, and as we developed into a modern culture, we became ignorant of the true understanding of these mysteries. The keepers of this knowledge and the mystery schools were forced to go underground, in order to preserve and keep these sacred and ancient teachings safe. Since then, these teachings have been referred to as the 'hidden knowledge' and until recently, the mystery schools have been a secret institution. Secret societies and organisations once again gained widespread attention through the 'cloak and dagger' novels of Dan Brown[54].

The primary duty of mystery schools was to serve the cosmic/ spiritual light and keep the ancient knowledge alive. Many forces on the planet have attempted to remove or eliminate this knowledge from the Earth. For within these teachings are the greatest secrets the world has ever known and the greatest power that has ever been available to human kind. Slowly the knowledge is becoming available to us all, once again. With the coming of the internet, all is being brought into the open, while we continue to grow in our awareness. Human consciousness is now at a level where many are able to understand and grasp these universal wisdoms. Today these teachings are becoming commonsense, and secrecy is becoming something of the past.

Although these traditions and universal teachings can be found throughout human history, the lineage of the leadership, DNA activation, and mystery schools, can be traced back more than 3,000 years - even before the time of King Solomon the Great.

DNA activation and leadership development

Today King Solomon is widely known in different religions and leadership development circles, for his wisdom and success as a king. He was not only an extra-ordinary leader, king, statesman - but also a family man, and a lover of nature and humanity. Today people still wonder what made him great: Was it because he was intelligent, hard working, had perseverance and persistence? Was it because of his religion or what he knew about his allies? Or was it something totally different - something out-of-the-ordinary, something extra-ordinary?

We need to find the answers to the following questions:

> *What made King Solomon such a great and wise leader for his time? How did he gain access to all these wisdoms?*

Current information now coming to light, has revealed that King Solomon had a special method of doing things. He knew the spiritual and etheric dimensions well, and as stated in the Bible, Solomon was connected to God. This gave the 'extra' to an ordinary soul.

From history dating back to the time of King Solomon's rule, it is now known that he had all the wisest men from all over, come together in order to present him with the best methods of having himself, priests, and his rulers in government, be taught or initiated

43

into higher spiritual wisdoms. This was so that they would and could advise and rule, to the benefit of all. The method that was presented to him was no university degree or physical strength - it was the sacred method of releasing potential by activating new life-energy or spiritual DNA. DNA healing and activation became one of the methods in which the priests from all over, including Egypt, were initiated. This was while these wisdoms were kept secret from the general population, for fear of their use being abused and misused.

These wisdoms were passed down from generation to generation - usually to priests - in the form of sacred spiritual teachings, initiations, healings and activations. These leaders knew that when the time was ripe, these wisdoms would be released to the general masses. The time would come when people attained a new level of awareness, understanding, wisdom and respect for spiritual power, wisdom and understanding. This time has now come, and over the last two decades the information has been made available on the internet.

Over the last ten years this information has been used by political, business, and financial consulting firms, as well as religious and academic institutes. On a more personal level, these wisdoms are used in personal mentoring, coaching and training of executive leaders. These are people who are spiritually evolved and are committed to ensuring the quality of life for all on Mother Earth. They are the new leaders, with New Success DNA, and New Leadership DNA - who are ready and committed to accept their role as 'change agents'. As we are becoming aware that leadership is now for all, this now includes everybody. The downside of course, is that we could run into those who are not connected or activated, and who oppose the emerging of a higher spiritual consciousness and power.

Many spiritual masters, who were prepared to go through the initiations and prove themselves worthy of these sacred wisdoms, are now accessible to the general public. From now on, the path of success will never be the same again. Success is, in essence, the journey of the higher self and soul, versus lower physical ego-self. This inevitably will impact on our leaders, our leadership styles and leadership training and development. The question is:

> *What do we need to learn from the history of leaders and leadership?*

From this short history above, we find that the most prominent contributions to leadership and leadership training can be found in the examples set by King Solomon and Sun Yzu.

Leadership styles: King Solomon and Sun Tzu

> *"It is better to have self-control than to control an army."*

King Solomon

Modern scholars accept that the completion of *The Art of War* - the ancient Chinese military treatise by Sun Tzu, a high-ranking military general, strategist and tactician – took place between 766 and 221 BC[55]. It is composed of 13 chapters, each of which is devoted to one aspect of warfare. Much of the text is about how to fight wars without actually having to do battle. It gives tips on how to outsmart one's opponent, so that physical battle is not necessary. As such, it has found application as a training guide for many competitive endeavours that do not involve actual combat. His important contributions include the thought that strategy was not planning in the sense of working through an established list, but rather that it requires quick and appropriate responses to changing conditions. It is said to be the definitive work on military strategies and tactics of its time, and is still read for its military insight and relevance to other contexts of everyday life. At the same time, it also reflects underlying spiritual wisdoms[56].

The Art of War has been applied to many fields well outside of the military. Modern followers of Sun Tzu's philosophy include many current political, financial, social and business leaders, that include General Douglas MacArthur, and leaders of Imperial Japan who have drawn inspiration from the work. *The Art of War* has also been used as a benchmark for business and managerial strategies.[57]

In comparison to Sun Tzu, we find a leader like King Solomon. Like Sun Tzu, he also recorded his philosophy and theory, and his writings have been included in the Bible[58]. After his lengthy rule as king, he started to lose the ideals of his youth, becoming restless and unsatisfied. His writings in Ecclesiastes, proclaiming that "all is vanity", support the view that the world's wisest man had become a pathetic figure in his old age.

Solomon fell victim to his own trade agreements, beautiful women, luxury, influence and the influx of paganism. His heavy taxation of the people brought unrest and rebellion, while surrounding nations began to marshal their forces to free themselves of Israel's tyranny. However, the most serious uprising came from within the nation itself. They had forgotten their covenant with Yahweh, who had warned Solomon that the divine favour and protection which had been bestowed upon Israel, would continue only if their faith remained uncorrupted by other beliefs. If idolatry should be introduced, Israel would be punished and the temple would be destroyed. [59] Solomon's greatest problem was his disconnection from the spiritual dimension, and loss of devotion to the god of the Hebrew people. Over time, Solomon found another god – Mammon[60].

Mammon is associated with unjust worldly gain and gluttony, as an obsession with and investment in the power of physical possessions, positions, wealth, power, prestige and comfort that accompany this life style. The word also means 'that in which one trusts'. Within Christian religion, it was personified as a false 'god' of the world, a dark force from the underworld.

The result was a division of Solomon's united kingdom into two separate nations - the southern kingdom of Judah and the northern kingdom of Israel. Although Solomon had great beginnings, in the end his empire was torn apart, and that resulted in two separate nations - the southern kingdom of Judah and the northern kingdom of Israel.

The challenges that our current day leaders are faced with, are not very different from the challenges our ancient leaders confronted. The only difference can be found in the complexity of our world. However, fundamentally very little has changed - the human species *Homo sapiens* is still moving forward. We are still in the process of becoming more aware and conscious of the fundamentals of life - the same life force we all share.

CHAPTER 2

LEADERSHIP, MOVEMENT AND GUIDANCE

"Trust only movement. Life happens at the level of events, not of words. Trust movement"

Alfred Adler

Movement

Movement is the pulse of life - without movement we die. When we aim to guarantee quality living, we need to guarantee the quality of our movements. We move in various ways - we can run, walk, hop, skip, jump and dance to the rhythm of life.

Albert Einstein wrote:

"Dancers are the athletes of God"

To live fulfilling lives of health, wealth and abundance, we need to find the rhythm of life, hear the beat, listen to the music, and find the cue to partake or sit out from the dance - only to hear the cue and enter again. We move physically, mentally, emotionally and spiritually in different forms and different ways, but according to an unknown author:

"Only the wise can dance the rhythm of life"
If movement secures a quality of life, the next questions come to the fore:

> *What kind of movement will secure a quality of life in the future? Where are we going? What should we know, and what should we do?*

Leadership and movement

Leadership is synonymous with movement, change and guidance. Movement, and therefore guidance and leadership, are in essence a natural part of life. We find movement, migration and leadership as a natural phenomenon within our animal and human existence. Everything is already encoded into our nature, as part of being human. All we need to do is to rediscover what we already inherently have, broaden our awareness, and connect at a higher level of consciousness. The challenge is to take back what we forgot we have. Leadership development is all about remembering who we are, and living it to the full. Where leadership is concerned, we do not need to reinvent the wheel!

The question is:

> *What can we learn about leadership from our natural ability to move, migrate, navigate and change?*

Migration, navigation and guidance in nature

Animal migration and navigation are part of recorded ancient history. Records of bird migration were made 3000 years ago by Herodotus and Aristotle, while The Bible[61] also notes migrations. Animal navigation is the ability of many animals to find their way accurately without maps or instruments, and migration is usually marked by its annual seasonality. Many animal species, such as the swallow, insects such as the monarch butterfly, and fish such as the salmon, regularly migrate thousands of miles to and from their breeding grounds, while many other species navigate effectively over shorter distances[62]. Below we find a map of the most important bird migration routes[63]

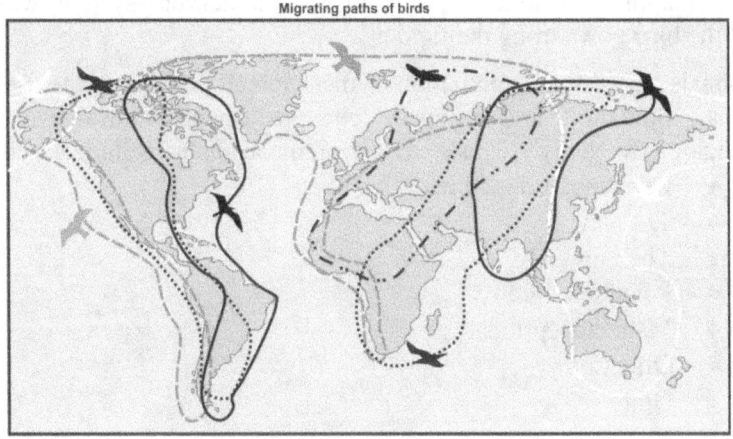

Migrating paths of birds

Global bird migration routes

The primary physiological cue for migration is changes in the light intensity or day length. These changes are also related to hormonal changes in birds. Navigation is based on a variety of senses. Many birds have been shown to use a sun compass. Navigation has also been shown to be based on a combination of other abilities, including the ability to detect magnetic fields (magnetoception), using visual landmarks as well as olfactory cues.

The ability to successfully perform long-distance migrations, can probably only be fully explained with an accounting for the cognitive ability of the birds to recognise habitats and form mental maps. It has been found that there is a strong genetic component to migration, in terms of timing and route. Migratory birds may use two electromagnetic tools to find their destinations: one that is innate, and another that relies on experience. A young bird on its first migration flies in the correct direction according to the Earth's magnetic field, but does not know how far the journey will be. It does this through a radical pair mechanism, whereby chemical reactions in special photo pigments, are sensitive to long wavelengths that are affected by the magnetic field. At this stage, the bird is similar to a boy scout with a compass but no map, until it grows accustomed to the journey and can put its other faculties to use, while experience teaches them to identify various landmarks. This 'mapping' is done by *magnetites* in the nervous system, which tell the bird how strong the field is.

Animals also use a combination of mechanisms, including the use of visual, olfactory, and magnetic cues to orient themselves, and navigate effectively[64]. These navigation mechanisms include:

- Remembered landmarks
- The sun
- The night sky
- Polarised light
- Magnetoception
- Olfaction
- Other senses

More recent research has found a neural connection between the eyes and "Cluster N", the part of the forebrain that is active during migrational orientation, suggesting that birds may actually be able to *see* the magnetic field of the Earth. This part of the brain and neural connections resemble the 'guide spot' in the frontal lobes in humans, the 'miracle in the middle' that also lights up and 'shows the way'[65]. We will focus on the role frontal-lobe functioning and 'mind wellness' plays in leadership and guidance in chapters 7 and 8.

The question that now becomes evident is:

> What about human migration and navigation?

Human migration

Human migration is physical movement by humans from one area to another. They sometimes travel over long distances or in large groups. Historically, this movement was nomadic, often causing significant conflict with the indigenous populations [66]. According to the International Organization for Migration's 'World Migration Report 2010', the number of international migrants was estimated at 214 million in 2010.

If this number continues to grow at the same pace as during the last 20 years, it could reach 405 million by 2050[67].

Various laws that govern human migration[68] have been identified'
while many factors influencing human migration have been put
forward. This includes groups of pulling and pushing factors.

- **Pushing forces**

Pushing factors include: not enough jobs; few opportunities;
primitive conditions; desertification; famine or drought; political fear
or persecution; slavery or forced labour; poor medical care; loss of
wealth; natural disasters; death threats; lack of political or religious
freedom; pollution; poor housing; landlord/tenant issues; bullying;
discrimination; poor chances of marrying; condemned housing; war.

- **Pulling factors**

Pulling factors include: Job opportunities; better living conditions;
political and/or religious freedom; enjoyment; education; better
medical care; attractive climates; security; family links; industry;
better chances of marrying[69].

The next question is:

> *Is there a connection between human DNA,*
> *genetics and migration?*

The answer is: Yes! We are currently experiencing a human genetic
migration. This important paradigm shift is going to impact on the
whole human race and nothing can stop it. It is not of our making as
it is a genetic migration that is now being triggered by our clock
genes and the Master clock. It is therefore important that our new
emerging leaders are well read and bred in the transformational and
transcending processes taking place. As we are all leaders in the
making, we all need to know about our current human genetic
migration.

Genetic migration

Genetic migration - also known as 'gene flow' - is the transfer of
alleles[70] or genes from one population to another[71]. Migration into or
out of a population may be responsible for a marked change in allele
frequencies. Immigration may also result in the addition of new
genetic variants to the established gene pool of a particular species or

population. Transfer can take place on horizontal or vertical levels. In the books *New Success DNA* and *Power Intelligence* we focus on the ability of genes to flow from one group to another.

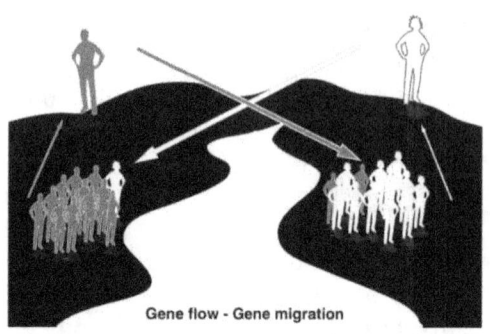

Gene flow - Gene migration

Gene flow and gene migration

Above we find a diagram of how people with different genes or frequencies influence other people by genetic migration or gene flow. It is nothing more than the emission of light from the chromosomes (*chromo* means 'light' and *soma* means 'body') or light bodies from a higher to a lower level. At the same time, we can consciously influence others to do the same. In the end we will find two different groups of people, separated by a barrier, veil or 'mountain' while others will be some way on-route between these two opposites - like below.

From this information we find that, with the current migration and new gene flow, we can expect the emergence of a new human gene pool – even a new human species[72]. We are returning to our roots and our original DNA blue-print and all this information is encoded into our DNA. This has also been confirmed by the latest scientific stem cell research[73].

Stem cell research

The term '*stem cell*' was proposed for scientific use by the Russian histologist Alexander Maksimov (1874–1928) at the congress of hematologic society in Berlin[74]. Stem cells are original cells containing our initial, original blueprint DNA with all the information of the healthy and happy person we should be. We have this all encoded as a blueprint DNA in our stem cells.

Living a life at any level lower or less than a fully functional, happy, successful, fulfilled and healthy human being, means that injury to the stem cells or a disconnection of the original DNA has taken place. This not only includes physical DNA, but also our emotional, mental and spiritual DNA. We therefore become 'dysfunctional' on all these levels. These dysfunctions can be caused by stress, infections like HIV/AIDS, physical injury like an accident; or be hereditary as *'the sins of the fathers get visited unto the children'*[75]. In a later chapter we will also focus on our mind-wellness and how we can develop HIV/AIDS of the mind and our spiritual disconnection from the 'God gene'[76]. Today we find that this can now be reversed by DNA activation, healing or enabling and that this could also include stem cell therapy[77].

We find stem cells in bone marrow, blood, amniotic fluid and embryos. Various 'stem cell therapies' are available in the form of stem cell preparations and/or powders containing specific 'sugars' as basic building blocks of DNA. The aim of stem cell therapy is to restore the original blue print of DNA thereby healing injury and illness. Although medical science primarily focuses on healing the physical DNA and body, we can expect that scientific research in Theology, psychology, psychiatry, social and other sciences, will now begin to focus on healing emotional, mental and spiritual disconnections at DNA level.

Stem cells are important not only because they contain our original DNA blue-print, they also have the ability to differentiate into many types of cells in the body and to self-replicate indefinitely. These blue-print cells can multiply and create more blue-print original cells – indefinitely! We can now re-create our unique self on all levels – mentally, emotionally, spiritually and physically. We can take back our authentic self on all levels, because all is encoded into our original DNA that includes the 'God-gene' in our stem cells. This process can be triggered in various ways that includes activating the frontal lobes of the brain, as we will later see.

The very nature of stem cells has intrigued scientists who foresee a day when stem cells could be used to replace diseased and injured tissue in patients, to screen and test new drugs, and help us to understand more about our fundamental biology and physiology.

The 2012 Nobel Prize for Physiology or Medicine was awarded to Sir John Gurdon, 79, of Dippenhall, England, and Shinya Yamanaka, 50, of Osaka, Japan, for work that revolutionised the understanding of how cells and organisms develop[78]. They share the prize jointly for their discovery that *"mature, specialised cells can be reprogrammed to become immature cells capable of developing into all tissues of the body,"* according to the Nobel Assembly, which consists of 50 professors at the Karolinska Institute[79].

Gurdon discovered in 1962 that the cells are reversible and Yamanaka discovered more than 40 years later how mature cells could be reprogrammed at a DNA level, to become immature stem cells that are able to develop into all types of cells in the body. This means they have found a way to reverse the ageing, disconnected and deterioration process and restore the original DNA.

These groundbreaking discoveries are now completely changing our view of life, human development and DNA specialisation. A whole new mindset, a new paradigm is emerging that will transform the way we think about and approach life and quality living. This also means that traditional mindsets will be left behind, while current text books need to be rewritten and new research fields also need to be established. The effect is that previous training material, methods, content and textbooks will be scrutinized, reinterpreted, rewritten or discarded. We can expect that new content, training material and books will from now on, be produced from a whole new mindset. We are also currently entering the level of quantum learning and quaternary education. Nothing will ever be the same again.

We will focus on the new paradigm, power-shift, change, transformation, transcendence, quantum learning and quaternary education, as well as the processes and positive and negative implications of this whole shift, in later chapters. For now – it is important to take cognisance of this major shift taking place – right down to our DNA and stem cells.

It is also common knowledge that when the paradigm shifts we also find new leaders in different fields emerging that include politics, commerce, education, psychology, business and social sciences, emerging. However – the most important leaders will now be the everyday person in the street. These are the people who are becoming aware of the influence of their authentic self and their responsibility to show the way. It is therefore an important time for all people to emerge with a new activated DNA from where they have been hiding – or even buried. The bell tolls!

The question is:

> *Do we also need to reinterpret our spiritual text and books like the Veda, Gita, Koran, Holy Bible and others?*

The answer is – yes! Leaders of the time always lead with the mindset of their time. Now the times and mindsets are changing. Even the Bible has a beginning and 'end' as spelt out in the book of Revelations. This means it is – 'back to the drawing board'. Most of our current leaders and teachers will all need to become students once more. School is not out yet! Many a leader in various sectors is in for a serious wake-up call if they think that they have arrived.

The questions are:

> *How should we reinterpret current mindsets and rewrite our 'manual' for successful living?*

Rewriting and reinterpreting current mindsets

From our spiritual text books, including our prominent religious books and scriptures, we find the story line of two opposing groups clearly coming to the fore. On the one side of the veil of the 'mountain[80]' we find the tribal minded hordes with their mindless disconnected views and tribal living. This symbolises unconscious, lower order tribal minded ego-driven masses with their disconnected or corrupt DNA (fallen ones). They are satisfied to live on lower discord octaves with lies, deceit and negativity, destructive power games, fighting and killing while crucifying all that is honest and authentic as well as the supporters of Light and Truth. With them we find their corrupt leaders who invest in maintaining their 'power over people' – the mindless, ignorant masses. Their most effective tool is to keep the masses uninformed, uneducated, unconscious and mindless. Their methods include lies, deceit, false promises, half-truths, delusional interpretations of facts and reality and motivation by fear. Religious scripts define this group as the 'corrupt ones', 'false prophets' or the 'adder generation' – referring to the reptile brain functioning, as we will later see.

We also have many an unsuspecting supporter who thinks they are doing the right thing by supporting these 'disabled' leaders that are found in various religious, academic, political, business and other contexts. Followers then become deeply disillusioned and disappointed when they find out that the leaders they trusted are turning out to be fundamentally corrupt while they implemented their self-serving, ego-driven self-destructive mindsets, methods and systems. This means many an unsuspecting soul will go through a rude awakening by the Truth that is now coming to the fore – and so will their leaders. Like all of us, they will have to go through this rude awakening and the whole transformational process of dying to the old and a new rebirth into the new season of existence. People are now finding out that their ladder of success is not only standing against the wrong wall. In essence they are climbing the wrong ladder – and so are their leaders!

On the other hand – a new generation going through their 'ego-self crucifixion' is leaving this old regime behind. They are the ones who are passing through the 'dark night of the soul' and are rising from wherever they are – purified, cleansed, healed and connected. They are the new enlightened leaders with New leadership DNA. These are people who know how to make their mark

Making your mark

The human race has over eons, always placed a sign, left a mark or symbol at the places they visited along the routes of their journeys. Journeys were marked so that others could retrace their steps or follow in their footsteps as necessary. Usually the travelers erected piles of stones or built monuments in order to make the statement "I was here". Other markers along the way include marking significant trees, natural sites like grottos, hills or mountains. Some used holy places like burial grounds, natural spots like waterfalls or rivers, while others used man made symbols like planting a tree, building a structure or planting a cross. Diaz planted his cross on the Southern point of Africa[81] in order to make a statement 'We were here - first!' Various religious leaders have also made their mark. Today we find different kinds of texts, scriptures and on a more physical level the symbol of the cross is used to convey specific information. Cross symbolism[82] can be found everywhere, and can denote positive and negative symbolism and includes crosses of various forms and designs, daggers, double daggers, swords and crucifixes. Christianity views the cross as the symbol of freedom. The Maltese Cross[83] is viewed as a universal and spiritual symbol that denotes the place physicality meets spirituality or higher dimensions. At this point, the nexus, the physical planes are overcome by the power of spirituality. It is said that Spirit is used to put out the 'fires of physicality'. This is also used as foundation for the symbol or logo for fire fighters.

Maltese Cross   **Logo of Firefighters**

Buddhists see a Bow tree as the symbol of the tree of life referring to the symbol of Buddha sitting under the bow tree are until he received enlightenment. In the end this can be seen as symbolic of our path up the mountain of life in the process of reclaiming our true identity and authentic self. This is encoded into our DNA this is where the authentic imprint or mark has been made.

The questions each one needs to ask are:

> *Whose markers am I currently following? Where do they lead? What is my marker? Where and when did I make my mark? What is my symbol or mark?*

New leadership is all about making your unique mark while climbing the mountain of life. Below you find our artists interpretation of this ego-defying and soul liberating journey up the mountain of Truth that includes various steps of self-development and self-liberation. Below we find our artists view of this liberating path up the mountain of truth.

The journey up the mountain of Truth

The journey up the mountain of Truth

Steps of self-liberation

Like all other study courses, we find teachers, learners and a curriculum. There are also various steps in this process that first demands an enrolment and commitment from a student. The student can become a servant student or 'chela' to the master or teacher. Many religious and other contexts refer to these students as their followers, apprentice, novice, student, trainee or disciple. Discipleship is the path a person follows in a teaching from a specific spiritual master in order to connect to the authentic self and obtain self-mastery and enlightenment.

On the path of liberating the authentic self and reclaiming the quality life we are desire and deserve, we can identify various steps, processes and teachings. These steps include being a student, disciple, friend (only by invitation), brother/sister (by sharing the same DNA) and then the anointed one or christed/enlightened one. Each step includes certain teachings and steps in self growth and development in self awareness. Self-discipline and self-mastery are the two most important tolls on this path of authentic success. This inner work is all rewarded by an initiation, ceremony and a celebration. It is something like graduating from college or university with your degree, diploma or certificate. At the level of self-mastery and enlightenment, the student becomes the teacher, guru or Master. This process of attaining self-mastery through self-disciple in the Truth, then repeats when the new master becomes the teacher. Our new enlightened leaders are also enlightened healers and teachers!

This was and still is the path of the training of authentic new leaders. These were and still are the fundamental teachings that were found in the ancient training of leaders in the mystery schools. Nothing has changed for – Truth can even be compromised.

We can expect that all over the globe different pockets of a new enlightened generation *Homo sapiens spiritualis,* will emerge until the pockets blend, become one and we all take hands. Just like building a puzzle by placing the right pieces in their place – all will contribute to the Big Picture. This new generation has moved beyond blind faith and now knows, meaning, has clarity and certainty, that we are created to live 'happily ever after' – it is encoded into our DNA. We were created to live 'heaven on earth'.

The questions we need to ask are:

On what side of the mountain am I now? Where do I want to be? What should I do in order to get there? Who and how are my current leaders showing me the way? Is it time to make a change and choose new leaders who can help me to develop my authentic self? How do I become someone with a new leadership DNA?

Not only do we have ancient teachings on how to restore our original blue print we also have help and assistance from scientist who can reprogram human cells and created new opportunities to study diseases on all levels while developing new methods for diagnosis and therapy. We now know that we can restore our cell memory and heal our fractured DNA. No longer are we victims of our physical reality. Although embryonic-like stem cells can be created in the laboratory from adult cells of the same organism, rather than using aborted fetuses or embryos, we can bypass this physical stage by connecting to our authentic self, our original potential and power on the 'universal net' or 'web of life'[84].

From this higher universal perspective and quaternary learning, we can connect to our spiritual, authentic higher self and download this information from the universal web. This new information and power will, can and does, restore our original blue-print DNA[85]. We are gaining a deeper understanding of how to restore our spiritual 'stem cell' by restoring our physical 'stem cell'. This means our human gene pool is changing as we speak.

The changing human gene pool

Our physical existence can be found on different levels of consciousness. On the first level we find our mineral world, with different crystals as the purest form of the Mineral Kingdom. At the next level we find our fauna or Animal Kingdom, and the Plant Kingdom or flora that thrives on the mineral world. We also find our fauna or Animal Kingdom that thrives on the two previous worlds. On the next level we find the human species, *Homo sapiens*, that thrives not only on the previous kingdoms, but also has a connection to the higher dimensions or spiritual kingdom, the 'Kingdom of God'. We now find the emergence of different 'human species' that can be identified by the level of consciousness they are connected to.

First we find what we could call a 'human subspecies, Homo *sapiens animalis'*. These can be viewed as humans who live their lives like 'animals'. They eat, drink and work like animals, and are mostly driven by instinct. Their lives are based on fear and they reflect a survival mode of 'fight or flee'. Many of these people are found in prisons, war-like situations, or are terrorists in the jungles or people on the outskirts of society. They are primarily connected to physicality and the earth. They are tribal minded and only have their primal third-level human DNA active. The rest of their multidimensional DNA has been deactivated and is identifiable as 'junk genes'. Their thinking is regulated by the primal brain or 'reptile brain' that is fear driven and responsible for sneaky, snake-like ways and stalking methods. From a spiritual point of view, these people could be viewed as 'primitive souls'[86].

In the following group, we find *Homo sapiens sapiens,* a warm-blooded human being who has learnt to survive in the 'jungles' of different cultures and societies. They live according to social structures and religious laws and rules, while conforming to standards set by the societies they live in. Usually their lives are very materialistic and filled with different 'cultured' ways, to survive from day to day. This group usually has DNA activated on level three, and their thinking is regulated by the middle brain or 'mammalian brain'. Many of our celebrities, pop artists and film stars who thrive on attention, public opinion and materialistic goals, function on this level. As this level is not fulfilling, they usually revert to substance abuse, addiction and jump from one marriage to another in search of happiness. From a spiritual point of view, they can be viewed as 'infant or teenager souls'.

The Changing Human Gene Pool

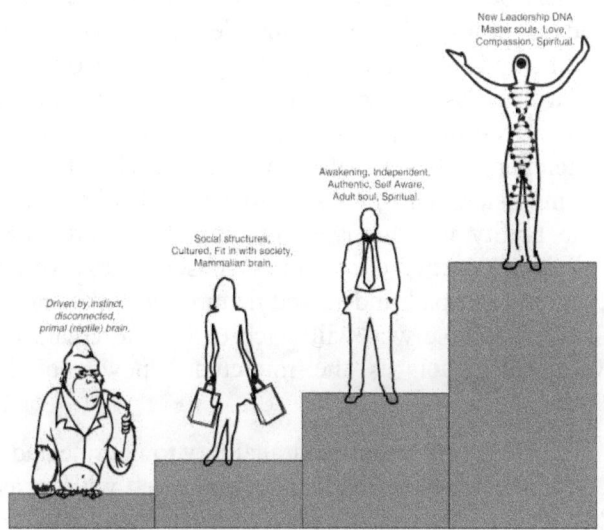

New Leadership DNA
Master souls, Love,
Compassion, Spiritual.

Awakening, Independent,
Authentic, Self Aware,
Adult soul, Spiritual.

Social structures,
Cultured, Fit in with society,
Mammalian brain.

Driven by instinct,
disconnected,
primal (reptile) brain.

The evolving human gene pool

We then find the emergence of *'Homo sapiens individualis'*, a person who is awakening and taking back their personal identity, self-expression and individual right to independent thinking and freedom. These are the people who are interested in growing and maturing, while fulfilling their full potential. This group started emerging on a full scale with the coming of the information era. Today *'Homo sapiens individualis'* is one of the fastest-growing groups on the planet. Information is doubling every year and social structures are being challenged by new information, thinking, change and transformation. Currently this group constitutes the larger part of our developed youth and leadership society, while tribal-minded youths and leaders still prevail in our less-developed countries. At this level their DNA has been activated up to the fourth level, while their thinking is primarily inspired by higher-order questions and challenges. The answers are found in the neocortex and by activating the frontal lobes. Here we find a group aspiring to move forward on a deeper spiritual path, by putting in the effort to consciously raise their awareness and fully access levels four, five and above. From a soul perspective they can be viewed as evolving 'adult souls'.

Over the last decade or two, a new 'species', *Homo sapiens spiritualis*, has been emerging at an escalating pace. These people have already gone though the previous learning curves, leaving the old ego-self behind. They are now forging forward into a higher level of spiritual awareness, knowing, understanding and attainment. Not only has their DNA been activated from level three through four and five, their temporal lobes are also being activated and light up with love and compassion. When we start to access this level we begin to develop the ability to co-create miracles. These are our 'master souls'. This is the next level of human consciousness we can aspire to. Here, we find our pathfinders and mapmakers - the leaders of the future. They are people who will teach us how to create miracles - people who will teach us the miraculous power of love and compassion.

From our understanding of our natural ability to migrate and navigate our way on Earth, we also find that no-one is left without assistance and guidance. This is a natural inborn instinct - it is programmed in to DNA. Migrating birds and animals do not question their inner guidance. There is, however, an 'unnatural' problem of communication and guidance where humans are concerned. For most people, organisations and even countries - something has gone wrong. We have become disconnected, our GPS is dysfunctional, and people, groups and even countries feel lost and alone. As a result, we find various leadership theories, styles, technologies and training. The answer, however, lies in the ability to reconnect to, activate and heal our natural inherent ability to move, change and navigate our way in this earthly existence we call 'life'.

Leadership therefore has nothing to do with academic leadership theories and training programs. It does, however, have everything to do with becoming your authentic self, activating your inner GPS, and influencing others to do the same. In this process we find our way home.

The following questions come to the fore:

> *How do we reconnect and realign with our inherent natural higher communication, guidance and navigational systems?*

Communication and guidance

For eons, people have been fascinated by communication and guidance from 'above'. Many would pay with their lives, if they believed that they had received guidance from a higher power, the gods/God, or higher spiritual beings. In our earlier history, it was believed that only a select few had the ability and right to guidance and communication from the heavens above. These were the 'chosen ones'.

Today, some still frown on those who proclaim to receive higher guidance and spiritual messages. Most people are still programmed with this collective social consciousness, that higher communication is just meant for a select few and the privileged religious and church elite. Others again believe that it is a lot of baloney, or derives from the 'devil'. However, this could not be further from the truth. People are becoming more aware, minds and structures are opening up, and we are not living in the 'dark ages' anymore. We are awaking from this long, dark slumber - we are becoming conscious, aware and enlightened. We are returning to our authentic source of guidance.

The questions that arise are:

> *Where do people - especially leaders - get their guidance from? How can we benefit from this knowledge and understanding?*

Different foundations and methods of guidance

From the earliest recordings of human history, it is clearly documented that different leaders of different cultures, religions and beliefs made use of different methods to obtain information on which they based their decisions. Their guidance became directional for all. They not only based their decisions on the information obtained, but also provided guidance to the masses that resigned to their will. This is relevant still to this day. From the beginning of time, there was only one of two options available. On the one hand, we find the multitheistic nations and their gods. On the other hand, we have the monotheistic religion and one universal source, or God. Everything, however, is not always clear-cut with right or wrong, good or bad - as we will later see.

We find many examples of different forms of guidance in multitheistic religions. This includes guidance from the priests, oracles or soothsayers. In ancient Egyptian history[87], we find the pharaoh as the high priest of all temples, the head of law and administration, and the commander of the army. The Egyptians believed pharaohs were half-man and half-god. Since only the pharaoh and priests were allowed to enter temples, ancient Egyptians had to ask the pharaoh to speak to the gods for them. This made the pharaoh very powerful in the minds of regular Egyptians. We find many texts confirming that pharaohs obtained information by calling on wise men, the astrologers, sorcerers and wizards for guidance[88].

On the other hand, we find that leaders of the monotheistic religion, found their guidance in two different ways. Monotheistic leaders made no decisions by themselves, but relied on direct communication from a higher power, almighty or God and divine personal revelation. Some leaders also called upon their priests and prophets for divination and guidance.

A few questions arise:

> *Are our modern-day leaders still making use of these methods today? What do we need to know and what do we need to do in order to ensure that authentic leaders take us forward into a prosperous future?*

In order to find answers to these questions, we first need to visit the different sources of guidance and information available to us all.

Different sources - different guidance

From the earliest days of humanity, many different methods of divination were used, and 'sorcery' was part of the social consciousness. However, it is important to understand the authentic meaning of the word 'sorcery'. In short it means *'sourcing information or guidance'*. The names of these people differ from place to place, and include the shamans, priests, prophets and psychics. We find different methods of gaining access to guidance or 'sourcing of information'. In ancient times, a 'sorcerer' or 'magician' was consulted. They were practitioners of magic, with the ability to attain or acquire knowledge using supernatural or non-rational means. The general preliterate[89] masses admired or feared their feats.

All over the globe, we find different 'sorcerers' and in different cultures, like the: Shaman in Peru, North America and other countries; *Kalku* from Chili; *Magi* from ancient Greek and Persian cultures; *Seids* from Scandanavia who worked shamanic magic; warlocks, wizards and witches from Europe; magic workers in the Greco-Roman World; *Onmyou* mystics from Japan; and *Bomoh* shamans from Indonesia and Malaysia. In Africa we find the witch doctor and the sangoma who still play an important part in everyday life. We can also include sages, prophets, priests, mediums, wise men or astrologers of the time.

We also find 'magic' in different religions. These powers could come from a light or dark force according to the person's personal orientation of character[90]. Examples of 'magic' in the Greco-Roman world are found in the various state and cult temples, Jewish synagogues and in the early Christian cathedrals and churches. These were important hubs for the ancient peoples of the Greco-Roman world that were representative of a connection between the heavenly realms or the divine, and the earthly planes or the dwelling place of humanity. The context of magic has become an academic study, especially in the last twenty years[91].

Another source of leadership guidance and information is found in the contact with ancestral spirits. Although Roman Catholicism is the official religion of Haiti, voodoo may be considered to be the country's national religion. Most Haitians believe in and practice at least some aspects of voodoo. Popular images of voodoo have ignored the religion's basis as a domestic cult of ancestral spirits. Adherents of voodoo do not perceive themselves as members of a separate religion; they consider themselves to be Roman Catholics. In fact, the word for 'voodoo' does not even exist in rural Haiti. The Creole word *'vodoun'* refers to a kind of dance, and in some areas to a category of spirits.

The belief system of voodoo revolves around ancestral spirits or 'family spirits', often called *loua* or *mistè* - who are inherited through maternal and paternal lines. *Loua* protect their 'children' from misfortune. In return, families must 'feed' the *loua* through periodic rituals, in which food, drink and other gifts are offered to the spirits. Haitians also distinguish between the service of ancestral spirits, and the practice of magic and sorcery.

Misconceptions about voodoo have given Haiti a reputation for sorcery and zombies. However, vodooists believe in a distant and unknowable creator god, *Bondyè*. As Bondyè does not intercede in human affairs, vodooists direct their worship toward spirits subservient to Bondyè[92]. Most vodooists believe that their religion can coexist with Catholicism. Most Protestants, however, strongly oppose voodoo.

Scholars often overlook that the entire northern area of Haiti is heavily influenced by West African, especially Congolese practices[93]. In addition, the Vodun religion, distinct from Haitian Vodou, already existed in the United States prior to Haitian immigration, as it was brought to the USA by enslaved West Africans. The transplanted Africans of Haiti, similar to those of Cuba and Brazil, were obliged to disguise their *lwa* or ancestral spirits, as Roman Catholic saints - an element of a process called syncretism[94].

Today, ancestral spirit worship is still very prevalent in Africa and is also found in Cuba, Brazil, Chili, Peru and Mexico[95]. In Africa, where mysticism and magic play a part in many people's lives, pronouncements from a 'sangoma'[96] can carry as much weight as those from governments[97].

The Zulu nation is the largest South African ethnic group, with an estimated 10 to 11 million people living mainly in the province of KwaZulu-Natal. Most Zulu people state their beliefs to be Christian. Some of the most common churches to which they belong are the African Initiated Churches - especially the Zion Christian Church and United African Apostolic Church, although membership of major European Churches such as the Dutch Reformed, Anglican and Catholic Churches is also common. Nevertheless, many Zulus retain their traditional pre-Christian belief system of ancestor worship, in parallel with their Christianity. In Zimbabwe we find the Shona, for example, who believe that there is an impersonal, omnipotent or principal creator, called *Muwari*, *Musikavanhu*, or a spirit which creates good and bad[98].

Although European colonialism, followed by totalitarian regimes in West Africa, tried to suppress Vodun as well as other forms of the religion - ancestral worship still prevails. This is because ancestral deities are said to be born to each African clan-group. Its clergy is central to maintaining the moral, social, and political order and ancestral foundation of its villagers, and it was impossible to eradicate the religion. Traditional leaders representing the African clan-groups are now part of governments and current political systems. In South Africa, Houses of Traditional Leaders have been established at national level and in some provinces, to carry out an advisory role in government[99].

Leadership in the East[100] is founded on deep spiritual philosophies that include key leadership lessons from Confucius, Lao Tzu and the Tao Te Ching[101]. It is possible to discern distinct generations of Chinese leadership[102], because both the Communist Party of China and the People's Liberation Army promote according to seniority. These groups of leadership have each promoted an extension of the ideology of the former, which in some cases influenced the direction of national development.

In the structure of Indian society, we find orthodox doctrines of Hinduism and the heterodox doctrines of Buddhism, with modifications brought by the influence of popular religions[103]. Weber believed that like Confucianism in China, Hinduism in India was a barrier for capitalism. The Indian 'caste system' made it very difficult for individuals to advance in the society beyond their particular caste[104]. Activity, including economic activity, was seen as unimportant in the context of the advancement of the soul. A large portion of the population, therefore, lives in poverty[105].

The unstable situation in the Middle East has been with us for centuries, and can be contributed to various factors. The most important factors that stand out are conflicting religious and value orientations, and the authoritarian leadership style of most Middle Eastern leaders. Because of this authoritative philosophy, Middle Eastern countries are often used as examples for Douglas McGregor's Theory X motivational leadership style[106].

Astrologers are consulted all over the globe, and even the defence and police forces of most countries make use of psychics. Methods of divination like tarot card readings and the I Ching, are still widely used, while fortune telling with the use of crystal balls, cards, and palm reading, are ancient forms of divination that are still widely consulted today. The same principles are used in African cultures, just by using bones and other traditional objects, while in Peru the reading of cacao leaves is highly revered.

A question still remains:

> *Where do our modern leaders get their*
> *information and guidance from?*

Modern guidance, for modern leaders

One of the most important leadership tasks is the responsibility to make fundamental decisions that impact on the lives of all involved. All leaders make use of different sources of information. As our information technology has evolved - the more informed and complex the decision-making process has become. Leaders should and do, surround themselves with knowledgeable people that include specialists in various fields. All depending on the leadership position, they also have access to the most up-to-date scientific information and the best technology currently available. Only the complexity differs from one leadership position to another. The information and technology available to the President of the USA is on another level compared to a father as the leader in his family, who can access all the information he needs from the internet. However, we find leaders accessing information and 'sourcing' higher guidance in different ways.

Astrology has played a role ever since the beginning of human kind. It was therefore not strange to find an astrologist like Joan Quigley rendering her services to the Reagan White House. Not only did Quigley volunteer her services to the presidential campaign, but she also later provided the Reagan's with guidance and information on a regular basis. In his book, Ronald Reagan[107] explains the best kept White House secret of his presidency. It was revealed that virtually every major move and decision made was first cleared in advance with a 'woman in San Francisco' - who drew up horoscopes to make certain that the planets were in a favourable alignment for the enterprise[108]. Ronald Reagan was also a deeply religious and spiritual leader, admired and trusted by many. This led to a vote of confidence and a second term in office[109]. Behind this all was the First Lady, Nancy Reagan, who not only supported the President's methods, but also instigated many of the processes.

President Roosevelt too, is said to have kept an astrological chart pasted to the bottom of his chessboard, for handy reference. America's Declaration of Independence, so the story goes, was signed only after the Founding Fathers made sure the heavens were in fortuitous alignment. In fact, astrology has played a part in public life as long as there have been politicians reaching for the stars. However, in the United States it has often been the women behind powerful men who looked to horoscopes or cards or clairvoyants - for guidance.

Other American presidents and/or their wives have made use of astrological information. This includes the founding fathers, Benjamin Franklin and Jefferson, and First Lady Betty Ford. Writer Sally Quinn, who investigated the capital's astrology habits for the Washington Post, says "I was amazed at the kinds of people who actually made political decisions based on astrological charts." But though many of the power elite consult astrologers, she says that "Nobody admits it." Contributions are also made by psychics and prophets, and Svetlana Godilla was among D.C.'s most popular seers[110].

Astrology has also played an important role in the leadership and politics of the France. The well-known French astrologist Elizabeth Teissier, was featured heavily in the media after she revealed that she had served as an advisor to the French president Francois Mitterrand, for a period of seven years. In her book, she claims that she used the stars to guide the president in choosing his every political move, including military actions during the Gulf War[111].

However, more than a century before the French Revolution, astrology was denounced as a discipline unworthy of study by Jean-Baptiste Colbert, who was then chief minister to the French monarch Louis XIV. Colbert founded the French Académie des Sciences in 1666, and a monarchical degree was passed which threatened to punish practicing soothsayers with banishment. Now, nearly three and a half centuries later, soothsaying has been rehabilitated at the Sorbonne[112]. According to statistics over the past two decades, the number of those seeking astrologers has nearly doubled. As for Russia, studies show that more than half of Russians believe in omens, and 42% believe in prophetic dreams. According to surveys, about 20% of Russians also believe in astrology.

Adolf Hitler also believed in astrology. He ignored the advice of an astrologer, Walter Sobottendorfa, to do nothing until after November 1923. Hitler however ignored this astrologic warning and gave the Munich putsch[113], after which he was imprisoned. Hitler then decided not to take risks, and from then on not only relied on his own insights, but also decided to include contributions from leading astrologers and other sources of information. He created a special research institution, and studies were designed "to harness in order to win in harnessing not only natural but also supernatural powers - of modern technology to black magic." It is in such an institution that William Wulff was hired in 1942 - who later became the court astrologer of the Third Reich[114].

Other prominent leaders who have made use of astrological guidance and information, include Indira Gandhi and Indian politicians. The involvement of astrologers in the affairs of Indian politicians are said to have always been at a 'state level'. Astrology is very popular with Indian politicians, as it has been with British leadership. Margaret Thatcher and John Major regularly commissioned astrological predictions from Marjorie Orr - a well-known astrologist from

Glasgow. Boris Yeltsin was also no stranger to assistance from astrologers. It is said that with their help, Yeltsin won the election. It is known that Vladimir Putin, at the time, requested astrologers to determine the date and hour of his inauguration.

It is common knowledge that many celebrities make use of astrology, and this includes people like Princes Diana and Marilyn Monroe.

In the United Kingdom, a research fund has been set up to investigate the potential of astrology, and in Denmark and Austria, business astrologers are active - with university backing. In India, the Education Minister has called upon all 200 universities to offer astrology courses, offering them each five extra places for teaching and support personnel. He has also demanded that all high schools teach Vedic mathematics and astrology[115].

In Africa we find *sangomas* having many different social and political roles in the community, that include divination, healing, directing rituals, finding lost cattle, protecting warriors, counter-acting witches, and narrating the history, cosmology, and myths of their tradition. They are highly revered and respected in their society. Illness is thought to be caused by witchcraft, pollution, the contact with impure objects or occurrences, revenge, or by the ancestors themselves. They believe that this could occur either malevolently, or through the neglect of ancestral spirits or if ancestral spirits are not respected. At the same time these occurrences could show an individual his/her calling to be a sangoma. For harmony between the living and the dead, vital for a trouble-free life, the ancestors must be shown respect through ritual and animal sacrifice.

Zuma's statement that *"God expects us to rule this country because we are the only organisation which was blessed by pastors when it was formed. It is even blessed in Heaven. That is why we will rule until Jesus comes back. We should not allow anyone to govern our city when we are ruling the country"* caused widespread concern with South African Christians and it was later re-interpreted. This confirms the very important, even defining role, beliefs systems and religions play in politics, government and leadership. At the same time, we have the question of the usage of 'muti'[116], especially rhino horn, in Africa and in Eastern leadership circles. The properties of rhino horn encompass more than an aphrodisiac, and can be traced back to the ancient times of the myths of the unicorn[117].

The story of unicorns has been with us, in one form or another, since the dawn of history. Its believed they were first described by the Chinese as a miraculous creature called the Ch'i lin (or K'i lin), a 'great unicorn', that radiated exquisite colours, had a voice like a thousand wind chimes, avoided fighting at all costs, lived for a thousand years, and had a horn twelve feet long. It was said that Ch'i Lin walked so softly that its hooves made no sound. Some believed this was because it was so soft-hearted, it did not want to crush the blades of grass beneath its feet. It was a creature of great power and wisdom, and would show itself at special times.

The appearance of a unicorn was always considered a sign of good fortune. When a ruler was just and kind and the times peaceful and prosperous, the unicorn would appear in a glade. It would also appear when a great leader was about to die or be born[118]. It is said that the pregnant mother of Confucius was visited by a unicorn before his birth. Although Confucius never wore a crown, he was revered by all. Through his teachings, Confucius probably did as much to shape China as the power of many kings and warlords combined.

The unicorn is also a legendary animal from European folklore that resembles a white horse with a large, pointed, spiraling horn projecting from its forehead, and sometimes a goat's beard and cloven hooves. First mentioned by the ancient Greeks, it became the most important imaginary animal of the Middle Ages and Renaissance, when it was commonly described as an extremely wild woodland creature, and a symbol of purity and grace, which could only be captured by a virgin[119].

The unicorn looks like a horse, from the forehead of which proceeds a single horn - like that of an ibex. The tail is tufted like that of a lion. Well known for being the sinister supporter to the royal families, it occurs in several coats of arms, like Arms of Saint-Lô, France; Arms of Líšnice, Czech Republic; Arms of Ramosch, Switzerland; Arms of Schwäbisch Gmünd, Germany; Arms of Eger, Hungary; Royal coat of arms of Scotland; and the official coat of arms of the United Kingdom of Great Britain and Northern Ireland, as below[120].

Unicorn   **Coat of Arms of Great Britain and Northern Ireland**

.

Reference to the unicorn were said to be also found in India. A creature in Chinese mythology is sometimes called 'the Chinese unicorn'. Other countries that have reference to the unicorn include Ethiopia, Japan, the QuéLy of Vietnamese myth, and China. In the St James version of the Hebrew Bible, we find the following reference[121]: "God brought them out of Egypt; he hath as it were the strength of a unicorn."

The appearance of a unicorn with its prominent single horn is revered as a symbol of wealth and prosperity, victory and conquest. The horn of the unicorn is said to attract two lovers, as the unicorn is attracted to the virgin. It was believed that the horn holds magical and medicinal properties. In the encyclopedias[122], the unicorn's horn was said to have the power to render poisoned water potable and to heal sickness. Until the 19th century, belief in unicorns was widespread amongst historians, alchemists, writers, poets, naturalists, physicians, and theologians[123].

Today, we still have this belief about the unicorn alive and flourishing in Africa and Eastern countries. The use of rhino horn is said to be a substitute for this power invested in the unicorn horn. While many organisations are fighting the battle against rhino poaching, we find many tribal leaders in Africa still making use of *muti* containing rhino horn. It was, however, reported that more than

500 tribal healers/sangomas have now vowed not to make use of rhino horn any further, and to support the 'save the rhino' campaign[124]. Sangomas are said to access the wisdom of the ancestors to cure ills and divine knowledge. They do this with traditional medicines, their muti, dream interpretation, bone throwing, channeling and possession. Dream interpretation, divination, tarot card reading and various other methods, are still prevalent all over the globe.

Rhinoceros horn   **Narwhal horn**

One repeated misconception is that rhinoceros horn in powdered form is used as an aphrodisiac in Traditional Chinese Medicine (TCM). It is, in fact, prescribed for fevers and convulsions. Efficacy for neither has been proven by evidence-based medicine. Discussions with TCM practitioners to reduce its use have met with mixed results, since some TCM doctors see rhinoceros horn as a life-saving medicine of better quality than comparable substitutes. China has signed the CITES treaty in 1993, however, and removed rhinoceros horn from the Chinese medicine pharmacopeia administered by the Ministry of Health. In 2011, in the United Kingdom, the Register of Chinese Herbal Medicine issued a formal statement condemning the use of rhinoceros horn. A growing number of TCM educators have also spoken out against the practice. In many instances, Narwahl and Gemsbok horn are used as substitutes.

From the above background, we find that many leaders seek higher understanding and guidance in different ways by using different methods. Most of the discussed practices are done behind closed doors - mostly without the people and public they serve having insight into their ways and methods. On the other hand, there are many leaders who view their position as a 'calling from God'. The

Dali Lama meditates at least four hours per day, in order to secure and maintain his spiritual connection and communication. A leader like Jesus Christ received his direction and teachings 'from above', while His disciples wrote on his teachings in the New Testament of the Holy Bible[125]. Mohammed also received his calling and teachings from 'above'. After his death, his teachings were published as the Quran[126]. The teachings of lord Krishna were made available to all in the Bhagavad Gita[127], while the Kabala is an integral part of the teaching of Judaism, Christianity, New Age, and occultist syncretic adaption's[128].

Joan of Arc was a spiritual visionary from childhood. It is said that she received direct help and assistance from the Archangel Michael. Through her vision, she received her calling to lead the French army to several important victories during the Hundred Year War. However, in the end, she was captured by the Burgundians, and handed over to the English in exchange for money, put on trial by a pro-English Bishop on charges of 'insubordination and heterodoxy', and was burned on the stake for heresy when she was only 19 years old[129]. During the Middle Ages, many spiritual visionaries, prophets and mystics were seen as 'witches' and burnt at the stake.

With these examples, we find various methods and investments in securing direct connection and communication with higher dimensions and spiritual realms, that include angels, masters, light beings and Source – God. Fasting, prayer and meditation are but a few of the methods still used in order to gain this quality of connection and guidance.

Leaders having visits from angels, direct communication with God, visions, dreams, intuitions and so-called 'paranormal' experiences, have been widely documented throughout history[130]. George Washington wrote: "I do not know whether it is owing to the anxiety of my mind, but this afternoon, as I was sitting at this table engaged in preparing a dispatch, something in the apartment seemed to disturb me. Looking up, I beheld standing opposite me a singularly beautiful being". Visits from angels and higher light beings have been widely documented. These methods of communication were previously not accessible to the general public, and they were left to the mercy of the leaders of the time.

When we look back on the history of human kind, however, we find one person in ancient history who stands out as the first to bring leadership to the people in a unique way. He heard his 'divine calling' to go out and teach the people to reclaim truth and take back their personal power, while creating a better quality of life for all. This message was conveyed, nearly 5000 years ago, by Zarasthustra[131].

Our first leaders - travelling teachers with a mission

The prophet Zarathrustra, also known as Zoroaster, lived between 3000 and 5000 years ago, and was born into a priestly family. He lived in Persia - what is now eastern Iran. He is called the 'the world's first philosopher'[132]. His teachings formed the core of a new monotheistic religion now known as Zoroastrianism. He is believed to be the composer of the *Gathas,* a selection of 17 hymns, valued as the most sacred texts of the Zoroastrian faith. They are organised in an easy to memorise sequence, where one song logically follows another. It was a collection designed to be taught to the preliterate and illiterate people. He created the first known group of travelling teachers, with a mission[133] to take the tools and teachings outside of their home area and tribe - to the people[134].

These teachers or missionaries were seen as the 'wise men from the East'. Magi or 'wise men' originated with the institution of the teachers, healers and leaders of Zarathustra. The Magi were educated in Bactria or modern Afghanistan, and sent out to all countries and people. Visits from the Magi were a time of celebration. They often brought new sciences, ways of building, farming, and new methods to better the lives of the masses. The Magi began at a time when Zarathustra's people were still nomads and violently raiding villages. They, however, taught a way of peaceful living in settled agricultural communities, and in harmony with nature. The Magi could travel from Persia or Babylon, or almost anywhere they wanted in the Middle East[135].

In the *Gathas*, Zarathustra sees the human condition as the mental struggle between truth (*aša*) and the lie (*druj*). 'All is one truth' and the 'free will' of human kind, is at the foundation of all Zoroastrian doctrine. These verses explain the divine essences of truth (*Asha*), the good-mind/God-mind (*Vohu Manah*), and the spirit of righteousness. We find echoes of his words in Judaism, Christianity and Islam. Zoroastrians were also known for their devotion to truth and wisdom and they place a strong emphasis on protecting the environment.

Zarathustra

Zarathustra was a revolutionary, and his views clashed with the traditional views, beliefs and values of the time[136]. The ancestors of the Persians were primarily animistic and pantheistic[137]. Their religion was made up of deified forces and phenomena of nature. The moon, wind and sacrificial fire were deified, and like many other solar deities, headed the Pantheon. As with the Egyptians, the god of the sun was also all-seeing and all-knowing, and was therefore the god of oaths, pastures, and cattle. Zarathustra spoke out against the religious establishment of his day, and as a result he secured their hatred and contempt.

The Persians maintained that the gods could be manipulated and appeased through the use of blood sacrifices. An animal, led by a Magi, would be taken to the place of slaughter. There it was slain, butchered, and boiled. During the ceremony, the worshippers would consume a quantity of a sacred beverage, known as *Haoma,* along with the meat of the sacrifice. Soon the sacred beverage would have its desired effect and the entire affair would rapidly deteriorate into an orgy. Still, to this day, blood offerings are believed to please the gods/God. Even in the monotheistic religions like Christianity, the 'blood of Jesus' is said to please God, open the spiritual doors, and pave the way to heaven. In African cultures we find sacrificial blood offerings to the gods and ancestors. This deep-seated collective consciousness and belief that the gods/God can be pleased by the sacrifice of human and/or animal blood offerings, still prevails all over the world.

The Persian monarchs of the time, however, tolerated different ideas and religions, and allowed the growth of the Zoroastrian religion to proceed without official impediment. Eventually they adopted Zoroastrianism as the royal monotheistic religion, insuring its survival down to the current day[138]. Today many researchers have drawn a direct genetic line between Zarathustra and Jesus[139]. The 'wise men of the East' knowing about the birth of Jesus, is only one of many examples of the connection between Jesus Christ and Zarathustra[140].

The 'wise men' were mainly astronomers of the time. They had the ability to read the stars, and interpret the fate that the stars foretold. It was later said that their teachings also included astrology, alchemy and other forms of esoteric knowledge. They were said not to be magicians, and did not do 'magic'. Their philosophy was taught verbatim only to specially identified and selected students. Their motives were pure, of sound-mind, good-mind or God-mind. They brought truth, honesty and integrity, quality living and all they did was to the benefit of everyone. Nobody was excluded.

The premises and methods of the wise men of Zarathustra differed greatly from the many sorcerers and wizards of the palaces. After the destruction of the faith and most of its written texts, by Alexander the Great in 333 BC, the Magi's ancient lineage was broken. This allowed other priests in other areas, such as Babylon and Assyria, to call themselves 'Magi'. There was wide diversity among the Magi. These later priests changed the liturgy and beliefs of Zarathustra, often blending them with Egyptian and Greek elements. These priests also relied heavily on astrology and prophesy to predict the future. It is they who are often written about in the Bible. Not all Magi were strict followers of Zarathustra, and today few true Zoroastrians use the term 'Magi' - preferring the name *Ashavans,* meaning 'followers of truth'[141].

The truth is that everyone has the ability to connect to and communicate with a higher power, truth, wisdom, source or God. We do not need shamans, wizards or any of the other mediums to do our connection and communication for us. We can view Zarasthustra as the first in history to lead by 'releasing the power within people' - in opposition to the leaders of the day who ruled by 'maintaining power over people'. Still today, the most important fact dividing current leaders is - the right use of power.

The questions are:

> *Why the explanation of these terms in a leadership book? Do leaders still make use of these methods? What should we know and what should we do?*

The answer is - yes, many of our current leaders still make use of these methods. We have the responsibility to understand where our leaders are coming from, where and from whom they get their guidance and information, in order to understand where they are going. We also need to secure the right leaders, in the right places, in order to secure a steady progress on growth, development and the quality of life for all. Everyone has the calling to place the right people in the right positions, in order to secure a safe transition into the next season of human existence. It is time to set the records straight - it is time to raise the bar where the quality of our leaders is concerned.

From the recordings of human history, it is clearly documented that any leader functioning independently, by ignoring and negating this higher spiritual alliance by rendering themselves as 'god', were doomed to self-destruct in the end. The destruction of their followers was therefore inevitable, as we find in the ancient history of the Aztecs.

Leadership lessons from ancient history

The Aztecs were a warrior nation that arrived in the valley of Mexico during the 13th century AD. History and legend reveal that they came from northern Mexico and called themselves *Mexica*. That term later changed to *Aztec*. However, according to records, the *Mexica* were led to the valley by a spiritual seer, called *Tenoch*[142]. It was revealed to him in a dream that he and his people must continue wondering until they come to a place that they would recognise when they saw an eagle flying with a serpent in its beak[143].

At the time of their arrival in the valley of Mexico, it was largely filled by a great lake. They also discovered that the surrounding land was already occupied by five other tribes. As these tribes were not keen on giving up their land, they all came together, conferred, and arrived at a solution. They would solve the problem by giving the Aztecs an uninhabited island in the middle of the lake. Here the Aztecs could settle, if they so pleased. However, the natives of the area knew that the island was infested with poisonous snakes, which they hoped would take care of their Aztec problem[144].

When Tenoch and his followers went out to the island, they saw a great eagle grappling with a serpent in its beak. This was the sign for which they had been waiting. Delighted, Tenoch declared that this was the place that he had been guided to look for in his dream. The snakes posed no problem to the Aztecs, for where they came from these were considered to be a great delicacy. Very grateful for their new home and with a well-stocked larder too, the Aztecs accepted the offer of the island and began building a new city, called *Tenochtitlan*, after its founder.

Within a very short time, the Aztecs flourished and became the dominant tribe in the valley of Mexico. Integrating with their neighbours, they formed a very powerful nation with Tenochtitlan as the capital. They united with the people of the Valley of Mexico, who taught them much about their religious beliefs and customs. For a while, they all lived in peace and prosperity.

To the northwest of Tenochtitlan lived the Toltecs, who were a blood-thirsty race. As part of their solar religion, they carried out human sacrifices on a regular basis. Over time, the Aztecs became alienated from the values and guidance once instilled by Tenoch and his followers, and adopted the same superstitious beliefs. They even took these customs and beliefs to absurd lengths. Under the leadership of Montezuma ll, the then king of the Aztecs, human sacrifice and especially the removal of still beating hearts, soon became the central mystery of their religion.

Silently, the younger Aztecs also encouraged rebellion amongst their subjects. It gave them the excuse to send in their army to take prisoners that provided them with a constant supply of human hearts to offer to the sun god. They believed that by doing this, they were feeding it with its favorite food - human life-force. Not only were they bloodthirsty, but they also worshiped a blood-thirsty god. According to these ancient beliefs, the blood-offerings ensured that the sun rose every day.

Historical records reveal that, for the consecration of Tenochtitlan's main temple alone, some 20,000 victims were sacrificed. It is estimated that at least 50,000 unfortunates were sacrificed each year. All this would have been a terror to their spiritual leader Tenoch, had he lived to see it.

Flag of Mexico

Needless to say, the Aztecs, under the leadership of Montezuma ll, became greatly feared and hated by all the neighboring peoples of Mexico. Their only hope was that the long awaited god-king, would return. It had been prophesied that this man, Quetzalcoat l, would reclaim his kingdom and set them free. As their only hope, the people kept this ancient legend alive. It was with some trepidation that Montezuma ll, heard that men with beards and white faces had arrived in his kingdom. This occurred in the year of the Reed - exactly the time predicted this arrival would occur.

On 4 March 1519, Hernan Cotes, with 11 ships and 600 foot soldiers, 16 horses, and artillery from Spain, landed on the coast of Mexico. He immediately started taking possession of the cities and the land. During a campaign lasting little more than two years, Cotes completely destroyed the Aztec empire. By the end of 1521, one of the richest countries in the world, which had up until that time been totally unknown to Europeans, became a province of Spain. Today, the flag of Mexico still contains the symbol of the eagle with a rattlesnake in its beak, as a remembrance of these times. The Aztecs are but a vague memory and part of ancient history. They lost the battle because their survival as a nation was totally dependent on the quality of their leaders, and the kind of leadership they were subjected to.[145] Their visionless leaders let them down

From ancient history until our modern times, we find that leaders and their leadership styles can make or break a country and nation. History also reveals that appointing and developing new leaders and leadership styles, was not always done in the way we know it today.

Conclusion

Nothing has changed where leadership is concerned. The fundamental principals regarding quality and good leadership in the beginning of human creation, are still relevant to this day. The fact remains: different gods, different opinions, different values, different directions and - different leadership styles. Where and to whom we are connected, determine our values and priorities, and influence the outcome. There is only one of two options: higher-value soul awareness and a dedicated spiritual path, or a lower ego-driven awareness and commitment to 'Mammon'. Mammon is the god of physicality and of money - the false god of ego or lower self[146]. This is all there is. These are the only two fundamental points of departure. This has got nothing to do with religion, the gods or God. As we found with Solomon, he had everything in the palm of his hand, but he was seduced by 'mammon' and became distracted and disconnected. In the end, he suffered the consequences, and self-destructed.

Leadership has everything to do with a personal awareness of, and conscious choice for, soul-centered values, of who you are, what makes you happy, and how you will get it and create a quality life. We become pathfinders, mapmakers and way-showers, to a fulfilling life of love and abundance for all. In the process, we find out how to serve others and the greater good.

In the next chapter, we will explore some fundamentals of New Leadership DNA.

CHAPTER 3

FUNDAMENTALS OF NEW LEADERSHIP DNA

Introduction

Leadership, success and quality living are inevitably interconnected. However, our definitions of success and perspectives of quality living differ, and therefore leaders, leadership values and leadership styles will differ. We find leaders on different levels[147], with different values and different styles.

The questions are:

> *What is authentic leadership? What are the fundamental principles of enlightened leadership?*

Fundamental principles of authentic leadership

In order to get to the root of leadership and lay a new foundation, we first need to understand the basic meaning. The word 'leader' comes from the word *leidð*, meaning 'to show the way by going in advance; to guide by taking by the hand; escort; direct; to go first as a guide; to be at the head of; to act as director or commander'. A leader is a person who influences others to change or move in a specific direction. This influence could be a guide to others on the path of life, business, family issues, sport, politics, economics, or any other context of life. It could also take on a negative direction of crime, negativity and corruption.

'Leadership' denotes a position to influence others to move or change; an office and ability to lead. However, everyone has the power and ability to influence others to move and change. We can directly influence others by taking up a leadership position, or indirectly by voting for leaders to take up leadership positions on our behalf. We also have the collective influence and responsibility to choose worthy, quality leaders, who represent our values, definition of success and quality living.

We could unconsciously influence the lives of every person we meet. This is not determined by our position or possessions, but by the influence and power of who we are. At the moment, we are awakening and becoming self-aware - self-conscious. We are learning about our authentic self and personal power, while re-igniting with our Power Intelligence[148]. This means everyone should be conscious of and educated in the emerging New Leadership DNA, in order to accept responsibility for our collective challenge. We need to become aware of our contribution in creating a quality future that will benefit all. We all need to become conscious of the influence we personally have in placing and maintaining authentic leaders in their leadership positions. Our choice of and support for leaders will reflect our value systems. At the same time, we come mindful of our personal power to influence others. This is what this book is all about.

Leadership always has to do with the perception of success, quality living, and how to obtain it. Leadership is all about ensuring a specific value system. This could be an individual perception that benefits only a minority, or a collective perception that benefits all. The perception of success and quality living are driving forces behind all leadership endeavors. Leadership is the ability to successfully ignite movement and change in the direction the leader or leaders see as a better quality of life. New Success DNA is therefore a prerequisite for New Leadership DNA[149].

All leaders have a personal agenda. Some ask "what is good for me" and "how many people will agree with me and will go along with my vision and value system?" or "what will serve me/mine best?" Some leaders ask different and broader questions: "What will benefit all of us?", and "how many can we benefit and take along?", or ... "How can I serve?" Identifying value-orientated and constructive or destructive self-serving leaders and leadership styles, starts with the answers to the questions:

> *Where are they coming from? What is their*
> *personal point of departure and value system?*
> *What is their personal agenda?*

If we understand where someone is coming from, what their point of departure and personal agenda is, we will also know where they are going and what to expect in the future. There are mainly two points of view. On the one hand, the vision and value system benefits only a select few. This represents an exclusive leadership style. On the other hand, the vision and value system is inclusive and benefits all. The vision is determined by the leader's vision of success and quality living. Followers will support a leader if they believe that they will benefit from the choices and the processes involved. Here we find an alignment and synergy of agendas.

The questions that guide this process are:

> *What do we want? Why do we want it? What*
> *must we do to get what we want? How do we*
> *create a better life for ourselves? (this could*
> *be an exclusive or inclusive 'self')*

Once these questions are addressed and the individual and collective vision of 'successful living' has been identified, qualified and quantified for those involved - it becomes necessary to get others to buy in to the vision, values and concept. Methods, skills, tools and contexts may differ from person to person, or group to group. In the end, all will agree on what is best for all in the group - be it an inclusive or exclusive group. This has the same relevancy for a group of terrorists, a group of Wall Street businessmen, youth leaders, a group of street children, or the G8 countries. Only the content will differ, and the answers to the questions will vary. The fundamentals always stay the same

The overall concept of leadership is the ability to obtain and secure successful, quality living - whatever the definition may be. Even if hardships have to be endured, the vision will still hold the group together, while they keep on agreeing on the underlying value system. This is the 'glue' that keeps everyone together.

If the value system loses its stronghold, the group will lose momentum, become 'unglued' and disintegrate. The leader will fall from grace. For decades leaders such as Mubarak from Egypt, Gaddafi from Libya, Mugabe from Zimbabwe, the Chinese government, and others, have ruled their people with an exclusive system that only benefited a select few. Previous governments in America, apartheid in South Africa, leadership in India, the Far and Middle East, and around the globe, all have histories of this inclusive leadership paradigm. Domination, dictatorship, intimidation, suppression, neglect and abuse of the majority are all part of this mindset that secures the quality of life for some at the expense of others. This is based on a scarcity mentality and a mindset of fear and survival. Now all is about to change.

As human awareness begins to expand, people start to ask: "What about me?" In order to maintain their positions, Presidents Mubarak and Gaddafi, the Chinese government, and other African and Middle-Eastern governments, have had to use force to secure their power and leadership positions. In the end, they will be overthrown by the same people who used to follow their lead.

The questions are:

> *What is changing and why are these changes occurring now?*

Nothing lasts forever. When we arrive at one point and start to become comfortable, there is always a trigger that initiates something new. New wants, needs and values begin to emerge as people become dissatisfied with the *status quo*. The new creates a new buzz, and a field of new energy starts to take hold and spread. Change and transformation become inevitable. We are presently in the midst of a power shift, as a shift in consciousness and awareness. A new mindset, value system and level of consciousness are emerging.

A good leader is a person who can anticipate and even initiate positive change that will benefit all. Bad leaders ignore and oppose these signs or can hijack the changes for their benefit only. Successful leaders identify the course to follow, show the way, and inspire others to buy in and commit to the new vision of success[150].

Authentic leaders are new pathfinders, mapmakers and way-showers. They can motivate, inspire, assist and guide others to change and move from one position to another. Not only do they give direction, but they can also create a new vision in the minds of others. They can provide solutions and implement relevant strategies in order to secure successful change. A true leader is a 'change agent' and a catalyst. Authentic leaders are alchemists[151] - changing lower-order human awareness into a higher consciousness of success and quality living for all.

The movement and change can either be positive or negative - all depending on the personal qualities or value system of the leader. This means we either have a positive or negative foundation for leadership or a leadership style.

In order to determine the fundamental point of departure of a leader, we need to ask the questions:

> *Where is this person coming from? Are they coming from a foundation of inner peace and positive values that will benefit all, or ... Are they ego-driven, with their value system only benefitting an inclusive group? Are their motives based on fear and are therefore self-destructive?*

Once we know the answers to these questions we can already determine the process and the outcome. There is only one of two possibilities. Our lessons from history, as we have seen in the leadership experiences with the Aztecs, give us some clues.

Different foundations - different outcomes

Tenoch was a well-known, well-loved, honest leader - valued and trusted by the Aztec people. The people knew that he had the welfare of all at heart. Tenoch's integrity and vision inspired the people to wander into the unknown with him, until they had proof of their land as promised. Tenoch was also a seer. He had special spiritual abilities, could envision the future, and interpret dreams. His faith and the faith of the Aztecs in higher dimensions of universal information and spiritual guidance, gave them the confidence and faith to leave their comfort zone, and to travel to an unknown destination in search of a better life.

However, change is never easy, but they all stayed true to their higher[152] guidance and vision of something new, bigger and better. What seemed to be uninhabitable to some became the 'promised land' to the Aztecs. Tenoch further succeeded in maintaining unity, and enhanced the binding force amongst all Aztecs. This made them a force to be reckoned with as a nation. Their influence soon spread and they became the dominant driving force of success and prosperity[153] in the region.

After Tenoch died, the values, faith, spiritual awareness and vision of the Aztecs dissipated over time. Each time a new leader was appointed, their guidance came from a lower level of consciousness. Forgotten was their initial connection to higher mind and spiritual guidance. As the Aztecs took on the beliefs and values of other bloodthirsty nations, the initial binding force Tenoch and his followers had instilled, became diluted, and then lost its hold. They become 'unglued'.

The destiny of the Aztecs under the leadership of Montezuma II was perilous. Montezuma II and his closest followers took their blood-thirsty rituals to the extreme. Primarily driven by greed, blood-thirsty ego-satisfaction, and fear, they negated the meaning of life and the value of prosperity for all. Without a common vision and positive leadership, their demise was swift and permanent.

Today we only find the remnants of this once powerful nation in museums or ancient history books.

Different foundations - different leadership styles

Positive leadership is ignited by a positive value system of peace and prosperity for all. This foundation is built upon universal or soul values and spiritual laws. This includes a vision of authentic success, abundance, prosperity, harmony and peace for all, and the solid uplifting universal values of honesty, truth, integrity, transparency and vision. There is an unseen universal driving force and higher guidance behind all the decisions and actions that propel everyone forward. This leadership style benefits all.

Un-authentic and also destructive leadership only benefits those in control, and is fundamentally built on a negative value system with underlying greed, control and fear. Fear is a destructive ego-driven force that ignites the development of self-serving systems, corruption, manipulation, intimidation and even annihilation of any opposition. At the same time, a negative fear-based system has self-defeating and a self-destructive processes as a default. Leaders who employ these destructive strategies are mostly unaware of these inherent destructive forces within their midst. This mindset includes a scarcity mentality with a deep-seated belief that there is not enough for all, while personal agendas and ego-driven laws govern the process. In the end, like Montezuma ll and the Aztecs, everything will and does self-destruct.

Self-mastery versus self-destruction

There is a growing consciousness and deeper spiritual awareness emerging within the general person in the street. Not only are individuals are rising up, but also groups, and even countries like Egypt, Libya, Syria and other Middle Eastern societies, are overthrowing outworn leaders and their rule of domination. A global awakening is taking place and change is inevitable. We can expect radical[154] change - a change that will touch on the fundamental values of life and the meaning of quality living, to take prominence. This means we can expect new leaders and a new leadership style to emerge, and also take predominance.

The purpose of this book is to provide guidelines during these changes, to those who also believe that there is something more and something better for all. These are the people who are prepared to take on the challenge and lay a new foundation for a new generation. First, we must know who we are and what we want, before we can decide where to go.

As we become more aware, we begin to ask the questions:

> *Who is the authentic me? What makes me successful and happy? Where am I going, and how do I get there? Who and what do I need to take along?*

We are being forced to re-evaluate our fundamental values and revisit our foundations. Great changes can be expected as many awake and change their very foundation and perception of life and quality living. The concept of success and successful living is taking on a whole new meaning. Living the 'good life' that includes money, fashion, cars and 'bling' is now making way for living the 'good life' that includes healthy living, protecting nature, and searching for deeper spiritual meaning. The definition of success is moving from ego-driven motives of obtaining positions and possessions, to a new foundation of the quality of persons we are becoming in the process of life. What we once viewed as symbols of success, like money, cars, and societal positions, are now becoming symbols of primitive, ego-driven values. People are becoming aware of higher spiritual values and definitions of success, and a whole New Success DNA is emerging. Once we question our own values, foundation and purpose, we become aware of still deeper questions.

These questions are:

> *Am I a physical being looking for a spiritual connection, or -*
> *Am I a spiritual light-energy being having an experience in a physical body on a physical planet*

The soul represents deeper, universal values, and the ego represents physical, earthly, individual values. We are either value and soul-centered or we are materialistic and ego-centered. The soul receives guidance from the divine universe, source or higher power - God. The ego receives guidance from Mammon - the god of physicality, the god of 'stuff'. One path leads to deeper universal values, true self discovery, mastery and authentic success. The other leads to self deception and in the end, self-destruction. Leadership is therefore either built on soul-centered values or on ego-centered values. These are the only two points of departure.

Ego-self centered leadership

The ego will find it difficult to answer the above questions as the confusion of world teachings does not give clear guidelines on who you authentically are. The ego-centered person is always self-conscious in the eyes of others and cares what other people think and say about them. They get their information from external sources and constantly need reassurance of who they are in the eyes of others. Self-importance takes on different forms. This person tries to prove their personal value to others and to themselves by acquiring physical possessions and social positions. This is the 'bling' of life. However, the 'bling' also has a sting - it never lasts very long. It is a matter of time before you come to learn that it is a meaningless existence - just repeating itself.

With the global recession and decline of international finances and financial institutions, many people and companies have lost everything. This has caused more than physical loss: also a loss of self, bruised egos and identity crisis. This means many people live a lie, built on a non-sustainable foundation of things or 'stuff", while employing different self-serving strategies. Sometimes these strategies include being important in the eyes of others, becoming rebellious, enforcing negative resistance, or opposing the *status quo.*

When external circumstances start to crumble and fail, an ego-driven person becomes unglued and fear-filled. They go through a stage of loss, pain, and depression, whilst experiencing an identity crisis. Anxiety and fear turns into manipulation, domination, intimidation and even violence. If they learn to overcome their ego-orientation, they can leave this stage behind - if not, they will have a prolonged stay in darkness and despair until they can identify with the authentic foundations of success. All self-serving and self-indulging methods are delusions that in the end lead to self-destruction.

The ego is driven by a hunger and fear that can never ever be satisfied. It constantly needs to be reassured, stroked, fed and boosted. Ego indulgences are very draining, as people live in constant frustration, anger, inferiority, arrogance, rejection, judgment, and conflict. In the end, people who are ego-driven *always* self-destruct.

Authentic leadership means first getting to know the ego-self and learning to manage and master personal self-defeating mechanisms before taking on the responsibility of leading others. Leaders are therefore born *and* bred.

SOUL-CENTERED	EGO-CENTERED
Self-aware	Self-conscious
Self-worth	Self-centred
Self-esteem	Self-importance
Self-care	Self-serving
Self-confidence	Self-delusion
Self-respect	Self-indulgence
Self-mastery	Self-destructive

Soul- versus ego-centred leadership

Soul-value centered leadership

The soul-centered person becomes aware of being an energy-spiritual, soul being, having a physical experience for a short time on a physical planet called Earth. Deeper universal soul values originate from a universal pool of values that underpin all of our reality, and are valid for everyone. There is the connection to a higher spiritual power or the absolute, many call God, source, the infinite, or any term you might use to explain a higher power or deity.

The soul or personal value system has an inner GPS (global positioning system) connecting to higher dimensions within the higher ether, spiritual realm[155]. It is from this realm that the soul receives direction and guidance. A description of the different dimensions was covered in the book *New Success DNA*, in more detail. Just like our GPSs receives message from the global satellites circling the Earth, the soul receives higher guidance for a universal source.

The summary below gives an indication of one of the two paths we could follow. There are seven steps that correspond to the seven steps of the pyramid of consciousness and development, which is discussed in a following chapter.

The soul-centered person knows the unique value of the self and the potential influence of each unique person, *warts and all*. They live a life of acceptance and non-judgment, and are above and below no-one. This is the person with true self-respect, high self-esteem, and self-value. They can see the big picture where everything is connected to everything else in a universal interconnected whole - that functions with precision according to universal laws, and remains in perfect balance and harmony.

The uniqueness of every soul on Earth has value and a unique imprint to make, a personal legacy to leave, and a role to play within the greater whole. Personal value is expressed in self-love, and love and care for others, nature, and the world at large. Self-esteem, self-value, and self-love are all part of a life of self-caring, while the path of life is explored with true self confidence, harmony, balance, faith, and trust in the deeper perfection of everything and everyone.

Many could see this as naïve, but it takes a lot of self discipline to focus on the positive, more than the negative possibilities. Everything you focus on grows. Here self-mastery, harmony, balance, and peace, form the basis of successful living. This foundation is non negotiable, and always leads to true success.

From the outline of the two different points of departure above, we find that the two power positions of leaders, and how they gain support, differ as well. As the waves of change become more evident, we can expect a fundamental shift from one side to the other. *Power over people* is changing to *igniting power within people*, and *power in numbers* is changing to the *number of powers* ignited in every individual. We will focus on these important issues in the next chapter.

Self-mastery and leadership

We have examples of many people who have mastered difficult

situations because of their level of maturity and self-mastery. Nelson Mandela, Martin Luther King, and Mahatma Gandhi, are just a few of the icons who have left a legacy of what non-violent, soul-centered leadership really is. The imprint they have made on the collective consciousness and world history, is a legacy of soul-centered self-mastery and value-driven leadership.

The word *mastery* refers to 'being an original from which copies are made' or 'to overcome or defeat', and 'he/she who is greater'. Self-mastery refers to overcoming the lower ego-self, delusional self or lie - while following inner soul-guidance and 'copying' the spiritual self or higher self. The only true foundation for successful leadership is truth and honesty with the self, others and the world. As the pace of change accelerates, all that is not truth, false, corrupt or broken, will be uncovered, rise to the surface, placed in conscious awareness and brought to light. These negative issues are now seeking recognition, solution and healing. The only resolve is to learn to lead with truth, honesty and integrity.

Leadership and integrity

The word 'integrity' is derived from the Latin words *integritãs* or *integer,* and is defined as "any intact unity or entity, whole, complete, perfect, virtuous". It refers to people with connected, centered, whole, and integrated personalities and identities. Their way of thinking, feeling, believing, and doing, are in harmony, balance, and are synchronised with each other. They are people with honest sincerity. Their lives are transparent, and there is an almost naïve openness and honesty - towards life and people in general. These leaders live a whole, integrated, clean, and creative life. Energy is not wasted unnecessarily. Herein we find a universal power, spirit, source and force at work.

The compelling force of each individual, group, company, organisation, and country, as well as the healing of mankind, can be found in integrity. There are five important components of integrity that need to be aligned and synchronised – our thinking, feeling, believing, speaking and active doing. Our actions speak louder than words. The world today requires powerful people who talk their walk, and walk their talk - in truth, honesty, and integrity.

The importance of leadership

People need and want strong leaders to show the way. Especially in turbulent times of chaotic, radical change, the need for leadership is prevalent. If the development and implementation of strong and grounded leadership is ignored, it could, and usually does, end in anarchy and destruction. Leadership always involves movement and change. We find two kinds of leaders, as constructive or destructive movement and change agents.

Constructive leadership refers to a person or group of persons, who take the wellbeing of all involved into consideration. Destructive leaders implement destructive values, methods and beliefs that only benefit a select few. The direction of change will depend on the inner dynamics, programming and subconscious patterns of the leader. This is where we find our New Leadership DNA. These inner dynamics include with whom and what the leader identifies, where the leader gets his/her guidance from, what kind of influence he/she portrays, and where or to what he/she is connected. A good leader is always first a good follower.

Leadership is a value-driven force that influences all involved. By understanding these forces and power surges that drive individuals, groups, nations and even the human race, brings us closer to understanding the new qualities of emerging leaders. These are individuals who can lead us into a prosperous future. We will be able to distinguish between constructive and destructive leaders and leadership styles. In democratic societies, we need to become conscious of whom we choose as leaders, and who we give these powerful positions to. As responsible citizens, we have to understand what power is and what the power-shift is all about.

Assessment

1. General assessment

From the above, draw up a list of values and personal traits that you think a positive leader should have. Use it as a checklist for yourself or for anytime that you need to give or receive guidance. Always ask: "Where is this coming from?"

2. Self assessment

Do your personal self-evaluation profile on the internet. Many websites are available, or go to the New Success DNA website and do the PI Success Profile[156]. You can use this information to develop a self-development programme and keep track of your progress. Plan your own programme and focus on the issues you need to master. Identify methods to move forward. Keep track of your progress,

In order to lay a sound foundation for developing New Leadership DNA, we need to once again start at the beginning, and ask fundamental questions:

> *What does this shift in consciousness really entail? What should we know about leaders and leadership, and what should we do in order to secure a safe transition into the next level of success, prosperity and quality living*

Leadership is not only meant for the select few any more. Everyone has to be informed about and trained in the fundamentals of New Leadership DNA. Leadership is changing from 'power-over-people' to a new perception of releasing 'power-within-people'. Everyone now needs to consciously accept responsibility for the influential roles we play, if we want to secure a positive transition into the future.

This is what this book is all about.

Notes

CHAPTER 4

LEADERSHIP, POWER AND INFLUENCE

"You don't have to be a 'person of influence' to be influential. In fact, the most influential people in my life are probably not even aware of the things they've taught me."

Scott Adams

Leadership and influence

Leaders are placed in very powerful positions, and are given the power and authority to make decisions on behalf of others. The decisions they make influence people, create change, give direction, and secure outcomes. How they manage this power and power-position, will depend on their personal and inter-personal dynamics. Their personal foundation and what they stand for, forms the foundation of all processes, procedures and outcomes that follow. The quality of a leader all depends on where they are coming from, and the quality of choices they make.

Most books on leadership outline what a leader should do. This book is aimed at who the authentic leader is as a person. The rest will flow from this core truth. When identifying, choosing and training a leader, we need to know the following.

We need to ask:

> *Where does this person stand on power and power positions? Where are they coming from?*

In the previous chapter, we found only one of two options available – ego-driven power and leadership that in the end is self destructive, or soul-driven power and leadership that is bound to higher universal guidance, personal self-discipline and self-mastery, and that benefits the greater good.

Soul-driven power stands for the positive use of power and power-positions, to the benefit of all. Ego-driven power has the abuse of power as default, as it benefits only the select few. This inevitably leads to destruction and disintegration. Leaders, and all people voting for leaders, should therefore have a clear understanding of what they stand for. Another take on it is the saying *"People who do not stand for something - fall for everything"*.

Leaders and their supporters should know the purpose of power and power-positions. The reason is, if you do not know what the use of something is - abuse (absence of use) is inevitable. All leaders should have a clear understanding of power processes, if they want to secure their leadership positions and maintain the progress of their people. This can only be done in one of two ways: maintaining power over people, or igniting power within people.

The questions are:

> *What is power? What is the purpose or meaning of power? How must this power be put to use? What will happen if this power is abused? What is the true role of a leader in a power position?*

The true role an authentic leader is to be of service to the people and to influence the greater good for humanity and nature.

What is power?

Aristotle coined the word *energy* as "active *power* at work", and the word 'energy' and 'power' are used in an interrelated way. Power takes many forms. Abuses have marred its use, whereas virtue has enhanced it. All power is subject to two primary qualifications under the classification of relativity: material-transitory and cosmic-universal. On a more personal level, we find power to be physical and metaphysical or divine.

In nature, we find electrical, chemical, nuclear, elemental and cosmic power. We also find temporal power, consisting of social influences, mass pressures, governmental and religious authority. On a more personal level, we find primary types of power that include personal, physical, emotional, mental and spiritual power. We find this in various forms and on different frequencies.

Power, or energy, cannot be annihilated, but can only change from one form another. Some forms of energy can be stored, others stay static, and some are dynamic and subject to a frequent change and transformation. At the very core of our existence, we find multidimensional realities of power and potential as 'power-on-hold'. Our total existence depends on the constant *energy-on-the-move*. The purpose or 'right use' of power, is to maintain the flow of life and quality living. The abuse of power or 'absence of use' in any form, leads to blocking of flow, disintegration, and the destruction of life. This is one of the cosmic laws to which everyone should adhere.

In living entities, energy is life force. Living organisms, with functions such as growth, response, stimulation and reproduction, are distinguished from dead organisms by the absence of these qualities. This not only applies to people, plants and animals, but also to organisations, companies, political parties, and even countries and nations who function as interconnected, living wholes. Companies, organisations and countries who commit to the positive use of power and release new potential, display signs of growth, development and progress. Those who abuse power and power-positions will self-destruct. An important fact to remember here is the universal law of: 'right use of power' – the 'right use of life-force'. At the same time, all power is interrelated and interconnected on a universal level, to form a cosmic web. At this level, everything is connected to everything else - like the 'internet' of life.

Power, and personal or 'psychic energy'

Jung[157] coined the term *psychic energy* as referring to the manifestation of the basic dynamics of life. He exclusively concentrated on the psychological aspects of the phenomenon. 'Psychic energy' is a collective term referring to human energy/power, generated from four different levels as physical, mental, emotional and spiritual energy sources. The utilisation of the power levels influence our behaviour and determine greatness[158].

Hawkins[159] identified a stratification of energy levels or attractor fields, existing according to corresponding levels of consciousness. He suggests that these powerful attractor fields dominate human existence, define content, meaning and value, and serve as organising energies for widespread human behaviour. He developed kinesiology - based on muscle response stimulus - as a science, over the last thirty years.

Csikszentmihali[160] states that creating physical objects requires both physical and psychic energy, and says that once we begin to use these energy levels or 'power tools', they start shaping our minds and actions. At the opposite end of this complexity of psychic energy development, is a form of "psychic entropy".

Research has revealed common factors found in strong personalities from all classes, as persons who are curious, try many things, enjoy influencing others, and are especially well equipped to affect the evolution of positive thought forms - because their beliefs, ideas and habits will be represented more frequently in future. Persons with 'psychic entropy' lack these factors. Positive leaders identify people with psychic entropy as power vampires or power parasites, and keep them out of their system

A human power-shift and the emergence of a higher-order self (or higher self) is taking place. People are now required to take back their personal power and to manage personal psychic energy. The focus on the development of self-actualisation and self-mastery reflect the emergence of this new consciousness. It poses the challenge of developing new thinking, a new intelligence, and even a new kind of human being[161]. Radical and fundamental change is inevitable.

Changing perceptions of power

From different scientific[162] psychological and religious perspectives in the West[163], reality is seen as a universal energy field, a quantum soup, a force-field of potential, power and energy-information. It is also defined as the spiritual, metaphysical, non-physical, quantum or virtual reality. This universal power or higher power is intelligent, omniscient, and omnipotent, and underpins and encompasses all levels and all layers of existence.

In the East this universal energy field is described as 'chi', 'qi', and 'ki', and defined as "breaths of life" or "life force"[164] This Universal Energy Field of Potential (Power) or the UFP, is seen as a vast morphogenic field of power, energy, potential and information. It is perceived as a sea of universal energy and unlimited information. It is a field of infinite possibilities. It is also viewed as the universal psyche, universal consciousness and universal intelligence, higher mind, or God mind. Our physical reality is holographic. It is a projection of thought or mind/Mind on the UFP[165], and the UFP coalesces into physical form[166]. Physical form is outcome only, and can change as our thoughts change.

We can access this powerhouse of energy-information and wisdom, by raising our consciousness, our awareness and mindfulness. We can co-create our own physical reality by being connected to the UFP, and can utilise this infinite potential at our disposal. It is scientifically accepted that when our thoughts, perceptions and information change, the energy levels change accordingly, and vice versa[167]. A power-shift reflects this change of perceptions, consciousness and thinking, and allows the flow of new information/energy through the system[168].

Developments in physics have a large impact on the perception of reality, and therefore on all perceptions reflected in psychology, education, philosophy, business science, leadership development and other disciplines[169]. When our perceptions of reality change, it reverberates in the changing of perceptions in all disciplines. This stimulates the flow of new information, while these changes impact on all contexts of life[170].

Einstein postulated, and Bohm and other scientists[171] concurred, that we live in and are part of a sea of energy-information or a quantum soup. From a metaphysical perspective, the quantum soup is defined as cosmic light or spirit.[172] We find the causality of all things physical within the quantum soup. It is the essence or source, from

101

which our physical reality is created. Physical reality is in essence 'frozen energy', 'frozen light', or 'spirit in form'. It is the tangible result or effect of consciously accessing and effectively manipulating the quantum soup. We can consciously develop the knowledge, understanding and different power tools, skills, competencies and strategies, in order to release this potential or 'power on hold' in the quantum soup, and precipitate the desired form in our physical reality.

Physical reality is effect only. All things physical are a holographic three-dimensional image of a projected image/Image[173]. The enduring truths of ancient wisdom also include the idea of levels or dimensions of reality. This is found in different levels of consciousness that reaches from matter to body, to mind, to soul, to spirit. Universal spirit is fully and equally present at all of these levels. It is the source, nest, God, ground or creation of the entire display[174]. Each senior layer transcends and includes its juniors.

The higher levels of reality and higher power levels can only be accessed and/or discovered by developing higher levels of awareness, mindfulness, consciousness and understanding. Transpersonal psychology has developed from these insights, with the aim of studying transpersonal experiences and the higher realms of consciousness, to include psychic, subtle, causal and 'nondual' levels[175]. Various leaders in the field of transpersonal psychology[176] declare that human beings have the capacity to access these higher states of consciousness, and move beyond.

A short definition of transpersonal psychology from the *Journal of Transpersonal Psychology*[177], suggests that transpersonal psychology "is concerned with the study of humanity's highest potential, and with the recognition, understanding, and realization of intuitive, spiritual, and transcendent states of consciousness". Issues considered in transpersonal psychology, include spiritual self-development, self beyond the ego, peak experiences, mystical experiences, systemic trance and other sublime and/or unusually expanded experiences of living. It has not yet entered the mainstream of the formal academic world and training in leadership, leaving a void to be explored. This requires a change in perception and a paradigm shift.

A paradigm shift in leadership theories

Reich developed the concept of 'bioenergy' and described it as a fundamental form of energy that permeates and governs the entire organism and manifests itself in emotions, as well as the flow of bodily fluids and other biophysical movement[178]. To Reich, 'bioenergy' reflected the process that goes on in the universe at large, and was a special manifestation of a form of cosmic energy that he called 'orgone energy'. His concepts resemble the Chinese concept of 'chi'. Capra refers to Reich as a pioneer of the paradigm shift that left no-one and nothing untouched[179]. This new way of thinking caused Reich to be excluded from the scientific community, to his persecution, and in the end to his tragic death.

Jung[180] referred to 'psychic energy', which he saw as a manifestation of the basic dynamics of life. He used the term 'libido', much in the same sense as Reich used 'bionergy', but exclusively concentrated on the psychological aspects of the phenomenon. Against this background, Hawkins[181] identified a stratification of attractor fields that exist according to corresponding levels of consciousness. He suggests that these powerful attractor fields dominate human existence and therefore define content, meaning and value.

Hawkins considered that these attractor fields and corresponding levels of consciousness, served as underlying organising energies for widespread human behaviour[182]. The implication is that, at a level far below conceptual consciousness, the body 'knows', and through muscle testing is able to signal positive expanding forces and negative dissipating and/or destructive forces.

Various perceptions from the East include the understanding of the human energy field or aura, and the chakra system. The chakras are defined as 'wheels of light' that function as vortexes through which cosmic/spiritual and physical energy interrelates[183]. These philosophies, once banned from Western thinking, are now evolving as the *New East*, while providing insight into the functioning of human energy fields and psychic energy. At the same time, we are gaining insight into the dynamics between physical, emotional, mental and spiritual energy levels.

The influence of personal psychic energy, attractor fields and corresponding levels of consciousness on human functioning and healing, has been scientifically proven and is readily used in healing practices[184]. We find for example that premature babies grow slower and even die, if they are deprived of the caring and nurturing qualities and positive influence of a mother or mother substitute. Aura readings, previously seen as alternative or New Age, and excluded from Western thinking, are now being scientifically investigated within traditional medical sciences[185].

On a scientific level, it has been found that the individual and universal minds are interconnected as part of a holographic whole[186]. Gaining access to the universal field is possible by means of our neuro-physiology and neuro-psychology. The whole human being, including the physical body, is an energy system, a system of information and power, with structure and form, giving access to a larger body of information and power[187].

Humans are manifested 'life force', 'chi' (East) or 'bioenergy', 'orgone' or 'spirit' (West). The body is part and parcel of the individual energy field within larger energy fields that can consciously be changed, developed and utilised by free will, to manifest a desired reality and successful outcome. The physical body is manifest in the person and not the person in the body as presupposed[188]. This has important consequences for the approaches to physical and psychological 'wholeness', wellness, well-being and healing.

A paradigm shift in leadership theories is taking place. There is a shift from leadership defined as leading people in a certain direction, to leaders directing energy and the power in the people. New Leadership DNA refers to the ability of a leader to become an energy engineer or alchemist. Alchemy is the ancient science of trying to turn lower metals, like copper or lead, into gold. On a personal level, it is the conscious ability to turn lower ego-driven potential into higher levels of human innovation and inspiration. Just like the alchemists, new leaders are becoming the alchemists, the new *gold smiths* of humanity.

Against this background, and in order to develop a deeper understanding of leadership and the influence on human potential, it is necessary to explore the various dimensions of reality, a bit further.

The question is:

> *What is reality?*

Power and reality

Human beings have intelligence[189] and free will and can choose how they will utilise their potential. It is therefore important to develop a deeper understanding of the levels of reality and methods of access that consciously or subconsciously influence choice and free will.

The *physical, material reality* represents levels of energy that have materialised or precipitated, vibrate or oscillate at different frequencies, and are visible as different forms and structures. These forms and structures represent different levels of information. Access is gained through our senses. Sensory perceptions are personally or collectively interpreted through our personal programming, value systems, and other filters[190]. Reality on the outside is therefore the projected meaning of reality within the self.

To change external reality, we first need to change our inner perceptions, filters, programmes and information-energy levels. As change takes place, individuals and organisations switch to a new wavelength that results in the emergence of new forms, structures and new levels of quality living[191].

The *quantum reality*[192] comprising atoms, electrons, protons and subatomic particles, is perceived as the smallest building block of physicality. We understand this reality through various scientific methods. At the same time, we can influence the quantum reality by consciously focusing thoughts, visions and dreams. Thoughts are electromagnetic impulses that can change the quantum reality and existing electromagnetic fields. These fields act as electromagnets that attract or repel anything within the field of influence[193]. This again organises matter and changes physical reality. This gives rise to one of the fundamental universal laws - the law of resonance - the law of attraction.

Behind this all and as a backdrop to everything, we find the *metaphysical reality - absolute.* Here we find the source/Source of infinite potential and possibilities. This is the place of silence. The metaphysical reality is an unbounded, unlimited, timeless, formless, sea of consciousness and universal intelligence that transcends and encompasses all previous levels[194]. Different religions use their specific dogma, methods and rituals as ways of understanding and accessing this reality.

Understanding multidimensional realities

The analogy of light is used as a common denominator within the physical, quantum physical, and metaphysical perspectives of reality. The colour spectrum represents different levels of energy and information[195]. Lower levels of the colour spectrum (red, orange and yellow) represent lower, less complex energy/information levels, while higher levels of the colour spectrum (blue, magenta and violet) represent higher, more complex information and energy levels. The ultimate challenge is to obtain a level of 'wholeness', unity and integration of all levels and colours, to produce white light.

The term 'enlightenment' is used by various Eastern teachings, and refers to the unity and interrelation of all things, the transcendence of the notion of an isolated individual self, and the identification with the ultimate self or higher self[196]. The challenge to reach 'enlightenment' necessitates an awakening, transcending lower-order values and beliefs, and the development of higher, more complex levels of thinking and spiritual values.

Zohar and Marshall use the term spiritual intelligence to describe the higher order, more complex metaphysical levels of consciousness[197]. The psychiatrist Stanlislav Grof says spirituality is an essential and desirable part of our existence, and might even be a critical factor for our survival on our planet[198]. These higher levels of consciousness (super consciousness) can be accessed through altered states of consciousness, higher sensory perception (HSP), intuition, faith, belief, meditation, yoga, prayer, silence, and various methods using induced substances.

When we gain access to the metaphysical dimension and universal consciousness, we gain access to higher levels of information, and higher levels of power. Developing new Leadership DNA includes accessing true power and encoded wisdom. Our new leaders are pathfinders and mapmakers. Wilber[199] says "Spiritual pioneers represent the growing tip of humanity forging a future telos through which the trunk of humanity is now slowly heading as a gentle persuasion". A summary of these dimensions and power levels are presented in the following table:

Reality	Physical reality	Quantum reality	Metaphysical/ Virtual reality
Focus	Material reality/stuff, physical things	Atoms, molecules, quantum soup, cosmic light	Universal Field of Potential (UFP) Source/ Spirit
Access	Physical senses, sensory learning	Science and scientific methods/ religion	HSP, vision, meditation transcendental practices, wisdom.
Levels of Awareness	Conscious Mind	Subconscious mind	Higher mind/ Super consciousness
Perspectives	Traditional and global views	Quantum perspective	Universal/ spiritual perspective
Intelligence	Pre-personal or tribal/ collective intelligence	Individual rational/emotional intelligence	Spiritual/ Power Universal intelligence

Accessing our multidimensions

Personal influence

A power-shift takes place when we become conscious of and understand the influence of thought, vision and focus on the movement of electrons and subatomic particles. We can learn to understand higher-order thinking, value systems, focus and attention, and consciously implement this new awareness. A new physical reality is created and/or altered by the quality of information, thought patterns, vision, attention, intention, beliefs and focus.

Ashby and Wiener[200] compared the functioning of the brain to computer images constructed from information from the electro-encephalogram (EEG) and defined the phenomenon as cybernetics. With the latest magnetic-encephalogram (MEG), the influence of how and what we think can now be reflected as an electromagnetic field that represents the level of information processed[201].

A consciousness of prosperity and success are therefore electromagnetic fields that attract people, situations, events and material things that resonate with the existing field in the proximity of the source. As thoughts, visions and focus can consciously be controlled, individuals can control their inner power and therefore choose what and who are allowed into proximity, or kept out of their lives.

Mind power specialists[202] have made these concepts accessible to the general public, thereby accelerating the shift in consciousness. Neuro-scientific research is further producing significant information in this regard, and at is producing important opportunities to explore the metaphysical reality at the same time[203].

The power to create physical reality

Scientists have found that the cloud or mist of subatomic particles or quantum soup have dual aspects. Depending on how they are perceived, these particles sometimes appear as waves, and sometimes as particles. The most important factor is that these particles 'light' up, become visible, and only come into existence when a person becomes conscious of, visualises, observes, and focuses on them[204].

When we focus on a thought or vision and pay attention, the silent quantum soup or UFP is disturbed. It turns into a *power pocket,* or 'light pocket' that resembles the focus, vision, attention and intention. Csikszentmihali[205] refers to these power pockets as memes, resembling the genes of genetics, as part of biology[206]. Different thought forms become different power pockets or pockets of light. Intelligent paths of access and communication interconnect them.

When these paths are open, energy flows freely, opening more innovative paths and processes. Negativity in any form, blocks these paths, restricts energy flow, and then these thoughts can die a silent death

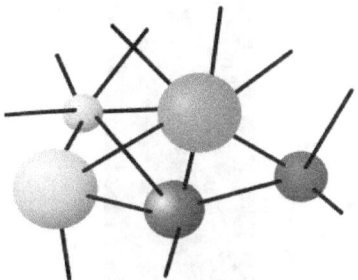

The web of life and thought forms as power pockets

When the thought forms are visualised and aligned with positive emotions[207], the energy creates a positive electromagnetic field, attracting people, objects and events in the proximity, whilst repelling negative experiences. Negative emotions attract negative people, objects and events, whilst repelling positive dissonant experiences not resonant with or sympathetic to the frequency[208]. Goleman gives deeper insight into and provides guidelines for the conscious management of these emotional processes, in his book *Emotional Intelligence*.

The power encoded in DNA

Within these power pockets (power packages, genes, memes, thought forms, light pockets), all the information and potential resources that are necessary to create physical reality and to be successful, happy and prosperous, can be found.

The latest DNA research has revealed that we not only have physical DNA with encoded physical information, we also have quantum and spiritual DNA[209]. Our DNA is multidimensional, encompassing all the dimensions - physical, quantum physical, and metaphysical realities. We have genes that, when activated, connect to the higher metaphysical, spiritual realms. This idea was postulated by geneticist Dean Hamers[210], the director of the Gene Structure and Regulation

Unit at the US National Cancer Institute, in his book titled *The God Gene: How faith is hardwired into our genes.*

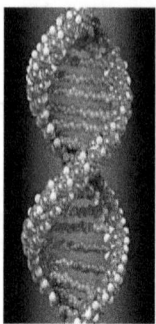

Genes and junk genes

The God gene hypothesis is based on a combination of behavioural genetic, neurobiological and psychological studies.

The major arguments of the theory are:

- Spirituality can be quantified by psychometric measurements.
- The underlying tendency to spirituality is partially heritable.
- Part of this heritability can be attributed to the gene VMAT2.
- This gene acts by altering *monoamine* levels
- Spirituality arises in a population because spiritual individuals are favoured by natural selection.

Although some scientists and researchers are critical of this theory, the fortunate part is that these disputes have placed the focus on the fact that there is an interconnection between genetics and spirituality and spiritual hereditary. The consequences of these findings have far-reaching effects for the everyday person on the street.

Biological hereditary and biological families are now making way for spiritual hereditary and a new spiritual family. Lifelong struggles with not fitting in with your biological family, now makes way for re-identification with a spiritual family that goes far beyond traditional teachings and biological genes.

Spirituality arises in a population because spiritual individuals are favoured by natural selection. The spiritual genotype has now become more important than the external phenotype, or physical appearance.

Today, spiritual teachings have wide scientific implications as well. The identification of a 'God gene', means that religion, science, psychology and spirituality will start to come together in order to provide deeper answers to the questions about life and quality living.

We also have dormant genes or junk genes[211] that are now being activated, thereby releasing new energy and information. A whole new consciousness is evolving - a whole new quality of human being. Not only New Success DNA is being ignited, a new kind of leader with New Leadership DNA, is emerging.

These are the leaders with the necessary awareness, knowledge, understanding and skills, that make them pathfinders and mapmakers. They will take the lead in igniting this infinite power and potential, while utilising it to the benefit all.

The power process and flow

When the three factors of connection to power source a chosen path or process and an envisioned outcome is connected, aligned, synchronised and in flow, the desired outcome will inevitably precipitate in form. Both Apter and Csikszentmihali refer to the importance of maintaining flow and the influence of flow on peak experiences and success[212]. Loehr and Schwartz[213] also highlight the importance of full engagement, and the connecting process, as part of the ascertainment of excellence. Affluence[214] is the successful outcome of this process. New success DNA leaders take cognisance of these important facts. Where and to whom they are connected is a fundamental ingredient of powerful, mindful leadership.

Disconnection, blockages and/or misalignment of this process leads to misused (abused) energy that causes destruction and disintegration. The terms like stress, burnout, depression and resilience are in essence all energy-related issues[215]. The challenge to overcome blockages and barriers, and to alleviate stress, burnout and destruction, necessitates new thinking.

Energy, change, evolution and entropy

Lamarck was the first to propose a coherent theory of evolution, for which Darwin later presented an overwhelming mass of evidence in favour of all living beings having evolved from earlier, simpler forms, under pressure of the environment. This forced scientists to abandon the Cartesian concept of the world as a predetermined machine, and to accept the universe as a constantly evolving and ever changing system of energy in which complex structures develop from simpler forms[216].

Physics however, found the opposite - a movement toward increasing disorder. This led physicists to the formulation of thermodynamics, the 'science of complexity' and a fundamental physics law, the conservation of energy. Energy can change form in the most complicated way, but none of it is lost. This led to the second law of thermodynamics, that of the dissipation of energy. Carnot[217] found that while the total energy involved in a process is always constant, the amount of positive, useful energy is constantly diminishing, and dissipating into heat, friction or other forms.

The term 'entropy' was introduced, and this assesses the measure of disorder. It is like walking up an escalator that is moving downwards. You have to put in more effort, in order to overcome the downward movement or entropy. To overcome entropy, living systems and living beings in a universe that continuously grows and evolves, need to stay open and constantly import new free energy and information from the environment and the cosmos as a whole, in order to survive[218].

These scientific findings are reflected within ancient wisdoms. All major world religions agree that unless individuals and groups alike, learn to raise their levels of consciousness, master the self, connect and obtain harmony with the cosmos, they will forever remain prey to the random forces of biology and society[219]. Within the 'change and order' or post-modern paradigm, these concepts are being revisited. The new information is being implemented within various disciplines, while stimulating new developments within philosophy, psychology, education, political, financial and business sciences, and leadership development.

Evolution, energy and information

Information forms a dynamic element taking centre stage in evolution theories of change, chaos and order. Information gives order and structure - which prompts growth. Growth and development define what is alive. It is both the underlying structure and the dynamic processes, which ensure life[220]. Information is therefore more than content and has a powerful organising function. New information organises matter into form - resulting in new physical structures. This is reflected in the term *in-form-ation*. The real system that endures and evolves - is energy.

Matter flows through the sea of consciousness while taking on different physical forms as required by the specific thought-form. When information changes, energy levels change accordingly, and new structures materialise. Change, growth and development take place through the flow of new energy and information, or energy-information. For a system to remain alive and constantly renew itself and move forward, new information at a higher more complex energy level, must continually be generated. It is a natural process of living systems to continuously renew themselves, and to regulate this process in such a way that the integrity of the structure is maintained[221].

The greater the ability to process new information, the higher the level of organising energy or power will be. Wheatly[222] says we need to have new information coursing through our system, disturbing the peace, imbuing everything it touches with new life. This can, however, trigger resistance from the status quo. Leaders and decision-makers who feel threatened by new information and the 'zero effect' of power-shifts, can try to secure their positions by deliberately blocking any new contributions and innovative ideas.

Individual and small groups and communities often understand the new paradigm better than large academic and social institutions, as these are often locked in old mindsets and repetitive thinking. Einstein said that problems created by a certain mindset cannot be solved by using the same mindset. Solutions can be found at a higher level of thinking – even a whole new paradigm.

An important question now arises:

> *How can we, as leaders, access different levels of power?*

Accessing power

In order to access different levels of power, we first need a deeper understanding of the functioning of the brain, our neuro-physiology, genetics, physics, mind-wellness and the power-tools and skills at our disposal. This has already been outlined in more detail in the books *Power Intelligence* and *New Success DNA*[223]. For convenience, a short summary is presented on the next page, and a short outline follows in the next chapters.

In the next chapter, we will focus on leadership, influence, self-mastery and the cosmic law of 'the right use of power' power. This universal law states that, 'as you sow – you shall reap'. All misqualified energy or abuse of life-force will be returned to the sender in order to be clarified and purified. At the same time all conscious and positive endeavors to 'sow the good seed' will be honored as well. We are called to stand for what is good and sacred. In the process we can enjoy the fruits of our labor. Everyone therefore has the personal responsibility for their expenditure of life-force and the quality of their lives.

Notes

Power force	Tribal power	Individual power	Universal power
Brain part	Reptilian brain	Mammalian and neocortex	Neocortex and frontal lobes
Brain/energy Frequency	Gamma waves	Alpha/theta	Theta/delta
Personal practice	Seek external counsel	Internal reflection, meditation, yoga	Transcendental and spiritual practices
Power position	Power-over-people	Power-in-people	Unified wholeness and oneness
Power lies in	Number of people	Number of powers	Universal power
Primary focus	Tradition, religion, mentor, coach	Consciousness, introspection and interpretation,	Silence, now, mysticism
Dependency	Dependent/co-dependent	Independent	Interdependent and one with the universe
Power tools and social skills	Active/passive, manipulation, intimidation, domination	Self-aware, self worth, honour, respect, purpose, identity, self-love	Universal power-tools and laws - compassion, love, peace
Guidance received	From others, religion, nature	Introspection and interpretation	Inner GPS, HSP, higher dimensions
Dominant gender	Male	Male and/or female	Androgenic - harmony, balance
Change	First wave	Second/third	Third/fourth
Era	Pre-modern	Modern era	Post-modern era

Summary of the power shift - a shift in consciousness

Notes

CHAPTER 5

LEADERSHIP AND SELF-MASTERY

*"Evolution is a whole long story of **mastery**.*
It's being real. It's being human. It's being who we are."

George Leonard

Introduction

Numerous methods and thousands of different examples have been used over the decades, in order to explain leadership styles, methods and leadership mastery. Here we do not want to unnecessarily repeat old information, because new challenges demand thinking 'out of the box'. When taking all this into account, we can ask the question:

> *Can we learn some new leadership lessons from a series like Harry Potter?*

Leadership Lessons from Harry Potter[224]

In this now world-renowned series, we find fantasised and dramatised versions of the conflict between the forces of light and darkness. In the middle, we find a young boy, Harry Potter, having special powers that he inherited from his parents. His parents were both supporters of spiritual light and both were white wizards[225]. After they were killed by dark forces, Harry was left on his own to fend for himself. Harry was also a wizard, but he was not aware of his powers or conscious of these gifts. He needed to be taught how to use what he had already inherited, and he needed to attend a wizardry school. So Hogwarts School of Witchcraft and Wizardry, or simply *Hogwarts*, becomes the primary setting for the first six books of the *Harry Potter* series, by J.K. Rowling. The story is about Harry learning about who he truly is, what his authentic purpose is, and how to use his gifts for the greater good. Each book covers the equivalent of one school year at Hogwarts.

We get introduced to Hogwarts, a fictional British boarding school of magic for witches and wizards between the ages of eleven and seventeen or eighteen. In the story, the school was established between the 9th or 10th Century, with the motto, "Let sleeping dragons Lie"[226]. The climactic battle of the books, and the series, is set within the walls of Hogwarts. Children with magical abilities may be enrolled at the school at birth, and acceptance is confirmed by owl post at age eleven. Names are written down by a magical quill in the Quill Room, somewhere in the school, at a 'magical' child's birth, and only 'magical children' could attend Hogwarts.

The main story concerns Hurry's quest to overcome the dark wizard Lord Voldemort, whose dark aims are to become immortal, to conquer the wizarding world, subjugate 'non-magical people', and destroy all those who stand in his way - especially Harry Potter and what he stands for.

Since their release, the books have gained immense popularity, critical acclaim, and commercial success worldwide. As of June 2011, the book series has sold about 450 million copies, making it the best-selling books series in history, and has been translated into 67 languages. The last four books have consecutively set records as the fastest-selling books in history. The books have been made into an eight-part film series, the highest-grossing film series of all time. The series also drive much tie-in merchandise, making the *Harry Potter* brand worth in excess of $15 billion. One thing is for sure - J.K. Rowling got the world thinking.

Interpretations of the Harry Potter series, spans a variety of genres and themes. First, the novels fall within the genre of fantasy literature and coming of age novels, while containing elements of mystery, adventure, thriller, and romance. More complex interpretations include political subtexts, and themes such as normality, oppression, survival, and overcoming imposing odds. Similarly, the theme of making one's way through adolescence and "going over one's most harrowing ordeals - and thus coming to terms with them" has also been considered. The books could be said to comprise many other themes, such as power/abuse of power, love, prejudice, and the ever-present theme of adolescence, with acknowledgment of the characters' sexualities.

At the same time, the series has also had some share of criticism, including concern for the increasingly dark tone. Various religious conservatives have claimed that the books promote witchcraft, and are therefore unsuitable for children. A number of critics have criticised the books for promoting various political agendas. In the end, the interpretation of the books remains a personal choice.

Rowling has personally stated that the books comprise "a prolonged argument for tolerance, a prolonged plea for an end to bigotry"[227] and also pass on the message to "question authority and ... not assume that the establishment or the press tells you all of the truth". In her biography, Rowling said that, to her, the moral significance of the tales seems 'blindingly obvious'. The key for her was the choice between 'what is right' and 'what is easy', "because that ... is how tyranny is started, with people being apathetic and taking the easy route and suddenly finding themselves in deep trouble"[228].

From our background setting of the current shift in consciousness and emerging New Success DNA, we could ask the following questions from a leadership point of view:

> *What leadership lessons can we take from the Harry Potter series?*

Like various examples throughout history, the Harry Potter series also shows that there is only one of two paths to follow. On the one hand we have the 'Harry Potters', representing the 'light' concept of life and everything that is valid, truth, good, constructive, positive and upstanding. On the other hand, we find the 'Lord Voldemorts', whose dark aims are to become immortal, to conquer the supporters of the light, subjugate pre-literate or non-light people, and destroy all the magical light people and those of the light - the 'Harry Potters' of the world, all who stand in their way.

As we have seen in the previous chapter, we find that leaders receive their guidance according to their belief systems. The leadership value and belief system could be based on a religion, philosophy, personal opinion, or direct guidance from source, or communication with God. Many influencial persons who supported specific leaders included wizards, wise men, prophets, shamans, and others also share the same value and belief system and faith.

Leadership, truth and faith

Whatever we believe is truth, is our reality as 'truth for me'. Within our personal idea of truth, we develop our personal faith and belief systems. Whatever you believe is true, is true for you. Lawrence Kohlberg[229], who was well known for his research on moral development, faith and belief, has stated that all faiths, including traditional religion, go through the same developmental phases - although the content of the information may differ. He identified three prominent levels we all go through. Each time we become aware of a higher truth, we need to let go of the lower-order truths and perceptions. Where leadership is concerned - every time we raise our awareness, we automatically access new information and elevate our resonance. Our system of faith and direction change as well.

The first level Kohlberg identified is a level of making choices based on things we get punished for, versus things we will be rewarded for. This reflects the 'good boy/girl' value system. Laws and values are right or wrong, good or bad. Information is obtained from significant others, people in higher positions, or leaders. These 'significant others' and their truths usually go without questioning, for fear of reproach. Here we find external control. This is 'mindless' or blind faith.

The second level emerges when we start to think for ourselves. There is a trigger, and something happens, and we become mindful and conscious - we start to 'wake up'. At the same time we take back our power from 'significant others', or people we previously viewed as leaders or the learned. We now begin to identify our own truth and put new information to the test. A personal consciousness awakens, and new multidimensional sources are consulted. Here we start to find our own truth, while being open and objective to new information. We are prepared to discard old information, outworn beliefs, and the people and structures that endorse these outdated truths, if necessary.

Levels of faith

The third level represents an autonomic level of development, where seemingly opposing information can be integrated into a meaningful whole. This is the highest form of development, and different points of view are valued, respected and integrated - without judgment. Here we find internal control, self-mastery, and an encompassing point of view that includes universal laws and guidance. Man-made laws and views are measured up against universality and spiritual laws. This is the level of expanded awareness, of true knowing and understanding, and of wisdom. The level of blind faith is now being transformed into personal and universal knowing and understanding. From here we can now consciously access the universal web and God mind. Blind and personal faith makes way for higher knowing, understanding and universal wisdom that encapsulates all.

At the same time, a growth in our faith also depends on the maturing of our neuro-functioning and our ability to process new information. The tribal mind and blind faith progress to individual mind and personal faith, and them to universal mind and universal knowing and understanding. We are, however, now becoming aware of the miracle mind and frontal-lobe functioning[230], and the role it plays in manifesting miracles in our holographic physical universe.

Below we find a short schematic summary of neuro-functioning and faith.

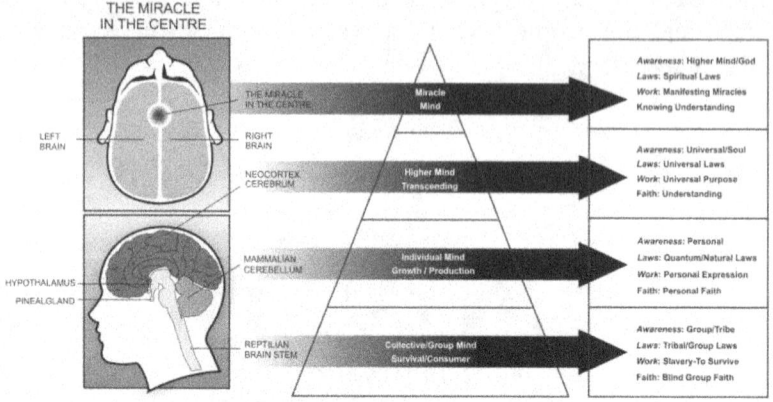

Neuro-functioning and faith

One question that still remains is:

> *What is faith?*

Faith is generally defined as "the confident belief in the truth, value or trustworthiness of a personal idea or a thing". It is the ability to believe in the non-physical or 'unseen'. This includes the assurance of, confidence in, and reliance on, what we believe is truth. This may include blind faith, personal faith or universal faith - but all still depends on where and from whom you get your information. We can summarise the dynamics of faith - e can say: "Faith is the conscious ability and choice to hold the truth, the vision, to hold the energy, or to hold the highest outcome in what or whom you believe to be trustworthy".

Our faith gets tested by placing us in difficult circumstances. The longer we hold the faith or vision in the unseen dimension of the quantum and universal realities, the stronger the imprint is made on the universal mind or 'heart of God'. When we 'hold the faith', it becomes manifest and lowered out of the fifth and fourth dimensional substance into third-dimensional physical reality. We create miracles through faith. Faith is the only method of co-creating with source - with God. Faith means holding the energy of truth up high - with passion, conviction and commitment.

The wonderful findings we are now becoming aware of, are that we have faith hardwired into our DNA[231]. We previously referred to Dean Hamers' contribution in terms of identifying our 'God gene' or 'faith gene' - as gene VMAT2. This means we have the beginning of miracles hardwired into gene VMAT2 in our DNA. We were created to become miracle makers. This is enough to make anyone smile!

All we need to do is to get reconnected to the divine heart and mind. It is here that we will find true faith. To many a person this means they will first need to disconnect from old outworn opinions and interpretations from previous programming and incorrect information learned or taught. We first need to wake up, get reconnected, and take back our power. We can then transcend blind faith and access the universal mind. When we place our faith and trust in this dimension, we find that miracles occur as a natural way of life.

From the beginning of human history, leaders were expected to create miraculous feats. Today this does not necessarily mean that leaders have to change water into wine or heal the sick. They do, however, need to make wise decisions and provide higher-order solutions for the challenging current day problems we are confronted with[232]. New leaders with New Leadership DNA are expected to be mystics in the making. They are the 'masters' of our time.

Mystics, masters, monasteries and mystery schools

Up until now, we have thought that mystics, sages and masters were the only ones who had the ability to consciously access the universal mind or God, and create miracles. A mystic is seen as someone who practices or believes in mystical or spiritual power. The word mystic comes from the Greek word *'mystikos'* meaning 'an initiate'. Mystics are specially revered as knowledgeable of different states of consciousness. They have personal experience of states of consciousness - i.e. levels of being - beyond normal human perception, including experience of, and even communion with, a supreme being or God. From this definition, we find mystics to be persons who have been initiated into higher states of consciousness, and who can commune with a higher dimension and higher being.

A sage is usually a man venerated for his experience, wisdom and calm judgment. Masters are seen as persons who have control over something, or someone. They are viewed as the victorious who can overcome challenges or as a victor, a teacher, schoolmaster or tutor. These are persons whose teachings or doctrines are accepted by followers, and are usually men and women of great learning. They are teachers qualified to teach apprentices to carry on their craft independently. Masters are also viewed as being an original from which copies are made. They are a principal and leading force, and leaders in their domain of mastery. The title Master/Mister is usually given to those who uphold the standard of mastery or excellence. We find grand masters in all walks of life, like our golfing masters, musical maestros, master chefs, or philosophical masters like Meister Eckhart[233].

A few commonalities are obvious where sages, mystics and masters are concerned. They all have been gone through a lengthy process of tutoring, learning and experiencing, whatever they chose to master. If it were golf or music, the teaching and training would include all that is needed to not only master that golf stroke or music principle, but also to move past the teachings of the master until they become master teachers themselves, while providing higher levels of attainment. Our music maestros compose their own music and do not just copy others, while golfing masters invent new golf clubs with new strokes. The question for the everyday person on the street, on a quest for true authentic success would be - what should we do?

Here we can learn from the mystics in their monasteries.

A monastery is a dwelling place of a community of persons, usually under religious vows, and especially referring to monks. It comes from the Greek word 'monasterion' that refers to 'living alone'. However, in the search for a deeper understanding, we find this all derives from the original Germanic word 'men', meaning to think, which refers to various qualities and states of consciousness. In a monastery, we can get connected to like-minded people and the shared states of conscious and awareness. A monastery is, in essence, a place where we can go, where we can connect to different states of consciousness.

The monasteries we know are secluded sanctuaries in the mountains, away from the general hustle and bustle of everyday life. In the tranquility of nature, mystics, masters and sages are taught deeper understanding and the ability to access higher dimensions - the ability to create miracles and change the quality of life. From these mystery schools and sanctuaries, they can influence our economics, politics and even the general vibe of a meeting.

The question then is: What about us? We all have our responsibilities and demands to attend to, payments to make, and people to take care of. There is not time to take off to enter a monastery or any other place for a lengthy retreat. Does it mean we are excluded from this new awakening? Can we awaken our miracle minds and become miracle makers without leaving our current existence?

The answer is, yes!

We too have our 'monastery'. We have an inner place or space where we can access new states of consciousness. We only need to learn who we are. We are the *Theoplexus,* the place love meets all[234]. This is our 'monastery', mansion or temple within. We can access this mansion any place and any time, and can co-create whatever we desire. This is what this book is all about.

Leaders as modern mystics in their mansions

Modern-day people are awakening, becoming miracle makers, and seeking to enter their inner mansion, and claim their rightful heritage. We are heirs to the Kingdom of God as we have it all encoded into our very DNA. We are the new generation of awakening souls who are becoming connected to a new level of consciousness. We are beginning to function within a new mindset, and on a new wavelength. We are accessing the frequency of miracles as we speak. However, this is nothing new.

The information and teachings that was once only available to those who were prepared to leave the world behind and retreat behind the walls of monasteries in secluded places, or enroll at mystery schools[235], are now being made available to all of us in different ways. Not only do our global networks provide us with access to spiritual information anywhere - downloads from the universal net and higher dimensions are infusing us with a new awareness, while our very DNA is igniting and releasing new potential that will take us forward. It is time ... and we are ready!

Our modern-day monasteries could be any place, and we can enter them any time. Our external circumstances are immaterial. It is this inner journey to our 'mansion within' that we have to embark on. We have to reconnect, master our inner demons, overcome fears, and heal our hurt and brokenness. We need to overcome the lower ego-self and reconnect with our higher self. We have to become one in body, mind, soul and spirit - to become healed, whole and holy.

In the process, we are learning to master the self and return home - back to our spiritual dwelling on higher planes. Today we are becoming modern mystics returning to our mansions in heaven[236]. Here we have access to all the treasures of heaven. All we need to do is master our authentic self, reconnect to source, and reclaim or heritage. The rest will follow - miraculously.

The question is:

> *What do leaders learn in their 'monasteries' or their 'desert experiences'?*

All authentic leaders have spent time in their monasteries. In history we find these experiences denoted as 'desert experiences', and on a more spiritual level we find this as the experience of the 'dark night of the soul'

Leaders and the 'dark night of the soul'

The 'dark night of the soul' sounds like a threatening and much to be avoided experience. Yet, perhaps a quarter of the seekers on the road to higher consciousness will pass through the 'dark night'. In fact, they may pass through several until they experience the profound joy of their true nature. Many seekers would encourage the 'dark night' experience if they knew what it was. However, to one engaged in the 'dark night', suffering seems unending.

The 'dark night' occurs after considerable advancement toward higher consciousness. Indeed, the 'dark night' usually occurs like an initiation before one of these special seekers is admitted into a regular relationship with higher consciousness. The 'dark night' represents the dying off of the old and letting go of the past - a death and rebirth experience. Here we find a 'switching over process' where one level dies off, while a new level is ignited. Below we find the spiral of life (a) that directly relates to the unfolding of our DNA (b). We find seven levels and seven octaves each representing a different level of energy-information, frequency and resonance. It is also good to know that the piano key board also has seven notes on seven octaves (plus four notes) as outlined in the book New Success DNA[237].

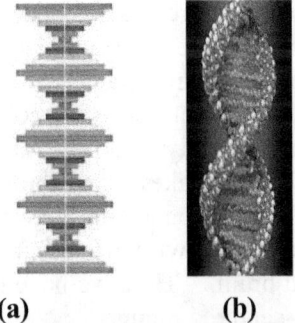

(a)   **(b)**

The 'dark night of the soul' - DNA activation

The 'dark night' also happens to those who do not seek human relationships, but immersion or unity in the higher consciousness. While the term 'dark night of the soul' is used broadly, its general meaning - in the field of higher consciousness - is a lengthy and profound absence of light and hope. In the dark night you feel profoundly alone - the 'shadow of death' experience.

Many people shy away from being alone, because they fear themselves and being lonely. However, everyone who has ever entered into these higher dimensions has gone through their 'dark night of the soul'. Many religions have analogies of this path into 'hell and back', and the analogy of the Temple of Solomon has been used over the centuries as an example of the journey into self[238]. This is not a skill to be learnt, but an experience you can only have by, and for, yourself. There is immense power in being by your self. All significant and influential leaders always first go through this desert experience or 'valley of death'. Here we let go of or die to the old synthetic ego-self, only to be reborn into the new. We find that death and rebirth are taking place at the same time and at the same place. This means that a break down and a breakthrough are also occurring at the same time and place. The direction you will go is a matter of personal choice. The quality of your life is therefore a matter of personal identification and your responsibility. We find ancient examples of profound leaders like Buddha and Jesus, and more recent examples like Mahatma Ghandi and Nelson Mandela - who come to mind. These are master souls who have left an indelible imprint on the fabric of life.

At a personal, collective, and even global level, we are all in the process of healing who we are. As we raise our awareness, we also become conscious of how we are physically, mentally, emotionally and spiritually 'wired' for the process of producing, creating and miracle making. All we need to do is to reclaim our power, grow in understanding, and consciously align with and enhance the universal processes at work. This all takes place through our higher mind or miracle mind. We find the connection between the higher universal mind and our personal mind within the seat of the soul - the frontal lobes of our physical brain.[239] Here we have to choose between ego-centered versus soul-centered living.

Summary

All authentic leaders first learn to master the self and the power they are given, while visiting their 'monasteries' – their inner sanctuaries. Here leaders become 'power intelligent' and learn how to change from *power over people* to releasing *power within people*.

In the next chapter, we will explore the fundamental principles of good and bad, successful and unsuccessful, constructive and destructive, and soul- verses ego-centered leaders and leadership styles. We will explore why some leaders make an indelible imprint that is revered over the centuries, and why some leaders, their leadership style and legacy, should rather be forgotten.

CHAPTER 6

LEADERSHIP AND NEURO-PROGRAMMING

Introduction

Leaders are in important positions because of the influence they have in the greater society. Individuals or groups play different roles within different contexts that include political, financial, religious, social or sport communities. They obtain these leadership positions in various ways. Some appoint themselves as leaders, others get elected by the group and others inherit their right to lead as we find in the monarchies of Sweden, England, Monaco and various African dynasties. Some leaders are functional and take the welfare of the greater community into consideration while others, who are less evolved – only take their own welfare into account, while negating any responsibility to society. The quality of their influence will be determined by the own inner dynamics.

The important fact is; the psychological functioning of leaders will determine the kind of contribution they make and the direction they will move. The rest usually follow. At the same time we are aware that most people strive for democracy where power is invested in the people. Groups of people functional as a whole and elected representative leaders exercise authority on their behalf. However, specific leaders are chosen by specific groups who come from a specific mindset. Although democracy has many advantages it also has a downside.

People choose leaders who they feel will enhance their value system and mindset. The problem is that a large part of humanity still functions on a lower, unevolved or mindless level of consciousness. This means they find it difficult to identify and choose competent, mindful leaders. This has become evident in the problems Egypt and Syria are currently experiencing. Unevolved people and groups with low levels of awareness usually vote for unevolved leaders. This results in a constant process of demise.

The challenge is to first to evolve to the higher level of awareness and independent thinking. Only then can they overcome the influence and need for dictatorship and ego-driven leaders. This could still take a while for the new leaders to emerge. At the same time we know that independent thinking and psychological functioning is directly connected to neuro-functioning.

In order to understand the emerging of a New Leadership DNA and new functional leaders, we first need to have a closer look at the personality dynamics and especially neuro-functions of people who aspire to leadership positions. At the same time we as the general public, living in democratic societies, need to become aware of the people we place in leadership positions. Leadership is the responsibility of everyone. This is what this book is all about.

The questions arise:

> *What should we know about psychological functioning of leaders and leadership styles in order to secure our contribution in placing the right leaders in the right places?*

The Triad brain evolving into a Quaternary brain

Paul McLean, a neuroscientist, sees the brain as a triad brain[240]. It primarily consists of three parts namely the reptile brain, the mammal brain and the neocortex. Each of these 'brains' has different functions and developed at different stages. The brain is further divided into a left and right part – each with its specific function and way of processing information, or thinking. Although the brain is more complex than the three parts, for the purpose of this book, we will focus on this basic model.[241]

The question we need to ask about people in general and leaders in particular is:

> *Where is this person/group coming from?*

We find some answers by looking at the different brains, with different thinking, different values and therefore different leadership styles.

- **The reptilian brain**

The first brain mainly exists of structures at the top of the spinal cord and includes certain parts of the brain-stem. Since it more or less has the same functions as the brains of reptiles, this part is called the reptilian brain. Like the whole brain of the lizard and the snake, the functions of this brain focus mainly on life-support, like the regulation of breathing, heartbeat, muscle movement and basic needs like eating, self-protection, the formation of a social hierarchy, reproduction and the instinctive selection of leaders.

The reptilian brain cannot learn and cope with new situations, but is mainly responsible for stereotyped behavioral patterns and predetermined needs and passions. The thought processes in this area are divided into two hemispheres.

On the left we find all the structures needed to think in a ritualistic, magical and territorial way. In the right part all the clandestine, devious, savage, barbarian, sneaky and stalking qualities are situated that appear mainly during times of war, and are observable in terrorists and assassins. When one feels unsafe, endangered or threatened, the reptile brain is activated and a choice is made between fight or flee. Fear is well-known to trigger and this phase is well known as the "fight or flight reaction".

At this level, a person is in an instinctive reactive mode and cannot think or function at a higher level of reasoning. This can be a natural reaction or an induced reaction through training and brainwashing or various methods of physical, emotional or neuro-manipulation.

When an attempt is made to encourage, activate or motivate people to act in a certain manner by means of fear or threat, a shut-down of higher systems takes place and this reactive, survival system is activated. This is best illustrated by strategies of extreme intimidation. Another example is when a leader rules by intimidation, manipulation or dictatorship.

Violence, in its various forms, is used to maintain their 'power-over-people'. They maintain their stronghold of fear, while implementing underhand, sneaky, and even ruthless strategies. These leaders and their supporters can be identified by high levels of corruption, white collar crime, lies, deceit and underhanded dealings. The labeling of a person or group as "snakes" is derived from this part of neuro-function.

Corrupt leaders and their followers live the illusion and are mostly delusional. Fear increases and creates more illusion – the lie – and no corrupt government, group or person has ever been left standing. Corruption has a self-destructive mechanism as default. As most people live unattended, fearful lives, this has left, up until now, very little place for openness, transparency, ethics, honesty and truth. The results are normally unproductive as a shut-down of productive systems takes place and higher neuro-functions close off.

On this level we find a vast body of information concerning 'reptilian leaders'[242] available and for decades various 'conspiracy theories' have been widely debated[243].

However, as soon as a person, leaders and groups begin to evolve, the fear factors are removed and truth emerges and safety and security can be restored. A shift to the next level of brain functioning – to a higher, more complicated system and level of thought, takes place. The second brain is then activated.

- **The mammalian brain**

The second brain, the so-called mammal brain, encircles the reptile brain and is therefore circular. Chemicals responsible for emotional reactions are produced here. It also controls biorhythms like sleeping patterns, hunger, thirst, blood pressure, sexual needs, body temperature and chemistry, metabolism and the immune system.

When we experience an overload of problems, danger or fear, this system shuts down and the person returns to the previous system. It means that anger, fear, emotional pain, relationship problems and disharmony can manifest in a physical stress reaction. This can take on different forms like an eating and/or sleeping disorder, sexual dysfunction, problems with blood pressure, concentration, memory loss and problems with the immune system that lead to chronic infection. These are psycho-somatic symptoms, or the body reacting to physical and emotional situations. Our health is a physical manifestation of the emotional climate of the world we live in.

This system is the centre of the information gathering system. Information from the external world is gathered by the senses, the eyes, ears, and skin, nasal and taste organs. The information is next transported to the thinking part of the brain, namely the neocortex, where it is further processed. The left side of this system produces organized, linear patterns and the right side produces impulsive, social, spontaneous, chance-taking and intuitive patterns.

Experiments show that the mammalian brain cannot function effectively if emotional blockages or emotional obstacles are present. High levels of negativity, threat, problems, arguing, scolding, shouting, fear, withdrawal, war or danger create barriers in the brain. The functions of the mammalian part can be switched off. This leads to apathy or emotional bluntness, a loss of the need to play, negativity and depression are only a few symptoms indicating emotional   barriers. Positive emotional stimulation like love, laughter, play and other forms of uplifting stimulation increase the release of endorphins, serotonin and other neuro-transmitters that stimulate brain development. In the book *Power Intelligence - Mastering the Miracle Mind,* we find a more detailed outline of the role emotions play in our level of stability and happiness.[244]

Once we have reached a certain level of emotional stability and maturity, further differentiation of the next system, the neocortex, can then take place.

- **The neocortex**

Over millennia a 'new' brain, the neocortex, evolved as an addition to the previously mentioned two 'brains'. This is the external, grooved part of the brain. We find it is underdeveloped, and the brain appears smoother in babies. The neocortex is a very complex structure with more than ten billion cells. It sorts the messages received by the senses. Reason, thought, purposeful and effective behavior, language, arbitrary muscle control and non-verbal ideas and vision are processes that develop because of the sorting and processing. This relatively 'new' structure provides a person with logic and reason. It is a specific thinking cap and is the seat of rational intelligence. We also find a difference between brain and mind. Brain refers to the physical entity; mind is the ability to connect to different frequencies and think on different levels.

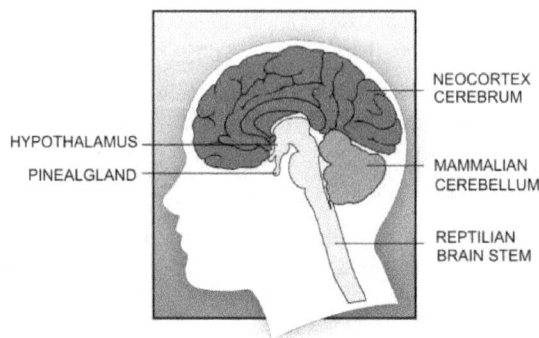

The triad brain

The processing of facts, detail and linear thinking are found in the left hemisphere of the brain. The right hemisphere processes conceptual, intuitive, imaginative, creative and holistic ideas that are evaluated and refined by the right part of the neocortex. Left brain thinking and development primarily dominated the Western world, while right brain thinking primarily dominated Eastern philosophies and thinking. The solution to more complex life problems now lies in whole brain and higher mind connections, thinking and development. Whole brain development implies stimulating the creative intuitive potential of the right brain and triggering left brain rational thinking to evaluate new idea before implementing it.

An inner harmony and peace can be created by quieting the mind, becoming still and integrating processes. It is here where new answers and ideas can be found. The person can now live a life of integrity from an inner core of peace and tranquility. This allows new creative ideas and answers to surface and flow from the inner core to the external world and contribute to life. This brings us to a next important part of the neocortex.

- **The temporal/frontal lobes**

A next level of the brain is currently being activated. For decades scientific research has been done by neurologists all over the world to determine if we have a special "power spot" in the brain. With special scientific sensor techniques it has been found that certain neural connections in the temporal lobes light up when a person is exposed to discussions of value, love, meaning, spirituality or religious topics. It reacts and lights up when we ask 'higher order' questions, like: What is love or what is the meaning and value of life? It was further found that there is a neural process in the brain devoted to unifying and synchronizing neural oscillations across the whole brain. This is where meaning and value are given to our experiences.

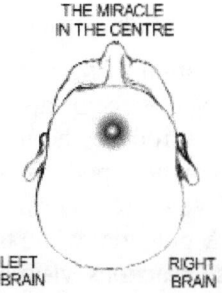

The power spot in the centre

This process literally binds our thoughts and experiences into one meaningful whole and places them into a larger meaningful framework. Here we connect to the higher levels of the etheric realm and become conscious of our connection to spiritual realms and the universal web. Not only do these frontal lobes deal with meaning and value, they are also the centre of symbolic communication and meaning like symbols, visions, sacred geometry, dreams or language. Terrance Deacon[245], a neurologist and biologist from Harvard, found that neither computers or higher apes could use symbols like language, as they lacked this frontal lobe facility.

This means we have a centre that lights up, produces energy when stimulated by asking higher order questions of meaning and value or

135

when we ask for guidance and vision. It lights up when we use different symbols like language, to explain our experiences. This centre produces the power and energy to bind, integrate and synchronize our thoughts into a powerful whole. This produces the impetus that can move us forward – even beyond boundaries. We can transform and transcend situations in the direction we choose to go and that have value and meaning. It is the 'power centre' we can activate and call on when we are innovative, creative, open, flexible and visionary. This is the level we need to access when leadership is involved.

It is in this centre where we find answers to our questions when reason or emotion cannot show the way. It is our 'guide spot', our inner GPS[246] that provides answers, vision and direction outside existing rules and boundaries and beyond known experiences. Here we find guidance beyond our rational and emotional intelligence or our physical senses. Here we connect to our 'God spot' and find guidance form a higher spiritual dimension.

At the same time the activation of these lobes ignites various other processes in the brain. Neuro-chemicals are produced while the pineal and other glands produce hormones that activate new reactions in the body. The whole body is ignited right down to the cellular and even DNA levels. Here dormant or 'junk genes'[247] can be activated, releasing new potential while taking us to new levels of attainment. We find these reactions visible in couples who fall in love or pregnant woman who have a certain 'glow'.

At this level, a fourth part of the brain is now being activated and a quaternary brain with all the associated functions is emerging on a large scale. This was previously only active in higher evolved human beings, sages and spiritual masters. Here we can connect to higher, spiritual dimensions and gain access to universal wisdoms. It is here where we find the edge between what we rationally know and an inner knowing or intuitive sense. This edge is the border between an inner knowing or ignorance, direction or being lost, between chaos and order. Here we can find our guide/Guide at the edge of our physical reality. We find our inner compass and direction beyond reasoning, outside our known boundaries, through an inner knowing, vision, intuition and a deep sense of meaning and value. Here the power and energy are released to make the move to the next level of development.

This power spot – 'God spot' – has wired us to become the people we are. When this spot lights up, our DNA gets activated and we find the potential for further growth, development, movement, transformation and evolution on the path of life. It is here where we connect to the big picture, to a larger meaningful whole and to the Universal Mind. Connecting with, tapping into, intelligently utilizing and managing this power is the challenge of the future as we stand at the cutting edge of human development.

Power is now found in silence and solutions are now found in flow and not in force. The brain is in constant contact with the rest of the body by means of the connective or nervous system – and with higher mind. At the same time the brain provides connections to different dimensions as the brainwaves can connect to different frequencies - just like a SIM card of a mobile phone provides a connection to a service provider.

More in depth explanations of these processes are explained in the books *New Success DNA* and *Power Intelligence*.

The nervous system

Understanding the nervous system is like comprehending an entire country. In the case of a country, we may consider it city by city, or in terms of highways and rivers. With the nervous system we can speak of independent systems that function inter-dependently as an interlocking whole. We find the Central Nervous System (CNS) is composed of the brain and spinal cord.

The spinal cord is composed of bundles of nerves running down through the vertebrae making up the spinal column. The Peripheral Nervous System (PNS) is all the nerves branching out from the CNS and re-branching to reach the farthest points of the body. The nerves end in different cells, tissues, organs and structures of the body. The importance of restoring the spinal biomechanical balance[248] will become significant in the future.

For now it is important to take cognisance of these connections, especially to the endocrine system and the pineal body, and the role they play in developing new leaders, and New Leadership DNA.

The questions are:

> *Why all the information on the brain, nervous system and nerve endings? What does this have to do with New Success DNA? How can we change our leadership DNA?*

Brain and mind

Our brain can be seen as the physical entity that receives and transmits messages – just like a cellular phone sends and receives messages. You purchase "airtime" for your cell phone from a service provider. This gives you access to a certain frequency on the information-energy highway. A call is made and a signal sent to the tower that connects you to the frequency. Your message is relayed to the recipient, the information is downloaded and a signal tells your friend there is a call or SMS waiting. Without any problems you can communicate whenever, wherever and with whoever you want – if of course all your connections are intact and enabled.

The SIM card with the micro-chip inside the cellular phone is responsible for the connections to different signals and frequencies. This is registered in your name – it is a personalised connection. You have to first register on the web before you can make use of all the information. Our brain and mind works in exactly the same fashion.

Getting connected

Our brain has the same ability as the SIM card and can access or pick up different dimensions or frequencies. We can consciously regulate these connections by changing the frequency of our brain waves. The example below shows that person 1 is connected to the biosphere, while person 2 is connected to the etheric level and person 4 to the astral level. Person 5 is totally disconnected, person 3 is connected to Higher (Universal) Mind and can "download" all relevant information from the universal net or web of life as needed.

All we need to do is: First know who your current "service provider" is. Ask yourself: Where am I connected? Do you have access and a personal connection or have you taken a path through a religion, nature, science, astrology, astronomy, education, and a relationship with a spiritual mentor, an ascended Master, angel or light being? Do you have access through other spiritual methods or gateways? You could be connected to the astral level or dark forces that inhabit dark dimensions. Ask yourself:

> *Am I connected? On what level? With whom?*
> *With what? Why? How do we get connected and*
> *why should we go to all the trouble?*

Because most people are disconnected from themselves, their soul and spirit, others around them and the Source of life, we need to make sure we are connected. Make sure you understand with whom you are connected and in what way. If you are satisfied – "renew your contract"! If not, disconnect, "cancel your contract" and investment and make a new, more satisfying connection. Getting connected and gaining access to higher, more reliable sources of information and power is one of our first steps in creating true, lasting success. The process could and does require a lot of inner work. We will, however, remain a shadow of our true self if we neglect this calling.

Leadership and mind-wellness

One of the secrets of life is to keep a tranquil mind, to be at peace on the inside, whatever is happening on the outside. Our state of mind impacts strongly on our physical health. A highly conscious and mature person is mindful of the importance of mind wellness and will focus on relieving personal stress and emotional tension while ensuring physical and mental health.

The questions are:

> *What is mind wellness? What is mental health?*
> *What role does mind wellness play in*
> *leadership?*

Mental health describes a level of psychological wellbeing, or an absence of a mental disorder.[249] From the perspective of 'positive psychology' or 'holism', mental health may include an individual's ability to enjoy life, and create a balance between life activities and efforts to achieve psychological resilience. Mental health can also be defined as an expression of emotions, and as signifying a successful adaptation to a range of demands. As we awaken, we also become more conscious of the quality of leaders we have in influential positions at the moment. Some leaders are mindful and aware of their personal contribution to the welfare of the whole. Others represent the mindless masses while serving their own ego-driven agendas.

The time has come to discern and understand the difference between mindful authentic versus mindless self-serving leaders and their underlying mindsets and agendas. We can expect mental health and mind-wellness to play a significant role in identifying and training competent leaders in order to secure a safe transition into the future.

In order to gain a deeper understanding of authentic leadership and New Leadership DNA, we will need to focus on leadership and mind wellness in the next chapter.[250]

Notes

CHAPTER 7

LEADERSHIP AND MIND-WELLNESS

Introduction

In the film *Forrest Gump*, with Tom Hanks in the title role, we find this inspiring man, who at the surface seems to be mentally handicapped, achieve the most extraordinary feats. He finds his happiness in his life-long love, Jenny. However, it is the seventies and Jenny was part of the Hippy, drug and sex-culture of the times. Jenny dies from an 'unknown' virus and Forrest is left with memories of love, fulfillment and happiness . . . and a son. Forest jr. is healthy, happy and very bright, and we learn – 'life is a box of chocolates'.

During the sixties and seventies many involved in the gay and hippy cultures contracted this then unknown virus. During these times people were caught unawares and they paid for their ignorance with their lives. Today we know about the HIV-AIDS virus and the global epidemic that has turned into a pandemic.

The questions are:

> *What is the HIV-AIDS virus and what does it do? Is there a 'HIV-Aids virus of the mind' that we need to be aware of in order to prevent being caught unaware and even pay for our ignorance with our lives?*

Virus infections

A biological virus is a small infectious agent that can infect all types of organisms, from animals and plants to bacteria. Since the first virus infecting the tobacco plant was discovered by Dmitri Ivanovsky in 1892, about 5 000 viruses have been described in detail, although there are millions of different types. Viruses vary in shape, are about 100 times smaller than bacteria and found in almost every ecosystem on Earth. Viruses are the most abundant type of biological entity and the scientific study of viruses is known as virology.[251]

The questions are:

> *What is a virus and how does it function?*

An 'infectious agent' like a virus is an information program or package in the form of genes on a RNA string that are capable of affecting the functioning of DNA in cells of living organisms. Computer viruses function in the same way by gaining access to our computers and rendering their programs ineffective. In the same way there are generic emotional thought patterns that could also affect human emotions and thought processes. As long as we are unaware and neglect to take the necessary precautions, we remain vulnerable.

These destructive virus programs could gain access and render us ineffective; physically, mentally, emotionally and also spiritually. The way this is accomplished is by disconnecting the initial connections to the authentic program – the blueprint of life. What all viruses have in common is that they can only live and function

142

within a host. Without a host – the virus is ineffective as it cannot fulfill its function.

The questions are:

> *What do we need to know and do in order to become immune to these viruses? Is it possible to become invulnerable?*

In order to become 'immune' we need to grow in understanding – we need to raise our consciousness and level of awareness. The higher and more potent the level or frequency we can access and maintain, the less susceptible we become to lower order destructive forces. However it takes time and effort to raise our conscious awareness – our frequency. It takes even more effort and self mastery to maintain a constant connection to higher levels when we are constantly bombarded with lower, destructive forces. Once we are fully connected and have healed the mind, we become 'immune'. If we do not achieve this level, we continue with a 'broken mind' or disconnected mind, the reason for our failures. Our success in life depends on us becoming conscious while reconnecting to higher mind, taking back our power and co-creating success and prosperity for all. We can create miracles. This is what Power Intelligence is all about.

Mind-wellness will play a significant role in the future. By becoming invulnerable to the influence of lower order influences, we can leave the old life of survival behind. We can die to the old self and be reborn, like the Phoenix, into whole new quality of living. We become free to embark on a new adventure of a fulfilling life of love and abundance.[252] In order to obtain this level of freedom, we need to grow in our understanding.

Understanding viruses

A biological virus consists of two or three parts: genes, made from either DNA or RNA that carry genetic information; a protein coat that protects the genes; and in some viruses, an envelope of fat that surrounds and protects them when they are not contained within a host cell. When the virus enters a host cell it connects an RNA string that is one part of the double helix DNA of the host. The host is rendered powerless. The new RNA of the virus takes over the DNA of the host and impairs the host DNA's normal functioning.[253]

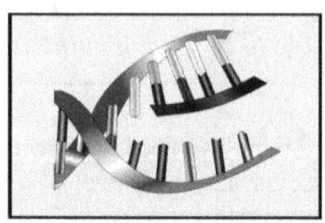

Virus conneting with DNA of host

Biological viruses spread in many different ways. Plant viruses are often spread from plant to plant by insects and other organisms, known as vectors. Some animal viruses are spread by blood-sucking insects. Each species of virus relies on a particular method. Whereas viruses such as influenza are spread through the air by people when they cough or sneeze, others are transmitted by contaminated hands, food and water or direct contact. The human immunodeficiency virus, HIV, is one of several major viruses that are transmitted during sex.

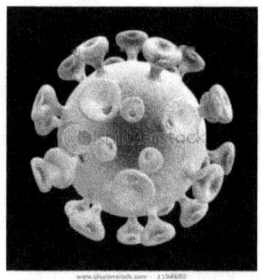

HIV–AIDS virus

Usually viruses are eliminated by the immune system, conferring lifetime immunity to the host for that specific virus. Antibiotics have no effect on viruses, but antiviral drugs have been developed to treat life-threatening infections. Vaccines that produce lifelong immunity can prevent some viral infections[254]. However, the problem with the

HIV-AIDS virus is that it disconnects the genetic material responsible for our immune system and renders the immune system ineffective. The virus shortcuts the flow of the initial information and the body loses its power to fulfill its authentic function. The physical body is then powerless to protect itself and becomes vulnerable to other infections. Once the HIV virus leads to AIDS, and if left untreated, death is inevitable.[255]

The viruses affecting our computers function in the same way. 'Trojan horses' or other forms of camouflage are used to gain entrance to our computers and cause the damage they were created for, that is – disruption of the flow of information. It costs time, effort and money to regain entry to the affected computer and restore the flow of information. Computer viruses have become a large concern in the information technology industry over the last decade. A computer virus functions in the same way biological viruses function.

An invader program with false, negative and foreign information, like the RNA-string of a biological virus, gains access to our computer files in various ways. The computer virus then attaches the corrupt information files to the unprotected open computer program, the corrupt file deactivates the initial function and the information flow is cut off. The computer program is rendered ineffective.

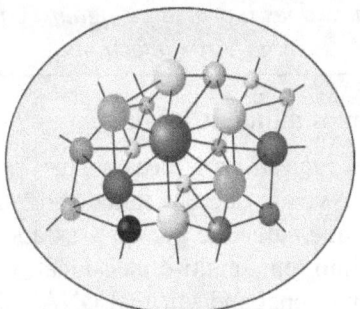

Invasion of computer virus in computer programs

There are people who specialize in writing computer virus programs in order to take control by deactivating the initial functionality of the computer. In this position of power the creator of virus programs manipulates the vulnerable consumer. Today we cannot think of purchasing a computer without purchasing an anti-virus program. It has become one of the largest money making businesses currently online.

In the picture above we find the invader's corrupt information program, depicted as dark, black thought-forms. It blocks the line of information flow of the original computer program, and the computer shuts down. Many computers and large computer systems have crashed (and died) before computer antivirus programs became freely available. Today, no one in their 'right mind' would use a computer to download from the internet without making sure that a computer anti-virus program has been installed and is up to date. In the same way no one in their 'right mind' will engage in unprotected sex with a stranger. It would be insane![256]

So far we can say that we have two points of departure. On the one hand we can be healthy, functioning from our 'right mind', sound mind or sanity. On the other hand, we have a dysfunctional situation operating from the 'wrong mind', unsound mind or insane mind. The disconnected DNA and unsound, 'insane' mind, leaves us vulnerable to HIV-AIDS-of -the-mind.

The questions that arise are:

> *What is this HIV-AIDS-of-the-mind that causes 'insanity'? What is this 'right mind' and how does it protect us against corrupt mind-virus infections.*

Mindful sanity versus mindless insanity

The answers to these questions are easy: This 'right mind' refers to the truth about who we are and our initial programming to function effectively as a unique authentic person – as a spiritual light being. This is encoded into our multi-dimensional DNA and includes physical, mental, emotional and spiritual DNA. We are connected to our 'right mind', our 'sound mind' or universal consciousness, via our DNA.

'Right mind' refers to higher levels of consciousness and awareness, the connection with higher intelligence, higher self, universal mind or Source. Once we are connected to this level frequency, we become immune to any other lower order connections. We are aware and can protect our self against unnecessary exposure to any of the lower frequencies and the bearers thereof. We consciously deny any access to dark, negative and corrupt influences, from self, other people, circumstances or substances that could jeopardize our emotional, mental, or spiritual connections, wellbeing and functioning. We secure and maintain our full sanity and functional ability to co-create with source, under all and every circumstance we may encounter on earth. We know and understand we can and should rise above circumstances. We can consciously raise our frequency and we can, and should create miracles. We only need to stay connected and function as we should – as authentic self, as light bearer and miracle maker.

The following questions are:

> *What does this HIV-AIDS-of-the-mind*
> *look like and what does it do?*

The answer is: This virus is the lie – corrupt information! It comes from corrupt sources and from ego-driven disconnected persons or groups on lower order, dark and corrupt levels. They consciously or unconsciously spread the misinformation, the lie, through their erroneous interpretations, teachings, values, beliefs, guidance and influence. We can directly or indirectly be exposed to the lie and erroneous teachings. The lie can be handed down from generation to generation. This means the HIV-AIDS-of-the-mind is not only contagious, but also 'hereditary'. Once the HIV-of-the -mind virus takes hold, it becomes a long and arduous struggle to survive. If you are not equipped with the correct tools and skills i.e. the truth, then loss of authentic living, or death, is inevitable.

The lie is any falsehood, untruth or half truth about who you are, where you come from, what your purpose is and how you should function. The lie disregards the truth of universal cosmic light, love, abundance, health, wealth, happiness, fulfillment of heart and soul and the ability to co-create with source. The lie negates the truth about your real identity as a spiritual light being with a physical body, heart, mind, soul and spirit. The lie denies your true heritage and disconnects you from your authentic, functional higher self, your spirit and your soul. The lie deactivates or 'steals' your soul. It takes control, renders you powerless, dysfunctional, mindless and even useless[257]. You feel lost, helpless, alone, worthless and afraid while living a meaningless life of constant survival from day to day. You become a captive of fear.

The lie represents the false image of the earthly ego and wants you to identify with this corrupt illusion. The lie disconnects you from your true identity and places a synthetic image in its place. Not only does the lie steal your soul and true identity, it wants to keep you mindless and 'insane'. It keeps you dependent, places you in bondage and holds you captive to lower frequencies and the destructive, corrupt, ego teachings and programming of the world.

The lie introduces the false ego self and places it in competition with the authentic soul self. The lie spreads false interpretations, confusion, dissonance, darkness, false notes, fear, disintegration and in the end, death. The lie clouds our thoughts rendering them dysfunctional while our heart, mind, soul and spirit are disconnected from the frequency of truth, wisdom, love and compassion – the frequency of miracles and true success. We individually and collectively become disconnected and fall 'out of love', out of 'paradise' and out of 'heaven'. We lose our power to lead happy fulfilling lives and the awareness that we can create miracles. We become 'insane' and lead unfulfilling and insane lives of the lie. It is from HIV-AIDS-of-the-mind we need to free ourselves.[258] We need to heal the mind and take back our sanity.

The challenge is to now break the stronghold of the ego lie and reclaim our power from illusion and corruption. We need to develop our Power Intelligence by becoming mindful and consciously setting the records straight. We are challenged to regain mastery of our authentic self and miracle mind, and co-create a fulfilling life of love and abundance. This is what this book is all about.

The question is:

> *What is the path back to authentic mindful living?*

Understanding the path back

Once you are caught in the corrupt web of the illusion of the lie, you get disconnected from your authentic self, your DNA is disconnected on various levels and self destruction is inevitable. You then revert back to lower order information and frequencies and the people who identify with these dark lies. People who share the same version of the lie form groups who want to make you part of their 'family of darkness and despair'. You can join one of these groups and remain here forever or – you could awake from this dark and depressing illusion, choose to reclaim your power and to heal yourself from this unwelcome invader, the lie – the corrupter. You can choose to reconnect to higher mind and use your inherent Power Intelligence. You then become free, feel free and you are free to live your authentic self.

Once you have woken up and become conscious of this destructive downward spiral, you choose to stop, turn around and head back home. You move to a new level of consciousness and embark on a new path of life and abundance. You ignite a whole new process and invest your time energy and money in growing in truth – freedom – love and compassion – light – Christ consciousness – sanity – the 'right mind'. You consciously disconnect and free yourself from the destructive path of the lie – captivity – anti-love – anti-light or darkness – Antichrist – insanity – corruption of HIV-AIDS-of-the-mind.

All corruption in any form and in any place arises from the infection by HIV-AIDS-of-the-mind. All corrupt persons, teams, organizations, governments and even countries as a whole, are consciously or unconsciously infected with HIV-AIDS-of-the-mind. Very few people, teams, groups, political parties or organizations, are however brave enough to admit their HIV-AIDS-of-the-mind status, and seek help. Corruption, the lie, then comes in many forms and with many faces. We find it in dishonest exploitation of power for personal gain and dishonest or illegal behavior by officials or people in positions of power, especially when they accept money in exchange for favours.

This means most people with self serving, ego-driven motives and intentions, are in essence corrupt and infected with HIV-AIDS-of-the-mind. Most people are currently vulnerable and living 'insane' lives. It is from this insanity and 'infection' we need to heal. We need to reclaim our power and put it to right use in our lives. If not, abuse or 'absence-of-use' is inevitable. A self-destructive life becomes inevitable. Herein lies the choice to become power intelligent. We need to pay attention to the wellness of the mind.

Once you can be objective and asses if you are disconnected or 'infected', as we do in order to attain our biological HIV-AIDS status, you can begin with healing the broken connections. You can then identify with a new group who share your 'right mind' of truth and who too function on the frequency of light, love and freedom. You develop a whole new spiritual family with a whole new DNA. At the same time you become aware of other people and groups who are infected with HIV-AIDS-of-the mind, and render your services. You open your heart, mind, soul and spirit and bring compassion, help and assistance to others. You correct the corrupt program of ego driven self service and change it to soul driven service and authentic success and quality living. You develop new leadership DNA and become a light bearer, pathfinder and mapmaker. You join hands with other like-minded ones and together we heal the body of light and find our way home.

It is from HIV-AIDS-of-the-mind we need to free ourselves.[259] We need to heal the mind and take back our sanity. We were created to heal from a self-serving corrupt lifestyle and place our authentic self in a functional service that will benefit all. We can heal the body of light – the Christ consciousness or 'right mind'.[260]

You choose to return to your authentic self, your authentic home and you live an authentic life of love, abundance, fulfillment and success. You consciously take back your power in body, mind, soul and spirit. You reconnect to your original blueprint, your authentic higher self. You 'fall in love' with your authentic self, your fellow human beings, with life on earth, with creation, the creator – God.

You embark on the journey back home. You heal your disconnections and you climb the success ladder of DNA back to your ability to co-create miracles with source. You gain access to the storeroom of the universe – heaven. You become aware of the *Theoplexus* and you consciously choose to become the *Theoplexus* – the place that Love meets all[261]. Your live your new life in love and abundance and yes – you understand how to create miracles!

Once we allow the corrupt agent, like the infectious virus, access, it affects not only the functioning of the physical body or a physical computer, but also affects human emotions[262] and thought processes. The questions are:

> *How do we get reconnected? What must we do?*

The power of our thoughts

Bruce Lipton's book, *The biology of belief*[263] illustrates how our thoughts have profound effects on our behaviour and on our genes. This, however, only occurs when our thought patterns are in harmony with subconscious programming, our soul and spirit. Lipton explains how the subconscious mind and the conscious mind operate independently. The subconscious mind repeatedly goes over the same behavioural responses from life. We respond to situations stored in our subconscious, which Lipton says is, "millions of times more powerful than the conscious mind". He further elaborates by stating: "genes are shaped, guided, and tailored by environmental learning experiences." His theory states that we are not the result of our genetic makeup, but rather from the influence of the environment—starting of course with our parents. He gives practical advice on 'conscious parenting', and believes that the best growth promoter for children is unconditional love. Our parents act as genetic engineers months before conception. All is encoded into our 'master cell'.[264]

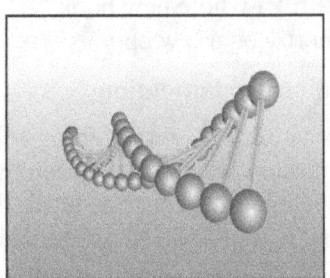

DNA with chromosomes

When we have a destructive thought or emotional pattern accessing our 'master cell', we can expect the same results we find with the HIV-AIDS virus. Not only do these negative thought forms and feelings invade our body and mind, our light bodies, our spirit and soul are also invaded and our higher connections are rendered ineffective. We then have dysfunctional or 'junk genes'. We have to reclaim and mine our lost potential from these junk genes.[265] All negativity, or low energy frequencies have the ability to disconnect us from higher frequencies, higher thoughts, higher mind and the heart[266] or source – God. One question still remains:

> *What must we do?*

In short – we need to heal and reactivate our multidimensional DNA.[267]

Healing the mind

You heal the self and connect to higher mind by accessing higher frequencies of information, truth and universal wisdom. Many times you first need to detox from toxic influences and people and unlearn lower order information in order to make place for a new mindset and new lifestyle. Dying to the old is not always easy or painless. This can be done by exposing yourself to new information and higher truths.

It helps to find competent people or support who can assist you along the way. If not, you have to do it n your own. There are a multitude of methods you can use in order to heal your mind and your DNA. This information will fill a whole new book.[268] For our purpose here, we will only focus shortly on a few options.

- **Physical and medical attention**

When a person is infected with biological HIV-AIDS, they immediately seek medical attention. Although HIV-AIDS-of-the-mind occurs on a psychological-spiritual level, the same care should apply. The physical symptom of HIV-AIDS-of-the-mind is 'burnout' that includes all the psychosomatic symptoms that accompany mental, emotional, physical and spiritual stress and fatigue. In essence, the body rebels against 'overuse' or 'abuse' in a mindless, HIV-AIDS-of-the-mind, plastic lifestyle of struggle and survival. But using the brute force of personal ego driven willpower to survive is unnatural and causes stress and further burnout. We are created to create success with effortless ease by increasing flow. The physical body is too fragile to withstand long periods of abuse, stress and inevitably 'burns out'.

The body cannot lie. All stress as mental, emotional, or physical strains are caused by disconnection to the authentic self and underlying fear and anxiety that leads to overwork. It may cause symptoms like raised blood pressure or depression. Depression is the symptom of a lack of authentic self expression. In order to heal the depression – you need to express your authentic self.

Depleted neuro-transmitters, for example serotonin, noradrenaline, dopamine and others as discussed, can be replenished with natural methods or medical assistance. All illnesses have underlying psychosomatic origins. We were not created to be sick – it is not 'natural'. When everything is in balance and functioning in harmony and flow, we also experience perfect health. However, with all the demands of physicality, we can and do become sick.

Medical attention should be given to the physical manifestations and all illnesses treated appropriately. These are however only the symptoms and not the original cause. The underlying emotional dynamics, disconnections and psychosomatic dysfunction, need to be attended to as well. We can also make use of other professional services.

- **Psychology, counseling, mentoring and coaching.**

Psychology has come a long way over time. Today, many psychologists are trained in the most up to date techniques. Like all people, psychologists use the techniques that suit their personality. As a psychologist, mentor or counselor, they walk their own path of life and adopt the methods that have become part of who they are. Many psychologists, counselors and mentors are also 'wounded-healers'. No academic training can give a person a firsthand experience of life. Mature counselors are people who can say 'been there, done that, got the T-shirt'. This level of maturity can be obtained irrespective of age. These are people who have learnt to come from heart and live their own truth.

Find a professional psychologist that you are confident will bring you truth and help you to find your own truth and authentic self. Choose someone who will be able to help you heal the hurt, heal the mind and heal your DNA. Unfortunately very few professional psychologists are currently trained in conscious DNA healing and activation.[269]. However, in the end you still need to help yourself. This is what maturity is all about.

- **Self-healing and self-mentoring**

You can start your own self-healing and mentoring processes by becoming conscious and aware of who you are and what you want out of life. Take all the steps and requirements you need in order to become fulfilled, happy and successful. Embark on a new adventure by attending workshops, reading new books, listening to new music and messages, while developing a new exercise and eating program. Do whatever it takes to heal your DNA and your life.

Currently there are various methods to heal your DNA that include the use of sound, light and also stem cell therapy. It is of course important to understand that all interventions have a positive and negative, light and dark side and must always be entered into with clarity and discernment. We can now also add to this growing list, the use of electromagnetic therapy.

Electromagnetic therapy and healing DNA

Science has established that electrical and magnetic energy exists in the human body. Some devices commonly used in mainstream medicine include the electroencephalogram (EEG) to measure electrical activity in the brain and the electrocardiogram (EKG) which measures the electrical patterns of heartbeats. The use of electrical energy to stimulate the heart when its rhythm is disrupted is known as defibrillation. Other devices such as magnetic resonance imaging (MRI) and trans-cutaneous electrical nerve stimulation units are also used in mainstream medicine.

Electromagnetic therapy involves the use of electromagnetic energy to diagnose or treat disease. Alternative medicine providers may offer low-voltage electricity, magnetic fields, radio waves, or other types of electromagnetic energy generated by electric currents for this purpose.

Electromagnetic energy includes electricity, microwaves, radio waves, ionizing radiation, and infrared rays, as well as electrically generated magnetic fields. Light is also a form of electromagnetic energy, and was addressed in the first chapter.

In contrast to the wide range of electromagnetic energy methods that have been proven for standard medical treatment, many of the alternative electronic devices promoted to cure disease have not been scientifically proven to be effective. Most of these devices claim to offer radio waves, electrical currents, or magnetic fields.

In general, practitioners of electromagnetic therapy all agree that when electromagnetic frequencies or energy fields within the body go out of balance, disease and illness occur. These imbalances disrupt the body's chemical makeup. By applying electromagnetic energy from outside the body, usually with electronic devices, it is possible to correct the imbalances in the body.

Practitioners claim that these methods can treat ulcers, headaches, burns, chronic pain, nerve disorders, spinal cord injuries, diabetes, gum infections, asthma, bronchitis, arthritis, cerebral palsy, heart disease, and cancer.

This research is currently part of standard medical intervention.[270] We can expect it to expand and include emotional, mental, psychological and spiritual healing as well. As our understanding and technology develop, we can expect new methods of healing our DNA to emerge.

Different frequencies activate and stimulate different parts of the physical and light bodies. Some of the frequencies we need to become aware of include the following:

Activates:	Frequency
Love	528 Hz
Pineal gland	936 Hz
Intuition	741 Hz
Light centres	432 Hz

However, DNA healing and activation is nothing new. It has been part of ancient spiritual practices for millennia. DNA healing is in essence spiritual healing – a reconnection with the universal mind, the 'right mind' or sound mind.

Spiritual DNA healing

Spiritual DNA activation in its currently available form can be traced back to King Solomon the Great over 2500 years ago, and is therefore not viewed as a new phenomenon. The technique was originally performed in the Great Pyramid of Giza to prepare priests, priestesses, oracles, prophets and high healers for positions of power and responsibility within their communities. The process of activating the DNA to the 24th strand and accessing the original blueprint is therefore seen as a very holy and sacred process.

These teachings, methods and skills have been handed down intact in an unbroken lineage, generation after generation to 'chosen ones'. Now these wisdoms have been made available and more accessible to the general public. These processes are still continuing daily, with or without our awareness. There is truly nothing new under the sun.[271]

At the same time science has discovered that the ability to live in faith is partially heritable. This led to the 'God gene hypothesis' that proposes that human beings inherit a set of genes that predispose them to believe in a higher power. This idea was postulated by geneticist Dean Hamers, the director of the *Gene Structure and Regulation Unit at the U.S. National Cancer Institute*. He wrote a book on the subject titled *The God gene: how faith is hardwired into our genes*. The God gene hypothesis is based on a combination of behavioural, genetic, neurobiological and psychological studies.[272]

The major arguments of the theory are:

- Spirituality can be quantified by psychometric measurements.
- The underlying tendency to spirituality is partially heritable.
- Part of this heritability can be attributed to the gene VMAT2.
- This gene acts by altering *monoamine* levels.
- Spirituality arises in a population because spiritual individuals are favoured by natural selection.

However, a number of scientists and researchers are highly critical of this theory. However, their criticisms drew attention to the idea of a connection between genes, heredity and spirituality. The consequences of these findings have far reaching implications for all.

Biological heredity and biological families are now making way for spiritual heredity and a new spiritual family. Lifelong struggles with not fitting in with your biological family now make way for a re-identification with a new spiritual family with a new spiritual DNA, that goes far beyond traditional teachings and biological genes. This means all have to be 'reborn' or reconnected in order to become 'spiritual heirs'. We have to heal HIV-AIDS–of-the-mind and reconnect the 'broken mind' with higher spiritual mind.

These spiritual teachings have wide scientific implications as well. With the identification of a 'God gene', religion, science, psychology and spirituality will start to come together in order to provide deeper answers to the questions about life and quality living.

At the same time a New Leadership DNA[273] is emerging. These are the leaders who will safely show the way into the future. One of the most important challenges of our generation is to identify and develop the 'leadership mind'. This is the responsibility of everyone and not just a select few. Only then can we be confident to remain on the right path of a fulfilling, enlightened life, here and now.

Notes

Notes

CHAPTER 8

LEADERSHIP, GUIDANCE AND THE FRONTAL LOBE

Introduction

We have found that the power spot has wired us to become the people we are. Here we find the potential for further growth, development, movement, transformation and evolution on the path of life. It is here where we connect to the big picture, to a larger meaningful whole and to the Universal Mind. Connecting with, tapping into, intelligently utilizing and managing this power is the challenge of the future as we stand at the cutting edge of human development. Power is now found in silence while solutions are now found in flow and not in force.

However, we need to consider the following questions:

> *Are humans the only species on earth that is specially equipped with an internal navigation system? If not – what can we learn from nature concerning change, movement and navigation?*

The answer is: No, humans are not the only species with an internal navigation system. We find animal migration, movement, change and navigation as a natural part of life as discussed in chapter 2. The next questions that arise are:

> *How do we activate this guide-spot and tap into all the potential that is at our disposal?*

In order to find answers to these questions we first need to have a look at the map of the brain and learn how the frontal lobes and 'guide-spot' function.

The function of the frontal lobe

The frontal lobe is one of the four main lobes or regions of the neo- or cerebral cortex. It is an area located at the front of each cerebral hemisphere and found in the brain of humans and other mammals. After lengthy debates is was found that the human frontal cortex was not relatively larger than the cortex in the other great apes – but was relatively larger than the frontal cortex in the lesser apes and monkeys[274]. In humans, the frontal lobe reaches full maturity only after the twenties, marking the cognitive maturity associated with adulthood.

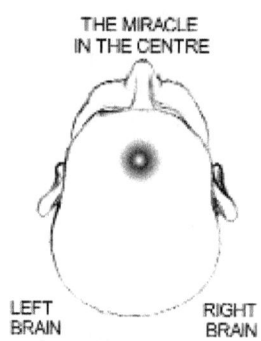

The frontal lobe

The frontal lobe is responsible for higher order thinking and behavior and is involved in movement, decision making, problem solving, and planning. The executive functions of the frontal lobes involve the ability to recognize future consequences resulting from current actions, to choose between good and bad actions, or better and best, override and suppress unacceptable social responses, and determine similarities and differences between things or events. Therefore, it is involved in higher mental functions. Here we find the seat of discernment, vision and higher guidance.

The frontal lobes also play an important part in retaining longer term memories which are not task-based. These are often memories associated with emotions derived from input from the brain's limbic system. The fully functional frontal lobe modifies those emotions to generally fit socially acceptable norms.

The frontal lobe also contains most of the dopamine-sensitive neurons in the cerebral cortex. The questions are:

> *What do frontal lobe functioning and dopamine have to do with our search for mastering our miracle mind?*

In order to find more clarity we need to have a closer look at frontal lobe functioning and we have to find out if there is any correlation with experiencing miracles.

The frontal lobe and neurotransmitters

Neurotransmitters are brain chemical messengers. These vital chemicals carry messages between brain cells and allow brain cells to 'talk to' one another. Trillions of messages are sent and received every day. The messages that are positive, happy, or upbeat are transmitted by the brain's happy neuro-transmitters, also technically known as Biogenic Amine/Endorphin System, to other parts of the brain. Messages that are negative, somber, disquieting or even destructive, are carried by the brain's 'sad messengers'. Most nerve centers receive input from both types of messengers. As long as this input is balanced, everything runs along on an even keel.

In order to master our miracle mind, we first need to understand the functioning of our neurotransmitters and inner communication system. There are three important neurotransmitters or 'happy messengers' – serotonin, noradrenalin and the dopamine system[275].

We will also need to shortly focus on the *amygdala* in order for us to gain a deeper understanding of and master the miracle mind.

The amygdala[276] is an almond-shaped group of nuclei located deep within the temporal lobes of the brain in complex vertebrates, including humans. Research shows that it performs a primary role in the processing of emotions and retention of the memory of emotional reactions. The amygdalae also send impulses relating to increased reflexes to facial nerves and for activation of dopamine, norepinephrine and epinephrine. It is involved in receiving input from our sensory system, our sense of smell and pheromone-processing processes. Pheromones are chemicals capable of acting outside the body of the secreting individual to impact the behavior of a receiving individual[277].

Studies also reveal that the volume of the amygdalae correlates positively with the complexity of social networks.[278] It was found that individuals with larger amygdalae had larger and more complex social networks and were also better able to make accurate social judgments. It is hypothesized that larger amygdalae allow for greater emotional intelligence, enabling greater societal integration and cooperation with others.[279] With today's widespread social networking we have to take this into account when looking to master the miracle mind. The amygdalae process reactions to violations concerning personal space[280]. We have a natural instinct to set boundaries and defend out personal space. However, these reactions are absent in persons in whom the amygdalae are damaged. The amygdalae appear to play a role in binge drinking while alcoholism is associated with dampened activation in brain networks responsible for emotional processing, including the amygdalae[281].

On a more positive note – Buddhist monks who practice *compassion meditation* have been shown to modulate their amygdalae during their practice. It was found that the increased activity in the amygdalae following compassion-oriented meditation may contribute to social connectedness.[282]. In order to master our miracle mind we will need to learn these techniques and clear ourselves of debilitating negative emotional memories, patterns, addictions and responses. This means we need to consciously reprogram the frontal lobe and amygdalae.

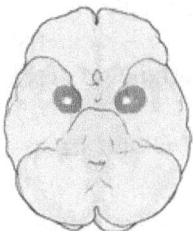

The position of the amygdalae in the human brain

Scientific research has also linked frontal lobe functioning with optimism.

The Frontal lobe and optimism

There could be deeper meaning to the common question: is the glass half full or half empty? Researchers like Vaughn[283] have found that optimism is directly linked to frontal lobe functioning. Essentially, the study found that in eternally optimistic people, the brain rejected bad news. Optimism also has health benefits that include lower anxiety levels, decreased stress, and improved health.

However, there is also unrealistic optimism that can be detrimental to our wellbeing. People who are unrealistic about their risk of negative events are more likely to engage in risky behavior such as unsafe sexual practices, consumption of drugs or alcohol, or investing in less-than-secure financial situations. In fact, a related study reported that optimism predicts the occurrence of alcohol-related negative events; higher levels of optimism predicted more negative events, despite facts and past experience supporting the risky nature of the activities.[284] A little pessimism, or even skepticism or realism, likely helps the fittest survive.

The authors[285] assert that this blind optimism is due to a malfunction in the prefrontal cortex that is supposed to update neural coding of undesirable information regarding the future likelihood of negative events. The brain is supposed to update personal risk factors when presented with negative information. Unrealistic optimism can be detrimental to our wellbeing. People who are unrealistic about the risk of negative events are more likely to engage in risky behavior.

The authors are not telling people not to have a positive outlook — optimism surely has its place — but they do insist that optimistic brains are not always functioning properly.

The frontal lobe dysfunction and stress

Various factors can influence frontal lobe functioning. We have already touched on the influence of stress. All of us have experienced some periods of overstress in our lives. Usually they will be of short duration. We live in such a highly stressed society in which at least ten percent of our population is overstressed all the time! These people, who have inherited a low stress tolerance, are fighting against what we generally could call 'happy messenger failure' every day of their lives. It rarely stops; and they are sorely afflicted.

If your total stress load is high enough to interfere with your brain's endorphin levels or happy messengers, then your body clock stops functioning effectively. You will find yourself having difficulty falling asleep, and frequent awakenings during the night, perhaps with vivid dreams. On waking, you will not feel at all rested. Next, you will note a lack of energy, lack of desire to get out and do things, and a lack of interest in the outside world.

Next, you could have aches and pains. Particularly common are chest, shoulder, back and neck pains. But, it will seem like you are aware of vague, uncomfortable feelings from all over your body. Along with increased sensitivity to aches and pains, there is a decreased sense of pleasure in life. Things that used to be fun or pleasurable do not seem enjoyable anymore. You feel overwhelmed by life. Now you may cry easily, and feel that you are "depressed". You may also feel quite anxious. Anxiety and panic attacks are common in people who are emotionally, mentally, spiritually and physically burnt out.

It is during these so called "panic attacks" that you feel as if you cannot catch your breath. The heart races in panic, the muscles ache and pain all over the chest. You may even feel light headed. You may have stomach upsets and diarrhea. Stress has caused your body to behave in strange and difficult ways. Under these circumstances, anxiety and fear are expected.

Shocking and traumatic experiences and enduring stressful times erode the body's immune system and many stress related, psychosomatic illnesses start to develop. This can include constant infections, sinusitis, headaches, blood pressure and heart trouble, cancer, allergies, skin rashes, renal failure and many more.

Damage to the frontal lobes can also lead to the impairment of mental flexibility and spontaneity. Talking may increase or decrease dramatically. People with 'verbal diarrhea' usually have an underlying emotional and/or neuro-dysfunction. Perceptions regarding risk-taking and rule-abiding are impaired and socialization can diminish or increase. Orbital frontal lobe damage can result in peculiar sexual habits while lateral frontal lobe damage reduces sexual interest. Creativity and problem-solving are diminished or increased, and a person can experience loss of smell and/or taste.

Autism and epilepsy in patients with frontal lobe dysfunctions and distraction occur more frequently as in those with Attention Deficit Syndrome (ADS). We also find illnesses such as Parkinson's disease and mental health issues such as schizophrenia associated with frontal lobe dysfunction.

The questions that arise are:

> *Are these neuro-dysfunctions and low levels of endorphins like dopamine hereditary? What role does DNA play?*

It is a known fact that epilepsy and schizophrenia are genetic mutations. Not only is the research done by the Human Genome Project assisting to alleviate these genetic mutations, but the Human Brain Project is also making widespread contributions to bettering the quality of life of sufferers. While this research has been primarily focused on alleviating disease, we also have a positive spinoff that is assisting us in coming to a deeper understanding of success. The next questions are then evident:

> *Is it possible to activate our own frontal lobe and stimulate new functioning? If so, how?*

Frontal lobe activation

As we have found, the frontal lobes are responsible for certain important functions, especially in the creating of miracles. More important is the fact that as our awareness and consciousness grows, we can consciously activate and stimulate the level of efficacy of the brain and especially the frontal lobes – if we know how. The question that follows is: how?

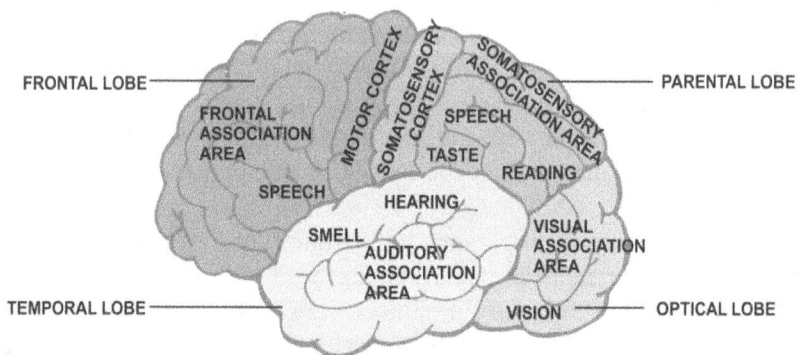

Frontal lobe functioning

It is possible to improve frontal lobe functions by engaging in activities that involve the frontal lobes. Such activities involve: problem solving (at the individual's current level of ability); learning new motor sequences (not practicing already learned routines); physical activity (particularly those that require solving spatial problems, like dancing); participating in new activities and going to new places, learning how things are related, similar or different, discussing pragmatics (how and why events or actions occur, and how meaning is related to context, culture, and expectations).

There are also many techniques to improve frontal lobe functioning in individuals with delayed or impaired frontal lobe abilities. [286]

The question that arises is:

> *Is there any connection between frontal lobe functioning and spirituality?*

The frontal lobe and spirituality

In the last decade, a number of studies have revealed the success of spiritual medicine. These studies come from a wide number of fields and deal with many aspects of religious and spiritual practice.[287] In their book, *Handbook of religion and health*, König *et al.* identified various factors that are influenced in a positive way by practices like prayer, meditation, attending church services and ceremonies. This includes the limitation of self-damaging behaviors such as smoking, drugs and alcohol and sex addiction. The social support network involved in religious belief and attendance at church and church services create a place of belonging with healthy social interactions.

It was found that a strong faith, positive relationships and positive thinking can strengthen the immune system, reducing the risk of cancer, improving general health and protecting the cardiovascular system. This field of research is now so large that it is not possible to review everything. What is however of importance is the fact that spiritual practices enhance our total wellbeing. With the right knowledge and skills we can now accelerate our wellbeing by consciously participating in spiritual practices like meditation.

There is now general agreement in the literature concerning the main changes that occur in meditation. The process of meditation initiates the relaxation response with a decrease in cortisol and blood pressure. This is especially noticeable in people who have practiced meditation over a number of years.[288]

However, one question still lingers:

What has this all got to do with creating miracles?

The frontal lobes, leadership and miracles

The frontal lobes are the final, highest and most advanced region of the brain. They are also the most recent part to develop. It is held that this part of the brain may have evolved to guide us in selecting the paths, strategies, and behaviors that would promote the best chances of survival[289]. Frontal lobe functioning is intimately connected to personality development, information processing, emotion, language, movement and executive functioning like planning, abstraction, judgment and movement. These are the personality traits we find in persons with a strong ethical character – those who live in truth and are incorruptible.

These are also the specific qualities that are necessary for the high level, executive behavior we seek in administrators, management, officials, directors and leaders. As this part develops and becomes active, we find the emerging of a new quality person and new leaders that will secure a safe transition into the future. It is here that our New Leadership DNA[290] is being ignited. The anterior part of the frontal lobes is connected to all other parts and controls not only emotional reactions but also the conscious ability to develop the personality and master the self.

Any frontal or temporal lobe dysfunction (FTD) refers to a disconnection with or deficit in this region. This causes problems in abstraction, planning, concentration, attention, reduced verbal production, mental rigidity and an inability to change a mindset. Mental disease in this area also interferes with encoding information, organization and learning, and can give rise to profound changes in character. Central to these disturbances we find a lack of self awareness, conscious self control and inappropriate social behavior.

This asocial behavior can be found in persons making rude remarks, violating the personal space of others or making inappropriate gestures. Persons with FTD develop problems with their own personal management and conduct as they become more passive about self. They could lose interest in personal hygiene and grooming and are stifled in their emotional ability to show joy, happiness or empathy for others.

Other symptoms of FTD include elevated appetite, an increase in oral fixations such as smoking, and sweet food cravings. Hyper sexuality can emerge that includes telling sexual jokes or compulsive masturbation[291]. Importantly, FTD correlates with hyper religiosity, devotion and belief.[292].

Although we find spirituality and even religiousness in both persons with active frontal lobe activity we find that with dysfunctional people they lack self awareness, self mastery, a mature personality and strong ethical character. By consciously developing these characteristics we move closer to the ability to fulfill our true function and purpose. We can enhance our ability to create miracles. The question is how?

It has scientifically been proven that meditation causes an increase in frontal lobe activity as well as an increase in blood flow to this region. The reciting of spiritual texts and passages, repetition of mantras and singing of spiritual verse also elevate the activity of this region. It has been found that by consciously activating frontal lobe activity we can substantially increase our ability to have spiritual experiences and even create miracles[293]. According to our definition, miracles occur beyond natural laws as we know them.

The next questions are:

> *Is it possible that we can override natural laws by activating higher frontal lobe functioning? If so, how?*

We have learnt that we live in an energy reality and that everything has a specific vibration and a specific frequency. In the book *New Success DNA* we focused on general frequencies we usually function on[294]. This includes alpha, beta, theta, gamma, delta and others. We also learned that it is possible to connect to specific frequencies and thereby enhance our abilities to learn, concentrate, remember, become innovative and even change one form to another just by changing the frequency.

Our questions therefore should be:

> *Is there a frequency for miracles that overrides natural laws? If so, how do we connect to this frequency, harness the power and utilize all this potential to our benefit and the benefit of others?*

We find the answer in the book *A course in miracles*[295] . Here we find a different point of view to successful living that now also includes miracle making. In order to come to a better understanding why *A course in miracles* holds this very important clue to miraculous living, we will first need to understand how thoughts become things.

Leadership, higher mind and guidance

There has always been a divide concerning leaders and communication with their gods or God. From a polytheistic view we find a different point of view on the task, purpose, guidelines and directions given to leaders through the communication with their gods than the leaders from a monotheistic approach – the one and only God – Yahweh.

The questions are:

> *How did the gods/demigods communicate with the leaders? How does God communicate with people? How are messages sent and received?*

The most important question is however: How do the thoughts of higher mind (gods/demigods/God) become things?

- **The 'seen' gods of polytheistic nations**

Worshipers of polytheistic nations could see their god/gods and made images of them out of stone, wood, copper, gold and other materials. From this point of view, the gods are visible or "seen" and communication takes place directly. This means that natural human senses are part of communication with the gods. This denotes a common realm – the physical realm, that gods and humans inhabited. Communication also includes oracles as shrines consecrated to the worship and consultation of a prophetic god, such as that of Apollo or Delphi. A prophecy could be made known at such a shrine in the form of an enigmatic statement or allegory by any person or agency considered to be a source of wise council or prophetic opinion.

- **The unseen God - Yahweh**

Guidance and information from the unseen Yahweh has raised various questions over time. The question is:

> *How do you communicate with an invisible God?*

God introduces Himself as Spirit – the unseen God – Yahweh. He communicates from a non-visible, spiritual position outside the physical realm and communication methods are beyond the natural physical senses of human beings. History reveals, however, that messages can be conveyed verbally through a cloud, telepathically, through holographic visions, dreams, divine encounters and oracles. Confirmation of these messages can be received through miracles or the confirmation of Angels of God, signs, or prophets.

We will focus on leadership, intelligence and guidance in the following chapter.

Notes

Notes

CHAPTER 9

LEADERSHIP, GUIDANCE AND INTELLIGENCE

What is intelligence?

Various researchers say that although the concept of intelligence is widely used, it remains difficult to define[296]. Many psychologists have taken a wider view of intelligence, trying to redefine intelligence in terms of what it takes to lead life successfully[297].

The Dictionary describes the word 'intelligence' as derived from two Latin words: '*inter*' meaning '*tween*' and '*legere*' meaning '*to choose*'[298]. Human beings are endowed with free will, the ability to consciously make choices. People have multiple choices on how, when and where to utilize their potential, 'chi', life force or energy to create and successfully manage their lives. Intelligence is now being linked to levels of success, consciousness, awareness and mindfulness. This means that the more conscious and aware we are the more intelligent are the choices we can make.

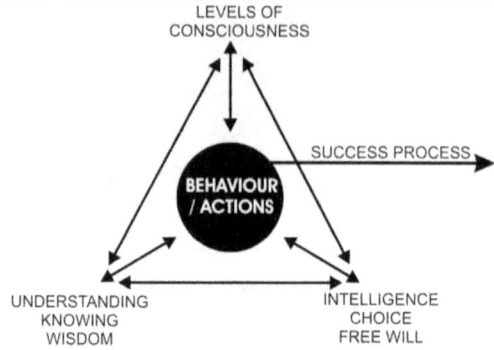

The dynamics of intelligence

Intelligence can be accepted as part of the dynamic interaction of levels of consciousness and understanding. These are two key competencies necessary for accessing and utilizing new potential or power-on-hold.

Different choices, different actions and forms of behavior are triggered by our personal, interpersonal, contextual, social, global and universal influences and dynamics.

Human understanding is evolving towards universal wisdom. Levels of human intelligence are evolving towards a universal intelligence that is represented by the levels of consciousness or power, universal wisdom and compassion and love. The interactions between wisdom, power and compassion, reflect the dynamics of multi-intelligence.

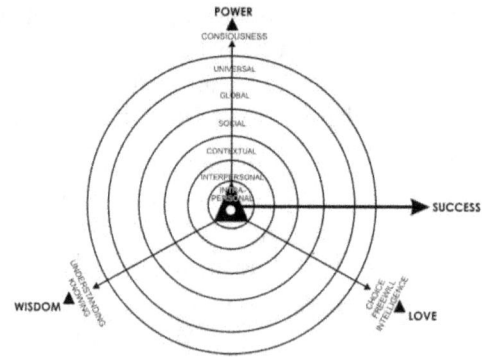

The Dynamics of multi-intelligence and Universal Intelligence

Human potential and human intelligence therefore have infinite possibilities. Against this background, it can be anticipated that as consciousness and understanding evolve, new intelligences will emerge and evolve. In the future this will take humanity to the next levels of understanding, power and success. Competent, intelligent leaders are needed to show the way.

Types of Intelligence

Many researchers have made distinctions between various types of intelligence[299]. Western perceptions of intelligence as active and rational differ from Eastern perceptions as passive and intuitive. Studies from Central, East and West Africa indicate that throughout Africa, intelligence has a wider social definition than it does in Europe[300].

Goleman introduced the concept of Emotional Intelligence, emphasizing the importance of identifying and managing emotions. The concept of Spiritual intelligence was introduced by Zohar and Marshall[301] in 1999. These authors argued that all intelligences may be linked to one of three neural systems, while those described by Gardner (citation) are variations of the basic IQ or intelligence quotient, EQ or our emotional quotient and SQ or spiritual quotient. These intelligences are associated with different neural arrangements that are connected to different frequencies and give access to different levels of information. This is refuted by the work of Hawkins on Kinesiology[302] in which underlying energy fields are interpreted by muscle tissue. It is further accepted that cellular memory affects consciousness, behaviour and leadership.

From the abovementioned, we find that intelligence is closely linked to success[303]. From further literature research, it was found that the definition of "success" as *the obtaining of goals* was in itself narrow and misleading. This necessitates a deeper concern and new approach to the interrelatedness of intelligence, success and leadership.

Intelligence, success and leadership

"Success" is informally and traditionally defined as "obtaining goals". The term "success", however, comes from the Latin root word *"cedere"* which is the same root word for access, process, proceed, excess, assess, exceed and excel. The word "success" therefore refers to a process with a specific purpose in mind. The words describing success can be used to identify the processes needed to create successful outcomes[304].

The first step to success is the ability to access and utilize different levels of internal, external and universal potential. Going within is therefore a prerequisite for going beyond known boundaries. This is reflective of the ancient statement of "so within, so without" and "so above, so below". We can define success as a process of consciously accessing internal and external potential and resources, releasing the energy, exceeding and excelling in the direction intended, assessing the progress and manifesting the desired outcome envisaged within time and space.

The success process is an intelligent process reflecting different levels of intrapersonal dynamics externally in different forms. The aim of developing new leadership DNA is to enhance these intra- and interpersonal dynamics by igniting new power and potential. The challenge is to create a new awareness of personal and universal power and develop our inner ability to become alchemists.

Alchemy

Alchemists of old are known for their experiments to try and transform base metals into gold. Although this was a challenge for natural sciences, the concept was used as an analogy in developing human potential. The ancient alchemists were also explorers of the spirit, whose experiments were aimed at finding keys to spiritual transformation as they attempted to transform the "base metal" of lower human potentials into the "gold" of higher potentials. Swiss alchemist and sixteenth century medical pioneer Paracelsus Von Hohenheim and his contemporaries, investigated and meditated on the principles of cosmic law[305].

For them, alchemy was a means to an end – the spiritualization of matter, the accomplishment of which would signify "as above, so below"; "so within, so without". These practitioners of the "all-chemistry" of the Universal Power were 'wholistic' in their approach as they sought nothing less than self-mastery and self-realization of their infinite potential and perfection of the physical matrix according to the Universal "Perfect Image". During the seventeenth century, Bacon[306]laid a scientific empirical foundation by pushing back limitations in the physical sciences, opening avenues to understand spiritual sciences.

Known for his investigations into alchemy, optics, mathematics and languages, he earned the title Doctor Mirabilis ("wonderful teacher") and a reputation as a wonder worker. As medieval philosopher, educational reformer and harbinger of modern science, Bacon developed the higher potential of his students and devotees as he instructed, mentored and inspired them in the "sacred sciences". Although these philosophies were and in many instances are still opposed by leaders of the Cartesian era, the new power-shift necessitates revisiting ancient theories and practices in order to come to a deeper understanding of and develop new skills and competencies necessary for the alchemic transformation of lower human potentials into higher order power and potential, thereby enhancing growth and development.

Rational and emotional intelligence

In the past, intelligence or IQ, referred to left brain linear thinking and problem solving strategies. In the mid 1990s Daniel Goleman showed that Emotional Intelligence or EQ, a right brain function, was of equal importance. It gives us the awareness of our own feelings and the feelings of others.

Whole brain functioning or integrated thinking became the challenge and buzzword of the 90s. As neither reason nor emotions can reach out beyond themselves, this meant we functioned within a closed structure and framework. We lived in a closed circuited world as reason and emotions have no power to go beyond what they are as thoughts and feelings. They have no transpersonal dimension.

This meant there was a void in the understanding of the complexity of life and the driving life force or power force beyond the human self. This left a hole at the centre of the self. Now we stand on the threshold of something new. There is something new in the air, a new vision, a new spirit, a new energy. And a third intelligence is emerging - Power Intelligence. The film the *Last Airbender,* has already opened the hearts and the minds of our youth as to the level of power we have within.

Power Intelligence is our ability to connect to our own unique and personal inner power source, Universal Power, Higher mind or God power, release this potential and focus on fulfilling our purpose. When the power is released it breaks through barriers and opens up new worlds and dimensions to be experienced. The outcome is prosperity, joy, health and happiness that can be shared with others. In this way a significant contribution is made to create a better life and a better world for all.

As we found in a previous chapter the power spot has wired us to become the people we are. It is here where we connect to the big picture, to a larger meaningful whole and to the Universal Mind. Connecting with, tapping into, intelligently utilizing and managing this power and inner GPS, are some important challenges of the future.

Our inner GPS

With our new technology scientists have identified a wave that is universal, that is in, above, and around everything. It is this universal power or thought that interconnects, synchronizes and harmonizes all other functions and factors. It has been found to be at the centre. It is at the centre of the universe and the centre of us as human beings, as people. This can be seen as the Power Intelligence spot. It is the place where we connect to God, Higher Power (or whatever name you choose), ask questions and receive answers and guidance for our path of life on planet earth.

This is where we consciously need to connect and know the Truth. We all have our own built in GPS to direct us in life and quality living. Leaders will form now on become more aware of this ability and consciously utilize this guiding force to the benefit of everyone. Ego-driven conflict and competition now makes way for value-driven cooperation and complementing contributions. They can only be achieved by quieting the mind.

It is in this stillness that we can connect to our personal power and listen to Divine Power and Truth. Here we find the energy and information to move to higher levels of functioning, health, wealth, meaning and prosperity. Very few people have consciously developed this ability and most people do not take the time to be still, understand and know! This means we are energetically or spiritually blocked.

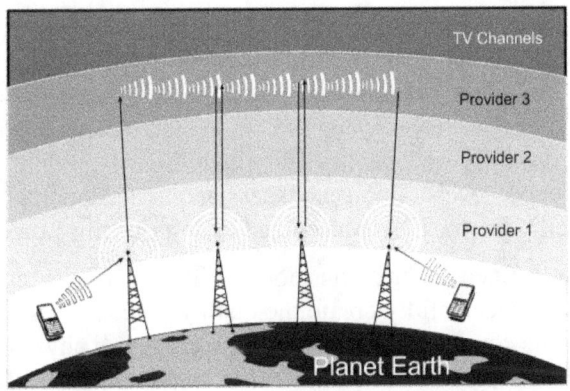

Getting connected: Cell phone with simcard

'Spirit' is an everyday term. There is a wonderful spirit at the rugby or tennis; or we have the general prevailing spirit of a company, organization or country. It is either positive or negative. When this spirit is positive, the energy levels are high and people and organizations are happy, work in teams, are productive and prosper. When the spirit is negative, energy levels are low and people are negative, despondent, unhappy, in conflict with each other and unproductive. Conflict, power struggles and power games are all part of this negative spirit.

The spirit of the Olympics attracts thousands of participants and millions of viewers from all over the word. This means that spirit is not only energy, but it also functions like an electromagnetic field or magnet. Spirit is an energy field that can influence the behavior, thinking, feeling and motivations of people who come in contact with it. It can be positive and open and develop new systems or it can be negative and break or close down systems. Not only is it energy, but information. Spirit is energy information in action. If you can change perceptions, mindsets and awareness – you can influence the spirit (energy information) and direct the actions of people. True leaders are becoming conscious of this powerful calling and responsibility by reclaiming their spiritual power and becoming power intelligent.

Power Intelligence

As the human race moves forward on the evolutionary path of development, it becomes evident that new innovative, intelligent ways and means are necessary to access and utilize deeper and more potent levels of power, of potential, and create new levels of health, wealth, prosperity, and quality life for all. This implies accessing new and deeper levels of consciousness and understanding. The term Power Intelligence or PI[307] was coined to describe this process.

PI can be defined as the conscious ability to utilize our infinite potential and successfully create the quality outcome desired. PI can be seen as the constructive use of psychic energy as physical, mental, emotional and spiritual energy levels, to create a quality life desired. PI is the conscious ability to manage energy and can be viewed as "energy engineering" or "energy intelligence" that includes physical, quantum physical and metaphysical (spiritual) perspectives.

Power Intelligence is the conscious ability to find new paths, maps and skills and develop new competencies to transform lower order potential and psychic energy into higher order, more potent levels of power, intelligence and success. PI therefore refers to the "alchemy" of human potential.

Statistics show that more than 90 % of people are religious. It has however been found that less than 1% of all people have developed spiritual power or power intelligence. This means that religion does not necessarily develop the individual power of people. Zohar says that the larger part of human society is spiritually blunted or powerless, impoverished and even "dumb". This means most people live religious but powerless, impoverished lives. This leaves only a few power intelligent, inspired "energy makers" in the world to take us forward. The rest are energy breakers and unproductive passengers ... and now an awakening is taking place.

Power intelligence means connecting to the personal power force and to an outside or transpersonal power or Universal Power or God. Power Intelligence is the ability to move beyond the self, to integrate diverse information into a meaningful whole and transform and transcend barriers, and overcome stumbling blocks. It is the power and energy that unifies, interconnects and synchronizes data across the whole brain.

Power intelligence is the ability to think in a holistic way, looking at the big picture and seeing the underlying processes at work. The brain processes information in the form of holographic wholes. Out of these processes we can move to the next level of functioning. Holistic comes from the Latin word "holis", meaning whole, healthy, wholly, and holy. This is the power of wholeness, healing and holiness. It is at the centre and unifies mind and body, reason and emotion, harmonizing and providing the power for growth, development and transformation. It is the active centre of potential and power, giving direction and meaning. Here we find the power of vision and values. It is this power that has to be discovered, connected to and put to positive use to its full extent in the future.

The Power intelligence of a person, organization or even a country refers to the conscious, clear connection to, communication with and management of energy. It is the collective ability to utilize all potential and is multidimensional or multi intelligence. This power centre can be a personal centre, organizational or Universal centre.

When people or organizations are in contact with their true potential and power centre they live powerful lives of vision, growth, development, innovation, progress, harmony, synergy, prosperity and success. The challenge is to train and teach people to get into contact with the power source, overcome stumbling blocks and taking responsibility for the direction of their lives. The challenge of the new era is to release this energy and create a spirit of power, progress and prosperity for all.

People are asking different questions such as: Who am I? Where am I going and why? This is the search for meaning. Power intelligence includes IQ and EQ, but places it in a larger framework of meaningful functioning. When developed and utilized, PI takes people and organizations to the next level. We then go beyond creativity towards innovation, inspiration and universal guidance. It not only provides the power to move, but includes a holistic, integrated framework that gives wider and deeper meaning to new levels of information and purpose.

Power Intelligence gives us the ability to break out of our restricting boundaries and claim a more powerful and successful life. Many people will make the move, many will stay behind. Each person has the responsibility to make the choice. We need to challenge people to get up and claim their power, their life force and move to the next level of prosperity.

PI refers to the inner power source that provides the energy and life force to think, feel, act and live at a higher level and in a meaningful way. This energy and information is encoded into our DNA. PI is the conscious ability to ignite and utilize our multidimensional DNA and create new levels of success. We have access through our neuro-functioning and brain waves and rhythms. The slower the brain waves, the more power we have. We consciously use the quicker brain waves or Beta waves in everyday life. Our power however lies in using slower brain waves.

Alpha power and many other Mind Power teachers have used these facts all over the world. There is however a deeper and more powerful level. These levels touch the emotions, belief and value systems. This is where we need to consciously reprogram the hearts and minds of people in order to release their potential, move to the next level of functioning and reclaim a life of health, wealth, prosperity and power. Power Intelligence is the conscious ability of activating new success DNA – in ourselves and in others.

Radical change is now inevitable. The very fiber of human society is undergoing fundamental changes. Some will be able to manage this paradigm shift while others will be left behind. In the process we are looking to new leaders to be pathfinders. These are new leaders with New Leadership DNA who will be conscious of mind wellness.

The questions are:

> *What is higher communication and how do we develop higher communication skills?*

Higher inter-dimensional communication

When we embark on a higher spiritual journey seeking for a new quality of life and guidance, we also need to understand how we need to communicate with these higher dimensions. We connect on different levels as we tune into different frequencies. These dimensions include our physical dimension, the etheric or quantum reality and the metaphysical or spiritual reality. Different parts of the brain have the ability to connect to different frequencies and therefore to different dimensions. Our guide- spot or inner GPS can connect to the higher frequencies. The information we receive from this level of connection, can be viewed as higher or divine guidance. However, to receive this information is one thing – to correctly interpret the information is another thing. The reason is that the universe communicates in symbols, signs, visions, dreams and sequences. It is our responsibility to learn to understand the language of the universe and de-code this cosmic communication.

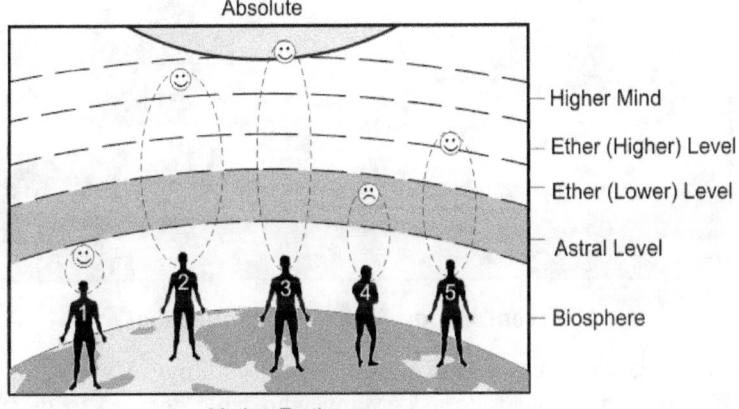

Absolute

Higher Mind

Ether (Higher) Level

Ether (Lower) Level

Astral Level

Biosphere

Mother Earth

Getting connected

The more aware we become the more conscious control we have over the self and the level or frequencies we can connect to. We are not just idle bystanders but have the ability to consciously co-create our reality. All we need to do is to become aware, take back our power and develop our Power Intelligence. In the process we can even co-create miracles. This is what the new emerging intelligence, Power Intelligence and new Leadership DNA, is all about.

- **Clairaudience or clear hearing**

You become conscious of the 'little voice' giving you direction. Although psychologists and psychiatrists would lift their eyebrows if they thought you 'heard voices in your head', the truth is that extensive research has already been done on the difference between hallucinations and messages from angels and higher spiritual beings[308]. The gift of clairaudience includes hearing the inner voice, that is warm, loving, positive, and sentences usually begin with *you* or *we*. Messages relate to your immediate concerns, and you are directed to take immediate action, including changing your thoughts, and to be more loving. You can hear someone call your name, or hear beautiful music. The messages are usually to- the- point and blunt, and include information about self-improvement or helping others.

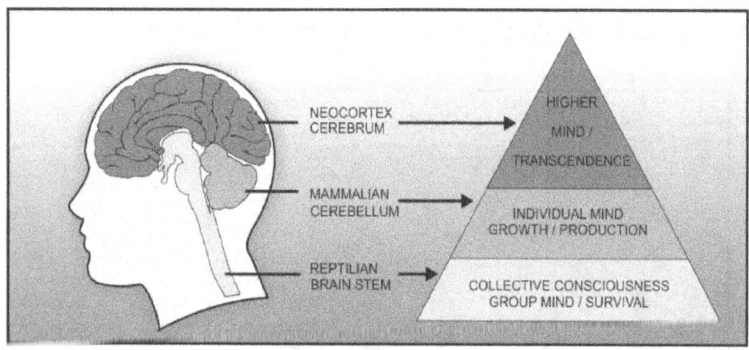

Different brains - different connections

With time, you learn to distinguish who is talking to you, and the best way to find out is to ask. Many who have decided to develop their spiritual senses, report a high- pitched ringing in their ears, even a shrill noise that could be painful and intrusive. Usually a physician will diagnose this as tinnitus, a disturbance of the auditory nerve. The ringing is a band of woven information, encoded in electrical impulses. Information from higher spiritual dimensions is downloaded for guidance, assistance and new information through this bandwidth—like a computer modem linking to the internet.

In the process we develop higher spiritual perception (HSP) and metaphysical communication skills that include:

184

- **Clairsentience—higher feelings or experiences**

This gift includes the ability to trust your feelings, especially your 'gut feeling'. This is the core of intuition and discernment, a legitimate and accurate divining device installed in you by source. In essence we are all naturally gifted psychic mediums. The only difference is that some people choose to acknowledge this gift and use it, and others don't. You find signs in feeling warm, cuddly, safe and secure, although you might be in danger. Often it is accompanied by a distinct scent or fragrances for which you can find no physical source for. You may feel a presence, someone touching your hair, arm, or shoulder, an indent in the bed as if someone was sitting there, or a change in air pressure or temperature. It feels natural, and you have a gut feeling that 'this is real'. In contrast with false guidance that makes you feel ice- cold, afraid, panicky, and with a gut feeling that 'this isn't real'. It could be accompanied by an unpleasant smell or sense of being alone.

- **Claircognisance—higher knowing and thoughts**

This gift includes higher knowing as 'I just know'. It seems you do know a lot, but are puzzled about how you came to own this information. Many inventors, scientists and futuristic leaders, have used their gift of claircognisance to tap into the collective unconsciousness, and access new ideas, and inspiration. Einstein's famous words: "I only want to know the thoughts of God, the rest is minor detail", confirms his reliance on his gift of claircognisance.

True, authentic experiences are positive and empowering. You receive explicit instructions about what steps to take, and receive exciting ideas, out of the 'blue', that energise you. You have a premonition about how something is going to turn out, or you receive new ideas for a business, book, or relationship. You have 'knowingness' that leads you to your lost keys, wallet, cellular phone, and you are assisted in finding the lost object. The ideas you receive ring true and make sense.

True divine claircognisance, is repetitive and positive. In contrast, we find false guidance that comes slowly as a response to worry, and has you thinking about worst- case scenarios. It leaves you depressed, hollow, empty, alone, discouraged, and abused.

- **Clairvoyance, - spiritual seeing**

You can receive visual messages or pictures, while sleeping (in your dreams), daydreaming or meditating. You see vivid colours, sparkles or flashes of light or repetitive instances of seeing a coin, feather, bird, butterfly, and rainbow or number sequence. What you see and the visual, symbolic message it brings is always service-orientated, so that it could help you and others. In contrast, we find false guidance in an ego-centred vision of you gaining at the expense of others, worst-case scenarios, and a feeling of force and struggle while you force the meaning you want to see into it. Spiritual seeing takes place through the 'third eye' or the pineal body, as discussed in a previous chapter.

With the development of the digital camera, higher beings have been revealing themselves to us as 'orbs'. Diana Cooper[309] was one of the first highly evolved souls to document these occurrences, and since then has received hundreds of photos revealing orbs. The orbs resemble a vortex of light that is in essence a porthole to the angels, masters or spiritual light beings. At the same time, we can connect to their frequency by just looking at photos of orbs. The best way to photograph the orbs is to take photos of nature, highly spiritual people, especially children, or new born babies, with a digital camera. It has been noted that the spiritual awareness of the photographer is important, and that orbs are more likely to appear on photos taken by evolved fifth level, rather than by un-evolved, third level souls[289].

- **Signs, symbols and animals**

The presence of certain birds, flowers, insects and animals, has special symbolic meaning. A bee is said to indicate the arrival of visitors while, an owl on the roof brings dire tidings, and the presence of a white dove symbolises the Holy Spirit in Christian religion. We find the use of symbols like the elephant, dragon, eagle, rose or lotus flower in religions and on the coats of arms of countries. The logos of teams, companies and organisations include signs and symbols with significant meaning. Feathers also have a special significance. Many believe that they represent the presence of angels, especially if they are white feathers.

While everyone felt the pinch of the recession, I also was going through a financial initiation. During this time I constantly found a brand new shiny 5 cent piece in just about every place imaginable. The most common place was right in front of the hypermarket, where everyone should see it. However, it seemed as if the coin was invisible to others, and only visible to me. The chances of mere coincidence were very slim. We also have personal symbols we exchange between loved ones. Rings are exchanged with marriage vows, while personalised items have a special meaning conveying a personal message that is only relevant to the giver and the receiver.

- **Bridging and channelling**

Bridges are established to connect the minds of a sender and a receiver. New information, guidance and healing can then be telepathically transmitted. Communication channels are opened between two or more parties, one being incarnated and the other in the spiritual realm. All depending on our level of awareness, we can connect to angels, archangels, light beings and ascended masters, and channel their messages, teachings and guidance. By combining all previous abilities with automatic writing, we can develop a personal library of valuable spiritual information. All our religious masters used these methods, and the information is documented in the sacred scriptures. We are taught to follow in the footsteps of the master/masters, and to do the same.

- **Somatic bridging**

Michael Newton combined the two terms 'somatic bridging' and 'therapeutic touch' to describe the method by which discarnate souls use directed energy beams to touch an incarnate body[310]. The film *Ghost*, with Demi Moore and Patrick Swayze in the lead roles, portrays this physical communication method between the living and the 'dead' (non-physical souls in spiritual realms). This involves bridging the 'gap' between physical and spiritual dimensions, and touching the body organs, whilst eliciting certain emotional reactions that can cause healing.

A body which is hurting can be touched by thought transmission. If these emotions are enforced by love and positive thoughts, the person will flourish. This is the reason we wish others well, send good wishes and bless others.

This is also the method Jesus used to heal the sick daughter of Jaïrus and to raise Lazarus from the dead[311]. Any negative projections can bring physical harm to the receiver and can even cause death. Verbal abuse, scandal, scolding, and telling lies about another, can physically harm them if they are not aware of these projections. Powerful methods consciously used for destruction are said to be one of the underlying causes of the destruction, famine, and poverty experienced in regions such as Africa, America, Haiti and China. Mother Earth, as a living entity, has to clear out all the negativity created over aeons.

Newton says that these skilfully applied energy beams can evoke recognition by sight, sounds, taste and smell. The purpose of somatic touch is to allow a person who is grief stricken by the loss of a loved one, to acquire awareness, that absence is only a change of perception and is therefore not final.

- **Personification of objects**

Personal belongings such as a ring or clothing can be used to communicate with a loved one. Newton reports that because men usually die before their wives, they have become very proficient in communicating with their loved ones, through personal objects. Missing persons can be found by gifted psychics, by holding anything that belonged to the departed person. They open their mind, while blanking out all other irrelevant thoughts. Messages are directly related to the missing person(s) involved. Police force units make use of the psychics, and so do governments and intelligence agencies.

One of my wonderful stories is of a man I met in a spiritual shop in Johannesburg. He was about six foot ten, perhaps even seven foot tall. We connected immediately, and I invited this interesting man home to visit with family. He had beautiful diamond rings on both hands. At that stage he was in the service of various diamond mining companies, as he had the ability to see diamonds under the ground.

- **Dreams**

Dreams and the dream state have been used to access spiritual information. Most dreams are not profound, and many specialists in the field believe that many dreams during the night are simply jumbled up absurdities caused by our circuits being overloaded throughout the day. If the mind is venting during sleep cycles, then the nerve transmissions across our synaptic clefts are 'letting off steam' to relax the brain.

Newton classifies dreams in three ways: firstly, we find the 'cleaning house' state. Many of our stray thoughts of the day are swept out of the mind, in Newton's words, as just 'gobbledygook'. There is however, a more cognitive part to dreams that can be divided into two, namely problem solving and spiritual messages.

Problem solving can include a person having a premonition about a future event, which can then consciously manage the situation and be prepared. Our level of consciousness and state of mind can be altered by dreams. During the dream state many grieving persons have found release from their pain. Problem solving through dream sequences is a process of mental incubation, because images appear that teach us ways to move forward. Spiritual dreams involve our guides, teaching souls, soul mates, and spiritual teachers, who come as messengers to assist us with solutions.

During difficult times *dream weavers* can assist us through emotional stress. Dream weaver souls engage in dream implanting. They can alter dreams by skilfully entering the mind of the sleeper and partially alter an existing dream, already in progress. On the other hand, the dream weaver can create and fully implant a new dream, from scratch. A meaningful tapestry of images is weaved and presented to suit their purpose. Creating and altering scenes in the mind of the dreamer is intended to convey a message.

We can also receive messages through:

- **Automatic writing**

This is a method to allow you to receive messages from higher planes. Doreen Virtue says that you can conduct automatic writing sessions with virtually anyone in the spirit world. It is a way to maintain and deepen relationships with angels, guides and masters. There are many individuals and groups, especially within African cultures, who communicate with their forefathers or deceased relatives. However, the value of automatic writing can also be found in the growing relationships with ascended masters and lady masters, Jesus, Buddha, the Ancient of Days (aka Sanat Kumara), Archangels Michael, Gabriel, Zadkiel, Uriel, Jophiel, Raphael, Charmael, and their Archaeï, angels and light beings. Archaeï are the complementary partners of archangels—just as we have a complementary partner as a soul mate or twin flame. You can be briefed as part of their spiritual mentorship program[312] and can receive information that will benefit all. The questions that then arise are:

For centuries, we have received messages from people who say that they 'talk to God'. People perceived that this gift was only bestowed on prophets, sages and holy ones. This not only includes prophets in the Bible, but also Mohammed who was responsible for the Koran he received from Allah. The disciples of Jesus and Buddha were inspired by the Holy Spirit and wrote down what they heard. More recently, we find the master Jesus Christ, communicating through the persons of Helen Schucman and William Thetford, Professors of Medical Psychology at Columbia University's College of Physicians and Surgeons in New York. These two professors were anything but spiritual. Both were atheists, their relationship with each other was difficult and strained, and both were primarily concerned with personal and professional acceptance and status. The statement Prof. William Thetford made: "there must be another way", changed the course, not only of their lives, but the lives of all who have studied their legacy in *A Course in Miracles*[313].

Every day, people claim to have direct conversations with God, ascended masters, guides, angels, light beings (such as Lazaris[314]), and archangels. Neale Donald Walsch[315] gives us new insight into the ways of God and life in his series of books *'Conversations with God'*.

No longer do we have to rely on pastors, preachers or earthly teachers to guide us. We are free to pursue a personal relationship with the ascended masters and lady masters, angels, archangels, and light beings. As religion and religious structures disintegrate and disappear, the only teachers who will be left are those who assist with the connection and communication with higher planes. We know now that it is possible to speak directly to God. This communication is not only preferable—but a necessity.

Health and receiving messages

The old saying: 'cleanliness is next to godliness', has universal merit. Spiritual leaders and teachers have always submitted their students to stringent tests of physical, mental, emotional and spiritual cleansing. In religious practices, this is known as 'fasting and praying', and in medical terms it is defined as 'detoxification'. Today, health practitioners and health spas all over the world, provide facilities and services that address all these issues. Medical physicians, psychologists and neurologists have determined that we too can develop these spiritual gifts and refine our spiritual senses and awareness, if we are prepared to do the inner work.

Brain health is becoming a major focus of our time. Neuroscience already provides us with machines that can harmonise our brainwaves and activate our neural system, in order to connect with a higher dimension. Brain wellness programs are freely available on the internet.

However, the downside is that there are forces wanting to take control of human thought processes. The balance between humans and the machine has and always will be a challenge. Films like *Men in Black* and *The Matrix* portray these issues in graphic detail. In the end, we can expect that technology will become outdated and viewed as 'primitive', while our spiritual senses and gifts further evolve.

The important question that arises is:

> *How will power and power positions change in the future?*

In the next chapter we will focus on the answers to this important question concerning leadership, power and power positions.

Notes

CHAPTER 10

LEADERSHIP
AND THE POWER SHIFT

Power and power positions

The definitions of *power* and *power positions* within philosophy, psychology, and politics, business and science are vast and conflicting. We even find different views reflected in Western[316], Eastern[317], African[318] and Asian[319] perspectives. However, in short, we can define a *power position* as a place or space where we have a choice. Here we have a voice and can make a choice in how to utilize and manage power/energy, release potential and create a better world for ourselves and others. Again we have only one of two avenues to follow – destructive or constructive use of power and potential. Whatever we decide brings about change that could benefit only ourselves, a selected few or all.

Power positions also come with responsibility or the 'ability to respond'. The bigger the power position, the more responsibilities arise. Leaders must therefore be clear on their stand concerning responsibility. On a personal level we all need to have clarity concerning how, for whom and for what we accept responsibility and take ownership. Because we are all interconnected at a deep universal level, no person, irrespective of their space, can neglect their ability to choose, to take ownership of and make their voice known. Failure to do this brings destruction.

Failure means: 'to cease to function properly'. This happens when we abuse our personal situations by compromising our personal influence. We can become the 'victim', the 'under privileged', 'previously disadvantaged', the 'less fortunate', the 'abused or battered' or any other label. We can choose to do nothing constructive and expect someone in higher places (or even God) to take care of us. Personal and collective destruction are the consequences of abusing our personal power position and negating our universal responsibility.

However, many may ask: "What can little old me do?"

The size of your power position could be very small or very big. Here size doesn't matter. What matters if the quality of influence – how you use your position. Take the position of the hungry children of Ethiopia for instance, compared to the power position of the President of the USA. The starving masses may think that they are powerless in their downtrodden positions. The truth is that the awareness of their plight has brought radical change to the consciousness of humanity and even caused the American President to move on their behalf.

The question is: Why on the face of this earth with what we call a civilized humanity, do these situations still occur? The answer is simple: It occurs because there are people abusing power and their power positions. There are corrupt leaders who don't care. Everyone is looking to democracy to solve the problem. They think that democratic governments will pave the way to prosperity for all. However, history reveals a different picture.

It has been said: "*If you think people are informed, cultured and intelligent – have another look at some of the leaders democracy has delivered.*" The questions go deeper and we need to ask:

> *Is democracy solving the problems of the world, or*
> *are more problems being caused by democracy?*
> *Could democracy alleviate the poverty in third*
> *world countries?*

The answers to all three questions are: No! Democracy is only a method – a means to an end – and not the end itself. The responsibility lies with the people and the quality of their leaders they choose. The people (or gods/God) give leaders their power positions and grant them permission to stay and do a job. This means every country, directly or indirectly, deserves the leader they have ... and now everything is changing.

Democracy, leaders and power positions

Within our growing democracies, we have the responsibilities to choose and vote for the right leaders. However, a large part of our global population comes from third world countries that do not have this privilege. Many of the people and the resources of these countries are being used and abused. A large percentage of the population is being deprived of dignity, human rights and personal free will by dictators and oppressive regimes.

We can expect that as the human consciousness grows, more leaders of the third world countries like in South America, Africa and even China, are bound to topple, as the people begin to raise their voice, take a stand and reclaim their personal power positions. In the future we will need to educate everyone in how to participate in democracy. As people awake, they need to learn *how* to choose and not *what* and *who* to choose – as this will infringe on free will. Educating people on the constructive use of their personal power and free will is becoming an important issue in social innovation and development. Learning how to identify true leaders and enforce constructive leadership styles, cannot be left to chance. Everyone has a power position in this regard.

Toffler defines one position of "power" as "purposeful power over people". Active or passive force or violence in different forms is used as an ultimate lever or power tool to gain command and secure a power position. Methods of power manipulation range from physical, emotional, sexual, intellectual, financial, information and religious intimidation, abuse and even 'violence'. Today national power in terms of wealth, monetary and military strength and capability alone, are not enough to secure power positions. The powerful impact of ideology, religion, culture and information cannot be ignored and can be abused in order to intimidate and maintain control over others.

Power is therefore not just a matter of quantity. It is important to recognize that the quality of power is becoming the most important factor in creating success and progress. The higher qualities of power found in higher levels of consciousness, spirituality, the Higher Self and the development of new power tools and skills, are enabling individuals, groups and organizations to take control of their lives.

People are taking back their power and becoming more independent. Potent skills such as personal choice, concentrated focus, intention, visualization, attention, attitude and interpretive and discriminatory action are now consciously being implemented. The arsenal of personal power tools are growing daily. This makes people less distracted by the external environmental, social and collective influences and collective responsibilities that are daily thrust upon them. People are starting to stand up for themselves. The destructive dependence/co-dependency patterns are being replaced with productive systems of independence and interdependence. Old, autocratic ego-driven leaders will in the end be removed.

Systems of power provide rules and boundaries that dictate power dynamics. At rare moments, the systems of power fly apart when all the rules of the power game change at once and the very nature of power is revolutionized. This is exactly what is happening today. Power, which to a large extent, defines us as individuals and as nations, is itself being redefined[320]. Power isn't just shifting at the pinnacle of corporate life, office managers, supervisors and military officers. Parents and teachers are discovering that workers and children do not take orders blindly as many once did.

The disintegration of authority and understandings of power in business and daily life are accelerating with global power structures dissipating as well. The acceleration of the process is taking place to such an extent that world leaders are being swept along by events rather than imposing order on them. Toffler predicts that, out of this massive restructuring of power relationships, there will come one of the rarest events in human history: a revolution in the very nature of power[321]. Beck and Cowan[322] refer to the crucible effect and predict the outcome to be something totally new, a seventh level of thinking, values and beliefs, even a new intelligence[323]. A power shift or shift in consciousness is taking place.

The power shift

A power shift is a shift in consciousness – a shift in awareness. The more consciously we live, the more we are in control of our lives. People for centuries have used different methods or power tools to gain control over the lives of others. This made them feel powerful and in control. As times change, so do the power tools change. To move with the time and still stay in control we need to understand the power shift that has taken place; we need to understand that there are new power tools and skills.

- ### Violence

The most widely used and most primitive power tool is violence. Violence comes in many different forms – physical, emotional, psychological, sexual. Many other forms of abuse have been used over the centuries. The primary underlying motive is fear. People try to gain control over others by creating powerful threatening positions and posing threats of pain, loss and suffering.

This was widely used throughout the past. People took control of others by physically or emotionally abusing them. Up and till the 1940s we had world wars and after that many smaller confrontations. The leading world countries relied strongly on their physical weapons. Clashes between different countries meant physical war. Business was done in a mafia-like style. Families and social structures were managed in this power structure of dominance and dictatorship. Today we do not have large scale wars. However, large scale violence, crime and abuse are still taking place. The underlying motives of many people to gain control by physical or emotional violence is still imbedded in the hearts and minds of many people.

- ### Money and sexuality

Money has always been a power tool. Up and till the 1970s it was the most fundamental motive of people of the technological era. Being comfortable and possessing expensive items placed people on higher ground and gave them power over others. There were the haves and the have nots - those with money and power and those without.

197

During this time sexuality played an important role. Banks and other financial institutes used their bosomed blond receptionists to attract potential investors. Marketing and other business deals involved money and sexuality. The Watergate scandal and the fall of president Nixon was caused by money and power being inappropriately used and abused.

This means that these power tools are not only relevant on a personal scale, but were and are still being used on a national and international or global scale. During the 1990s a power shift took place.

.

THE POWER SHIFT

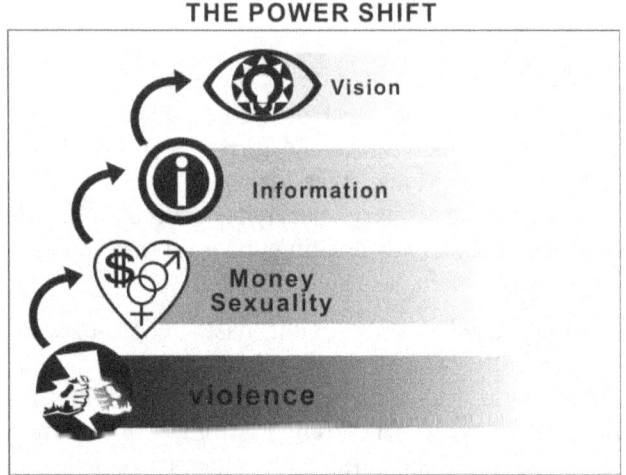

The power shift

- **Information**

Bill Gates and many others introduced a new power tool in the form of computer technology as the most important tool of the information era. Today a young child with the right equipment and the right knowledge and skills can hack the most scientific security codes of organizations like banks and defense forces. Although this youngster may not have any physical power, be sexually active or even get pocket money, the ability to process information puts this youngster in a power position. A power shift has taken place and so have the power positions. We are now in the information era. People are being empowered by training and use of information technology. Most

198

schools have computer literacy as part of the curriculum and many youngsters are growing up with this power tool. No organization can survive today without our modern communication technology. The question is: Can there be more – are there other important tools?

The answer is: Yes! One of the most potent and significant power tools up to date is emerging. This is the power of vision and focus!

- **Vision and universal force**

While the larger portion of the population is caught up in developing the other power tools to secure their power positions, there are those people who have moved to the next level of functioning. Communication technology as such has no power. It is a tool, a means to an end.

Many people are today looking past the other power tools and are focusing on a new vision for the future. Many people are today discovering the power of vision. Another power shift has taken place. This demands that we develop new knowledge, skills and power tools.

When we look at the previous chapters, we begin to understand the power of the mind and vision. The challenge of the future is to utilise this potential at our disposal. A new quality of leader is emerging and a new intelligence is emerging. Change is inevitable. These are leaders who understand the fundamental principles of success and use their influence to combat poverty and create affluence.

Leadership, influence and affluence

Affluence is generally understood as financial abundance and an exotic lifestyle. The true meaning of affluence, however, comes from the verb '*to flow'*. Affluence is an action – not an outcome. Success and affluence are about maintaining flow – what goes up, must come down – what comes in, must go out – what you give, you will receive – what you sow, you will reap.

The result of maintaining flow is that there is never lack. You have and get what you need – when you need it. Our needs are constantly met. We don't always get what we want – we always get what we need. The things we need are always for the fulfilling of our soul purpose. When our purpose is aligned with the higher purpose and benefit of all, all the necessary resources will flow to us. We will *always* have enough of what we need, when we need it. This is affluence – being fulfilled.

There is a well known story of the German evangelist, Reinhardt Boncke. As the number of followers grew during his visit to Africa, he realized they needed an enormous tent to accommodate everyone. The cost was exorbitant. When someone asked him, "Where will we get all the money from?" he replied, "From wherever it is". He got his money and his tent.

People, and especially leaders who are ego-driven, have a constant longing and want for more. Their personal brokenness, loss, pain, deprivation, abuse, lack of insight, intelligence or pure ignorance, drives them to want more. Constant wanting, desiring, hoarding and clutter are symbols of the blockage of flow – a lack of affluence and also a lack of true influence. Unfortunately many uninformed followers always want their leaders to live up to their expectations, placing a burden on the shoulders of the leaders to constantly want more and get more. Want always reflects an inability to be really satisfied on the inside. Want is a lack of fulfillment.

People who are constantly wanting and needy look to external things and others to fill the void they have on the inside. They work for attention, more power, more possessions and more influential positions. The truth is – this never works. The void stays and grows bigger while life remains empty and unfulfilling. The only things that work are healing the void and igniting a new flow of life force or energy. Affluence or flow is our natural state of abundant living. Anything else is unnatural. True leaders know and adhere to these universal principles and deeper truths.

Wants and needs of individuals, groups, companies and organizations are some of the most potent driving forces on the planet. At the moment a radical shift in the basic wants and needs of the human race is taking place. People who understand and can consciously master these forces become innovative pathfinders and mapmakers. They are our leaders of the future. This also determines the kind of power these leaders ignite within their followers.

Leadership and alleviating poverty

Most leaders have to contend with the issues of alleviating poverty. The same word for success from the Latin *"cedere"* is the same root word for the word "abscess" or "absence of success". Any blockages of the power process lead to stagnation and the absence of the success process. This is the root cause of an abscess. Poverty is an "abscess" on a large scale.

Apathy, complacency, boredom, fear, anger, depression, guilt, trauma, and pain are reflected in stress, conflict, illness, crime, violence and decay. This represents the blockage and nonalignment of the power process causing stress and stress-related symptoms that impair the quality of life. Hawkins says that poverty or "poorness" can be seen as a quality characteristic – a limited self-image. This intrapersonal flaw results in a scarcity mentality and the scarcity of resources.

Although alleviating poverty is not only on the list of priorities of most leaders it is one of the priorities of the international community as well. However, there is still a widespread ignorance about the nature, causes and impact of poverty. This often results in inefficient strategic planning for poverty alleviation[324].

Poverty, as the inability to utilize potential, negation of personal power and/or the negative, destructive use of potential, is first and foremost a result of energy and educational concerns and then a financial and political issue. The mere redistribution of wealth will therefore not solve the challenge of alleviating poverty.

The challenge of alleviating poverty and creating prosperity for all lies in healing destructive patterns, educating individuals, communities and organizations, aligning potential and creating personal and collective success.

Unfortunately, once a leader and group have lost their power and power position, decay and destruction inevitably sets in. True leaders know how to maintain the momentum of growth, development, empowerment and self-mastery. They know where they stand.

Power over people vs. power within people

Leaders are given authority and power positions – be it by the gods/God, the people, by their positions or by themselves.

In order to maintain their ego-driven power positions, leaders enforce their power over people. These leaders negate the responsibility to give the people voice and freedom of expression. Robert Mugabe of Zimbabwe, like many other dictators, finds his country in ruins after more than two decades of rule. The same is applicable to the Apartheid regime in South Africa. In the end *power over people* cannot be sustained and disintegration and destruction are inevitable. From now on we can expect many other countries to learn this lesson.

The shift is now to release and harness the *power within people*. Developed value/soul driven leaders have a deep insight into the power potential of all people and harness this potential in order to obtain the ultimate goal of a better quality life for all. However, before being able to release power within people, a leader should be able to master the self and develop their own power Intelligence. By gaining this new level of awareness and developing the new mindset or paradigm, they understand that power does not necessarily lie in numbers anymore.

Power in numbers vs. number of powers

Today the masses that are given the democratic right to vote for their leaders have shown that many developing countries do not have or cannot identify quality leaders. This means that these countries are still stuck with ego-driven forces causing havoc on the global playing fields and in individual lives. Strikes, protest marches and various other forms of resistance are marking the way of the greater majority now reclaiming their power, taking responsibility and raising their voice against corruption, lies, deceit and abuse.

Complacency is over. The power previously found in numbers is dwindling. Leaders now come to realize that the more people who are dissatisfied, angry and disillusioned, the greater the destructive force at work. However, new Leaders with new leadership DNA are consciously focusing on and developing new success DNA in others. The power of pure numbers is changing.

The atomic bomb dropped on Hiroshima during the Second World War is a good example of the power shift from the power in numbers to the number of powers. The destruction it caused is a reminder of the consequences of the destructive force of abusing power over people. It took only a handful of people and one very powerful bomb, against a far larger number of people with traditional weaponry, to change world history.

Now, there is a positive revolution taking place. A new, more powerful, positive explosion is being ignited in humanity. A genetic 'atomic explosion' is being ignited. New success DNA and new leadership DNA is being activated in different ways, as we speak. This is changing the course of human history for the good.

True leaders are now consciously developing new power tools and power skills in themselves and others. They surround themselves with people with a new consciousness and develop new success DNA. All we need is a 20% new success DNA conscious generation in order to create a critical mass and tip the scales in our favor. With 50% of the population under the age of 25, this could be achievable within the next five to ten years. They will then take over the leadership positions from current leaders who will be 'weighed and found too light'.

A new generation of power 'heavy weights' is emerging. They are prepared to put their new found power, a new consciousness and awareness, to the use of creating success, prosperity and affluence for all. This new generation is awake, informed, conscious, mindful and powerful. They are aware that we are evolving into a new species - *Homo sapiens spiritualis*, that has a new level of consciousness and a new intelligence – and a new kind of DNA.

Against this background we can accept that by understanding human consciousness and releasing new levels of human potential encoded into our multidimensional DNA, will become one of the major focus points of the future.

Human potential and empowerment

During the 1950s, Maslow (1962) spearheaded the school of humanistic psychology as a reaction to the dissatisfaction with the mechanistic orientation. The emphasis was placed on self actualization as the positive development of human potential on all

New Leadership DNA

levels that included spiritual, transcendental or mystical aspects of self actualization.

The leaders of this movement coined the term Transpersonal Psychology to describe a movement that was directly or indirectly concerned with the recognition, understanding and realization of non-ordinary, mystical or "transpersonal" states of consciousness[325]. They placed themselves in a position that differs radically from that of most major Western schools of Psychology which have tended to regard any form of religion or spirituality as based on primitive superstition, pathological aberration or delusion about reality[326].

Potential refers to a healthy tension between higher and lower levels of physical and psychic energy – a tension between "what is and what could be". Potential is "energy on hold". We can release potential by choice and action. We can turn possibilities, opportunities and capabilities into existence.

The aim of self-mastery and empowerment is to learn to consciously manage thoughts, visions, desires, emotions, choices, actions, the self and life as a whole. We can consciously active new success DNA. Raising the awareness that we are personally responsible for the quality of our lives has now become one of the most important social challenges.

Empowerment entails more than giving permission and providing opportunities and resources. It includes the intra-personal ability to transcend existing internal and external boundaries, release and develop new potential and rise above psychic entropy and negative, lower order internal and external barriers. This necessitates energizing people from the inside out. By implementing higher order thinking, igniting new energy/information levels and developing new understanding, even a new intelligence, we can change outer physical circumstances.

In the next chapter we will focus on leadership and change.

Notes

204

CHAPTER 11

LEADERSHIP AND CHANGE

Paradigms and paradigm shifts

One of our basic needs in life is the need for purpose and a meaningful existence. Success is about finding meaning. People are searching for a new definition of success, of a meaningful life, a new level of functioning, and a new frame of reference through which life can be perceived and managed successfully. People are looking for answers to the questions of our time. They are looking for a new paradigm.

Thomas Kuhn[327] coined the term 'paradigm' that refers to a frame of reference, injunction, method or experiment that is not so much concerned with thinking but with doing. However all our actions are the outcome of a specific line of thought. In simple terms, a paradigm is a way of perceiving life while allowing us to choose our actions or 'doings' accordingly. It is a window or framework with certain boundaries, rules, values, opinions and solutions that give meaning to life. This means the old outworn paradigm, values, ideas and perceptions need to be challenged and discarded to make way for the new mindsets and ways of perceiving life that then reflects in our actions or doing.

Every time we go through positive change we release new energy and can move forward. Change is the discovery of a new perception of the world, a new approach to successful living, happiness, prosperity, abundance, meaning and life. This means we must see, think and act in a new way. The most important point, however, is that we must reinvent ourselves and our lives, for 'new wine in new wineskins'. Leaders take the lead in the process of reinvention and change. They are our pathfinders, mapmakers and bridge-builders to the future. In essence, everyone is a pathfinder, mapmaker and bridge-builder. Everyone has leadership capabilities.

The questions that arise are:

> *What is changing and why?*

What is changing?

Problems experienced worldwide today are more demanding and complicated than any problems experienced in the past. What has changed? It's easy – people and their world have. Life, problems, value systems, beliefs, technology and managing life in general are constantly changing. Most people are under a misconception that a phase, institution or specific life pattern will, and has to, remain intact forever. The truth is that nothing remains forever! A country's government, a relationship, marriage, organization, company or any other level of functioning or paradigm is only temporary – part of a specific phase, era or period.

Some people are of the opinion that they will remain in the same position forever, only to receive a separation allowance. Or that the children will remain at home forever, only to discover that they have flown from the nest. Or that a relationship will last forever, only to discover that they have separated in some way along the line. Some believe that political, social, economic or religious institutions are the alpha and omega, only to experience the disintegration of it all. We find that careers, marriages, family structures, political beliefs, religious, social and business institutions, as well as social values constantly grow, develop, reach a pinnacle, integrate, disintegrate and restructure once again.

Unfortunately we were taught that we are 'strong' when we keep things as they are and should always maintain the *status quo*. The only lasting thing on earth is constant change, growth and development. It is the core of life. As soon as disintegration becomes visible, anxiety and uncertainty erupt. Very few people are prepared and very few understand what is happening. However, if we understand the process, it will be easier to manage and cope with change. Leaders need to be able to identify and take the lead in a constantly changing environment.

From the known to the unknown

Life is like the board game, Snakes and Ladders. We start at the bottom and in the course of time advance step-by-step, from stage to stage, until we reach the top of the ladder – only to discover that it is time to move from one ladder to another. This move is not always easy. We must leave the known and enter an uncertain world. Once we accept the challenge and move, our whole world changes. If the snake does not bite us, we find ourselves at the bottom of the next ladder. We start at the bottom once again – at the 0-stage of the next phase. This is the zero-effect of change that refers to going back to the beginning or 'getting back to basics' as a new foundation needs to be laid. Ego-driven leaders find this stage difficult to master. They try to maintain the status quo because they have built their lives on ego accomplishments of the past. Their endeavors to override the zero-effect actually accelerate the pace of change. In the end this leads to self destruction and they get left behind.

The positive side is that we get another opportunity to move upwards. If we use all the opportunities we can reach the top of a new ladder. It means exchanging one step for another. Letting go, new input, learning, development and new action are required every time. Growth, learning and advancement are all part of positive change. We can now express a new kind of life and vitality - a new kind of self-expression.

The opposite is negative change or a negative spiral of disintegration, pain, hurt, failure, loss, ignorance and deterioration. We lose our self expression and become depressed. Depression is a situation caused

207

by lack of true self-expression. People who are constantly depressed are unwilling, unable or uninformed about change. Life requires an attitude of excited discovery – of passion, vision and expectancy of surprise and amazement – of miracle mindedness. There are many opportunities in life. The problem is that we do not always acknowledge them.

With a positive attitude, belief and conviction that life is good and rewarding, we are open and able to recognize the opportunities and abundance in life. What we do with these opportunities remains a personal choice. Unfortunately there are some people who do not want to open themselves to life and make an extra effort to learn and grow. They are stuck in a rut on the ladder of life. There are those who prefer selecting the positive from difficult circumstances. They change every difficulty and problem into an opportunity for learning and growing.

It reminds one of the three children who survived the nuclear bomb attack on Hiroshima. While being astounded at the devastation around them, one of them suggested: "Let's work – let's build a house." By the time the rescue workers arrived, these children had already built a shelter. They did not allow themselves the luxury of wasting productive energy on their misery, loss, pain or devastation. Their time, energy and means were applied positively – irrespective of the circumstances.

There are those who prefer getting stuck. In the career world they are perceived as blockages or boulders in the channels. They do their work mechanically, accept their salaries every month and seek excuses not to grow, make positive contributions or be productive. Relationships stagnate and disintegrate because of the fact that people do not develop, grow and change. Work and relationships become boring, dull and a burden – a way of surviving. Without new insight everything will ultimately disintegrate.

Even people who have experienced tragedy can refuse to give up and instead move on. Although pain and loss in life is not of our choosing – what we do with the experience is a personal choice. A new life requires us to move on irrespective of the circumstances. Not only life becomes new, but the whole person becomes new!

At the top of the ladder we find two possibilities. We can cling to our comfort zone, or accept that a stage (ladder) has passed and move on to the next stage or ladder. There are those who are willing to make the move and leave what is familiar behind, either out of necessity or because of a spirit of discovery. The first step to reinventing a new life is to accept the challenge! The next ladder, however, has to be approached from the bottom.

Change results in a zero-effect: New learning, new knowledge and new skills. The ladder has to be conquered from scratch. The pitfalls, or snakes, in life are very important factors to consider. For example, when a person loses their job, experiences divorce, is declared bankrupt or when a loved-one dies, they could fall into a deep despondency and depression and think life is over. Sometimes it is an intermediate setback. Sometimes we find total bankruptcy. To remain in the game of life, it is necessary to know life has stumbling blocks that can be turned into stepping stones. Nothing ventured, nothing gained.

Sometimes it could be to one's benefit to experience loss, pain or failure. It can place you on a new path in life. Retirement, political change, divorce, death, loss, disappointment or any other tragic occurrence can provide a new perspective on life and create the opportunity for new self discovery, growth and new meaning to life. Change, movement and growth remain a choice.

Generally it is easier to remain where we are – in our comfort zone, with all that is familiar. To remain in the same occupation, church, relationship, political party or social group is easier and safer, but it can limit our growth. Alternatively, one can choose to make a move. However, this is not always easy. We must leave the safe structures of what is known and challenge the unknown. This in itself leads to anxiety, doubt and uncertainty. Change demands courage, conviction and a willingness to leave the known behind and live life at its fullest. What is required is an understanding of the phases of change, so that we can manage it.

Stages of change

Although there are diverse points of view regarding the various stages of change, in essence, five can be distinguished. Each of these stages has its own demands, responsibilities, methods, laws and rules. In order to adapt to change and grow in the process, it is necessary to understand and consciously move through every stage. You can then determine the most effective course to get you out of the chaos created by change. Here is a summary of the various stages.

- **Stage One**

At this stage everything seems under control. Individuals, families, organizations and communities manage periodic problems realistically and effectively. The people are content with the situation. Families flourish, companies are productive and communities fulfill the individual's needs. However, individuals, families, communities, companies, political parties, church communities and other institutions can exist in this state for only a limited period.

Yesterday's solutions become today's problems. The stage has served its purpose and has been outgrown.

- **Stage Two**

Our first introduction to this stage is the awareness of something lacking – something is wrong. Since true insight into the problem is lacking, the actual origin and root of the problem cannot be established. There are signs of unrest, uncertainty, discord, dissonance, separation, problems and conflict.

Individuals do not experience the same success, happiness, fulfillment and contentment as before. Parents can no longer control their children. Marriages disintegrate. Companies are less productive. Political parties lose ground. Religious institutions experience turbulence, economies start to plummet and countries experience unrest.

Habitually, we try to deny and ignore the problems. The same patterns of the *status quo* are followed – but now with more commitment, devotion and force. We find growing resistance to change taking hold. CEOs fight for economic survival, government leaders defend their policies, parents attempt to set more boundaries, social, cultural and religious organizations apply more rules, laws and stricter discipline. Companies and individuals work more and harder. One partner in a marriage tries harder to keep the other partner happy and satisfied. Religions persist with greater devotion and commitment to their doctrines and everyone keeps on doing more of the same. This brings a certain amount of satisfaction. People feel they are addressing the issues and are not complacent. For a while 'things are back to 'normal'. However, the perception that everything is fine only lasts a short while. In truth, this is the silence before the storm – the illusion is about to be exposed.

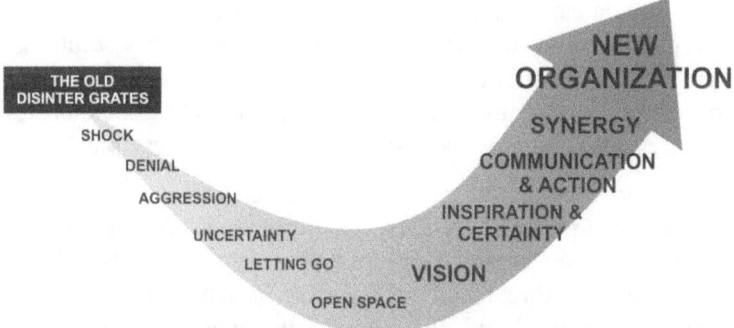

The process of change

Sooner or later, a critical point will be reached – but not yet.

Now damage is caused by continuing to do more of the same. If you keep doing more of the same – you keep getting more of the same. The conflict worsens and the separation between people increases. Depression, recession, stagnation and disintegration become inevitable. Attempts to remain on the old path become more difficult as old mindsets, patterns and solutions are no longer effective. However, a point where the fundamental paradigm, system, and structures of the *status quo* are challenged has not been reached as yet.

This leads us to the second stage of this phase.

Because our understanding is no longer functional we regress to the past and the good old days when everything seemed to be in order, and where, according to us, life, discipline, happiness and fulfillment were still intact. At this stage, we become nostalgic for the past because we thought everything was still OK. The focus on historical events, new religious practices, a sudden interest in animated forces, traditional healers, angels, devils, demons, the 'evil eye' or *tikoloshe,* all form part of this stage. This brings us to stage three

- **Stage Three**

Increased barriers and frustration are experienced during this stage. This results in various anti-social and self-destructive behavioral patterns, for example alcohol and drug abuse, violence and crime, physical, emotional or verbal abuse, chaos and irresponsibility. A state of frustration, aggression, resistance and struggle against the *status quo* escalates. The rebellion persists because there is more clarity regarding the underlying problems and their solutions. However, the existing boundaries, written and unwritten laws or comfort zones, prevent any form of advancement. These boundaries and structures could be moderate, strong or even impenetrable.

The *status quo* has inbuilt punitive measures that could contain personal and even physical dangers, should the laws and boundaries be challenged or overstepped. Think of a member who wants to leave a gang and who is threatened with death, or when a child starts outgrowing the family and the parents threaten to disown him because he does not honor his father and mother. In this way judgments of demonic influences or digression are voiced if a person questions a religious practice. In the career world such people could be discounted for promotion or be threatened with dismissal.

Resistance at this stage is tremendous! Conflict erupts.

Conflict could be directed externally, like the struggle against dictatorship, oppression, drugs, women or child abuse. It could also be internal, such as the inner struggle that a person experiences if there is no work or marital satisfaction. This stage is characterized by struggle – struggle with self or in a marriage, family, community, congregation, organization or even in a country. People now become conscious that they are at a crossroad.

Fear of change, fear of making new or even wrong choices or doing the wrong thing can render people powerless, helpless and victims of the situation. They stagnate at the crossroads of life, constantly regressing back into the past. However, when they find the futility of searching for answers while reminiscing, the direction can change. The next phase is marked by striving to the future. Only two routes can provide an outcome – revolutionary or evolutionary change.

Revolutionary change is always accompanied by force or violence of some sort. Frustration, anger, disappointment, fear or hate, can fire a person or group to actively resist situations and/or forcefully break down barriers. Most people first try this method in some or other way. Emotional, verbal, financial, sexual, psychological and other forms of violence always bring destruction and no-one is left untouched. History reveals that in various instances where leaders thought that violent, revolutionary change was the only option it resulted in war and more destruction. However, leaders such as Gandhi showed us the way of passive resistance and FW de Klerk and Nelson Mandela have shown us the path of non-violent change.

With evolutionary change, we consciously seek for, find and implement constructive and creative solutions to these problems. We make a conscious choice to move on and beyond perceived barriers by thinking new thoughts and breaking through to the next stage.

If we don't follow an evolutionary or revolutionary path, we get stuck at the crossroad and can stagnate here forever. Change is always triggered by a choice, followed by action. How we make our choices and where we get our guidance and information from, will determine the path we follow and in the end determine the outcome. The only way to get out of stagnation is to make an informed decision. Competent leaders know where they get their guidance from and can make informed decisions that will benefit all.

Difficult problems require new, different and complex solutions found in new thinking and changed perceptions and ideas. The change needs to occur firstly within the self, before the external world can be changed. Think of a case where one marital partner believes that should the other person change, the marital problems would be solved, or where the employer believes that production could be increased if the employees work harder.

The reinvention of a new self with a new mindset, a new paradigm, must first take place before real change in the world situation can commence. Change and renewal starts within the self. The time has come to reach from within the new self, with new success DNA, to the outside world. We then live from the inside to the outside, and not from the outside in. We exchange ego-driven values for soul-driven values. It is like shedding the skin of an old life – dying to the lower ego self.

'Dying to the self' does not imply that a person ignores and destroys the self, but refers to the process of dying to our egoic identity based on separation while identifying with and upholding our authentic identity as pure awareness or consciousness. In this process we dissolve the old paradigm, leaving hurt, pain, loss and disappointment behind and discovering a new lease on life and success. It takes place by opening the mind, heart and soul, while continuously renewing thoughts, discovering new purpose, exploring new passions, avenues and possibilities and focusing on quality living.

The true meaning of life lies in constant transcendence of the old and discovery of the new. Should new insight indicate that the known structures or *status quo* are not the end goal or only solution then new evolutionary options come to light. The structure becomes one of many possibilities. New solutions, a new paradigm and new meaning are searched for! When all the comfort zones are left behind, we reach the next stage.

- **Stage Four**

This stage is characterized by rapid change. The old stage is left behind and we focus on the future with new commitment and energy, while removing the remaining stumbling blocks. We take back our power and the responsibility for and control of our lives. The past no longer determines the present or future. This stage is characterized by a high level of energy and activity. This exuberance results in a series of creative reactions, utilisation of resources and responsible commitment to the creation of a new person or stage. Think of the person who looks forward with excitement to a new career after the loss of his job or a lifelong companion, or who realizes that there could be a new life with another partner. Life gets new meaning. Old patterns make room for new structures and patterns that will serve us better in the next stage. We understand that 'this too will pass'.

However, this stage could also have negative side effects. A high stress level is characteristic of this level for example in a relationship where one partner grows faster than the other. Should too much energy, excitement and pressure to advance to the next step manifest too soon, resistance is triggered. Setbacks follow as old mindsets, past comfort zones, fears, boundaries and defense mechanisms are re-established and the process of change is slowed down or stopped.

Eventually, if we do not fall back on the old patterns or stagnate in more of the same, new paradigms and a new life emerge.

• **Stage Five**

The new paradigm, and life, would obviously originally be unclear. The boundaries are not clearly understood, demarcated or visible, and new values, rules and guidelines have not been established. As the change and transformation process advances, the new paradigm becomes clearer. New boundaries, rules and structures are defined. New ways of thinking and solutions are implemented and creativity is the order of the day.

Change and growth have taken place. There is a new vision, new objectives and a new purpose in life. This stage will only continue for a specific time, and then it will be necessary to go through the process of change with the same measure of uncertainty and chaos, once again. A new life, a framework with new content, new insights and new prospects provide new purpose and meaning.

The purpose of this last stage is to search for new and creative solutions to questions, problems and needs of the time. This stage requires new paradigm thinkers. These are leaders who are willing to challenge the *status quo*, provide new creative solutions and to assist with the implementation of new innovative solutions, irrespective of resistance. Only people with vision, determination, persistence, purpose and courage reach this stage. Others get lost along the path of life.

The waves of change

Alvin Toffler[328] made us aware of the different waves of change during the 80s. Since then change has escalated at an unprecedented pace. Modern information and communication technology have made our world not only small, but also instant. A change in one part of the globe immediately influences the whole globe as messages get sent over our social, global and satellite networks. What once took fifty years to change, today takes only moment. The waves of change

215

are also taking place at an increased frequency. This means that before we can internalize a change, the next wave is already upon us. In the end we will find that all we have is constant change.

Many leading authorities[329] on change have given guidelines on what we can expect. We find a short summary at the end of the chapter.

Time for change

The best time to move or make a change is when chaos and uncertainty are at the highest level or when everything is stagnant and dead. This usually is the best indication that the previous system has disintegrated. There are choices to be made and lessons to be learnt. If one forfeits the opportunity to learn and move on, it could happen that the same lessons would be repeated, the same ladder climbed from scratch and the same situation is repeated. This could continue until we stagnate or die or on the other hand learn the lessons and move on.

Change sometimes takes place gradually, for example when a person retires and has already prepared for the next stage. It sometimes takes place by means of a sudden leap. In such an instance we refer to a quantum leap – from the top of one ladder to the zero-level of the next. Think of a sports hero who has suddenly been seriously injured and who can no longer take part, or someone who experiences the loss of a partner, or someone who suddenly loses his job. This means a person suddenly moves, without warning, from one position to another.

This kind of change is normally associated with great shock and trauma. Even for governments, change can be sudden and unexpected. A ripple effect is created and the economy, commerce, individual households and the individual can be affected. The results of change are not always visible on the surface. It is therefore not possible to anticipate the full extent of any change.

A situation of this nature can only be approached with faith and trust. It means that people with a strong inner core, a belief in themselves, their Creator or Higher Power and their place and purpose in the Universe, can make changes with greater self-assurance. Planned or sudden – the attitude with which change is approached and managed remains a personal choice.

	First Wave	Second Wave	Third Wave	Fourth Wave
Guidance from	Tradition/ ancestors.	Group/ ego awareness	Inner self /Self aware	Higher Self Divine core
Brain part used	Reptilian brain/Limbic system	Mammal brain & left hemi-sphere	Whole brain: left and right neocortex	Union with universal - One mind/ Frontal lobes
Driving force	Feeling Instinct/ fear	Reason	Reason & intuition	Integration of all. HSP
Mindfulness awareness Lives in	The past	Present	Future with focus on present	"Spacious present" Now.
Sense of time	Rhythm of nature	Chronos time units	TimeSpace & process	Universal Now /Kairos time units
Foundation/ faith	Authorities	Scientism, Religious dogma	New 'spiritual-science'	Intuitive knowing / Understand
Economic Unit	The farm	The factory	The office	Free form
View of natural world	Animism	Control & utilizing resources	Cooperation with nature	Oneness with nature
Basic form of energy	Wood	Fossil (oil/coal) Hydro-carbons Nuclear	Solar, hydro, silicon, nuclear hydro-carbons	Universal Field/ Spirit/ (electro-magnetism/ ether.)

Waves of change

217

Notes

CHAPTER 12

LEADERSHIP AND TRANSFORMATION

Transformation

Einstein said the world (paradigm) that is created on a certain level of thinking, doing and believing creates problems that cannot be solved on the same level of thinking, doing and believing. The future can therefore not be explored with old outdated paradigms, traditional thinking and outlived patterns. Development cannot take place by merely extending the existing boundaries and manipulating various ideas.

If the paradigm shifts and thinking changes, the form, pattern and structures must also change. The new structure becomes the container of and represents new thinking and information. New wine cannot be poured into old containers. The containers will break and the containers, as well as the wine, will be unusable. The new structures, rules and patterns are the new containers. One cannot exist without the other. The future is found in new ways of thinking, creating new structures and form – 'new wine in new wine-skins'.

Whether change takes place within an individual, a family, community, political party or even in a country as a whole, the principles remain the same. First of all there must be a change and shift within the self. This could be an individual self or a collective self. Think of the example of a family where the father dies. Everyone has to process the new information and situation within the self. A reassessment is necessary to handle the situation. The new situation also changes the structure of the family. There are new roles and new responsibilities. Issues not realised in the past now become visible, like the importance of a proper will and testament. Structures also change when an organization goes through an economic rise or fall or a political party gets a new leader or position in government. This calls for new thinking.

Change is sometimes anticipated, for example, when a company gives the employees enough time to prepare themselves for termination packages, a closing down, dismissal or retirement, or when the possibility of future promotion exists. This restructuring of life is less chaotic and traumatic since the individual has enough time to get settled in the new structures. The change is evolutionary and people have time to grow into it. The disadvantage is that people sometimes adjust too slowly and thereby postpone or slow down the changing process, growth and development.

The quantum leap

Change sometimes happens radically and immediately. The new information and situation are not anticipated and the new structures are not in place. Think of a sudden lapse in the economy and the subsequent insolvencies and dismissals; or a sudden change in the family structure caused by death, divorce or an unplanned pregnancy. The change takes the form of a quantum leap - a sudden leap from one situation to another. During this leap the future is normally unclear, without any planned structures and on the surface it looks chaotic.

People who understand the principles of chaos and order can make a quantum leap and excel in the chaos without feeling threatened. Not all people can cope with chaos. It is however, a normal part of life, change and growth and therefore people should be trained in the theory of chaos and order. The bigger the change the more chaos occurs. On the other hand, the greater the chaos, the better the opportunity for a new vision, ideas, structures, order and pattern to arise. In other words, the more chaos there is, the greater the opportunity to initiate transformation, growth, development and something totally new.

Chaos and order

Our world is never static. We live in a world that is dynamic and constantly changed and formed by interaction. At the same time we live in a universe of order. The human psyche is designed to function better under circumstances of harmony, balance, peace, order and stability. With constant waves of change, the following questions become relevant.

> *What is order? How can we establish order within the chaos? How do we develop structures that can move with change and still maintain order?*

Research clarifies our understanding of chaos and order. These are opposite sides of the same coin. The one contains the other.

A combination of ordered structures and patterns represents an organism's real identity, while chaos or disintegration exists and change takes place, all at the same time. A person's external appearance, for example, is maintained while a constant renewal process takes place. The skin is renewed on a daily basis, just like the stomach lining, retina and hair.

People do not only function physically, but also psychologically and mentally within a constant process of renewal. Renewal of the self and the world by means of disintegration or chaos and restructuring and order result in the development of constant growth, development and progress. People should learn to be patient and comfortable with uncertainty and chaos. It is a normal part of life.

In every situation potential chaos and potential order can be found. Certain triggers instigate the applicable reaction. If the system has served its purpose, a process of disintegration and subsequent chaos would be triggered. Underlying the chaos, a new pattern of order, form and structure develops. A point is reached where the two systems interchange and for a while it looks as if stability has been obtained. In reality a new system or form is being further developed while the old system and form disintegrates further. Chaos is replaced with new order, structure, form and new life. It also gives new meaning to life.

This situation prevails until the pattern has served its purpose, and chaos and disintegration once again replace order. The pattern is repeated. Change and growth involve the death of the old and development of the new. It will never come to an end, because it is life!

Transformation and development

It doesn't mean that everything developed so far should be discarded. The new paradigm contains a lot of what currently exist, only in a different form. The life cycle of the butterfly can be used as an example.

The life cycle starts with the egg – containing the potential, ingredients and codes for all future phases. Growth takes place within the egg and the circumstances inside of the egg are ideal for the development of the contents. Transformation takes place at a certain stage and a new form, a larva, surfaces. The larva cannot exist inside of the egg (old structure). Where a structure (egg) is useful at one stage, the same structure is no longer sufficient after the transformation process. If the larva remains within the eggshell, it will die.

Transformation in nature is known as metamorphosis. Metamorphosis firstly means an increase in size and secondly a change of shape or form. Since the skin determines the external form, transformation takes place if the old outgrown skin (reference or framework) is shaken off. Where the increase in size represents a constant process of growth, the change of form happens sporadically.

The process of metamorphosis can vary in degree. Some insects reach maturity with very little change in size, while others experience a radical change. If the life circumstances radically change, an organism will be able to adapt and survive if it undergoes a radical change itself. If this does not happen, however, the organism will not be able to adapt and will die.

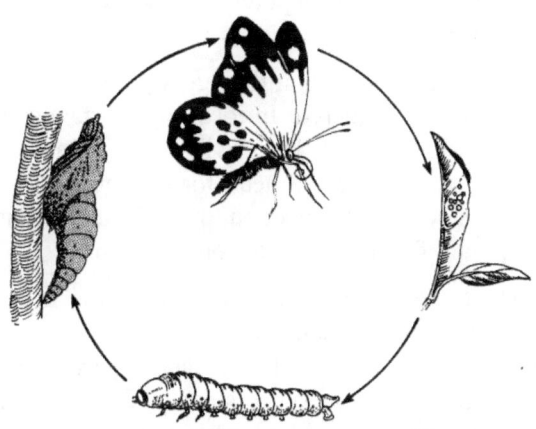

Metamorphosis – natural transformational processes

Shedding of the old skin (paradigm shift) takes place as the old skin (framework) disintegrates and is left behind. At the same time cell division (growth and development) takes place. Disintegration and restructuring take place simultaneously. As the old cells (framework) die, a new skin (framework) progressively replaces them. By means of the constant process of growth, transformation, development and shedding of the old during metamorphosis, a new form emerges that is better suited for the new circumstances.

Change initially takes place internally, and then becomes externally visible. Change initially takes place in the brain as control centre of the organism and manifests externally in the new life form that has adapted to the requirements of life. The organism does not only change to survive, but also to make a meaningful contribution to life as a whole and to live a purposeful life. The purpose of life can only be found by means of constant growth and adaptation to changing circumstances.

It is a path – the Path of life. It involves constant development of the unique potential of the self and other people, to effectively and productively manage the world and live a meaningful life.

Developing potential

The potential for all the phases of life is encoded in the DNA of the egg. All that is needed, from butterfly to larva to cocoon and back to butterfly, is already available as potential in the DNA. We as humans function in the same way.

Transformation takes place when the egg's potential to develop into a larva is activated or triggered. In ideal circumstances the egg will develop, change shape and a larva will hatch. Time and again an activator or trigger announces a need for change at the end of each phase. The larva goes into the cocoon, the old stage disintegrates and the new stage, that of a pupa in a cocoon, develops.

Disintegration of the old and development of the new have taken place. The same thing happens in order for the pupa to metamorphose into a butterfly. The essential parts and codes have always been present in every stage of transformation and development. By means of the emergence of novel structures, transformation takes place and a new entity appears.

These cycles of transformation and development exist in nature, but also apply to all other systems including, countries, groups, companies, organizations, families and individuals.

If this is our natural state, the questions are:

> *How does it apply to us as people? How can we transform our lives?*

Firstly, the old life has to be closed off and left behind before a new life can emerge. This process is not without insecurity or pain – but it need not be. The butterfly does not resist the change and experience pain, anxiety or insecurity going through these phases. There is an inborn 'knowing' that this is as it should be. It doesn't struggle, get upset, resist, fight or run away. It just takes life as it is. To live life to the full we need to understand how to just "be". We need to learn to live in the Now and just be. Most people live either in the past or they live in hope for a better future. Life is for living in the Now, just as it is. This is a great lesson for all of us – to let go and just "be".

Many people are under the impression that a good life only entails the good times and they seek fun and pleasure to 'prove' they are happy. Some try to ignore problems and questions of life in an attempt to escape pain and struggle. The truth is that it is precisely the struggle with life, questions and problems in us and in the imperfect world that leads to transformation, growth, development, change and eventually a new life.

The story is told of the man who saw a butterfly struggle to get through a small hole in the cocoon. Intending to be of assistance, he cut open the cocoon only to later find a dead butterfly. How was he to know that the struggle to escape had to take place, since life-giving liquids pumped into the butterfly's wings are necessary for the next life cycle? By lessening the butterfly's struggle, he in reality denied it the opportunity of development and in doing so, took its life.

When people try to escape from their problems or try to ease the situation for themselves and others, the same could happen, as was the case with the butterfly. They don't become strong enough to fulfill life's demands and die to life. Some people even try to return to their cocoons by returning to their comfort zones. The irony is that although the cocoon served a purpose and maintained life at one stage, in a next phase it can be deadly. When problems are tackled with courage, diligently and with persistence, change and development take place.

The necessary potential is discovered time and again. A new phase with a new form and life-style continuously develops. The transformation that takes place in people is not necessarily characterized by external changes, although these can manifest under certain circumstances. Someone losing a loved one can suddenly look old and defeated or a newly married couple glow with happiness.

Transformation in people firstly takes place in the deepest essence of the self. This new life is triggered in a person by internal and external factors or triggers. As the change surfaces and moves to the outside world, other people and aspects of life come into contact with the change and new entity and are also influenced. A person's transformation manifests in the new and changed way he or she manages life. The world now is also changed and when the world changes, people also change. It is a mutual, interactive and continuous process. People find the very meaning of life in constant growth and change.

We are now looking for and are in need of a new kind of human being, with more developed inner qualities so that we can meet the demands of the new era. This means we will have to go through the transformation process into a new era. The direction and quality of the transformation cannot be left to chance. A sound knowledge of the path we need to follow is necessary to guide people into the new millennium. We need new thinkers and visionary innovative leaders.

Outdated leadership and management styles won't be effective in the new paradigm. New styles have to be learnt and new leaders must take initiative to successfully reach the new level.

Transformation of *Homo sapiens*

Humans, known as *Homo sapiens* are the only living species in the Genus *Homo*[330]. It is accepted that anatomically modern humans originated in Africa about 200,000 years ago, reaching full behavioral modernity around 50,000 years ago[331]. Humans with their highly developed brain are capable of abstract reasoning, language, introspection, and problem solving. Other higher-level thought processes of humans, such as self-awareness, rationality, and 'sapience' or wisdom, are considered to be defining features of what constitutes a 'person'. A fully conscious person has a high level of awareness and deep self-knowledge that also includes:

- Authenticity: a wise person is conscious of and understands the authentic or higher and shadow self.
- Sincerity: A wise person seems sincere and direct with others.
- Knowledgeable: Others ask wise people for advice.
- Integrity: A wise person's actions are consistent with his/her ethical beliefs.
- Maturity: a wise person has a mature character and acts with insight and wisdom.

- Leadership: A wise person is usually chosen for a leadership position by other knowledgeable or 'wise' people.

People on the same level of consciousness group together and identify a leader who represents the group consciousness.

At the moment *Homo sapiens* is going through a transformation and many individuals, groups and even nations, are finding this transitional phase very difficult. Not only are climate changes causing havoc, the financial, religious, political and even cultural stages are changing. The emerging of new leaders with new leadership DNA has never been more important than at the current moment. However, many evolving countries are getting rid of their previous dictators, but very few people are in the positions to take groups of people to the next level. This means groups and even countries can go through a series of 'trial and error' until, out of pure exasperation, they will call for authentic leaders to come forward. This means that the greater population also has to evolve in order to be able identify new leadership DNA. Leadership is now not only for the select few. We all need to become more aware and grow in consciousness and make our voices heard – especially where identifying and selecting leaders are concerned. As part of the species *Homo sapiens,* we find different people functioning on different levels of consciousness.

On the first level of consciousness, we find our mineral world with different crystals as the purest form of our Mineral Kingdom. The next level we find our Flora, the Plant Kingdom that thrives on the mineral world and our Fauna or Animal Kingdom that thrives on the two previous worlds.

On the third level we find the human species, *Homo sapiens,* that thrives not only on the previous kingdoms, but also has a connection to the higher dimensions or spiritual kingdom, the 'Kingdom of God'. We now find the emerging of different 'human species' that can be identified by the level of consciousness and the level of spiritual awareness they are connected to. The species *Homo sapiens* is undergoing a transformation as we speak. From different points of view we can identify a variety of 'human species' according to their level of consciousness and self awareness[332].

First we find '*Homo sapiens animalis*' as humans who live their lives like 'animals'. They eat, drink and work like animals and are mostly driven by instinct. Their lives are based on fear and they reflect a survival mode of 'fight or flight'. Many of these people are seen as 'cold-blooded animals' and found in prisons, war-like situations; they may be terrorists or people on the outskirts of society. They have little or no self awareness, a low level of consciousness, and are primarily connected to the Animal Kingdom, while their connection to physicality and the earth is viewed as the only reality.

However, we also find these 'animal' souls in modern day leadership positions in governments, religion, finances and others contexts of life. They can also function in the 'jungle of society' but ignore social standards, values and laws. They are ruthless and psychopathic leaders without any conscience, empathy for others or remorse.

These people are materialistic and earth bound and only have their primal third level human DNA active. The rest of their multi-dimensional DNA has been deactivated and is identifiable as 'junk genes'. Their thinking is regulated by the primal brain or the 'reptile brain' that is fear driven and responsible for sneaky, snake like ways and stalking methods.

The following group we find is *Homo sapiens sapiens,* a warm-blooded human being who has learnt to survive in the 'jungles' of different cultures and societies. They have become conscious of the world around them and are caring and loving parents. They live according to social structures and religious laws and rules while conforming to standards set by the societies they live in. Usually their lives are very materialistic and filled with different cultured and/or religious ways to survive from day to day. This group usually has DNA activated between level three and four and their thinking is regulated by the middle brain or the 'mammalian brain'. Many of our celebrities, pop artists and film stars who thrive on attention, public opinion and materialistic goals, function on this level. As this level is not fulfilling, they usually revert to substance abuse and addiction, and jump from one marriage to another in search of happiness.

We then find the emergence of '*Homo sapiens individualis*', a person who is awakening and taking back their personal identity, self-expression and individual right to independent thinking and freedom.

This group started emerging on full scale with the coming of the information era. Today *'Homo sapiens individuals'* is one of the fastest growing groups on the planet. Information is doubling every year and social structures are being challenged by new information, thinking, change and transformation. Currently this group constitutes the larger part of our youth and leadership society. Their DNA has become activated up to the fourth level while their thinking is primarily inspired by the neocortex. Here we find a group aspiring to move forward on a deeper spiritual path by putting in the effort to consciously raise their awareness and fully access levels four, five and above.

Over the last few decades a new 'species' called *Homo sapiens spiritualis* has been emerging at an escalating pace. These people have already gone though the previous learning curves, leaving the old ego-self behind. They are now forging forward into a higher level of spiritual awareness, knowing, understanding and attainment. Not only has their DNA been activated from level three through five, their temporal lobes are being activated and light up with love and compassion. When we start to access this level we begin to develop the ability to co-create miracles. This is the next level of human consciousness we can aspire to. Here we find our pathfinders and mapmakers, the leaders of the future. They are people who will teach us how to create miracles – people who will teach us the miraculous power of love and compassion. Like the emerging butterfly in nature, we find the true transformation of the species *Homo sapiens* taking place here. The emerging of a transformed human species, *Homo sapiens spiritualis,* is taking place before our eyes.

What triggers transformation?

The questions we should ask are:

> *What triggers transformation? How does transformation influence leadership? How should we manage change and transformation?*

We have a built in clock that triggers change and transformation at different time intervals. This is all encoded into our DNA as 'clock genes'. Scientific research has revealed how the clock genes function and regulate the processes in our lives on all levels – physically, emotionally, mentally and spiritually[333]. We also have a 'master' clock as part of our circadian rhythms (biorhythms), that harmonises and synchronises all our processes with the greater universal web or matrix on a DNA level. We are preprogrammed to change and function with the greater good of the cosmos and the 'cosmic clock'. These processes are primarily triggered by light that includes physical and cosmic light. Chronobiology, the study of the influence of light on our DNA and cell functioning, is providing us with fascinating information about ourselves and the world we live in[334]. It is therefore important to understand these processes currently taking place because our light intensity from the sun and also cosmic light intensity is changing as we speak. This means our inner clock genes are been triggered into action – without us even knowing!

The changes in day and night, light intensity, seasons, and our biorhythms trigger certain reactions in the body. Radical changes take place every five to twelve years with an average of a seven year cycle. It takes the body about seven years to completely transform – meaning we have a totally new body every seven years. Certain stages of change and transformation can be demarcated by our age and the position we have on our earthly time-space development line. In new success DNA we outlined not only our levels of development, but also the ages when we achieve these milestones. Every human change we undergo also includes physical changes that encompass our hormonal cycles and the influence on our physical functioning – right down to cellular level and our DNA.

At the same time we find global and universal influences that trigger change and transformation. Our seasons have a direct influence on how we manage our life. We are becoming increasingly aware of the influence of climate change on our quality of life. The next step is to become aware of the solar, astronomical, cosmic and universal influences and how they trigger radical change and transformation.

We can once again refer to the development of the butterfly. As mentioned before, the necessary codes for each phase of the life cycle are encoded. From the literature it is indicated that when the larva hatches, a new phase emerges - not only with regard to the environment, but also regarding the feeding process. A juvenile hormone in the larva's brain keeps the larva immature. With sufficient intake of necessary foods the juvenile hormone is eliminated and the larva transforms to the next, more mature phase. Should sufficient foodstuffs not be taken in, the larva remains immature and dies. This principle of transformation is applicable to people as well.

Transformation is triggered by the intake or processing of large quantities of the right information and acquiring new skills at the right time. Transformation takes place through learning. Learning and internalizing new information triggers new electro-chemical reactions in the brain, stimulates neuro-functions and ignites new potential in our minds, hearts and even our DNA.

Nothing will be as important in the next era as creating a culture of learning and to make the necessary information and skills available to everyone. The era of information, data processing and the power of the mind has already replaced the technological era. Our new leaders will need to take this into account.

This new paradigm will have far reaching effects on our perceptions and appointment of leaders and leadership training, as we move from a stance of 'power-over-people' to a new leadership position of 'releasing power-within-people'. Leaders will need to be informed and trained in new success DNA, the management of change and transformation while climbing the ladder of success.

In the next chapter we will focus more closely on the ladder of success and the change and transformation it entails.

Notes

Notes

CHAPTER 13

LEADERSHIP AND NEW SUCCESS DNA

New Success DNA

Leadership and success are synonymous. We choose leaders who we hope will contribute to our personal and collective fulfillment and success. Now, against the background of constant waves of change and transformation – even the definition of success is changing. A New Success DNA is emerging and the kind of leaders who will come to the fore will evidently change as well. A New Leadership DNA is inevitable.

The questions we can ask are:

> *What will success look like in the future? What kind of leaders will emerge in order to meet our needs and assist us in becoming successful?*

What is authentic success?

Success is a relative concept. It means whatever you want it to mean. Success is meaning. To develop new levels of success – we need to uncover and become mindful of new values and deeper meaning. New success DNA[335] is about awakening to a new purpose and quality living with deeper meaning.

Many individuals, companies, organizations, and even countries and their leaders, chase after and acquire physical things – money, possessions, position and a social image of success. The "bling" of life. However, the "bling" also has a "sting". It doesn't last very long because it loses its meaning. You constantly need to repeat the whole process in order to stay on top. Ask yourself: Who would you be if you gave away, or lost, all your possessions, your work, financial security, health, relationships, or social position? Many people have gone through this process. Natural disasters, recessions, epidemics and illness have claimed many lives and possessions. Most people see this as devastating loss... but, could this be a form of success too? We all accept that we will have a sense of loss, anger, and frustration in situations that seemingly are not going our way.

The first thing we have to do is to get clarity on the following.

> *Is success defined by: (1) what we have and are acquiring – our physical possessions and positions – or – (2) who and what we are becoming in the process?*

If your answer is number one, you will need to focus on putting all you efforts into acquiring more possessions, positions and social acceptance. This is ego-success and is never fulfilling, never satisfying, and it never lasts – it is an illusion. People who look for this kind of success are living with false perceptions of success. They will consciously or unconsciously seek leaders who will assist them in obtaining this goal.

This means that these leaders also need to share these values.

If, however, your answer is number two, you will need to learn who you really are, what you are designed to do, be and become – and then do it! This comes from your heart and soul[336]. It is soul-success that is fulfilling, lasting and "true" success. They will seek leaders who share these values and will assist them in reaching these goals.

Everyone has hidden agendas. These agendas are formed out of our desires, and the needs and wants that determine our choices. However, most of these driving forces are subconscious and we are not aware of who we really are and what we want. So, in order to determine where you stand where leadership is concerned, ask the questions:

> *Where am I coming from? Am I doing this for ego gratification or - Am I feeding my soul?*

Once we can honestly distinguish between the two answers and points of view, we are well on our way to true success and we can identify the pathfinders and mapmakers – the leaders of the future who can assist us in getting there.

These are people, individuals, groups, mentors, coaches or friends who can – 'walk the walk and talk the talk'. They are leaders with new success DNA who know how to help, assist, support and guide us on this path of true success as a journey of personal self-discovery and self-mastery. The success symbols obtained along the way are markers of the success process and could be diverse and varied. The important point is to stay on the path.

The questions are:

> *What does this path look like? What kind of leaders do we need on this path?*

The path of success

We all are leaders because everyone can influence others in a special way. Leadership is about having influence and using it constructively. The only thing that differs is the amount and the kind of influence that we have. This determines or power position. Leadership positions are moving from ego driven power-over-people to soul driven development of power-within-people. Power has moved from power-in-numbers to the number-of-powers. New leadership DNA emerges when we transform old outworn mindsets, methods, skills and tools into new mindsets and power-tools, when the soul emerges and takes prominence over the ego.

Each person has the choice to choose where they want to go and what they want to learn. The challenge is to consciously move from one level to another and gain new insight and become more of who you are with more powerful tools and skills to create a quality life.

Leaders understand this process and help and assist us in becoming who we are, overcoming fears and stumbling blocks and acquiring new insight, understanding and skills. This means that true leaders have also walked the path and are a few steps ahead. They are the pathfinders and way-showers into the future. A short summary of the different levels and what they entail[337] follows.

- **Level 0: Infra-red. In the basement.**

This is the dark or night side of life. Just as growth and development take place within the womb, so we too can go into regression or darkness to survive and to grow. This is the survival mode. The aim is to be able to control the physical world. The lessons we need to learn here are related to surviving physically, intellectually, financially, emotionally and biologically.

This triggers our basic survival instinct or fight or flight reactions.

Negative stumbling blocks we need to overcome include self-destructive behavior, substance dependence, malnutrition – physical and emotional abuse, warlike conditions – being on the 'war- path', extreme shock conditions, revenge and bitterness, negativity, destruction and obsessions.

Here we need to overcome the fear of danger and threats to personal survival and safety, attack, violence on all levels, to include physical, emotional, religious and intellectual values. The basic need at this level is the need for safety. The strengths include the ability to act on survival instincts and overcome fears and negativity. The underlying value lessons are:

- Life is valuable.
- There is a purpose and meaning in life.

The following are the triggers that indicate it is time to move on.

* Overcoming danger or danger is over.
* Overcome challenges and problems.
* Accepting and understanding the value and purpose of life.

Once we have worked through all this it is time to discover the next level.

Level 1: Red milestone

Here the lessons are related to group survival. The aim is to contact, manage and control the group, team or family. This can be within a personal or a business 'family'.

The lessons we need to learn include

Managing our physical world, producing and receiving stimulating information, coping and surviving as a team, family or tribal group values and ways of thinking; coming from religious, ethnic, business, academic, social, political, family views and values, providing material necessities like shelter and food, controlling and managing the group, team or family. We learn how to relinquish power to the group authority figure; find individual physical safety in the group; accepting responsibility for the group, tribe or team. We find family and group safety – 'warm nest' syndrome; bonding – being together. Important are team, group loyalty and justice; basic traditional and cultural beliefs, traditions and values. We learn the value of cultural, group dignity and honor; feeling at home and part of the family. We identify with the family, group, "ubuntu", law and order.

Negative stumbling blocks

The negative stumbling blocks we need to overcome include: Desensitization, where physical senses are impaired, blunted or deadened. Not belonging /not part of the 'family'. We fear feeling separate; fear of responsibility; afraid of or not accepting authority; People nurture negativity, bitterness towards cultural/tribe, group, person or team. Develop an inability to cope. Feeling disconnected insecure and unsafe. Fear being victimised by group or tribe or feeling culturally victimised. Not identifying with or rebelling against family, group or "ubuntu" law and/or authority figures.

Strengths

The strengths we need to develop include: Tribal, group, team or family identity and community development. Ability to bond, belong and accept responsibility for team, group, tribe or family. We can accept honor code; develop support systems, loyalty, a sense of safety and a sense of connection. Here we learn to overcome fears and negativity.

Fears: We need to overcome the fears of: abandonment, loss of physical order, superstitions, magical forces, ageing, victimisation by group, tribe, team or family.

Needs: Fulfillment is achieved by meeting the basic needs of: Being in control, with logic, order and structure; achieve physical and material comfort; belonging, being grounded and accepted while serving others, the community, tribe, group, family or team.

The underlying value lessons:

- All is one – The team, group, family are one.
- Honor family.
- Honor all tribal families and human communities.

Experiences: Here we need to experience: 'I am safe, secure and grounded - I am part of the 'family' '.

Triggers: Triggers we need to identify and move on:

Triggers include: discord between tribal values and growth values; tribal, group, family power too restricting; challenging toxic tribal, group or team power; need to filter tribal values that are negative; an urge to keep useful, positive values and traditions; separation from tribal values that no longer support our growth; separation from people that no longer support our growth.

Once we have learnt these lessons, overcome the fears and heeded the triggers, we move on to the next level.

Level 2: Orange milestone

At this level we learn lessons related to interpersonal relationships. The aim is effective and productive interpersonal contact and control on one-to-one basis. Here we start discovering our power within relationships. This is fundamentally ego based and we strive to compete, achieve and be accomplished in the eyes of others.

Positive lessons:

These lessons include: Achievement and accomplishment; competition – winner takes all; relationships and friendships on one-to-one basis. Positive control patterns: all relationships have different energy levels and need to be managed and/or controlled; working relationships and financial partnerships; managing money; sexual relationships; making egocentric choices and setting boundaries; ethics and honor in relationships; power and control and creativity.

Negative stumbling blocks: We need to overcome negative controlling; power games; quick pleasures and fast money; conflict; negative destructive competition; abuse of power/position/money and sexuality.

Strengths : The challenges and strengths we need to develop include: The ability and stamina to survive physically and financially on one's own; work and professional ethic; experience power in relationships; defend and protect self; setting boundaries; positive competition; striving towards a goal and taking risks; recover from loss and negativity; the power to rebel; leave boundaries and re-establish life; sound business and financial practices; meaningful relationships on a one-to-one basis; personal and professional decision-making ability; positive attitude towards money and sexuality.

Fears: Here our fears we need to overcome include the fear of: Losing control; being controlled or dominated by others; intimidating powers, situations or events; loss of the power and health of the physical body.

Needs: Our needs include: The experience of a positive one-to-one relationship/s and meeting ego needs. These include the need to achieve, accomplish and compete.

Experience: We experience fulfillment by: Experiencing power, success, status and influence. To give and receive: physical things, money, sexuality etc. while mastering emotions (power).

Value system: The underlying value system is: Honour one another.

Triggers to move on: This includes: A meaningless experience of money, pleasure and sexuality; feeling caught – entangled or imprisoned; experiencing boredom and emptiness; unfulfilling, meaningless relationships; unproductive power games; asking "but what about me?"

After we have gone through this whole process it is time to move to the next level.

Level 3: Yellow milestone

Here the challenge lies in attaining personal power and personal peace. This is where we start finding the answers to the questions: Who am I? Where am I going and why? Personal meaning now starts to overshadow group, team and family values. Here we find our personal power as inner peace.

The positive lessons: Positive connection with the self; clear self-identity; inner personal power related to external world; self-esteem; self-discipline; self-respect; self-confidence; living in integrity; personal honor; personal intelligence; physical abilities and skills; accepting responsibility; making decisions; stand up as individuals; maturation of ego; investment in self-development; inner peace and self-love.

Negative stumbling blocks to overcome, include: Lack of personal honor and power; egocentric approach; loss of integrity; lack of accepting responsibility; inability to make decisions; lack of inner power and courage; feeling insecure; lack of self respect and self-discipline; disconnected from the self and inner power source; minimum self-discovery and development; lack of self-love.

Strengths: The strengths we need to discover, include: Discovering who I am; own inner power; integrity; self-esteem and self-worth; self-respect; self-discipline; self-growth; coping with crisis; courage to take risks; generosity, appreciation and gratitude; ambition; strength of character; valuing life; ability to generate action.

Fears: There are various fears we need to overcome: The fear of criticism; rejection; looking foolish; failing; responsibilities; commitment; all fears related to physical appearance.

Value lesson is: Honor oneself.

Experience: Here we need to experience who 'I am'; my own personal value and worth; personal power; living in integrity; peace and personal growth and development.

The triggers to move on are: Sharing who 'I am' with others; the search for higher meaning in sharing, teaching, learning. Learning to be thankful, humble and expressing gratitude.

These first three levels can be seen as the primary school of life. These are the material or pre-personal levels. It is the level of objects and events, the levels where the group and relationships tell us what to do and how to manage our lives. Up until here we have focused on interaction and competition with external power – living from the outside in! From here we start moving from the outside in and start looking for information and guidance on the inside. We do not allow ourselves to be governed by outside events and objects as in the past.

Here we start finding radical change - a quantum leap; a change from the pre-personal to a personal reality – as truth for me. We change from the perception of a physical reality to a quantum reality. Here we make a transition. Some people will stay behind and others move forward to discover this new perception of reality and meaning.

Level 4: Green milestone

The introduction to the leap can be found in seeing reality from a quantum perspective. Here we find information on the inside and the outside. Outer knowledge is objective and the inner knowledge is intuitive. We start to know ourselves from the inside out.

Lessons: Here the lessons are related to understanding, intuition, empathy, tolerance and forgiveness. We can openly give and receive higher values: healing, love.

Aim: The aim of this level is the meaning of conscious living, forgiveness, reconciliation and love for the self, people and nature and God.

The positive lessons to be learnt include: Meeting emotional needs of the self and of others; experiencing the beauty and hearing the messages of nature; listening to the heart, the true motivator;

trusting: "Let go and let God"; detoxifying the body and soul; healthy living; letting go of negativity and destructive patterns; compassion and forgiveness; goodness; tolerance and compassion; healing of wounds; reconciliation and bringing together; conscious living by experiencing each person and situation to the full.

Negative stumbling blocks to overcome include: Hate and resentment; toxic emotions; hurt and pain; separation and brokenness; keeping negativity alive; unforgiving; blame shifting; procrastination.

Strengths: Our strengths can be found in: Inner peace and centeredness; love and forgiveness; compassion; dedication to work, others and life; experiencing beauty; inspiration; hope and trust; healing oneself and others; embracing the positive; inspirational living.

Fears: Here the fears we could meet along the way and need to overcome are: The fear of intimacy, being close, loneliness, commitment, emotional weakness and betrayal.

Needs: We experience fulfillment when our needs are met through developing insight and understanding, exploring, love, responsibility to love and knowing what love is.

Underlying values: The underlying values include "Love is Divine Power" and "love changes everything"

Triggers to move on: We know it is time to move on when there is a: A new search for meaning. A need to walk the path to a higher purpose and Plan. A need to live a full life of integrity and love at a higher level.

LEVEL 5: Blue milestone

Lessons: Here we find the lessons related to: Truth, honesty, open communication, inspiration and unlimited discovery.

Aim: The aim at this level is to: speak my truth as truth sets you free, make creative contributions and inspiring discoveries, communicate openly and honestly.

Positive aspects to be developed include: Developing will power; integrity; choice; detoxifying the body, mind soul and spirit; being

242

open and fearless; positive speech and communication; aligning personal will with Higher will; truth and faith; inspirational discoveries and creative contributions; being non judgmental.

Negative aspects: The stumbling blocks we need to overcome include: Lack of will power; lack of choice; lies and dishonesty; toxic psyche and spirit; lack of integrity; lack of faith and trust; little or no creativity and inspirational contributions; being separated and alienated from own will and Higher will.

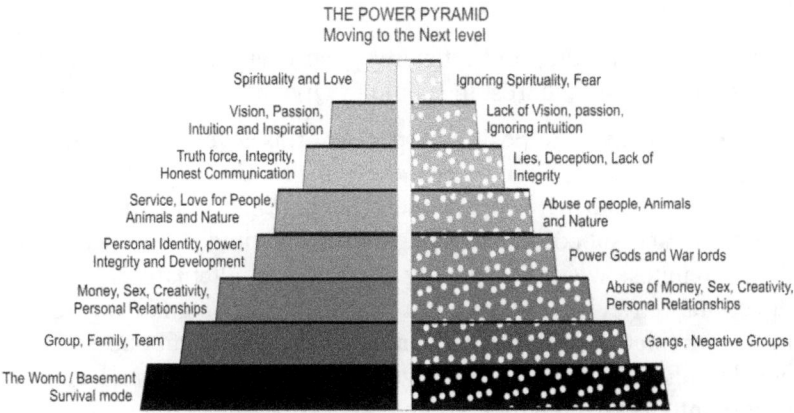

THE POWER PYRAMID
Moving to the Next level

Spirituality and Love	Ignoring Spirituality, Fear
Vision, Passion, Intuition and Inspiration	Lack of Vision, passion, Ignoring intuition
Truth force, Integrity, Honest Communication	Lies, Deception, Lack of Integrity
Service, Love for People, Animals and Nature	Abuse of people, Animals and Nature
Personal Identity, power, Integrity and Development	Power Gods and War lords
Money, Sex, Creativity, Personal Relationships	Abuse of Money, Sex, Creativity, Personal Relationships
Group, Family, Team	Gangs, Negative Groups
The Womb / Basement Survival mode	

Summary of the levels of change and transformation

Strengths: Here we find the strengths of truth and honesty; identifying and aligning life with higher purpose and calling; honor and integrity; keeping your word; faith and trust; inspiration and true creativity; the ability to walk your talk and talk your walk.

Fears: The fears we need to overcome include giving up power of choice; being out of control and powerless. This level also includes all previous fears at deeper level.

Needs: The needs we need to meet to obtain fulfillment include understanding our higher purpose in life; making contact with higher Divine plan; living inspiring and creative lives.

Experiencing: Here we need to experience truth and honesty; wonder, beauty and inspiration.

Underlying values: Surrendering my will to Higher Truth or Divine will; seek only the truth.

The triggers to move on include the ability to say "Thy will be done" or "all yours" and to seek the one and only Higher law, path and truth.

Level 6: Indigo milestone.

Lessons: Here we find lessons related to vision; integration and being one; getting the big picture.

Aim: The aim is the understanding that everything is connected to everything else; the trust to submit to Divine Power and processes.

Positive aspects: The positive aspects of this level include holistic, integrative thinking; connecting everything to everything else; expansive, mental reasoning; understanding and evaluating beliefs, conscious and subconscious thoughts and attitudes motivated by fears/strengths; wisdom; opening the mind to alternatives; internal direction; retrieving power from "false truths"; connecting to the universal mind, Higher Mind, universal Power; symbolic sight or developing the inner or "third eye", developing vision and gaining insight into underlying patterns and processes.

Negative stumbling blocks: The negative stumbling blocks we need to overcome, include an inability to reason logically; unwillingness to understand new truths, values and beliefs; unwillingness to change attitudes and beliefs; inability or unwillingness to access subconscious mind; mistrust of inner "voice" and internal direction and vision; unwillingness to open mind.

Strengths: The following strengths can be developed: Seeing interconnectedness; holistic, integrative thinking; wisdom; intellectual abilities; evaluation of thoughts; openness; being non-judgmental; inspiration; vision; receiving and generating innovation, creativity and action; command over the elements; manifesting by commanding energy to become matter.

Fears: The following fears need to be overcome: The fear of truth; realistic judgment; discipline; confession; one's shadow (dark side) and attributes; unwillingness to look within; external council.

Needs: The following needs need to be met in order to experience fulfillment: To have an answer to the question: Why?; the need to find meaning; to experience reverence, compassion, devoted service and universal love.

Underlying value: I love myself, I love others and I love God - the Universal or Agapé love.

Triggers to move on include wanting to find the answer to the question: Why? We move on because of a deep need to grow in awareness, find a deeper understanding and the search for higher meaning.

When all the lessons are learnt and questions answered we move to the next level. The breakthrough to the next level again is like moving from school to university or college. This again indicates a leap. Here we move from the personal to the transpersonal level.

According to Deepak Chopra, here we move from the quantum reality to the virtual reality. Here we make another transition where some will stay behind and some will move forward.

Level 7: Violet milestone

Here we find lessons related to wholeness and unity with the higher consciousness and the Divine will.

Aim: Wholeness and living the "I am".

Positive: The positive aspects we need to develop include the presence of and connection with universal Divine and higher Power; spiritual insight and understanding; vision, intuition, love and grace; prayer and meditation; living in the now; miracles; hope and inner peace.

Strengths: The strengths include connecting with the "God spot"; seeing the big picture; understanding the higher, universal purpose; inner guidance; trust, hope, and faith that transcends ordinary human fears; insight into the roots of disease, poverty and negativity and the healing thereof; devotion and inner peace; love.

Fears: The fears we need to overcome relate to the fear of spiritual issues; spiritual abandonment; loss of identity; loss of connection to life and the people around us; our "dark side"; closeness, connection, love and caring; death.

Needs: Meeting our spiritual needs, as we are spiritual beings; to live fully within time and space of the earthly now; living meaningfully in the present.

Underlying values: Living full, meaningful lives in the present.

Triggers to move on: We move on because of a search for deeper meaning. As spiritual beings there are no barriers or death - just a change of form. When our earthly purpose is completed, we pass on from one form to another and move on. Here our physical death is the trigger to move on. This time we transform – not from level to level, but from one dimension to another..

Below we find a summary of different levels of consciousness and different levels of leadership.

Summary

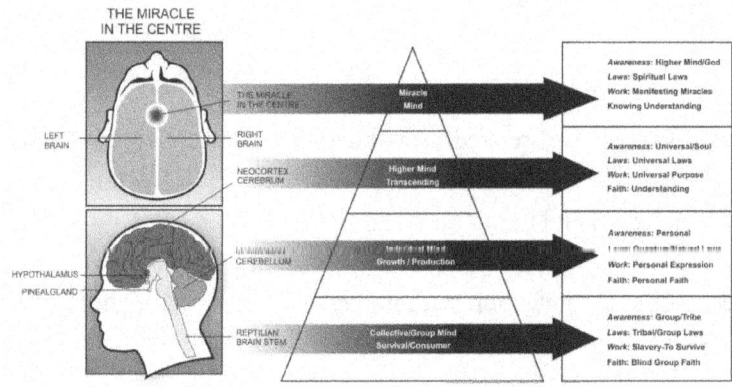

Notes

CHAPTER 14

LEADERSHIP AND MOVING FORWARD

Letting go

The Bushmen know that the survival of the group depends on them traveling light. When the elders become a burden, they leave them behind and move on. To them, this is part of life. In so-called developed cultures, this seems barbaric. The underlying principle, however, is to travel light. This means discarding excess baggage and distancing yourself from people that keep you from moving forward. In order to manage these stages, we need to understand the dynamics and processes at work. With this information we can decide how to move forward and who will be left behind.

Every time we leave unnecessary baggage behind, we become lighter, more energy is released and we can move faster.

The questions are:

> *How do we move forward? Where does*
> *it start and who will stay behind?*

Where does change start?

Change or a shift always starts to develop outside or on the periphery of traditional systems, structures, organisations, thoughts and beliefs. It develops, gains momentum and shifts from outside the external structures to their inner core. As soon as the core of the system changes, the transformation is complete. Normally this occurs through resistance, struggle and pain. The *status quo* does not easily give up its power position.

Creative and innovative people searching for answers to existing problems, find solutions in new ways of thinking and structures. It starts within the depths of the self – just like new life starts inside the invisible world of the womb. Many see this as the universal womb of innovation and creation. The answers to all our questions and problems are encoded within – not only within our hearts and minds, but within every cell and in our DNA.

With the right stimuli and correct triggers, the latent potential and even the junk genes in every cell are stimulated. An awakening takes place and awareness grows. New energy-information is released. It shapes new ideas, methods and processes and takes on a new form and creates new structures. New solutions are born. A new life force moves from deep within, outward.

When problems arise, innovative people will creatively start searching for answers and solutions. The solutions are found within a strong inner core of an inner or higher "knowing". This is more than faith and includes a connection to a higher universal mind without any rational explanation. Innovative people "just know". They have a gut feeling of excitement, knowing understanding and live from this "fire in the belly". This ignites all the other processes. Once momentum is gained it only needs to be sustained. There is nothing as powerful as an idea for which the time has arrived.

These persons live from this strong inner core to the outside. They provide positive solutions, change life around them and make the world a better place. They are the new paradigm thinkers – creators, initiators and facilitators of change, growth and development. They normally function independently, outside traditional groups' formalized structures. As soon as the time for their ideas has arrived, they come to the fore in order to address the problems and issues at hand. They then disappear as soon as the problems are solved. The new ideas spread to people whose lives depend on new information from external sources. These people live from the outside to the inside.

Change and new ideas take shape in the hearts and heads of individuals. They then form groups who think and feel the same. Eventually the individual and the group influence the general overarching structures and organisations, the country and even the world as a whole. A paradigm shift takes place from outside political, educational, academic, religious, family, company or community structures to the inside.

In order to stimulate growth and change, people must receive the new information from the outside and be newly equipped. At the same time the structure and rules of the organization will and do change. Because everything happens simultaneously, external experts are used to facilitate change and growth and help to integrate the various parts.

The following example serves as an illustration: Within the family the children grow up and in their teens they expect their parents to view and manage them differently. Parents on the other hand, have their own agenda. The time arrives for change and movement to take place. A knowledgeable person, such as a counselor, adviser or psychologist as objective outsider, can identify the conflict and indicate how to eliminate the stumbling blocks. New knowledge and skills are transferred and restructuring of the system is facilitated and integrated.

The same applies to groups, companies, organizations and governments. Change, growth and progress are the fruit of the cooperation and work of all the people involved. Should it be managed incorrectly, people, families, groups, companies and even governments deteriorate into a constant process of conflict without creative solutions being identified. A constant process of self-destruction and disintegration then follows.

The hierarchy of change and productivity

Personal competency is a prerequisite for positive change and productivity within the group, team and even a country as a whole.

The quality, relevance and suitability of personal skills and knowledge determine personal competency. Personal competency determines personal effectiveness and productivity that lead to personal achievement within certain contexts or circumstances. Self-knowledge, -mastery and -management are the basis of successful personal functioning and leadership in any situation.

The personal achievement and quality self-mastery of each individual member of the group, determines the competency of the group. Group competency leads to group efficiency and productivity that in turn determines group achievement. The achievement and management of the group form the foundation for the management of a total organizational efficiency, competency and productivity.

The success of any organisation therefore depends on the skills, effectiveness, productivity and success of each individual and group. Today we will find that the quality of our people will become more important than the acquired skills. Skills can be taught – being a quality human being depends on a personal value system.

Hierarchy of organisational productivity and success

In the light of the changing financial and political dispensation and situation in countries, political parties – companies and institutions are obliged to provide their employees with various training programs. Skills training and training in areas such as labor laws, affirmative action and transformational leadership, however, represents a fragmented approach. New thinking, skills and knowledge of the person as an individual are often ignored. A new foundation of thinking, values, belief systems and skills will now be laid so that the achievement and prosperity of the group, institution, organisation and eventually the country as a whole can be secured in the future.

It represents a diverse process very few organisations and companies can cope with. Some will take a short cut, but realise too late that the time and money spent did not provide the expected results. However, there are those who have an understanding of and insight into the process and who are willing to make the necessary investment. Time, money and sacrifice should be rewarded with increased creativity and productivity.

Each person, organisation and company should accept the responsibility of being equipped with new knowledge, skills and vision. The success of the change will not only depend on every institution or group, but also especially on the willingness of every person to think, learn and do anew. The biggest challenge for leaders of the new paradigm is the management of people and human resources during change. It is increasingly necessary for individuals to identify and master their reactions, responsibilities and roles in order for the change to take place with maximum effectiveness and productivity.

Who will stay behind?

It is important to understand that all persons grow and develop according to their potential and self-structure. Change is sometimes difficult for some and sometimes even impossible. It is therefore not possible to take all people along on the path of change, growth and development. The question is: How can we identify these persons, manage them and understand why can't or don't they take part in growth, development and change?

The following characteristics inhibit a person's ability to change.

• **People with rigid, perfectionist personalities**

These people find it difficult, even impossible, to go through the chaos and pain of change. Their inner stability and security depends

251

on the maintaining order in the outside world. Their feeling of safety is directly related to the structure, order and stability in their existing circumstances. They avoid and resist any change in order not to be subjected to chaos and uncertainty.

- **People with personal problems and an identity crisis**

The inner energy of these persons is mainly focused on their problems. Little energy is left for growth and transformation. They are people who do not know who they are and who cannot determine and define where they are going.

- **People who are anxious and feel intimidated**

These people experience a lot of anxieties, threats and mistakes. It sometimes takes them a lifetime to assert themselves within a specific context of life and feel safe. It is unlikely that they would take part in anything else but trying to feel safe.

- **Arrogant people**

Arrogant people are over-conscious of their own importance. Their exaggerated pride and obsession with their own achievements result in them not changing for they would have to leave it all behind.

- **Selfish people**

Some people are primarily ego-centred. They are constantly self-centered and self-focused and the wellbeing and development of other people are of little or no importance to them. Selfish people would not make any changes if it threatens their comfort. They would rather resist any change and fight the new ideas and the bearers there of. They would do anything to defend and maintain their comfort zone. They would rather sacrifice other people, laws, systems and structures in order to maintain their own identity and their point of view. To change would mean a loss of ego and therefore a loss of power, especially power over people.

- **People without the intellectual ability to change**

Change demands certain insights and intellectual abilities. There are people who do not possess these abilities and therefore cannot take part in the process of change. They passively go with the flow, or actively sabotage change and the new paradigm. These are our 'passengers' who are in it for the ride and 'go with the flow'.

- ## Saboteurs or executioners

Development saboteurs are people inside or outside structures who believe there is only one way to solve a problem – their way. They feel threatened by the new information and people. All the negative results of a paradigm shift manifest in these people. The execution occurs when new ideas, solutions and strategies and the initiators thereof are hypercritically judged and condemned.

People with new ideas usually get "crucified" and ostracized by these judgmental persons. There is no chance of positive, constructive criticism or healthy opposition. They are found within structures like the family, marriage, company, school, religions, political parties, academic, cultural institutions or organizations. They constantly feel threatened.

They usually try to cope with change and the new paradigm with negativity, threats, accusations, attacks, judgment, denial and aggression. These people feel uncomfortable in a positive, happy, uplifting situation of growth and development.

This kind of leadership style can result in a lot of personal and organisational damage. It sometimes takes a long time to get rid of malicious and harmful people, groups or organisations and their harmful influence. They are sometimes removed from the system at high personal, organisational and even financial cost. Once outside they system they could still pose a threat by trying to gain access to the structures once more. These people find it difficult to move on.

These people sabotage, handicap and deliberately inhibit any new ideas, transformation and growth. They denigrate and depersonalise the initiators of the new thinking and actions and try to minimize or even eliminate their influences. James Lundy[338] correctly identifies three fundamental contributions when he says: "Lead, follow or get out of the way." It is crucial to identify, rehabilitate or remove these people from the system in time, if progress is to be secured.

Because their self-serving systems have self-destruction as a default, they eventually cause their own downfall and find themselves outcasts from the main stream of life. They usually live outside the structures where they can do the least damage as embittered people. The question is: What should we do about these people? The answer is - nothing – let the dead bury their own dead. The challenge is to move on.

Who will move to the next level?

We can be identified four types of people who will take part in change, namely: The pioneers, the initiators, developers and followers.

- ### The pioneers: The new thinkers

Pioneers are individuals who can creatively identify and initiate new solutions to problems. These people think in open systems and acknowledge the fact that people, groups, institutions, organizations and even countries move from one plateau or level to the next. They understand the flow of change and can integrate what is applicable from the past with what is required for the future in the transformation process. They search for integrative structures and have a wide vision and insight. New paradigm pioneers are aware of the fact that everything functions holistically is integrated as a living whole within the oneness of the Universe. They think holistically and improve the well-being of the whole and not only the fragmented parts.

The new paradigm pioneers have X-ray vision and can identify differences and problems under the surface. They have wide panoramic sight and insight and are constantly open to new information and ideas. They can cope with and manage different people and situations and value systems and aim at facilitating a common vision and synergy for all. They are competent, effective, disciplined people with deeper, fundamental and universal personal qualities. At the same time they have developed and are equipped with various coping and leadership skills that will benefit all.

The new paradigm pioneers are not people who can be manipulated and dominated. They are not necessarily found in the normal corridors of influence and prestige, but rather on the periphery of power and mainly outside of the structures. They do not attempt to be on the foreground, unless contributing to the solution of existing problems.

The new paradigm leaders are the innovators of new ideas, solutions, structures and answers to problems of life until another power shift occurs. They are very conscious of their time to step down and retreat out of sight. Some stay active while leading from behind. They make excellent mentors and coaches for upcoming new leaders.

Various characteristics of the new paradigm leaders and pioneers, can be distinguished: They are people who can take initiative and think in open systems as opposed to established, ideal situations. They also think in terms of flow and flexibility and can integrate natural differences in an evolutionary flow.

While millions of people move through the various stadiums of growth, each one experiences his/her situation as ideal, but not for the organisation in the whole. New paradigm leaders search for integrated structures to manage the complex mobility of a living system. The new paradigm leader thinks and plans for the total population and not a specific group. Because of this the new mindset they do not lapse into the categorisation and labeling of people in historical stereotypes and stereotyped categories. They rather relate everything to everything else in quantum parts

New paradigm leaders don't get stuck in small fragments or compartments. They have a need for a common vision, integrated structures and focused strategies, energies and resources. Effective solutions for complex situations are found by taking the bigger picture and the whole into account. They are comfortable with criticism and opposition. While taking the whole into account they act on behalf of all involved.

These pioneers believe that all people should be willing to simultaneously understand and influence the search for solutions for complex situations and problems. They focus on the functioning of the whole, while inspiring the development of individuals and the parts they represent. They have an ability to observe everything through holographic scanning that refers to their ability to literally and intuitively 'see' the big picture and know what is going on behind the scenes. This is more than faith and includes clarity and certainty. These pioneers have moved beyond blind faith or even personal individual faith and they have a deeper knowing, understanding and wisdom.

New paradigm pioneers and leaders are the products of the information era. Their sensory systems are continuously open to the flow of data from all possible sources. They have the ability to think in the past, present and future and retain perspective and continuity, and are susceptible to new ideas. They condemn politics based on intimidation and power games, the blockage or distortion of information and find the aggressive defense of personal agendas and terrain unnecessary, since everybody has a place in the sun. These leaders have developed a heightened awareness and function from a higher consciousness. Their senses are finely tuned and intuition plays a big role in their scanning of the environment.

At the same time they can implement a variety of problem-solving strategies. They are knowledgeable in the management of various levels of human and/or technological development and change in complex environments. They can think on their feet and are agile and flexible.

Innovative leaders are competent, fearless, tough, resourceful and cheerful. While attaching high value to autonomy and personal freedom they enjoy something new and have an interest and passion for personal challenges and doing unique projects. They respect competency, are unselfish, possess high ethics and a strong sense of responsibility. They are not dominated and manipulated and only support something if it has merit. They display courage in difficult times and can still laugh, play and have fun. While addressing issues in earnest and with dedication, their sense of humor usually brings light into many a dark situation.

- **Initiators**

These thinkers are people who get in touch with the new ideas, the thoughts, values, structure and rules at an early stage. Although they did not discover or invent the new paradigm, they are open and receptive enough to understand, extend and integrate the new. They are especially ready to undergo change. They are the initiators of the new values, thoughts and paradigms in their groups, structures and organizations.

While others are still struggling with the old solutions within the status quo, they already initiate and implement the new on a small scale. They mainly function within structures and attempt to introduce change to people within the structures and the status quo. They are mainly found within groups, academic institutions, business structures, and political parties, sporting circles, and cultural groups, religious or church boards and in social communities.

Others can perceive them as the devil's advocate; those that that handicap the traditional status quo, stirrers, conflict makers or problem creators. Initiators normally clash with the establishment, institutionalized structures and the procedures of the status quo. Sometimes they can break through the old mindsets and calcified structures and create a new field where more and more people can realise the deeper meaning of the new mindset. They can also think and work independently and are not discouraged by resistance and punishment.

Should a change in the status quo not occur and expectations of change are limited, they leave the system and will move to better circumstances. Today it is important that new paradigm leaders and initiators are identified and supported in their efforts to facilitate and develop innovative change.

- **Trainers and developers**

As the new paradigm develops and gains field, more people are trained and developed. Some people find it more difficult than others. Trainers should be identified, trained and equipped with the new information and skills in order to train and develop larger groups. Trainers and developers are those people within structures who show an aptitude for the new mindset and can be trained in order to facilitate and develop the new information in others. Innovative leaders will invest in training competent trainers thereby broadening the basis of leadership.

- **Followers**

Followers are those who are willing to follow other people towards change without resistance or questioning. They adapt to the new thoughts and skills and accept that, should their identified leaders support the change, everything should be in order. Followers form the largest percentage of any group or community and therefore the importance of effective quality leadership cannot be emphasised enough.

What should be done?

Nothing constructively happens without something being done. The question is: What should be done?

- **Break away from outdated ideas and structures**

Accept that change and that power and the paradigm shifts have come to stay. This means there is no turning back. The time has come to break away from outdated ideas, mindsets and ways of thinking and believing.

- **Open the systems.**

People should make themselves available to become new, to learn and think anew.

- **Change attitudes and dispositions**.

Attitudes should change. Negative, envious and hostile attitudes should make room for healthy competition, compliments, co-operation, synergy and support.

- **Identify and develop quality leaders.**

New leaders should be identified and developed early on, in order for them to assume leadership at the right time.

- **Invest time and money in training**.

People should be introduced to and trained in the new paradigm. More time and money should be spent on leadership training and development for all. Unfortunately we come from an old mindset where personal responsibility and a valid learning culture did not develop. The time has come for all people to accept responsibility and be willing to invest time and money in education and development. It can no longer be a luxury for a selected minority, but is a necessity for all people if progress is to be ensured.

- **Develop new, flexible structures**

New structures should be established in order for different ideas and contributions to be coordinated and integrated. The whole is bigger and more effective than the individual parts. Not only should different people be brought together, but they should also be exposed to people from other contexts, cultures, religions, and backgrounds; the life-world extends and boundaries are moved.

- **Stimulate creative thinking and living**

The opportunity for stimulation of creativity and holistically integrated thinking must be created and the creators should be rewarded.

- **Develop the entrepreneur and innovator**

Innovation and developing entrepreneurs are at the backbone of a developing organization, country of even the human race as a whole. However, not much effort is put into developing entrepreneurs. The high level of unemployment and the vast majority of young people who are without jobs after graduating from school or college, underlines the importance that each individual needs to think about becoming an entrepreneur and/or self-employed. New comers to the workforce have to face the reality of scare job opportunities for unskilled and inexperienced individuals.

At the same time universities and colleges are filled to the brim and young people have to turn to other avenues of income. This opens new door for entrepreneurs who should be supported, trained, mentored, guided and encouraged. All economies are positively influenced while the creation of job opportunities has a positive effect on the crime rate, drug- and alcohol abuse, divorce and family disintegration, violence, murder, psychosomatic illnesses and the general well-being and mental health of all.

- **Improve the flow of information**

Information is represented by organisation, structure and pattern. As soon as structures become too rigid, the flow of information is obstructed and productivity impeded. A constant flow of information has to be ensured and secured. Advanced communication technology resulted in global information being available every moment of the day. Mobility, open communication and interactions should be priorities and individuals should be informed of global events.

- **Implement new paradigm leadership training**.

Change is inevitable and the traditional leadership and management techniques can no longer be maintained. Holistic, integrated leadership and management should be implemented and people should be trained in these areas.

- ### Develop self-management and self-mastery

Change takes place in individual s before they can change their circumstances. The extensive task of introducing people to themselves, with the purpose of self-evaluation and self-mastery within the bigger whole, should not be underestimated. Because of the complexity of life, it is becoming increasingly difficult to manage large groups and organisations. The time has come for the individual to accept responsibility for self-mastery. The biggest task for the coming decade is firstly to bring people into close contact to and connect with themselves and then others. Secondly, we need to train people in self-mastery. The challenge is big and has to be accepted as a priority in order to ensure progress.

- ### Protect nature

We live in a physical world that includes Mother Nature, a living entity. We are also part of Nature that includes our Fauna and Flora. Beyond this we find our Mineral World and all it has to offer. Up and till now this natural world has been providing us with and abundant of resources while making our physical stay comfortable and enjoyable. However, Mother Earth has been plundered and abused by unconscious humans and their mindless search for luxury, comfort and technological progress. During this process their mining, farming, fishing, manufacturing and polluting practices have had a negative influence on our habitat. It has also caused a serious global wound we find as the hole in the ozone layer this is daily still deteriorating while contributing to climate change. At the same time we are becoming aware that many of our natural resources are running out.

With our current raising of consciousness we are therefore also called to honor Mother Earth and protect her treasure house of resources. This calls for supporting conscious awareness of the importance of nature conservation and the responsible, mindful use of our natural resources. Usually this task was forwarded to governments, companies and organizations. However, each person is now called to do their part in recycling, conservation while developing healthy sustainable living practices. Quality living is taking on whole new dimension as everyone now needs to go 'green'.

• **Stimulate vision**

Each person has his own unique place to fulfill and contribute to it. People must accept responsibility for their own life and development. Everyone should have a clear vision and objective. The following sayings are important: "Blessed are those who aim at nothing, they shall hit it every time"; Blessed are those who expect nothing from life – they shall not be disappointed"; Blessed are those who run in circles- they will be called the merry-go-round"

Everyone's personal vision could then be integrated with a group vision. Ultimately all the visions should synergise to form an encompassing vision for the group, team, organization or country – certainly one of the biggest modern challenges is to:

Reclaim your soul – the higher values of honesty, truth and integrity.

Develop a new spirit of growth, development, prosperity, health, wealth and happiness for all.

This represents the unseen world as manifest in the physical world. People should be made aware of this unseen dimension and the effect it has on everyday life. All this needs to be taken into account to successfully enter the new paradigm and dimension.

• **Accept the challenge**

There are no such things as problems – only lessons to be learnt. The so-called problems of life are in essence opportunities and challenges to learn and to grow. Challenges must be overcome to make a success of life. Everyone should be called upon to accept the challenge.

Summary: What should be done?
• Break away from old, outdated leadership and ideas.
• Open up the systems by allowing new information to flow freely.
• Introduce people to the new paradigm and train them.
• Overcome the resistance towards change and new Paradigms and new leadership DNA.

- Co-ordinate and integrate seemingly opposing or new ideas and recommendations.
- Stimulate higher values and integrative thinking.
- Invest time, money and the self in development and self-mastery.
- Improve access to and the flow of information.
- Protect nature.
- Reward creative and innovative thinkers.
- Develop the entrepreneur.
- Stimulate and improve mindful management leadership.
- Develop self-management and self-development.
- Stimulate vision.
- Integrate all resources - human, natural, information, financial and technology.
- Develop a new spirit of responsibility, growth and development.
- Develop understanding of the power and effects of thought.
- Challenge people to live in abundance.
- Accept the challenge.

Notes

CHAPTER 15

LEADERSHIP AND MANAGEMENT

Differences between leadership and management

History has taught us that leaders in power positions can have a positive or negative influence on evolving processes of human development and the path of the human race. It has become necessary to identify and develop positive leaders in power positions to secure a safe transition to the next level. This cannot be left to chance. There is a difference between leadership and management.

A true leader is someone who can show the way by walking the path in advance. They can guide, escort and direct. These are the people who can give direction when change occurs – they know the way, go the way and show the way. They are mature people who have developed all the power tools and skills and are prepared to accept the challenge and responsibility of giving guidance and direction.

Leadership is activated when people, group, organisation or team need to find answers to questions of the time and move from one level to another. Leadership refers to a person's ability to give direction and build momentum for the thoughts, visions and actions of others. A leader is an individual or a corporate body who can trigger energy, stimulate innovation and a new dynamics, create vision. They can direct action and movement towards a new and higher goal and meaningful purpose. Others will follow. This process follows the same path as we have discussed in the previous chapter. Some individuals, groups or organizations will move forward and some will stay behind.

True leaders become significant when there is a need for direction. They have a life history of being prepared for the task. They can really say: 'I know. I show and I go the way.' They can say 'I've been there.' These are persons not only in contact with themselves but also with other people and their personal purpose and function. They have consciously or unconsciously connected to their higher power or with God. Here they find the inspiration and direction to lead with confidence.

The need for inspirational leaders

With the newest technology and the identification of the 'guide spot', we will now be able to consciously train more leaders for the future. Management refers to the ability or manner of controlling, supervising or handling something. A manager is a person who is in charge or current processes. Leadership takes place within open structures and systems and aims at discovering new ways of thinking and new direction. Management takes place within these set directions or structures and gives substance to the outcome of the process. Leadership, movement, change and action are all integrated. There is a need to develop more people who can accept responsibility for direction, action and vision. Part of the process is the effective management of change, action, processes and progress.

Managing the negative consequences of change

It is important to understand and manage the negative consequences of change. Negativity uses a lot of energy and if not managed properly can influence people, relationships, families, businesses, organisations and even a country as a whole. We need to have clarity concerning the damage these negative consequences can cause in order to effectively manage the transformational process.

Negative consequences of change include:

- **The zero-effect of change is experienced negatively**

A paradigm shift always results in a zero-effect. This means old ideas, achievements and values are not necessarily valid in the new paradigm. The zero-effect can have negative consequences for many people, because of their inability to cope with it. Think of a person who makes a career change and has to find his feet from scratch. Think of the arrival of an unplanned baby and a new household routine. Another example is the paradigm shift involved in the demilitarisation of the police force. Years ago a person could enroll in the police force with the objective of becoming colonel or general. When he eventually reaches this level, the paradigm shifts and rankings disappear. It can be extremely demotivating.

People become negative and unproductive and stagnate in the system or leave it. If the paradigm shifts, achievements of the past are of no consequence. People, who in the past, assessed or measured their personal value in terms of successes, can struggle. The general, professor, doctor, minister or pastor who have been successful in the past, can be embarrassed by the zero-effect of the new paradigm. Think of a medical practitioner who builds a large practice around his specialty and who accepts that it will last forever, but who does not keep himself informed of new development in medical technology. He loses patients as the news spreads that he makes use of outdated methods. One moment a person is very successful, the next moment they become unknown because of the zero-effect.

In reality a very successful past can limit one's perception of the future, and can block the willingness to explore and develop new horizons. These people are the ones who say: "Just as I thought I knew all the answers, somebody changed the questions." A person's identity, their ability, skills and positions are determined by the paradigm in which they function. When change takes place, the zero-effect has the result of this person losing a certain understanding and insight and identification of the self.

There are various examples related to the changes in government or police services where the white male reigned for a long time. People of other races and women served in subordinate positions. Because of the paradigm shift and the subsequent affirmative action and highlighting of women's rights the white male experienced the zero-effect of paradigm shifts. In many cases it results in an identity crisis. It requires new insights and new developments to solve this problem and utilize the problem's potential.

- **People stagnate in a survival mode**

People have to climb the ladder of life all over again. Some cannot accept the challenge. Instead of exploring the new situation and developing the self, people lose courage. Stress symptoms develop and individuals use their poor circumstances or bad health as excuses not to accept responsibility. They can apply to be declared medically unfit or for early retirement. In this way their skills are forever lost to society.

Many people stagnate in a survival mode that to them seems to be the best alternative. The actual problem is the fact that people are lazy. They are too lazy to think, reason or do something new. They prefer to survive in an outdated system because they are merely too lazy, comfortable or afraid to develop another system. Responsibilities are left to others or even to God. They believe everything is OK and follow an ostrich technique or implement fighting, sulking, praying, or fasting and think life will become better. This, however, is not true.

After fighting, ignoring, praying, thinking and talking, something has to be done. Nothing happens until you do something. Doing something new is the trigger that a new stage has begun. People stagnate in their old situations because they are too afraid or lazy to do something new. They think and believe someone in a higher position will accept responsibility for them. They create their own pain by not accepting responsibility for themselves, their development and their quality of life.

- **Uncertainty and chaos are viewed as destructive.**

People suddenly find themselves in a position unknown and even inaccessible to them before. Because of a shortage of knowledge and skills, they experience problems adapting to and coping with the demands of the new paradigm. For example the person who gets a job they are not qualified for as a result of affirmative action. How well meant the affirmative action principles may be, it results in anxiety, uncertainty, and chaos and unproductivity of an individual. Many people experience this chaos as negative. They do not understand that chaos is a normal part of the growing process.

Change can make people feel cheated. They experience discomfort, pain and loss. Most people experience pain as being negative. Pain, however, is a motivation for action - something needs to be done. Some people are unable to change uncomfortable and negative feelings into growth and development. They feel threatened by the unknown and try everything to stop renewal. People who have to adapt to divorce, the death of a loved one, career change, retirement and other forms of disintegration, feel that they must avoid the unknown, chaos, pain and uncertainty at all costs, and in various ways try to counteract the change. Resistance, alcohol, drug and medication abuse, gambling and the search for fun and pleasure, strikes, conflict and protest against change, withdrawal or emigration, are all examples of escape.

- **An inability or unwillingness to learn**

People resist change, because they are not willing to become students of life. A personal inability exists to prevent people from opening up or being accessible to new experiences. They are either afraid, too lazy to think, or merely do not have the inner strength or value and belief system to make these shifts.

- **Ego or identity problems**

People who link their ego and identity to the old paradigm and the position and status it held for them, experience an identity crisis and feel as if their whole being is threatened by change and renewal. Ego or identity problems result in people resisting change and a paradigm paralysis can occur. People can be immobilised while they still could have made a significant contribution. Rigid, arrogant people consider themselves strong if they do not change. They are also scared that others will consider them weaklings and as losing the competition or struggle should they surrender. They persist in discarding new ideas and try to prove their strength – sometimes against their better knowledge by resisting. It means they limit their own growth through a rigid ego and a false sense of identity.

- **Rivalry, competition, jealousy and envy**

267

People feel threatened in an atmosphere of competition, rivalry and power play and try to defend themselves, their boundaries, philosophies and paradigms. Each one builds his/her own ivory tower and the system becomes closed and exclusive. Only those who do not seriously threaten the status quo are listened to. People who are continuously in competition with others and who need to prove themselves do not easily accept new ideas from others. New ideas and a new paradigm are experienced as a threat. It does not matter how good the proposals, ideas and solutions are for the problems of the time, they are ignored or rejected. As a matter of fact, the better the new idea is, the bigger the resistance of the status quo. These people cannot apologise, ask forgiveness from others or compliment other people. They would rather gossip about or discredit and insult others. They depersonalise their opposition.

- **Conflict**

Conflicting ideas, thoughts and paradigms lead to conflict that is manifested in various ways, like an increase in crime, violence, murder and suicide and stress-related illnesses and the abuse of women and children. There is an increase in alcohol and drug abuse and drug lords especially, exploit the youth. Relationships become strained and impaired. The situation further deteriorates since people cannot find meaningful solutions to their relationships and problems. The chaos and uncertainty of change threaten people and negativity and conflict become rampant.

- **Laziness and complacency**

People are sometimes merely too lazy, arrogant or complacent to make the efforts to grow with the time and to change. Complacent, self-righteous, lazy people believe that things are normal and should be kept that way because they are used to it. This occurs in people who are comfortable with the old paradigm, because it used to work in the past. Arrogant self-righteousness occurs in people who believe they know everything and cannot be taught anything. They are of the opinion that things are wrong, happening too fast and must be postponed or stopped. An arrogant person normally does not have a creative vision of the future, and lives within unquestionable boundaries. They are content with what is, without wondering about what could have been. Edward de Bono (1992) describes it as: "If your horizons are limited and you lack any vision of what can be, you become complacent in what is."

- **Disintegration, unproductiveness and uncertainty**

Traditional thinkers believe that all new ideas that could contain uncertainty and chaos, should be ignored, banished, or rejected. They believe the traditional paradigm can be kept in place by excluding novelty and its advocates from the system. Success is measured by the way the status quo is kept in place. Change and the new era are not easily accepted.

The reality is that if new information, suggestions and ideas are not allowed to flow freely through the system, it stagnates, becomes outworn, worthless and eventually disintegrates. It is one of the main reasons for the disintegration of marriages, relationships between parents and children, political parties, companies, academic and religious institutions and governments. Personal, group and organisational productivity also fall victim.

One of the main problems we encounter is the high level of unemployment and the low productivity in the current labor market. This is the result of this deep underlying problem.

- **Uncertainty regarding leadership and management**

Another negative consequence of a paradigm shift is that people become uncertain of their leaders. New leaders appear and are a threat to old leaders. Old leaders become aware of their inability and insufficiency to fulfill the new requirements. A power struggle can develop and old leaders who are not prepared to change or waive their positions will fight the new paradigm and the leaders thereof, to the best of their ability. Leaders of the old paradigm are eventually replaced by the new thinkers and leaders. People in general become uncertain of who would be suitable to guide them to the next phase.

Most people expect a leader or manager to always be there to guide and lead them. Should it not be the case, uncertainty and a loss of direction occurs. An example is a political change in a country. The leading party disintegrates and there is a search for new leaders and new parties with new vision and solutions for the problems of the country. People start searching for new direction and new leaders emerge. All are influenced by this change.

People realise that traditional leadership and management styles, methods and training no longer work. What used to be the alpha and omega in leadership and management training now becomes the initiator of chaos and disintegration. Degrees, diplomas and training in traditional, old-paradigm leadership and management now become an obstacle to progress. Academics at universities and colleges, who did not grow in their personal development training, self-management and leadership skills, experience themselves and their philosophies as part of the problem and not part of the solution.

Traditional leadership and management decline and in some cases completely disintegrate. A need for something new starts developing. This starts from the outside of traditional structures and moves to the inner core. This means that traditional academic training could only implement new leadership and management training long after it has already been implemented by creative organisations.

- **Lack of vision**

People not only become negative, demotivated and unproductive, but life loses its direction and leaves them without any vision. A big problem in a country is the lack of a common vision, direction, and purpose. Without a common vision, people lack the synergy or 'together energy' that will take them forward.

The negative consequences of a paradigm shift must be managed and turned around into something positive should an individual, in specific and organisations, companies or a country in general, want to successfully move to the next level of human existence.

Summary of the negative consequences of the paradigm shift

- Successes of the past are no guarantee for the future
- People can experience an identity crisis
- The paradigm shift results in a zero-effect
- People stagnate in a survival mode
- Paradigms, theories, philosophies and structures are seen as the only perception of what is right. Leaders then serve the paradigm and not the progress of the people.
- People, their well-being and progress are of less importance
- People are afraid of the future

- There is uncertainty of who the actual leaders are
- Old paradigm leadership and management methods no longer work
- Rigid, arrogant people perceive themselves as strong and resist change
- People become demotivated and unproductive
- A limited vision of the future prevails

Positive consequences of change

The positive consequences of change and transformation include:

- **The challenge of the zero-position**

Individuals who used to be teachers and skilled persons in the old situation, find that they become students, followers, and uninformed and unskilled people in the zero-position.

Think of the capable housewife and chef who has to learn to prepare food in a microwave oven from scratch, or a person who is not computer literate and has to go on a computer course with children (most probably primary school pupils). Such situations could be experienced as humiliating, or as a wonderful opportunity. Past conflicts can be solved if people are willing to be humble and sincere. It requires tremendous adaptation.

Should an individual bridge all the negative aspects and humbly develop an open and learning spirit, he could succeed in correctly managing the situation. Such an attitude leads to a great extent of growth and maturity.

Since the new paradigm has new demands, past successes no longer count. Growth-orientated people face life with the philosophy that there must be constant renewal and they understand that everything becomes outdated and we need to move on. They don't rely on past achievements for success. They realise that these successes and highlights only apply to a specific period and then we need to move on. They travel light through life and leave unnecessary baggage, relationships, successes, achievements and failures behind. They know this can prevent future growth.

- ## A growth orientation and learning culture develops

The new paradigm results in new challenges and opportunities for discovery. People who are growth- and development orientated, grasp all these opportunities. Life becomes a training school and expedition. These people know they cannot grow without learning. They are students of life and are open and accessible to new learning situations.

The new paradigm stimulates everybody to accept responsibility for the quality of their own lives. A willingness to work for and contribute to success for all develops. The level of work ethics and productivity increases. Because everybody accepts responsibility their own identity is strengthened. People become conscious of who they are and the new awareness places all on a new path of success. Chaos and pain no longer result in disintegration of the self. The self is continuously evaluated in terms of true self-consciousness, the overcoming of problems and the subsequent growth. Self-image and self-confidence improve. The new paradigm provides an opportunity for all to develop their unique potential. Negative competition is cancelled out and nobody's identity is therefore threatened.

- ## Success has a new definition and meaning

Success is now defined by who we are becoming over what we are acquiring. The igniting and utilizing of every person's unique potential now become the ground for success. Acquiring physical possessions and positions are seen as ego-driven, lower order values. Although people have enough of everything at a high level of quality, the importance of physical possessions and positions make makes way for a value system of success and prosperity for all.

- ## People and progress are served

Change which does not serve the interests and well-being or progress of mankind and nature, in reality is no progress. Growth-orientated people will make shifts if it is in humanity's interest and involves the releasing of potential - even if it means a surrendering of their views.

- ## Chaos is accepted as a normal part of life

People who perceive pain and chaos as uncomfortable and less gratifying, but a normal part of life, more readily search for opportunities for growth and development. One of the biggest challenges is to teach people that although chaos, uncertainty or pain are experienced as negative, it cannot always be avoided on the path of growth and development. Chaos and pain can be transformed into development and growth.

In the new paradigm, the open and flexible individual is seen as a strong person. The rigid, inflexible person, who wants to prove a viewpoint with power, strength, manipulation, domination and aggression, is perceived as weak. Think of the construction of a bridge. Should a bridge be built inflexibly, it will crack and weaken with the first change in temperature and circumstances. Provision is made for the change, by building the bridge in such a way that it is flexible and able to react to external situations. Flexibility increases the strength and life span of the bridge. A person functions in the same way.

- **Synergy and motivation increase**

The new paradigm thinker understands that synergy or "together-energy" has better results than negative competition. Instead of defending their own paradigm with competition and resistance, the new paradigm thinker supports people who are already moving in the same direction, and in doing so, strengthens their influence.

Negative competition and wasting time and energy are avoided. The new paradigm results in everybody accepting responsibility for the self, the team and the organisation and therefore share responsibility for leadership and management. It has far-reaching consequences for the identification and development of leaders, and leadership- and management styles that will be discussed later.

- **People focus on the future**

The growth-oriented person believes in the future. The pain, sorrow, disappointment and achievements of the past are forgiven, forgotten and left behind, and within the new paradigm everyone takes part with responsibility, enthusiasm and persistence and builds the future.

In Nietzsche's words : '*I am chiefly interested in the future because I am going to spend the rest of my life there.*'

- **Vision**

An open, impartial person purposefully works towards a clear vision of where he/she is going. The breakthrough of a new vision leads to the birth of a new life. Where the old paradigm used to be closed, with no future perspective or vision, hope, enthusiasm, and new expectations are created in the new paradigm.

Summary of the positive influences of the paradigm shift

- The zero-effect results in humbleness, honesty and sincerity.
- The achievements of the past are no longer counted on.
- A growth- and learning orientated culture develops.
- Chaos and pain are experienced as a normal part of life.
- The progress and prosperity of people and the world are served.
- New leadership styles develop.
- Work ethics and productivity increase.
- Strength and mobility develop.
- Self-responsibility, identity and self-image improve.
- Synergy and motivation increase.
- Future orientation develops.
- A new spirit develops - a new togetherness - a new Ubuntu.
- There is new purpose and meaning to life.

Managing resistance to change

Most people experience a natural resistance to change. Why the resistance? The answer to this question can be found in the nature of paradigms. As mentioned earlier, a paradigm is a reference framework with certain rules, values and ways of thinking, that sifts and filters data. Paradigms establish boundaries and successful methods are identified to solve problems within a specific context. Information in agreement with an already known paradigm, could be easily identified and accepted, whilst unknown and unexpected information and ideas challenge and threaten the existing boundaries and the status quo. New information (or the new paradigm) results in anxiety and uncertainty and disturbs the status quo. Various reactions are identified. Initial aggression and denial of new information could manifest in various ways, for example to humiliate, mock, attack, deny or ignore the person in possession of the new information. This reaction arises from an individual's first experience of a threat to their comfort zone.

Resistance could indicate that an individual is uncomfortable with new information. Various reactions are possible. It could be denied or eliminated, or the person could indiscriminately submit to change, or an attempt could be made to thoroughly analyse, evaluate and think through the new information, and come to a realistic decision. One of the most important aspects of change is that it represents a process. People move through the various stages in their own time with their own ability, aptness, and vision - some faster, and some more slowly. Should these processes be understood, change can easily be managed and guided. It is when ignorance exists and the various stages are not interpreted or managed correctly, that negativity and problems are perceived as insurmountable.

Various mechanisms could also be implemented to keep the new paradigm away. As the new knowledge becomes available, an individual could become more aggressive, more insulting, denigrating and denying. Various examples could be found in everyday life. Imagine the father who cannot accept that his child thinks differently, or an employer who cannot accept that the employees can make a positive contribution. A leader cannot accept that the citizens do not accept his dictatorship and intimidation any more. A violent repression of the protests of the people usually follows – as we have found in Libya. Leaders could intimidate people physically or emotionally blackmail them with remarks like "you will go heaven if you vote for". Sometimes people could be threatened with revenge or they could be totally rejected.

Think of the students or workers who suggest a completely new paradigm for the solution to academic or business problems. The new ideas could be changed to suit the old ways of thinking, or individuals who feel threatened could disapprove of or ignore the suggestion. This usually is the first sign of total disintegration. Maintaining the old paradigm becomes a priority and more of the same is done with greater conviction. This results in more chaos and disintegration, and change becomes inevitable.

A known case is that of the two young Swiss watch designers who approached the Swiss Watch Association with a new and strange alien watch design. The association was of the opinion that their existing world quality products could not be improved on and the new design was not patented. A few weeks later the designers displayed their invention at a watch exhibition. The manufacturers of Seiko and Texas Instruments noted the potential of the design and the quartz watch was born. Seiko, a Japanese manufacturer, started to control the market. Within a year the watch industry in Switzerland crumbled and tens of thousands of people were unemployed. The restoration process took approximately ten years.

The more innovative and creative the new paradigm, the further away the new information would be from the old traditional paradigm and the less visible and understandable the new

information would be. Individuals, academics, politicians, religious or community leaders will fail in the anticipation, interpretation and integration of new, meaningful information. Such people are bound by tradition rather than a desire to assist humanity.

Strong beliefs and traditions blind a person towards new and creative solutions. Paradigm blindness develops. People then have an inability to bring about change when active action and creative actions become necessary. Paradigm blindness and paralysis are the main reasons for resistance to change. Although a paradigm shift cannot be prevented, the negative results must be identified and managed in order for transformation to be productive and successful.

People not only resist change because they are blind to the new information, but also because the new information is perceived as not practical, or negative. Those who introduce and facilitate the new paradigm are perceived as impractical and difficult to understand. A yearning for the good old days when everything used to be under control – when there was discipline – develops. It looks as if the new paradigm only creates chaos and uncertainty, which is negative and should be avoided at all costs There is a lack of inner certainty. Personal certainty is determined by the circumstances surrounding the person – one lives from the outside to the inside.

Should the environment and circumstances be calm and under control, people feel safe. As soon as change occurs, they feel threatened and try to avoid the change at all costs. Those who react like this are normally intellectually and/or emotionally immature, short-sighted, complacent, arrogant or plainly too lazy to grow. They are especially not equipped to measure up to the demands of a constantly changing world.

The question is:

> *Why would people resist change and transformation?*

Reasons for resistance

Below is a list of reasons why people resist change and transformation.

- **Paradigm blindness**

It means most people cannot see the new paradigm, since its contents cannot be integrated within their existing framework.

- **Inability to learn**

Every new situation results in new opportunities and new experiences. Some people are unwilling, or do not have the ability to study. They will naturally resist any change.

- **Fear that something might be lost**

People with this fear believe that certain rules, ideas and viewpoints will last forever and that their losses will be immeasurable should it change. The fear is created that the good old days, when everything used to work, will be lost in the new paradigm. This tendency is experienced over the full spectrum of humanity, for example the manager who clings to old management styles, parents who desperately cling to old education methods, or religious people who cling to old rituals, methods and applications.

- **Ego and identity problems**

The ego refers to the outside concrete reality and self as reference point. A person's own importance, achievements, qualities, prosperity, identity and ego have always to be protected. These concepts relate to a person's perception of him/herself. It includes the feeling that there is correlation between the person's perception of himself and the perception of other people. There-fore there is continuity in life. When development of the ego and identity takes place in harmony, the inner core is in harmony with characteristics such as reliability, honesty, success; hope, willpower, love and caring develop. These people are flexible and open to change. When development of the ego- and identity however are unsuccessful, a person becomes rigid, the ego is threatened and they find it difficult to change within the self. Adaptation becomes difficult, ego- and identity problems are created and change becomes a threat. Change and ideas outside of the self will obviously lead to a lot of resistance.

- **Stagnation in the comfort zone**

Within their own personal comfort zones people is exactly what it says – comfortable. They are normally arrogant, complacent or lazy and do not allow the disturbance or discomfort through change. These persons are like babies who cry at the least discomfort. As soon as they experience discomfort they protest in some or other way. The methods are less obvious than crying but the principle is that the discomfort be relieved. Adult persons can manage discomfort, and when necessary, can leave their comfort zones.

- **Lack of vision**

Vision is the ability to see in the unseen, an insight and under-standing of where you want to go. A person in a comfort zone also has a lack of vision and will resist all change. The questions are:

> *How does a competent leader manage*
> *resistance?*

A wise leader understands the stages of change and the general reactions people go through when confronted with something new.

Managing reactions to change

To eventually arrive at the new identified destination, the reactions of an individual must first be identified and managed. Should these personal reactions to change be ignored, the process could lapse into destructive anxiety, uncertainty, aggression and destructive chaos.

- **Shock and aggression**

An individual's first reaction when confronted with brand new information, ideas and values, is shock and aggression. The shock indicates that the individual's boundaries are tested and questioned. We experience shock because of the rapid increase in new information and the subsequent inability to keep track. The modern person suffers from information shock. The existing framework of knowledge, values and coping mechanisms are threatened and the information shock worsens. Aggression and or denial are the easiest ways to defend this sensitive inner core and reference framework and is an attempt to keep the new information out and maintain the status quo.

- **Denial and aggression**

Denial can be implemented with aggression. Negativity and blame form part of denial and the inability to integrate new with existing knowledge. People actively attempt to keep new knowledge out of the system by not allowing somebody an opportunity to speak, or by ignoring them. People in a position of power, who are threatened, easily belittle and depersonalise the new paradigm thinker. Insults, criticism and gossip are the order of the day.

- **Uncertainty**

Should new knowledge, values and insight persist, one of two things can happen. An individual can persist with rigid ways of thinking, avoidance, aggression or denial. Such a person could spend a lifetime in bitterness, denial and a search for the good old days. Nothing new and productive however, is implemented. More of the same is being done with more devotion, commitment and persistence. Re-organisation takes place, but the parts are merely shoved around within the same reference framework and it does not work. More determined attempts and harder work are attempted, but no progress is made.

A situation that used to be very simple is now filled with questions and uncertainty. This is where the choice must be made between returning to the comfort zone of the familiar, or persistence in the search for new answers, information and insights. Many people are afraid of this search and uncertainty and return to the known. They prefer the pain and discomfort of a familiar situation over the uncertainty of the unknown. Uncertainty can only be overcome with courage, belief and inner conviction, and in so doing, the old paradigm is discarded.

- **Letting go**

Should a person realise the futility of the struggle to maintain the old, a stage develops where there is a disconnection and the old is discarded. Old, outdated values, thoughts, people and actions are identified and replaced with new ones. The inner core and guide of life is rewritten and the new skills and equipment for life are added. An inner cleansing process takes place. All the outdated and subconscious experiences, patterns, ideas and rules are brought to the foreground and are consciously evaluated to be maintained or eliminated. It could be a very painful phase.

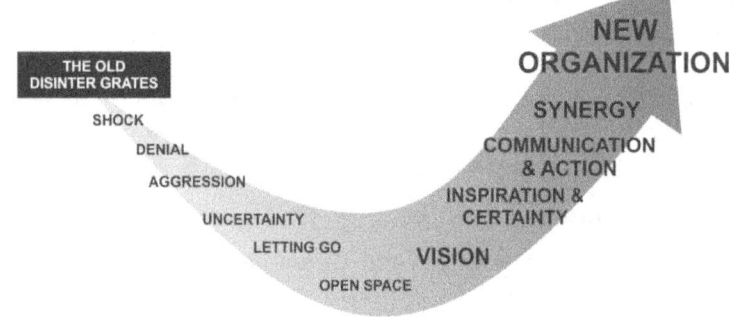

Managing people's reactions

People, who experience pain as being negative, make very slow progress or no progress at all during this stage. Should a person be willing to go through the painful pruning process, pain is converted into a growing pain. An opportunity for something new arises. A new life is waiting to be discovered.

- **Open space and inner peace**

Although the old has been disconnected and discarded, the new is not always obvious. The chaos could result in people longing for what used to be good and even return to the old paradigm. This is where room must be made for uncertainty: An open space where the old is finally disconnected, but at the same time an opportunity is created for development of the new. People, who believe that change in life must occur with immediate clarity and order, find this open space of uncertainty and silence very difficult to cope with. Once again the danger of returning to the old, well-known comfort zone exists. The management of this open space and silence is crucial and people must be equipped to positively manage the uncertainty and discomfort with patience. This is where the choice is made to finally cross the Rubicon.

- **Creativity and vision**

At this stage new solutions are searched for. Creative ideas and a new vision become clearer. Time, money and energy are invested in the discovery and development of new ideas and values. A new energy field is created by new visions, thinking, values, contact, communication and information. A better understanding of this new energy field of life increases and momentum starts to build up.

- **Communication and synergy**

Synergy as the integration of energy or "together-energy" replaces initial resistance. A critical mass or momentum is reached and a breakthrough takes place where the old boundaries are left behind. A kind of new communication develops even a new terminology, language and culture. It could happen that friends from the past have been outgrown and that communication has ceased.

New points of contact, new people and new situations are investigated. People who speak the same language look out for each other. Not only do they share the same interests, language and vision, they join forces to realise their vision. The invisible vision becomes visible. People take part and a new field is created and concretised. The spoken word becomes reality and a new structure is created.

The new phase and organisation

The new organisation has new boundaries, values and rules. To constructively contribute, people must be trained and equipped for the new situation. Learning and development are characteristic of the growth of the new. Just like birth, the creation of the new organization is sometimes very painful. It is however necessary to understand and manage the negative consequences in order not to do injustice to the growth and development. This new organisation will grow and reach its peak, and then the process will repeat itself. This will pose a new challenge to leadership and management.

Notes

CHAPTER 16

LEADERS AND THEIR SUPPORT SYSTEMS

Leaders and the people who surround them

Leaders are known by the people who surround them. A leader is only as strong as the people who follow – without a group of followers nothing can be achieved. Leaders also know the people who follow their lead. The quality of interaction and kind of dynamics between leaders and followers will in the end determine the outcome of the change and processes envisaged. There are only one of two options – positive or negative outcomes. In order to lead and manage people, leaders have to first sharpen their people skills.

With the right knowledge and skills leaders can transform every negative situation or stumbling block into a stepping stone. Understanding negative issues can contribute to positive interpretation and acceptance as part of the path of life. We have the challenge to turn energy breakers into energy makers.

Understanding energy breakers

- ### Negative attitudes

By nature life has much negativity. Negative factors have to be managed and transformed into positive, creative and stimulating solutions and opportunities. Negativities result in an emotional shut down or draining of energy. As already described in Part one, the brain switches off when an overload of negativity occurs. This kind of negativity cannot be converted into positive opportunities and solutions, because the insight, understanding and energy basically do not exist. Negativities like fighting, moaning, complaining, sulking, verbal attacks and such, result in a deadening of the senses. Positive energy and creative solutions cannot be released. People become a victim of their own circumstances and this can manifest as a physical ailment or illness.

- ### Physical illnesses

Many of our physical illnesses are psychosomatic symptoms. The mind, and how we think and believe, influences or gets encoded into the physical body, just like the external environment gets encoded into annual rings of a tree trunk. Biography becomes biology. The body follows the way the mind operates. As the mind is programmed so we biologically become programmed. This means that the negativities, strains and stresses of life wear the physical body down and one can become sick.

In his book, *Ageless Body, Timeless Mind*, Deepak Chopra explores the body-mind-relation and gives guidelines how to live a healthy life. The book *Why People Don't Heal And How They Can* by Caroline Myss, has become a global best seller in this regard.

Healthy living starts with a healthy lifestyle in body, mind and spirit. We need to keep our life and energy levels in balance or we become sick, passive, unproductive, tired and bored. This is the illness called entropy.

- ### Entropy

A person with entropy is someone whose attitude and actions towards the self, fellow human beings and the world as a whole, are energy draining. These people are energy thieves, because they take productive, uplifting energy from the system, but do not make a productive contribution. Examples are people who are often negative and embittered. They moan, gossip, create problems, but do not provide solutions. They are found in all contexts of life: In families, marriages, businesses, in communities, at work, in meetings, in politics, church, sport and other contexts. This means that should personal beliefs, behavioral patterns and social structures become rigid and remain closed to new information and energy, the person, or community cannot adapt to the changing situation. The creative process of evolutionary change or evolvement cannot take place and eventually stagnation, degeneration and disintegration will prevail.

The biggest problem people face today is the danger of negativity, boredom, stagnation and entropy. The increase in unemployment, psychosomatic illnesses, riots, conflict, drug- and alcohol addiction, war and crime are all signs of disintegration. Negativity, a lack of purpose, productivity, vision and constant fatigue are all part of entropy. Entropy, just like negativity, has become one of the power games of our time.

- **Negative power games**

People who have discovered their unique value, vision and purpose are excited about life. They can generate a lot of energy, stimulate action and function in a mature self-sufficient way. This makes us feel good, happy, successful and full of life. There are, however, persons who have not discovered this ability. They desperately need to obtain energy from others in order to feel good. These people need to feel they have power and are in control. This is how power games arise.

Power games can be manifest in two ways: as active or passive power games. James Redfield describes this in his book *The Celestine Prophecy* as control dramas. Active power games include intimidation and manipulation in every possible way. From physical and verbal assault to more sophisticated manipulation and intimidation as with fear, guilt and blame. Passive power games include the silent treatment, poor me looking for pity and attention, or the victim. A person can move from one power game to another in order to obtain enough attention and energy to feel good. Potential is ignored and opportunities are missed on the path of life while people use and abuse their own energy and that of others. Most people are caught up in one or many power games. The awakening needs to include our awareness of subconsciously participating in needless power games, stop and change the process and utilise all potential in positive creative ways.

- ## Co-dependence

Although people playing power games at a conscious or subconscious level do not experience the health, wealth and happiness they desire, very few have the inner power and courage to challenge the system and break loose. This means people find themselves caught up in co-dependent relationships. One person can be an active manipulator by blaming or putting the other person down. The other person can revert to the poor me or victim situation or become aloof in search of positive input. The real underlying insecurity and search for love, power and security is never identified and people can spend their whole life living this way. We need to break free from co-dependent destructive relationships and power games in order to discover our true potential and inner power, love and wisdom.

- ## Excusitis and blamitis

The word "excusitis" may sound strange. It is the illness of the excuse and normally develops when a problem has to be solved or responsibility has to be accepted for a task. Involvement, participation and inputs are needed. People, who normally do not want to do anything, play power games and make excuses to get out of the situation. Excuses normally sound nice, good and right, but are mostly unrealistic. The following excuses are familiar to all of us: "I can't do it, because I am too busy, too young, too old or too ill." Negative or unacceptable excuses, like: "I am too lazy, unorganized, too comfortable, you owe me, I don't want to work, I am undisciplined" are seldom heard. Excuses are usually camouflaged lies the person accepts as the truth, because it means he/she does not have to accept responsibility. A healthy, responsible person usually is someone who is already involved and contributes to life and who doesn't have to make unconvincing excuses.

Just like flu can develop into pneumonia if not treated, "excusitis" can develop into "blamitis" without treatment. Now someone can be blamed for the responsibility, task, assignment or problem. With blame or accusation there are usually two underlying objectives: (1) The person finds a reason not to do anything positive and (2) someone else is held responsible and loaded with feelings of guilt. Excuses and the blaming of other parties or institutions are general. Think of: "I am unhappy with the government not keeping its promises", or "Teachers can no longer discipline the students", or "My marital partner does not keep me happy", or "My employer does not treat me fairly", or "The church is not doing its work" etc. etc. It is particularly visible in comfortable, afraid, lazy, unhappy, bored and emotionally immature people.

These are those people who cannot or will not be productive. Power games, excuses and blame are used to soothe their feelings of guilt, and to make them feel better. The responsibility for thinking, of plans of action and solutions is left to others. All ages are vulnerable. Children say they are too young, the aged claim to be too old. It is usually people who are of the opinion that others or the world owe them something. The unavoidable result is that nothing positive, constructive or creative is being done. A general negativity and passivity reigns, problems are not solved and tasks are not completed.

The danger is that it is contagious! Blaming, accusations and excuses are conveyed within certain groups, households, families, churches, political parties, companies and communities. It could also be passed from one generation to another, which means that "excusitis" and "blamitis" are not only contagious, but also hereditary. Creative and positive thinking are smothered, positive growth and development are limited and stagnation, deadness or entropy takes over. These conditions are sicknesses of our time. In turn these sicknesses result in being unproductive.

- **Being unproductive**

One day a bee on a window sill used all his energy in an attempt to fly. Unfortunately one of the wings was missing and he could not get up and fly. The energy it used, only resulted in the bee spinning around, without any results. This was such a waste of life force energy. The bee eventually died of exhaustion. There is a big difference between the unproductive use of energy and the ability to do constructive, creative, effective and productive work. Similarly, most people are missing a wing. They run around in circles, going nowhere while wasting time and energy. There is a lack of constructive or productive inputs. In the end they can fall down and "die" of exhaustion.

Statistics have shown that 90 percent of humanity is: unproductive, unsuccessful, ineffective, unreliable, uninformed, without vision, lazy, comfortable, lazy to learn, going nowhere, passive and waiting to see what happens and under the impression that someone or life owes them something. It means that the responsibility for progress has to be carried by a mere ten percent of humanity. This is very hard work for a very small group of people.

"Work" can be defined as "physical or mental effort aimed at doing or making something"; it can also be defined as "the use of energy"; or as: "a physical or mental effort or activity directed towards the production or accomplishment of something".

From the above definitions it is clear that the ability do work includes more than the completion of a physical task. Work means the productive use of the total potential, abilities and powers of the holistic integrated person – body, mind and spirit. Productivity means that actions result in something new – a new product – a new, more effective innovative way of thinking and doing. This something new is the outcome of productive work or labor. It means that in each piece of productive work or labor, physical, mind and spiritual energy is invested. The outcome of the product is more than the separate parts.

- **Poverty**

We live in an abundant universe. We were created not only to manage the abundance, but to enjoy it and live happy prosperous lives. The word "poverty" refers to lack. This means an inner lack of productivity and an inability to create a prosperous life. If thoughts are things then poverty in its concrete form is the manifestation of the inner lack and inability of people to trigger and activate physical, mental and spiritual potential and stimulate creative energy, prosperity and progress. There are very few people who productively apply their life energy and accept responsibility to develop their full potential. Very few people can create abundance, meaning most people therefore live in poverty.

As a body, mind and spirit being we can and should make a positive, productive and creative contribution to the world as a whole. Health, wealth and happiness are the result or outcome of living and managing the path of life on purpose. Unfortunately most people have not found this path and have become slaves instead of creators of our world and life. This is because most people are paralysed by fear.

- **Fear**

Fear is caused by the expectation or anticipation of danger, pain, loss and disaster. Fear is a feeling of dread, anxiety, apprehension, disquiet, panic-consternation, trepidation and the like. A supposed or real threat triggers a specific pattern of thought and a fear reaction takes place. This activates a person to fight or flee. Feeling fear results as a physical reaction, causes a shutdown of systems in the brain and we can become mentally and even physically paralysed. The things we fear are mostly in our own minds.

Statistics have shown that 90% of all the things we fear and are afraid of never happen. The rest we can usually cope with and even find creative ways to learn from threatening situations. People with fearful ways of thinking project these thoughts onto the outside world and in fact attract these situations to themselves or find ways of proving they are right. This means they find danger and threats around every corner. This means we can overcome every potential threat just by the way we believe and think and then act appropriately. Fear remains one of the biggest stumbling blocks on the path of growth and development. A fear of failure, rejection, being ridiculed, attacked, made fun of or even just ignored are of some of the fears that can keep us from acting and doing something new and creative.

- **Passivity and Procrastination**

Passive people are usually lazy, locked into their comfort zones, complacent or paralysed by fear. The more they procrastinate and do nothing, the less really happens, the less they are motivated to do something. These persons lack an inner motivation and vision and take life and people for granted. Actions are the cutting edge between thought and physicality. Creative thoughts and visions become concrete and manifest in the physical word through our actions. If you do nothing, you get nothing.

The questions arise:

> *What do energy makers look like? How do we make a shift from being an energy, breaker or vampire, to independence?*

Turning energy breakers into energy makers

People within negative, destructive personal situations, groups, families or communities, usually demonstrate a loss of energy, openness, flexibility and a lack of solutions, creativity and productivity. The result is destruction, decay and poverty. In contrast, positive people, groups, families, communities, businesses and countries who are committed to developing their authentic self and unique potential, show high energy levels, creativity, variety and flexibility. They are progressive and therefore prosperous.

If disintegration and entropy and the related illnesses are processes, what should we do to prevent them? The answer can be found in the meaning of "life" and "energy".

- ### Producing energy and new life force

Energy means work, the ability to do something. The only way to stop entropy and the destructive process of power games and disintegration is for each person to produce energy and work towards the development of their full potential and unique gifts, talents and make a positive contribution. It means that only through positive, purposeful decisions, functional actions and creative attempts something positive and constructive can be produced, or created. If the farmer learns the lesson that without planting, he won't have a corn crop, he can change his attitude, expectations, disposition and inputs. The first step would be to realise that it takes productive work and positive inputs to ensure growth, development, productivity and progress.

Since entropy takes place by itself, it takes extra energy-inputs to initially counter the natural energy drainers. It then requires a further positive energy-input to direct the process in a positive, productive direction. A lazy, unmotivated, bitter, negative person, afraid of work, has little chance of being productive or successful – there just isn't enough energy. The less we do, the less energy is available, and the more easily deterioration takes place. Growth and development require energy and hard work. This work refers not only to physical actions, but also to the power of our thinking.

- **The power of silence**

As mentioned before, the physical world started off in an invisible world of ideas and thoughts. Few people take the time to

become quiet and determine what and how they think and do and ask where they are going. Thinking requires us to physically become still while stilling the heart and mind, in order to produce effective and productive solutions. These ideas are then converted into actions or productive work. It takes time and effort to let go of the beta levels and enter alpha levels of functioning. One grows in the direction you work hard for, and one has to work hard to grow in the direction of your choice or your vision. Each time we think, do and work anew and creatively, energy is released. This energy is life!

- **Joy and enjoyment**

We are called to act at all stages of our life. Nothing happens until we do something. Each of us is called to enjoy the life we've chosen and to find actions that fulfill our destiny. Destiny is what is happening to us today, not just what will happen to us in the future. We create our future and so our destiny by doing what we need to do today. We need to enjoy every action, every step on the path of life. Even if it is just watching a cloud, washing dishes, filing papers, or talking with a friend, it will make a difference. The future is created in the now. The more we learn to live to the fullest, overcome stumbling blocks and be grateful in the now, the more we can live on purpose and find peace, success and happiness.

No system however, can last forever. It means that nothing is permanent. Systems stagnate and disintegrate without positive growth and effective actions. Evolutionary change is actually forced upon us. Even to remain at the same place, we have to move ahead. Life is like an escalator that goes from top to bottom. We have to move upwards against entropy. In other words, we have to keep on moving to remain in the same place. If we want to move ahead nobody can afford to sit still or retire. The solution for negativity, poverty, fear, procrastination, wasting energy and entropy lies in the simple principle - think new and do new. In this process we can grow and develop.

- **Growth and development**

A person, family, social system, business or country must be permanently willing and busy at cleansing, healing, learning and growing to ensure growth, development, change, prosperity and happiness. We need to constantly apply available energy more effectively and productively and use less energy. It means that old methods should be stopped and weeds and thorns on the field of life must be removed. It is not possible to plant a field filled with weeds, thorns and thistles or paint a rusted house and expect success. If the house cannot be restored, it has to be leveled and a new one built. The same applies to a field. If the farmer finds that it will take too much energy, time, money and effort to clean the old field of distils and thorns, he can decide to rather plough a new field. Relationships and situations, in which the pain, hurt, disappointment and unhappiness of the past cannot be sorted out, cannot grow. Sometimes relationships or situations have disintegrated, crumbled and repair is difficult or impossible. They should then be ended so that the participants can move on.

This situation takes place in a natural way in marriages, families, households, communities, the church, politics, careers and other situations. We now know that it is an essential, although not less painful, part of growth, healing and repair. The keys to growth can be found in thinking, working and focusing of our time and energy. Work will lead to burn-out if not alternated with rest and play. What should we do? Working, learning, playing, resting and enjoying are simple keys to growth and a full life. Nothing, however, lasts forever.

The answer to this dilemma is included in a very important fact of life, namely – love. Work hard and learn to love. No person is too old or too young for it. Everyone should be empowered and have the opportunity to make an inspired contribution.

- **Empowerment**

The word "empowerment" means to provide with energy, power and strength. It includes creating opportunities, resources, equipment, knowledge, skills, support and methods for the optimal development of potential. It is not affirmative action. Affirmative action does not necessarily release potential and energy. It can even have the opposite effect. Placing people into situations they are not equipped to cope with can be counterproductive. Each person therefore has a responsibility to empower themselves and others. It is this energy and power that contributes to growth development and productivity. People need each other to contribute to the process of generating energy, growth and development.

- **Getting Connected**

Synergy means together energy. People were not created to be alone. Although we are challenged to be independent and responsible, we are not expected to do it alone. People are supposed to find at least one person in their life to discover together the "dance of life" in harmony. Herein lays a quiet inter-dependency. It is something one simply cannot find on one's own. It can only be discovered in togetherness – independent, responsible, mature, self-actualising but together. In synergy, doing together, learning together, being together, lies healing and wholeness. Herein lies the solution for the separateness of mankind.

- **Synergy**

Synergy means together-energy. Synergy is created in a group or team who think, visualise and act together. The visualisation, thinking, interaction, planning and activities of groups or teams result in the physical manifestation of ideas and visions.

- **Create a new field**

To ensure productive growth and development, it is necessary to remove all stumbling blocks on the path of progress. First we need to make an assessment. Negative destructive processes must be stopped on purpose. Unproductive patterns should be replaced with a new process of thinking, working, learning, playing, growth and development. Very few people accept the challenge of seeing the truth of situations. The truth of deterioration, failure, wounds and negativity can be painful. People can even avoid this cleansing process, because it could be accompanied by pain, loss and a feeling of failure.

Some people fear doing away with the old and familiar, although negative, patterns. It can be a comfort zone and they feel safer to continue within a negative situation than to enter the unknown of a new situation. A good example is that of the person who walks down the road with a nail in his shoe. If the discomfort and pain can be avoided and endured long enough, one can get used to it. The advance, however, is very slow. A dilemma arises when a simple question is asked, such as: "Why don't you remove the nail from your shoe and run the Comrades?" It is the awareness of the long repressed pain and discomfort and the responsibility to do something new and different, that makes people shy away, and to fear and deny reality. There is only one of two choices. The person either prefers walking their paths of life with the nail in the shoe, or they decide to stop, remove all nails, allow the pain to pass, wounds to heal and then attempt the path of life with new motivation and strength.

No growth can take place without the healing of old wounds. But where do we start healing, change, growth and productivity? The answer lies in the person. A person needs to commit to go through processes of healing and learning.

Learning

People are the most adaptable and adjustable beings on earth. They have the ability to effectively manage the challenges of their own human nature and to meet the demands of life. In doing so, we adapt. Each adjustment to a situation means that a person has found an acceptable answer for a specific life problem. By managing and coping with situations and demands we bring about internal and external changes. This means we are continually adapting and adjusting in a certain direction and will hopefully be able to manage life more effectively. It means that a person cannot change and adapt without solving problems and questions and discovering new answers and learning methods. No person can grow and develop without any challenges to face or problems to solve. You cannot grow in a space of 'nothingness'. How difficult it may sound – many people need difficult circumstances in order to learn. The ego is a hard taskmaster while the soul is the revered teacher. We are the students and we are here to learn.

According to the law of entropy a person who does nothing, will in any case stagnate and deteriorate. People however, usually experience any change of direction as problematic. There are simply only two directions of change. If problems, questions, demands and crises are ignored and managed ineffectively, a void develops within the person. Qualities such as denial, procrastination, lies, fear, rigidity, ignorance or rejection develop and a person becomes increasingly ineffective in life. By constantly following this pattern, people eventually face a barrier in life. It is only when they get stuck that they are prepared to look at the negative patterns of thinking and coping. Sometimes the road back is very long and difficult. People can find themselves in a great deal of pain and distress. This could be prevented if negative patterns are identified and turned into consciously living a positive and full life.

Chaos vs. Synergy

The opposite is also true. Every time a person openly and honestly evaluates a problem, demand, responsibility and crisis in life, effective solutions can be found. The process of identifying and implementing answers, solutions and more effective coping strategies stimulates growth and development. Winners are people who are not scared to honestly evaluate and cope with what life throws their way, irrespective of the pain, disappointments, failures or misfortunes. In essence life is like a gymnasium. No person goes to the gym, picks up a crossbar with balloons and expects to become fit. You only become fit to the extend you can master weights, apparatus, cycle, and exercise. Every time we master the demands of life, we learn some-thing new and become fitter. An adult person is someone who is fit for life. It is usually somebody who already had the opportunity to exercise. Lazy or scared people cannot become fit for life. Similar to athletes, life's winners are not born, but made.

They are people who make healthy, productive choices and adaptations and are willing to learn and grow. In this we can find meaning in life.

- **Develop new knowledge and skills**

To effectively overcome stumbling blocks and adapt, people firstly have to gain knowledge regarding themselves and the world we live in. We need to know our own potential, needs, dreams, visions and the self. We also have to learn and understand the advantages, disadvantages and dangers, as well as the inherent laws and principles of our world and the universe. It is this willingness to learn that enables people to grow and overcome any obstacle. Apart from new insights and knowledge, people who develop effective skills are able to assert themselves and play a constructive role in society. The knowledge and skills represent the theory and practice on our path of life. The one cannot function without the other. As mentioned before, knowledge and skills won't only differ from community to community, but rapid change will result in knowledge and skills becoming more complex and will change from time to time. This means we are in a constant process of learning and developing new insights, knowledge and skills.

- **Communication and the evolving person**

Before we can manage our world in a meaningful way, we firstly need to get in touch with ourselves as unique persons. We refer to intra-personal contact, our subjective world where a person is in relation and communication with the self. How we think, feel, believe our motivation and driving forces, are but a few components we need to examine. It is through these inner perceptions of the own self, or inside world, that a person gets in touch with, sees and communicates with the outside world. We see the world then not as it is, but as we are. It is therefore necessary for us to change our own thoughts, feelings, beliefs, and motivation to overcome stumbling blocks in life. Change and adjustments then take place in the outside world. We always speak to ourselves first, before speaking to others.

A mature adult person, in a constant process of personal growth and development, keeps to the path of fulfilling their own potential and tries to live the true and honest self. This demands honest communication with the self.

Secondly, we are in communication with other people and things. Here we refer to interpersonal communication. A person learns to understand, accept and manage the differences in people. Thirdly, a person communicates within a certain context, for example within a career, marriage, family, politics, church and the world as a whole. Fourthly, people can be in contact and communication with their Creator, Higher Power or God.

It is in this invisible spiritual dimension, free from time and space, where solutions, guidance and answers to questions, problems and objectives for the concrete here and now can be found. This is metaphysical contact and communication that gives a higher dimension to meaning in life. How it is lived within various religious systems and patterns of beliefs remains a personal choice.

- **Meaning**

Meaning can be found in the growth and development of the contact points and communication spheres of life. Deeds without good relationships are empty, meaningless and lead to ill health. The healthy person living a meaningful life, not only manages life effectively, but has meaningful relationships with the self, with others, within different contexts, the world and their Creator. As a path it includes constant growth, development and discovery process. The adaptable person, therefore, is not only a person who is open and willing to learn, but also someone who can maintain good relationships on all levels and experience life as meaningful. Change includes change in relationships and a search for meaning. It starts within the relationship and communication with the self.

- **Understanding**

The word "understanding" – refers to "clarity and certainty". At one or other stage of our lives we need to have clarity and certainty about who we are, were we are going and why. We all have the ability to step out of the self and look back into the self. We can observe and evaluate our experiences, thinking, beliefs, feelings and actions. Through self reflection and self assessment we can evaluate the results and influences of our thoughts, beliefs, feelings and actions. We must remember that this self-reflective ability only exists in people. An elephant cannot evaluate its trunk or the ageing of its ears or the influence of the breaking down of trees on the environment. It is not necessary. For people as intelligent rulers of the planet this self- reflection and assessment form an important part of growth, development, adaptation and therefore, survival. Only to the extent we know ourselves, accept, understand, and make effort for the development and living of the inner potential, fulfill our purpose and enjoy life, can we love ourselves and other people like ourselves. Understanding and loving other people is the result of understanding and loving ourselves.

- **Love**

It was not possible within the reference framework of people, the church, society, business structures or political parties in the past see (Part 1) to value the life of a unique person. Rules, laws, paradigms and systems were of much more importance and it was believed that people were subordinate to 'the cause'. It is however, not possible to be honest and true to yourself, and to sacrifice yourself for the cause, before you have actually come into contact with the self. Naïve sacrifice without self-knowledge, self-insight and self-love is suicide.

Honesty with the self and the search for truth result in the discovery of the path of love for the self, others, our world and universe we live in. This discovery of love is the discovery of life itself. The old paradigm of self-sacrifice was rather a denial of and escapes from the self and the pain, discomfort and problems of reality. People preferred ignoring or repressing the true self, lived a lie and tried to be accepted and fit into a world of rules, laws and power. The outer image conformed 'comfortably' to the norm while this behaviour produced internal discomfort. White plastered tombs on the outside, but full of skeletons on the inside. This time is over and the time has arrived to open up all these graves, no matter how uncomfortable. It is in self-acceptance and the discovery of self-love that a person is freed to serve their fellow human beings and make a positive contribution to the world.

- **Higher consciousness – a new awareness**

Without self-evaluation we merely obey programs from the genes, or social codes and cultural heritage. Unfortunately, this will not ensure the future of the human race in the next century. A self- reflective consciousness allows us to write better programs and plans of action. We can now take responsible and mature decisions that not only influence the self, but also the group, the whole and the course of the future. With the right decisions and actions we can ensure a positive change and the transition to a higher level of functioning in the future. We unfortunately take our conscious reflective abilities for granted. A higher consciousness is taking place and more sensitivity is being created in many people. We need to wake up and discover new insights - a whole new vision!

- **Vision**

A new creative idea develops in the mind of an architect, for example. A building takes shape in the mind and ideas and manifests in the physical world. Thoughts become things. The invisible gives birth to the visible. The implications of this are that we can learn how to manifests the potential of the invisible world of thought in the visible physical world. Vision is the ability to see into the unseen. It is the understanding of potential and ideas. Each vision can potentially give birth to a new entity, structure, solution, order and life. It is in the invisible that transformation, growth and change take place. The invisible becomes visible in our tangible world. Without vision there is an emptiness, void and death. The new paradigm is a future vision-oriented paradigm.

Vision is a field of energy – a projected thought form. Each person's individual visions and ideas take shape in an unseen world. They gain momentum by reinforcing the thoughts and vision. It means an electro-magnetic field is created by our thoughts, words and communication. If it is united with other people's creative ideas, visions and discussions, synergy takes place. The new paradigm sees potential in the invisible. It is a living universe of unlimited potential just waiting to serve mankind. Here is contact, a new interaction, a new spirit and new life. Life must be seen as a living whole with everything connected to everything else. Each individual part, however small, fits somewhere and the sun shines on everyone. There is enough for everyone to live in abundance and prosperity.

We create our own reality by seeing into the unseen. We create our own reality according to our inner visions, dreams, thoughts and desires. A new vision of inner peace, health, wealth, happiness and prosperity for all is forming in the hearts and minds of many people. All over the world an awakening to new visions and higher dimensions is taking place.

- **The awakening**

An awakening to renewal, growth, love and the transition to higher dimensions is taking place within persons, groups, communities, organisations and some countries all over the world. More and more people, irrespective of age, gender, creed or color are hearing the call, an inner voice. The wakeup call can come softly or with a loud bang! We can hear the call and answer or we can continue to ignore that inner, hollow feeling of emptiness.

Many will choose to ignore it for a lifetime. Many are now prepared to answer the call, wake up and do something. This awakening to a new value system and the creative path of life, love, growth and development is increasing. It is primarily being experienced in America and Europe from which we can learn.

It means a total new view of life. A whole new era, a new value system, new terminology and even a whole new language has begun. It starts in the self. In essence it implies an awakening from a long "sleep". We can discover that we were living in a nightmare. This awakening will lead us to a new perception of the purpose of life. As we discover the truth we become free to live life abundantly.

- **Freedom**

Responsible people are free people. They are free in responsibility and not free from responsibility. These persons can let go of the past and progress to the future. They want to live life to its fullest. They are people who are switched on in themselves and live from the inside to the outside. They are not co-dependent and do not rely on unnatural support systems. If there is need, the support systems are activated, and as soon as the need has passed, they withdraw to live an independent and interdependent life once again. They support others when necessary and then withdraw to give the person space and an opportunity to live independently and to grow.

There is a healthy balance between giving and taking. From a strong inner core they reach out to the world. They can unselfishly serve others unconditionally. These are the people who activate others to get up and take control of their lives. These are the people who start a revival.

Awakening, revival and renewal

The word revival means "to live anew", "return to life", "show signs of life", "become powerful again" or "the restoration to use, acceptance, activity, or vigour after a still, dormant and inactive period of obscurity". The time has come for people to return to life, and to accept responsibility for the world and its people. We need to remember who we are. It won't be like a flash of lightning, but through inner activation of each unique person to release all the potential and inner energy, in order for us to become who we are.

It means most of our traditional support systems will have to be left behind. We need to live a responsible interdependent synergistic life. It reminds one of people in intensive care in hospital. They are connected to the heart-lung machine, kidney machine and intravenous system to keep alive. They are on a support and survival system. It is an artificial life from the outside to the inside. Machines and other systems think, do and make decisions on their behalf.

Being connected to the support systems means the loss of the ability to live life to its fullest. They cannot move, grow and develop and enjoy life without these systems. Should these systems be switched off, they could possibly lose the little life that's left. The truth is that one cannot always be connected to support systems. It has to stop somewhere. The systems should be switched off – the person either dies or starts living a self-sustaining life again. It will all depend on the person being "healthy" and strong enough to maintain a meaningful life. Most people function this way.

Most people are connected to external factors and measure their quality of life accordingly. A marital partner who thinks that the other person should accept responsibility to make him/her happy, or parents who are of the opinion that their children should achieve, so that they can look good, or older people who believe children should take care of the elderly because responsible precautions were not made for old age. There are people who believe that the government, life or even God owes them something. Life becomes a tug-of-war, a power game. There are very little signs of living a full independent, happy, responsible life.

There is another side to the coin. There are those who always want to play the role of the support system. They take care of the weak and the wretched. They are also connected to an artificial life system, but it is based on helping others. These people believe that they are doing well by helping everybody and taking care of everybody. It is often no less than an escape from the meaninglessness of their own lives. There is little sign of a happy creative life as they are always accepting responsibility for the lives and troubles of others. Such people enjoy the weaknesses of others, because it makes them feel good and strong. They sometimes even make an effort to keep others dependent against their will. In this way an unhealthy balance between taking and giving is created.

Csiksentmihalyi[339] summarises this as follows:

"Oppression is a condition in which the psychic energy of one person is controlled by another against his or her will."

Nobody was born to be oppressed, as nobody can grow in these circumstances. The one group takes and the other gives, and both groups become dependent. It remains a lose-lose situation. Co-dependent people, who do not make the effort to live life at its fullest, and expect others to do it for them, will always be among us. It is part of life – but it needs to stop!

People are now challenged to make a choice and live life and fulfill their purpose and place in the world. Not everybody is willing or capable of doing so. It means that the progress of the world will have to be carried by a smaller group of independent, responsible people.

No person or group can indefinitely carry the world on their shoulders. The more complex the world and humanity become, the bigger this group of independent, creative, responsible people have to become. This cannot be taken for granted. The time to challenge people to awake, arise and live life has arrived.

CHAPTER 17

LEADERSHIP AND

TRANSCENDENCE

History

The new paradigm demands courage and the willingness to take steps into the unknown. In order to survive and grow we need to move beyond the boundaries of our time. Our willingness to go through transformation and development is important. The ability and willingness to transcend will determine in what way we will reach the other side.

Transformation means to "take a on a different shape or form". The word "transcendence" comes from the words 'trans' that means "on the other side" and 'send' that means "sends". Transcendence therefore means "send to the other side", or "send outside of the boundaries", or to "move the boundaries of the existing life world." In order to do this we need a special power that will defy the laws of gravity, the habits of our programming that pull us back. Here we find the ultimate manifestation of power and progress.

Change and growth within the self and the transcending boundaries do not take place separately, but simultaneously. This means that the boundaries of the self, as well as the boundaries and perceptions of the world we live in, have to be replaced and enlarged. A mature person is constantly busy testing and moving the boundaries of the self and the world. It does not only require knowledge and skills of the here and the now, but also courage and willingness to enquire about the unknown, and to search for what could be. There is not only the willingness to take chances, but also the ability to enter the unknown. Life is like the Comrades marathon. Each step is a challenge and each person has to decide how they are going to run this marathon of life.

In the Old Testament Joshua accompanied other spies to the Promised Land on the other side of the border. Their aim was to determine the possibilities of a better quality of life. While the other spies returned with negative reports, Joshua spoke of the land of "milk and honey". Not only did he move outside the boundaries of perceptions, he identified the potential of the new country and was willing to win it over. From his perspective he saw what others were unable to see. Joshua was open and receptive to the new and could therefore transcend. Similarly, Columbus, Dias and other explorers undertook dangerous voyages of discovery and found new continents and sea routes. Neil Armstrong was the first man on the moon. Today, journeys into space are routine.

People are increasingly overstepping their own physical possibilities and we experience unknown achievements in sport, research and other contexts of life. Not only are the physical boundaries moved, we move outside technological borders every day. In our recent history, the Wright brothers introduced aviation and Alexander Graham Bell invented the telephone.

Today more astounding technological revolutions are taking place with the introduction of the very advanced computer and communication technology. Bill Gates and many others have caused major changes through their developments. By continuously moving the boundaries, we discover a new world, develop and win it over. History is made by people who move outside of their boundaries. What do all these people have in common? How is it possible to constantly move the boundaries? Is it possible in this rapidly changing world for something to be permanent and substantial? What does it mean to the everyday person in the street?

If we want to understand the full extent of the power of transcendence, we have to understand the full extent of the dimensions of reality we live in. We are body-mind-spiritual beings and function as such. It means that transcendence too has to take place within these three dimensions of reality.

Transcending boundaries

In this process of change, transformation and transcendence, we need to break through many barriers and mindsets and move beyond current boundaries. We are making a multi-dimensional shift than will include new realities. We need to move our boundaries to include:

- **Physical reality**

Physical transcendence means moving boundaries on a horizontal and vertical level. People have been prepared to move their physical boundaries when necessary. The move from one place to another, from one country, office, home or building to another, becomes lessons in life. The knowledge gained, can be ploughed back into life. This reality is found within the first three levels of our 'university of life'.

Here we need to develop the skills and tools to manage our physical reality and world in the most effective and creative way. Transcending the physical dimension on a vertical level refers to looking beyond the physical domain into a quantum and virtual reality. Although we use levels to identify these dimensions, they are all integrated, all is one. These have been described as parallel realities. We move from being consciousness of one reality to a higher consciousness or awakening to a higher dimension or reality. We then transcend the boundaries that kept us within the darkness of the unknown.

- **Psychological or quantum reality**

Psychological transcendence refers to the psychological move, especially the renewal of thought. Thought is quantum reality. Changing our ways of thinking includes an emotional and inner shift of the total self and self-concept. We not only stretch outside of the boundaries of the self, but also outside of traditional, cultural, political social, academic and religious boundaries. It could also manifest in a physical move where a person can no longer continue in a specific situation, relationship, career, church or training institution, and then moves, changes or searches for answers elsewhere.

The quantum leap takes place here where we start to understand the power of thought and how we create our own reality. Moving beyond boundaries means understanding the limitations of our self-structures and thought patterns and accepting the challenge to move beyond to new discoveries.

Level 7	
Level 6	VIRTUAL REALITY
Level 5	
Level 4	QUANTUM REALITY
Level 3	
Level 2	PHYSICAL REALITY
Level 1	

Different realities –different leadership

- **Spiritual or virtual reality**

In every person there is a deeply rooted need to transcend spiritually – to make contact with a higher power, deeper dimension, the Divine Spirit or Source. Meditation, yoga-exercise and prayer are applied in an attempt to get in touch with the transcendental. With certain concentration rituals some even succeed in experiencing how the spirit leaves the body. Spiritual transcendence is directly related to spiritual growth and entails the development of the ability to see, hear, feel, taste and smell in the invisible dimension, higher dimension or within the dimension of God. Here we will to enter the spiritual reality.

The path of success and prosperity

We cannot take the process of transcending and claiming the "promised land", for granted. It is a Path, a spiritual journey. It is not the path to health, wealth, happiness and prosperity. Prosperity is the Path. It starts as change within the self, then of the personal life contexts and then as change in the world. With new knowledge, insights, values and visions, we can move the boundaries of our self definition. Disintegration of the old boundaries in all dimensions of the self has to take place. A broadened perspective and a new self-structure develop. The new paradigm will take shape outside the boundaries of old traditional, cultural and religious values. Many values and visions will stay the same and many will change as values change and integrate, to form a new paradigm.

When we go through the zero-effect of change, we again have to ask: Who am I? Where am I going to and why? All the advantages and disadvantages of the paradigm shifts are experienced in the self, before it can take place in the world. Some will find it easier than others. Some people will be able to manage the transformation and transcendence in the self on their own, will be able to appreciate it and think anew, and will therefore be able to discover the new life on the other side of the boundaries. Others will remain in the cocoon of life to continue there with their lives or stagnate. This happens because of their stagnated souls. It remains a personal choice. As mentioned before, the biggest wars of today are fought within the self.

Franklin D. Roosevelt said: "*Men are not prisoners of fate, they are prisoners of their own minds.*"

Each person lives within the boundaries of contexts, such as career, marriage, family, politics or church. As soon as change, stretching, enlargement and a shift in the self takes place, there has to be change in the boundaries of the life context, to be able to accommodate the new self. Old contexts will have to be enlarged to make room for the new self. If this change does not take place, the context will fall away or the person will have to return to the original. An example is a person who has developed and can no longer continue within the boundaries of a career or relationship. A choice has to be made between the change of career or relationship, to a situation where there is more room for growth and development, or back to the old familiar comfort zone. It remains a personal choice whether these boundaries are going to be moved, or not. Deepak Chopra[340] says: "In the process of letting go you will lose many things from the past – but you will find yourself."

Contexts therefore also go through the shifting of boundaries or transcending. A new game with new rules develops and the zero-effect is then experienced within life context. Two people from different cultures find each other and decide to spend their lives together. Traditional marriages as religious and cultural institutions, do not apply to this new situation. The rules of the game have changed and with it the boundaries of the contexts they used to function in, have been transcended. A person for example, makes a change in career and starts his own business. He starts with very little and has to build a career and financial context from scratch. It requires maturity and wisdom to direct and manage this transcendence.

- **Death**

So far only transcendence of life has been discussed. Real meaning, however, can be found in lives opposite. We can understand and appreciate light if we experience dark, joy if pain has been experienced, summer after winter and life if there was death. Death means amongst other things, the transcendence from this world to the next, and the end of this earthly existence. Many people are anxious and uncertain about physical death. Myles Munroe (1994) explains it as follows: "Death in its simplest form, is the termination of potential." How many people have value after this death? Health and medical services are viewed as priority in most countries and a lot of effort is made to improve the quality of the physical life. Little attention, however, is paid to a psychological or spiritual death and all the potential that is lost. The fact is that our physical life on earth, bound to time and space, gives us a limited time to develop the full body-mind-spirit potential and to discover and enjoy life. The limited time here cannot be taken for granted. We need to make the best use of each opportunity, to use time to live the fullest lives now.

To live life at its fullest, death has to be taken into account. Everyone will transcend the boundary between life and death. This is where life's meaning lies. Victor Frankl (1985) identifies four aspects that give meaning to life, namely: Life: Life provides opportunities to discover and contribute. The circumstances or quality of life or health does not matter, everyone can decide how they want to live: positively or negatively.

Death: People can choose how they die and there are only two choices: positive or negative. Death makes life meaningful, because we realize the time is limited to do what we have been called on to do.

Work: Productive labor makes life meaningful. A person, who has developed all opportunities and potential productively, leads a meaningful life. For someone who has not discovered the true meaning of work, life remains meaningless and empty.

Love: To be able to give and receive love, makes life meaningful. The opposite of love is not hate, but death. To live is to love, and to love is to live. As death is inevitable, we all need to ask what we are here to do with our lifetime.

- **Life**

The natural, ideal state of human beings is one of love, happiness, a full life, pleasure, progress, prosperity and abundance. People and the world however, are imperfect, and the path of life is full of boundaries, obstacles and stumbling blocks that can keep us from claiming these fundamental rights of life. Problems, pain, hurt, failures and disappointments can keep us from the realisation of dreams, wishes, needs, visions, ideas and the development of potential and discovery of opportunities. Life provides the challenge to transcend the boundaries the world has created. It requires a positive perception, purposeful and deliberate decisions, hard work, persistence and perseverance to overcome the problems and obstacles and live life to the full.

Life is like the discovery of the potential of a gold mine. To live life at its fullest, and fully explore and enjoy the opportunities of life, the boundaries of life have to be moved. A full life means to overcome obstacles and resistance. The word "win" mainly means to open up, and be explored and discovered, like a mine, to persevere with effort and to solve problems, and eventually be awarded a price or award. Everyone busy developing their potential is a winner.

The Universe has all we need for an abundant, creative, prosperous life. We have the responsibility to accept the challenge and live life to its fullest and create the reality we desire. It means creating love, happiness, abundance and health, first in the self, then in our personal context of life, and then in the world as a whole. A whole new world is being created by persons hearing the call, who start to do something and manifest their own world. Miracles are taking place at a large scale as we override time and space.

People from all over the globe are awakening to a new World Vision. Leaving the old behind, creating an abundant life, transcending the boundaries of the self and communities and even contributing to a positive forward movement of people, organisations and even countries as a whole, requires creativity, inspiration, courage, faith and power. We already have everything to undertake a safe journey. The destiny and arrival is secure. All we need to do is awaken, release the power and claim what is already ours. It is and remains a personal choice.

Notes

CHAPTER 18

LEADERSHIP AND BEHAVIOUR

History and behaviour

Most experts believe that modern humans evolved in Africa about 100,000 years ago. During the Ice Age, in a landscape that was frozen for long periods of time, inhabitants had to develop skills and effective behavioral patterns in order to survive. As the landscape started changing so did skills and behavioral patterns change. For the greater period of their evolutionary history, modern humans have survived as omnivorous hunter-gatherers. Their migrations led to the occupation of every continent, with the exception of Antarctica, by 11 000 BP.

Human cultures developed skills and patterns of behavior very different from any behavior found in prehistoric species. Behavior common to modern man included communication through the spoken word. Art became a vital part of human life. People carefully buried their dead and had some concept of religion and life after death. Some people stayed grain collectors, while others developed their hunting skills to a peak. Later human developments – farming, civilisation, huge population growth, industry and control over nature — have occurred in the relatively tiny period of ten thousand years. As human development went through different stages, ranging from the Stone, Bronze and Iron Age, and the more recent Technology and

Information Eras, we can identify certain skills and behavioral patterns relevant to each of these periods. These behavioral patterns needed to be developed to secure the survival of the species at the time. With the turn of the millennium we too entered a new era demanding that we develop new skills and behavioral patterns that will enable us to continue to evolve safely to the next level.

The power of our actions and behavior

Action refers to the transmission of energy, force or influence. Being active means being – able to move. It is a state of doing something and refers to a series of movements. Our actions are the physical manifestation of our thinking. Behind every deed and action we find our thoughts, feelings, motives, values, visions, beliefs and all the other power tools we have discussed. The unseen quantum and virtual reality manifest in the physical reality through our actions and deeds. Every movement that we make transfers energy that can transform our physical reality and therefore our lives. Our deeds and actions are very powerful. Research has shown that very few people are very successful in what they are doing. Less than 1% of all people have a personal plan of action; the other 99% are not living powerful, innovative inspired, creative and prosperous lives.

On a more global scale most organisations, companies and even countries are less that 45% effective in what they are doing. This means most of us are using outdated, inappropriate or ineffective strategies and action plans. We are wasting valuable energy and, therefore, life. It is like making an investment of $1 and receiving a return of 30c. Within financial terms this would be seen as a bad investment that needs to be corrected. In life terms, however, very few people have the understanding of how they are making bad investments with their lives. This too needs to be corrected. Most people do not know how. Very few people know who they are, what they desire and how to get it. Most people are unsure of what they are doing with their lives. The time has come to be conscious of how we invest our time, energy and our lives by being conscious of what we are doing. If we want to lead powerful, successful and prosperous lives we need to understand the true power behind our actions and behavior.

Many theories on behavior have over decades evolved from different perceptions. Behavior refers to how we act, react, function or perform in a certain way under specific circumstances. As one action is triggered, it starts a series of actions that result in a behavioral pattern. Behavior is power in action. When we repeat certain actions, the patterns are laid down in the neuro-physiology, as discussed. These behavioral or action patterns develop over time and form habits. Some behavioral patterns are effective and functional and should be reinforced, while other patterns become outworn and ineffective and should be stopped and replaced with more suitable behavioral patterns.

These patterns form the foundation of our life management. When life changes we need to change our behavior. This means we firstly have to break out of our old patterns and habits before we can develop new patterns. This has to start within each person. A new success DNA leader understands these principles and makes sure that all who follow their lead adhere to a very clear and concise code of conduct.

Personal behavior

As we have discussed, every person is unique and therefore has a unique personal behavioral pattern. As every movement we make brings about an energy release that has a result in our lives, we need to understand the positive and negative consequences of our actions.

As we are unique persons we make a unique contribution to life as a whole. Understanding how to develop power actions and behavioral patterns will take us forward. Actions refer to what we physically do by using the whole body, but the two most important power action tools that bring about the greatest effect, are using our hands and our speech. Actions speak loader than words and the word is mightier than the sword.

Personal behavior is the result of all we have discussed in the previous chapters. Each of the checklists refers to certain actions and behaviors. In working through these lists and identifying new aspects to work on, new patterns of effective coping behavior will emerge that will contribute to a more effective and prosperous future and give meaning to life. As we develop this within ourselves we too can contribute to groups, teams, organisations, companies, countries and life as a whole.

Reality	Physical reality	Quantum reality	Metaphysical/ Virtual reality
Focus	Physical Material reality,	Atoms, molecules, quantum soup	Universal Field of Potential,UFP, Spirit.
Access.	Physical senses, sensory learning	Science and scientific methods	HSP,Vision, meditation, transcendental practices,
Levels of awareness	Conscious	Sub-conscious/ unconscious	Higher (Super) consciousness
Perspectives	Traditional views.	Quantum perspectives.	Universal perspectives
Approach to faith	Blind, pre-ecognitive group faith.	Individual / Personal faith	Universal knowing & understanding Wisdom
Approach to work	Burden,slavery Survival.	Self-fulfilling	Universal calling.
Intelligence	Pre-personal tribal / group collective intelligence	Rational and emotive Intelligence	Spiritual/ Power Intelligence
Approach to time	Past	future	Now

Organisational behavior

Organisational behavior

Organisational behavior is in essence the collective behavior of all participants within a specific context. The whole is, however, more than the parts. This means that every organisation has a unique behavioral pattern with a unique contribution to make.

Organisations function as a whole and all the universal principles underlying personal behavior is applicable to the collective behavior. The time has come not only to change our personal patterns, but to change and enhance organisational behavior to secure success and prosperity for all.

Changing our behavioral patterns

There are three steps in changing our behavioral patterns – detoxification, detangling, and reclaiming life.

- **Detox**

Toxins are harmful, destructive, fatal, negative, or poisonous substances, people or situations. They cause injury, illness, destruction and even death. Detoxification is the process people and organisations need to go through when wanting to reclaim success, prosperity and life. When looking at the situation in the world it is obvious we have a lot of healing and cleaning up to do. We have left the battlefield with our wounded people and societies and are now entering a stage of rejuvenation and energising people and organisations. People accomplish much more by playing together than fighting. It is now time to challenge the perceptions of the battlefield and change it into the playground. This takes place on the physical, psychological and spiritual levels, or detoxing the physical, quantum and virtual realities.

Physical detoxification refers to cleaning up ourselves and our physical world. We have physically poisoned ourselves by what we put into our bodies. The artificial production of foods with colorants, flavourants, preservatives and other unnatural substances have alienated us from healthy living. Today the health industry, propagating fitness and healthy eating programs, is a booming business. A healthy body houses a healthy mind. The cleaning up of our own personal world includes not only personal health and welfare, but cleaning up our personal living space and our environment. Cleaning up clutter and beautifying our own living space and environment creates a new clean atmosphere and promotes flow – the essence of life.

- **Healing perceptions**

Every thought entails a segment of the world we see. We see the world through our own perceptions of brokenness and attack. We see the world we have made but do not understand and see ourselves as the makers of it. The world we see, is the world behind our eyes. There is no point in trying to change the world. The world we see is the outcome or effect of thoughts and is therefore incapable of change. The world we see now will go away when the cause – our thinking and believing – changes. By letting go of negativity, hurt and pain we heal our thinking and our perceptions and we heal the world.

- **The power of vision**

Healing the person will take centre stage for decades to come. Healing our bodies and minds clears our vision. We are then able to clearly see into the virtual reality. With clear vision we will remember the truth about ourselves and our abundant world. This is true vision – the ability to see into the unseen and manifest it on earth.

- **Detangle**

Tangle means to mix up and or intertwine in a confused mess. People and organisations that are tangled up are trapped in awkward, complicated, confused involvements with people and situations. These persons feel trapped, confused, bewildered, out of touch with themselves and life. Consciously identifying these situations and people and letting go of them is an important part of reclaiming your life.

- **Reclaim your life**

It was part of our broken perceptions that we experienced reality as threatening – like a battlefield. We have been programmed to battle with others and with ourselves. Most people have self-defeating mechanisms that keep them from prosperity. We have been alienated from who we are and what we desire and can achieve. These negative patterns have caused us to give away our power and misunderstand our potential. When we achieve something or become rich, we believe we need to feel guilty as though we do not deserve it. Most people then become their own worst enemies and engage in self-defeating behaviour.

These people can be found in all walks of life – from the hobo in the park to the MD of a big company. We need to consciously change these self-defeating patterns and reclaim what is rightfully ours – life in abundance. We reclaim our life by reclaiming our power and take back the control and responsibility for the quality of our thoughts, actions, beliefs, feeling and attitudes. We reclaim life by reclaiming and developing our power and inner strength.

Power actions for power people

Successful people have fundamental actions and behavioral patterns in common. Copy these and start your own process of success.

- #### Managing prosperity

Prosperous people have a prosperity consciousness. They think and manage their world in terms of positive outcomes. Once we understand our true power to create the life we desire, we have the responsibility to manage it well. Looking after ourselves and our assets says that we care. It sends out a message of respect.

Everything we respect will return to us. Cleaning, fixing and protecting against decay are just a few ways of managing your physical prosperity. Investing time and energy in uplifting relationships and connections is hard work. People need to know you care and value them for who they are. If prosperity is a condition, then creating and managing this condition is a responsibility we need to accept.

- #### Managing money

Money is not success. Money is the outcome of success. Success is focusing, staying, acting, behaving and living on purpose. Money is the physical manifestation of the exchange of valuable life force or energy. The more energy, the more value, the more money.

Focusing on and worrying about money is a self-defeating mechanism and ineffective behavior. How can we expect to be successful if we confuse the purpose with the outcome of the purpose? It is like putting the cart before the horse. A sound knowledge of financial management is the best investment any successful person can make. Managing money effectively, responsibly, with respect and without fear creates a powerful field of attraction. You can multiply your assets by being in control of your money.

People and companies who do not understand these money principles can strive their whole lives to be rich and affluent, but never will obtain enough. Money does not make you rich. It is the attitude you have towards yourself, people and life that makes you rich. The outcome is money — in abundance!

- **Energy economics**

Like money we need to know how to invest our life force or energy.

Wasting time, energy and our authentic selves on meaningless issues is self-abuse. Letting go of people and the past, reclaiming our power and investing it in effective meaningful actions, relationships, projects and situations secures the outcome of prosperity and happiness.

- **Caring and giving**

Prosperous, successful people know that we live in an abundant universe and that there is enough for everyone. They are happy about the successes of others, even about progress of their opponents and competition. They care and give freely and understand that as we give to others we give to ourselves.

- **Enthusiasm and inspiration**

Prosperous people are exited and enthusiastic about life and the challenges they meet. They know that they already have everything at their disposal to turn stumbling blocks into stepping stones. Excitement, eagerness, lively interest, happiness and inspiration all trigger powerful actions that create the world they desire. These people are not afraid and have a zeal for life.

- **The entrepreneur**

The entrepreneur is an innovative enthusiastic, inspired, person who is able to trigger a process, create a viable business opportunity and implement it successfully, regardless of the resources initially available. True entrepreneurs do not primarily focus on finances, as they know that financial success will follow their purposeful actions. Prosperous people are not only creative and innovative, but can recognize and exploit business opportunities and develop vital factors that make positive contributions to their success. They constantly develop the entrepreneur within themselves.

- **Plan of action**

Prosperous, successful people have a plan of action. They know who they are, where they are going and what they want. This plan is usually written and revised regularly. They erect milestones on their way to indicate if they are still on the right course. They are not afraid to change direction when necessary.

- **Gratitude and humbleness**

Powerful people are humble. They show respect to and honor themselves and others. They are connected to their core and are happy and unpretentious. They are filled with gratitude and are aware of imperfections as part of being human. They can take a lower stance and laugh at themselves. They focus more on being good human beings rather than on being powerful, wealthy and successful. They never use their power in inappropriate ways. Only powerful people, who have experienced true greatness, can be truly humble. Their power is under control and focused on the welfare for all.

Powerless people however abuse power positions and need to be in control in order to overcome their inner fear, negative feelings, self-defeating mechanisms, feelings of unworthiness. These people mistake inferiority for true humbleness.

- **Living in the now**

The Now is not necessarily a reference to time. It refers to a time-space reality. The Now is a place where everything is It is a place and way of being – a connection with the universe and being One. It is a level of consciousness where you have access to everything you need – now.

Most people live either in the past or the future. We all, however, have the responsibility to create our lives – now. The past is just a memory and the future a vision. The present is exactly what the word means - a present, a gift. This is our "real time". Experiencing and savoring every moment to the full, living and loving to the full en being grateful for every moment is one of the power keys to life. Prosperous people do not waste time and energy on past mistakes and unhappiness. They humbly accept life and live life as abundant as they can. They live life as if…! Living in the now, according to what you visualise, makes it manifest in your life. If you want to be successful and prosperous, start living it – now!

- **The power of silence and centeredness**

Truly successful people are free from worry and fear. They know we live in an abundant universe with unlimited potential. We need to be still and centred in order to connect to this power spot and power guide we referred to in a previous chapter. The power of silence lies in connecting to our power source at a deeper level and to effectively monitor and direct our actions and behavior.

This could take about thirty minutes in the morning and thirty minutes in the evening. Many people say they do not have the time. The fact is, when our actions are not effective the first time, most people do have time to do it again. When we are quiet and centred, our actions are synchronised and effective, productive and innovative. We do not waste time by repeating everything. Being quiet is a time saver. The bigger the assignment, the more important the need to be still becomes. Being still does not mean sitting still. It is an inner harmony, centeredness and alignment that synchronises everything with everything else.

- **Learning, growth and development**

Prosperous people are open to new learning experiences. They understand their curriculum for life as we discussed in a previous chapter and are prepared to walk the path. They are prepared to think for themselves and are driven by internal direction and motives.

These people do not only learn from their mistakes or by "hindsight". They are focused on their purpose, vision and experiencing life to the full. They are motivated and directed by their inner guide and learn from their visions what they need to do. They do not waste time but learn in "foresight". The most successful and prosperous people will start to invest more time visualising and focusing their actions on effectively and abundantly creating the future - now.

- **Love and compassion**

Prosperous, successful people are in love with life. They can give and receive love and happiness and appreciate happiness, success and beauty. They are at peace with themselves and life and are not only connected to themselves, but to others and to their Higher Power. Power people have made a conscious choice to be all they can be and create and enjoy a life of happiness and prosperity. The world is therefore a better place and generations to come have a sound foundation to build the future on. Everyone has the choice to take part in this adventure.

- **Attitude**:

Aircraft have an attitude meter that determines the altitude.

Altitude refers to how high we move or are elevated above a specific level. Elevation is the process we undertake to move from one altitude or one level to another. In aerospace the altitude refers to the direction and orientation of a space-craft. Altitude is therefore not only how high we are but includes orientation and direction. It is the inner flight plan that gives direction to our action.

Attitude comes from the Latin word 'aptus' meaning 'fit'. We too determine our fitness in life, our altitude is determined by our attitude. Attitude is an orientation of character and refers to our inner fitness and overall condition, direction and ability.

When our attitudes are negative, focusing on attack, disaster, failure, loss or poverty we become subject to negative forces and allow them to pull us down. When our attitudes are positive, we are centred and focused on our purpose, visions and values, we excel and defy the forces of gravity. We can go beyond the limits or standards – we perform at a higher level and exceed our own boundaries and expectations. We have the power to constantly function and live in a state of excellence.

We have been given the power to create the life we desire. The only things keeping us back are a lack of knowledge, fear, and false perceptions. We all have the power to overcome these stumbling blocks and create the happiness, meaning, and prosperity we desire. It is a personal choice and responsibility to be part of the emerging generation of power intelligent people – the leaders of tomorrow.

Programming for success and prosperity

Using the checklist we can draw up a plan of action. We can reprogram our lives for happiness, prosperity and abundance by developing the following.

- New information and skills
- New thinking and new feelings
- New actions, habits and behavioral patterns
- Vision and dreams
- Challenges
- Intuition
- Affirmations
- Plans of action
- Meditation /prayer
- Being grateful and valuing beauty
- Doing to others as we want done to us
- Happiness and prosperity
- Enjoying life in abundance
- Living in the Now
- Inner peace and love
- Practicing a positive attitude and sustaining a prosperity consciousness

Notes

CHAPTER 19

LEADERSHIP AND FUTURE DEMANDS

Introduction

In order to prepare for a new approach to success, now and in the future, we need to have a look at what the future might hold. On the one hand we do have the prophets of "doom and gloom"; while on the other hand we have more optimistic views. I believe that the devastating predictions refer to the dying off of the old mindset and lower ego self and the rebirth of a new awareness and higher consciousness – the emergence of a new, fifth dimensional human being. The questions are:

> *What changes can we expect? How should we prepare?*

Many authors[341] have given their views on 2012 and beyond. What follows is a short summary of various contributions with a glimpse of what we can expect and need to prepare for.

Changes we can expect by 2030

By taking all the current available information into account, we can make a short summary of the changes we can expect in the future:

- **Radical fundamental change**

We can expect change to escalate at a rapid pace. The wants and needs of people will change from being basic ego self centred, self serving and materialistic to a universal spiritual consciousness. Materialism, power games, manipulation, deception, corruption, and dominance will make way for equality, cooperation, honesty, truth, integrity, ethics, responsibility, and healthy living. Our perception of money, management, leadership, success, business, business structures, are changing to encompass the new consciousness. People will start to see their common humanity, rather than differences in culture, creed or religion. A new foundation of healthy, balanced living in harmony with nature and humanity, on all levels of existence, with a deep awareness of, and connection to, spiritual reality, will predominate.

The human species is evolving from a three dimensional being which refers to the lower levels of basic functioning. Fourth dimensional human being begins to think for themselves and accept responsibility for their quality of life, while fifth dimensional human beings are totally spiritually aware and conscious and can co-create with the spiritual dimension. People as fifth dimension human beings with activated DNA will predominate.

- **The unfolding of *Homo sapiens spiritualis***

The new kind of human being is evolving from a third dimensional, physical, ego-driven species, to a fourth dimensional, self driven state then to a fifth dimensional, spiritual human being. Each of these levels refer to the levels of development of the power pyramid and the three levels of neuro-functions – the primitive reptilian mindset, the mammalian or caring mindset, and the neocortex with the frontal lobes, connecting us to the higher mindset and spiritual vision.

As we literally upgrade our mindsets or frequencies by letting go of lower order mindset frequencies, we consciously connect to higher spiritual information, guidance and solutions. People will begin to open up spiritually and psychically and begin to communicate telepathically with others on a soul level.

With new spiritual sight, people will be able to access and see into other dimensions, while accessing new information from angels and elementals alike. The human species is unfolding from *Homo sapiens* to *Homo sapiens sapiens* to *Homo sapiens spiritualis*.

The higher spiritual, positive self, will take predominance over the lower ego-self, while a person consciously chooses to live in love, peace, and harmony with self, higher spiritual dimensions, others, and with nature. A consciousness of respect, integrity, honesty, care, and the welfare of all, will produce a new level of success and abundance.

Wise souls are now coming to earth in order to help with the transition. They are compassionate, caring and loving people, who will help those through this difficult time of loss and pain. At the same time, they hold the new consciousness, anchor the light in physicality, bringing hope and peace to those in turmoil, while laying a new foundation and assisting with the initiation, building and development of fifth dimension communities.

- **Going green**

Harmony with nature will play a major role in everyday life, Mother earth will be taken into account as a living system that needs to be taken care of, while she takes care of us. This means that the use of pesticides in nature would be viewed as destruction, while good organic food, pure water, clean air, peace, quiet and harmony will benefit all. As the veils between the physical and spiritual dimensions lift, the feeling of oneness will escalate, and the growing sense of belonging will unite individuals, communities, nature, and spirit world. The definition of success will move from ego centric, to soul centric definitions, with deeper spiritual values and meanings of success.

- **Energy resources**

As our natural resources start to run out, we will seek new forms of power and new developments in eco-energy, by harnessing water, lightning, and wind, as new power sources. Solar energy, captured into compact batteries, will provide a large part of our energy. Other forms of eco-energy will be derived from earth magnetism, pyramid power, crystals, and plant energy. Technologists are already, unconsciously or consciously, at work to bring about this new technology. Harnessing energy from the oceans for global use, will be one of the common international projects once peace has been achieved. Nuclear power will still be one of the viable sources and will continue to produce energy for all. Our oil based materials will become less acceptable and already the plastic container industry is finding alternative, more eco-friendly ways of packaging. It is estimated that our primary sources of oil and gas will run out by 2012 and we will be living on reserves till new forms of energy are accessible. This will make travel more expensive.

- **Transport**

The lack of fuel will limit travel in the future, necessitating us to use alternative forms of transportation like trains, boats, bicycles and walking. After this period all our current transport will be seen as "old-fashioned", while it is envisioned that after 2033 individuals will be able to travel with their own little helicopters and cover longer distances in larger airborne and hovering transport.

- **New social communities**

As our natural resources dwindle, smaller communities will be formed by fifth dimensional people who choose to live in co-operation and for the higher good of all. Ego based systems, will make way for interdependence between individuals and communities. Within fifth dimensional communities everyone will be supported as they learn and experience how to live naturally. Communities will be formed on the basis of spiritual values and co-existence with less barriers and separation. Without discrimination on the grounds of colour, race, age, religion, or creed, the barriers between people, families, groups, societies, cultures and even countries will fade, leaving place for openness and freedom of movement over current boundaries. Spiritual marriages beyond the values of traditional, cultural and religious boundaries and laws will form the cornerstone of these communities bringing a new awareness of the higher value and role of men, women and children.

- **The raising of the feminine**

As the raising of the feminine escalates, to balance the current masculine patriarchal system, a new kind of masculine and feminine consciousness will emerge. Here the role of men and women are based on their spiritual calling, and soul-centred contribution, giving rise to a new perception in relationships and marriage.

- **Marriage**

In the future marriages will be built on soul and spiritual attractions and connections and not necessarily on current physical, religious, social or cultural values and prejudices. Marriage will involve a relationship between two mature persons who find their partner to be a soul-mate or twin flame and are prepared to commit themselves to a monogamous relationship in order to serve the higher good of each other and the whole. This means that each partner is already connected to their soul purpose living a balanced, integrated, centred, and soul-fulfilling life. These commitments will be based on a mutual agreement of optimum soul development and the raising of the spiritual consciousness within the community their communities. At the same time, it will bring a new orientation towards sensuality and sexuality.

- **Sensuality and sexuality**

As the feminine consciousness rises, women will take in their rightful place beside a man while both are in touch with their masculine and feminine sides, This will bring about a deeper understanding and respect for gender differences and sexuality. As every person will be respected and valued, the exploitation of women and sexuality will cease, making way for genuine love, respect, and a new kind of sexual fulfilment. This is founded on mutual appreciation and value of the masculine and feminine body and energies. The growing awareness that the masculine and feminine psyche and soul are not necessarily found within the corresponding body, and that we can find a masculine soul, or energy, in a feminine body, and a feminine soul, within a masculine body, will make way for more acceptance of homosexuality. In the end, this also will fade out and we will have an androgynous society, with the balancing of the male and female energies within one person choosing to share a fulfilling soul-centred relationship with another androgynous life partner. Sensuality and sexuality will take on a spiritual meaning, while the responsibility of children and raising a family will become the responsibility of all.

- **Families**

Within fifth dimensional families we find family life founded on spiritual principles, soul development, and fulfilment. Extended families that include multilayered age groups and generations will form the basis of fifth dimensional communities. Children will play an important role in their own education, while the aged maintain an active productive life contributing the welfare of the whole community.

- **Babies and children**

It has already been found that recent education systems do not meet the needs of the current youth. As we enter into this twenty year transitional period, it is expected that the new babies to be born will require a different kind of understanding and attention. Many of these children already have more strands of DNA activated than their parents or peers. These children are seen as "indigo" or "star" children who have an innate knowing and wisdom beyond the years of others. This can only be related to their direct connection to higher dimensions. It has already been found that many babies currently born to mothers with HIV-AIDS have an inborn immunity to the virus that can only be related to DNA that overrides the viral effects. At the rate this phenomenon is escalating, it is estimated that nearly 20% of babies will be born with their 12 strands of DNA activated in the future. These children are telepathic, clairvoyant, and psychic on every level, and have extra-ordinary gifts, like the ability to teleport, levitate, communicate with other life forms, and heal. They need special understanding and nurturing parents, so that their special abilities can be developed and nurtured for the greater good. Adults will start to give children what they need, rather than what we want from them. This approach to children, education, and parenting, will bring about the development of happy fulfilled children living their soul purpose. Soul satisfaction will be the criteria for success, instead of the ego gratification of today.

Indigo children were first identified by educators in Canada. They mapped the way for the raising of consciousness after becoming aware of the influx of these babies in other countries. Some need special feeding, as their bodies are very sensitive to current food manufacturing methods. Allergies and other physical ailments have been diagnosed that are usually resolved by correct eating habits and healthy living. At the same time indigo children need special attention in order to develop their spiritual gifts. If not they become passive, or disruptive, within traditional systems, placing added responsibility on quality parenting. Many hyperactive children labeled ADD or Attention Deficit Hyperactive Syndrome, need less medication and more stimulation in order to develop their full potential. Not all hyperactive children are however necessarily indigo children. It is expected that the percentage of indigo, crystal, and rainbow children being born will escalate over the next ten to twenty years, placing a new challenge before the doors of the education systems of the world.

- **Education**

The rising of consciousness brings with it a new perception of the value of the soul, especially as it pertains to children. Children and education will be approached with the sole purpose of utilising the full potential of each child. Where government policies and parental guidance previously demanded conformity from the youth, it will now be replaced with respect and appreciation for each life, and the contribution each soul makes to the whole. Children will be allowed to develop their own unique talents, while making their contributions available to the common good. Parents will take each child seriously, while teachers and educationalists will develop new policies and programs for maximum utilisation of potential.

Smaller schools that are the responsibility of all inhabitants of the community will be one of the binding factors that keep communities together. The curriculum will include spiritual teachings and practices for all, while traditional religions, dogmatic separation and exclusivity will fade and become irrelevant. Music will be played in schools, as the harmonious sounds heal and soothe children, so that they can learn more easily. The main focus of education will be on healthy, natural living, while developing your soul purpose to the benefit of all. As most children will be indigo children, they will have guidance in themselves as what they do need to learn, and the contribution they need to make.

- **Emerging new intelligence**

The world is starting to see the rise of a new, quality human beings who has reclaimed their souls, and are connected to their higher selves. This process means reclaiming power invested in the ego and the lower ego self. By reclaiming personal power and detaching from old outworn view, beliefs and life styles, we find the rising of personal power and a new kind of intelligence – Power Intelligence. PI is the conscious ability to utilise your infinite potential to the benefit of all. These are people who accept responsibility for the self and their quality of life. They make their own choices, accept responsibility, demand freedom, honesty, peace and fairness. Co-operation and co-creation are part of successful living, while dictatorial leadership with "power-over-people" loses its hold and makes way for releasing the "power within people".

- **Aging**

Aging, and the effects of aging will be outweighed by the ability to consciously activate, or renew DNA, while older generations will be honoured for their wisdom. Aging in the end will become irrelevant as there is a sense of being healthy, alive, alert and useful. A general feeling of love, contentment and happiness will prevail, which will keep people healthier. Death will occur when the soul purpose has been completed, and accepted as a natural part of the journey of the soul. Solemn mourning at funerals will be replaced with happy celebrations.

- **Architecture**

Architecture has already started to move towards the building of self-sustainable, self-sufficient homes, and fifth dimensional communities will respect nature and the environment. Everything is "going green", while the use of synthetic building material is being replaced with natural building material, in harmony with nature as the mindset of "less is more" takes over from a materialistic mindset. Many architects are specifically called for this purpose, while others continue on the path of ego gratification – the bigger the better.

- **Food supplies and eating habits**

The focus on healthy, balanced living is already having an impact on the production of food, while at the same time food prices have soared. This is igniting a new awareness of the necessity to be self-sufficient. Organic farming, and a diet of fresh fruit and vegetables with plant proteins, will form part of the fifth dimensional community's food supply.

As eating habits change, and the pace of life becomes more harmonious and balanced, it can be expected that health issues will change as well.

- **Health and healing**

Health is, or should be, the most natural state of being. It is the complete sense of harmony, wellbeing, or being "whole", that brings true health. As societies awake and become more conscious of the true essence of successful living, our health care systems will change accordingly with an attitude of "prevention is better than cure". Self healing will become a way of life, and medication and doctors will be replaced by education and training in health issues and personal healing. This will have far reaching effects on the training of health care professionals, the pharmaceutical industry and the operation of medical aids.

- **Weather and farming**

As our climate continues to change, our foods supplies will at first dwindle and farmers will be forced to change their farming practices and agricultural policies. Smaller multi-produce farming will serve the local communities, while export and import will dwindle. Self sustaining groups will no longer be dependant on imported goods, as most of them will be able to manifest whatever they need. "Simplistic living" will be the keywords to life. At the same time new farming methods and sources of food will be ignited in innovative ways while all live in harmony with nature. The use of pesticides, hormones and artificial methods of producing food will come to a halt, while people become more health conscious and focus on organic healthy foodstuffs, and their producers.

- **Commerce and trade**

Money is a symbol of exchange, and the word "currency" refers to the flow from one hand to another. When the exchange occurs with honesty and integrity, fairness and openness will flow, providing benefits all. In accordance with the Mayan prophecies, the world economy started to crumble in 2007. Deceit, dishonesty, corruption, and unfairness, will further cause the disintegration of our monetary systems and world economies. Those who have forfeited the privilege of open flow, by lending non existent money with high interest rates, while benefiting the rich above the poor, and doing business based on corruption, gambling, and greed, will be exposed and will disintegrate. Our monetary systems will continue to collapse, while a new system emerges based on honesty, integrity, and fairness. As there is a return to an honest, open exchange of services and produce, the necessity for banks and financial institutes will diminish. We will once again implement the barter system and the mutual exchange of goods, while co-operation and sharing for the highest good will take highest priority. This will cause the identification and obsession with money to dwindle till money as method of exchange method becomes irrelevant and is replaced by more practical methods of exchange.

As our power sources dwindle, transport will become scarce and expensive, resulting in substantial impacts on commerce and trade. Soon it will not be economically viable to export food and goods around the world and countries will need to become more self sufficient and self sustaining. The value systems of countries will start to change. Many countries who base their economy primarily on export, will find that although their economies dwindle, that their countries will become more self sustaining. Spiritual awakening will lessen the demand for material goods.

- **Work and employment**

With the dwindling of our energy sources, accompanied by a change in transport methods, less travel will be undertaken necessitating smaller, multi-functional, self-reliant communities. Work within these communities will be based on soul-satisfaction, and contribution to the success and welfare of all. People will learn to contact their inner self, and connect to their soul purpose, and higher self, in order to determine what purpose needs to be achieved, and contribution to be made. Personal gifts and talents will be put to use in the community, while expressing the true self. This will have a decisive impact on education, training, employment, and our monetary system. Personal satisfaction, self mastery, service, excellence, and career fulfillment will be priorities in the workplace.

- **Change in demographics**

At the moment the world population is growing at an accelerated pace. It is estimated that our planet and natural resources can only accommodate about 16 billion people. At the moment our natural resources are running out, and we will not be able to sustain over-population for very long. China has already experienced the effects of overpopulation, and their law that couples only have one child, is their contribution to the overpopulation dilemma. South Africa, a country with the highest level of HIV AIDS patients, already has to cater for more than two million orphans. Global population is predicted to drop considerably over the next two decades, as population growth declines and natural disasters, viral infections, natural disasters and other causes claim many more lives. As the death toll rises, each soul departing will also take a little bit of our negativity with them, in order to help cleanse our planet.

At the same time, the human heart is opening to the suffering of others, as was experienced with the earthquake in Haiti. Natural disasters, global health issues, and other human trials and tribulations are already opening the boundaries and borders of countries, making people more accessible to each other, in order to bring relief to those suffering. At the same time a deep respect for all the differences in culture and nature is emerging and awareness is growing that our differences are just skin deep.

We can expect different countries, races, and religions to begin working side by side in mutual respect, and in order to reach joint decisions on strategies geared towards the greater good of all.

- **Business**

The collapse of large, dinosaur businesses will continue until they no longer exist. They will be replaced by smaller businesses with a business paradigm of honesty and integrity based on creating and producing for the highest good of all. The emphasis on people making a soul contribution to the workforce will demand a business ethic of mutual respect, cooperation, integration, and harmony. Synergy, as "synchronized energy", igniting organisational potential, and implementing personal empowerment, will emphasise unique contributions, while creating an atmosphere of harmony and peace.

Poor working conditions, and children in the workforce, will not be tolerated, while support will be given to poorer countries by more affluent countries, that open their hearts and purses for the highest good of all. Businesses who honour their staff members, nature, clients and humanity as a whole, will continue to be successful and prosper, while those who ignore these values, will in the end self destruct. The business paradigm in the future will move from ego driven business, to successful soul centred cooperation driven business paradigms. Corrupt, ego driven individuals and groups will fade into obscurity.

- **Technology**

As we start to reconnect and activate our spiritual DNA, new advances in spiritual science and technology will take premise over our current technology that will become outdated. This means no computers, internet, email, cellular phones, Facebook, or Ipods as these communication technologies will not be necessary. The new technological advancements will bring a greater sense of freedom, leaving more time to connect to nature and each other. A quality life will be spent outdoors and outdoor sports will become more popular than ever.

- **Disintegration of dogmatic religions**

The original purpose of dogmatic religion was to provide a comprehendible framework with relevant information concerning spirituality to the masses on a level they could identify with and understand. Religion offered comfort and hope to the masses at a time when they were disconnected, at a low level of consciousness as people were unable to understand true spirituality. These meant that the masses were not in a position to access and comprehend the higher spiritual world without assistance. Shamans and spiritual leaders such as priests, pastors, and "wise men", whom it is assumed had higher insight, would interpret the information for the masses and teach or preach to them – usually from "higher authority". This meant that the masses were given interpretations and guidance outside their own understanding and had to accept this as truth. Different religions emerged that were initiated by different leaders of the time with Christianity, Judaism, Hinduism and the Moslem religion, as some of the current major lines of belief. Religion has been a divisive force between people, cultures, countries and individuals for millennia. As dogmatic religion fades away, one single spiritual system will emerge, based on one truth and one spiritual reality, uniting all souls of the light into one collective whole. In the Christian tradition this is seen as "the healing of the body of the Christ".

Each religion has an underlying theory or dogma and religious practices that are meant to assist the believer on the path of ascension, enlightenment, higher spiritual understanding, and attainment. However, many reasons for the distortions of these teachings are now being uncovered. Mostly the spiritual information has been distorted by the egos of those who would aim to maintain control over the unthinking masses, while others distorted the information out of a lack of a deeper connection, understanding and interpretation. Mostly this information was accepted at face value. Most of the religions have however gained, and still keep control over the masses, by spreading fear and limitation. This stronghold of dogmatic religion can be expected to become "unglued", as the raising of consciousness brings individuals into direct contact with their own inner wisdom, without any need of external input. This awakening could, or could not, be accompanied by inner guilt and conflict, as the new information clashes with traditional dogmatic teachings. Some groups will revert back to known religious dogma, while other will gain access to higher spiritual understandings, and leave traditional religion behind.

- **Higher consciousness and spiritual living**

Spirituality on the other hand, is seen as a cohesive joyous light /Light and love, in everything and between everyone. There are no barriers, no divisive theories or practices, as spirituality only talks of love, inspiration, success, empowerment, and oneness. The journey of the soul on the spiritual path is the most important focus – more important than earthly possessions and positions. The awakening of the masses includes the awakening of the soul to a higher spiritual awareness and consciousness. As changes occur, it can be accepted that traditional religions will make way for higher spiritual attainments.

At a deep level everyone wants to be kind, loving, happy, successful, and prosperous. Everyone wants to love and be loved. From the lower third dimension level of consciousness people are quick to criticise, judge and condemn. The consequences are seen in the separation in marriages, families, religion, cultures and countries. With the emergence of the new fifth level, spiritually the hearts and minds of the masses will begin to open and heal. Then it will be easier to connect and live in harmony with all. Peace will rule the day.

With fifth dimensional spiritual vision, we will be able to see and understand the hearts and minds of people, while accepting them unconditionally with love. Nothing will be hidden. Truth, trust, integrity, honesty, faith, and love, will form the basis of all relationships and communication. At the same time co-creation with Source, manifesting and miracles will become a way of life. This is true success.

- **New leadership and management**

As the paradigm begins to shift, our leadership and management styles will shift as well. People will become bored with jobs and tasks that do not meet their soul needs, and productivity will decline in companies having 'skills development' but no 'soul development' policies. Leadership will move from a basic tribal 'power over people' style to a soul and value-centred leadership approach, releasing 'power within people'. Management functions will broaden as they move from task orientation to include people and soul orientation. We can expect that as the pace of change accelerates, that the turnover of leadership styles and positions will do so as well. This means that leaders may be rapidly replaced by more evolved, value guided, soul-centred individuals. The emerging new leaders will function as new pathfinders and mapmakers, while instilling deeper soul values and spiritual wisdoms. They are the Magi of our time.

Their main goal is to function as we were predestined to function – as light bearers living a fulfilling life of love and abundance. Although our purpose is predestined, we have conscious choice and freewill to choose how, when and where we will utilise this universal gift of cosmic light potential. We can choose the quality of lives we want to lead. New Success DNA leaders are servant-leaders, showing the way back to our destiny, that is – authentic living. Not only do they serve the people, they also serve the greater good of all.

However, most of these new DNA leaders are still submerged in physicality and caught up in the ego packaging of everyday life. Unconsciously they are waiting to fulfill their divine calling. When the time is right the clock-genes will automatically ignite a whole new awakening process. When the unconscious becomes conscious it creates chaos while challenging the status quo and causing havoc to ego-systems. Chaos escalates as the old systems disintegrate, simultaneously causing destructive forces to rise and defend their illusion and lie. It does however help if we are conscious of these processes and do not get caught up in the down-draught. The challenge is to rise above the circumstances.

The time is now arriving for new leaders, and this means all of us who have chosen to become light bearers, to emerge from this silent slumber and also take in our rightful positions on the market place and platforms of life. The truth is – wake-up calls are now load and clear. The bells are beginning to toll!

The bell tolls

As the time and tides are changing, the signals to get up and get out are becoming loader and more frequent. Wake-up calls are already being heard far and wide – one after the other. In a country like South Africa we find the power struggle has come full circle. On the national news recently, bodies lay strewn in the streets while photos of bloodshed, tears and wide-eyed youths licking their spears were sent out into the world[342]. President Jacob Zuma announced to the country that it had lost its values – the ANC has lost its soul. Opposition parties call for the resignation of the President.

During the week of writing this chapter, South Africa was shrouded in mourning for the death of brothers as fellow countrymen turned on each other. This takes us back to the Sharpeville Massacre of 21 March 1960[343]. This wakeup call for South African, who represent the cosmic human power centre and host the Cradle of Humanity, shows in essence that nothing fundamental had changed and power has just shifted from one group to another. The power battles and ego-driven struggles for survival have been with us all this time, just cloaked in different wrappings with new names. Fearful hearts and the ego-driven value systems remain. This reminds us of the lessons learnt from the ancient Aztec history of Tenoch and Montezuma II[344] that in the end, ego power leads to self-destruction.

Now, the bell tolls, not only for the leaders in South Africa, and especially Africa, but for leaders all over the globe. We can expect Africa to awaken and see the light. Dark Africa is becoming enlightened. The rest of the world will follow!

As the bell tolls, these new leaders will come to the fore and take their rightful places. They will begin to fulfill their calling. However, this is not meant for a select few. This is a call for everyone to take their rightful place. Everyone therefore, has a leadership calling. This is a call to come and make your unique mark on the fabric of life. Only the authentic you and your original unique presence can fill this space. Like building a puzzle, we are called to make our contribution to the big picture and the universal body of light[345]. There are those who hear this call who are taking back their soul, reclaiming their 'soular' power[346] and are fulfiling their rightful unique place.

On the other hand, there are also those who are choosing to turn a deaf ear. We can expect that they will become further disconnected and their potential disabled while moving deeper into the darkness of loveless lies and deception and the lower resonance of the unsound/insane, fragmented fearful mind.

This idea is best captured in the well-known phrase of John Donne[347] in: *'For whom the bell tolls'*.

> *'Perchance he for whom this bell tolls may be so ill, as that he knows not it tolls for him; and perchance I may think myself so much better than I am, as that they who are about me, and see my state, may have caused it to toll for me, and I know not that'.*

The time of the New Earth and the Golden Age of 'heaven on earth' to emerge is here. The bell tolls for us all! Do you hear it calling? You are called to bring your piece of the puzzle to the table. You are called to bring your authentic self and take up your place at the banquet table of the universe. You are invited to join the adventure we call life.

The call for everyone to bring their part to the table

In this process we find people assisting others to do the same. These are our New DNA Leaders who have heard the calling and accepted higher authority to take a stand for what is right, true and authentic. Others will follow their lead. In the process the Golden Age begins to emerge for the benefit of all. The questions are:

> *What does this Golden era and New Earth look like? What should we as leaders do in order to assist in guiding others?*

Leadership, the New Earth and the Golden Age

The *New Earth* and *Golden Age* concepts are nothing new. This mindset has been part of all prominent religions and spiritual teachings for eons. These spiritual concepts refer to a level of human consciousness and world experience radically different to what we are experiencing at the moment.

The New Earth, also known as the *New Jerusalem* or *City Foursquare*[348] is the archetype or blue-print of the Golden Age. In religious terms seen as a city of cosmic light that exists on the etheric or quantum plane (heaven) and will be lowered to earth when the time comes. This is the authentic *Holy City,* representing sacred geometry or holy perfection.

The City Four Square metaphorically represents the four sides of the pyramid of enlightenment or rising of the consciousness of light or Christ consciousness. As a human race we will come full circle with the lowering of the New Jerusalem/City Four Square/New Earth, according to cosmic law, 'so above so below'. This lower process is done not by us – but in and through us. We are the Theoplexus – the place the love- resonance meets a troubled world. We are the Chalice – we are the Holy Grail.

The Golden Age denotes a new season of enlightenment for the human race. A new quality human being, *Homo sapiens spiritualis* with a newly enabled DNA, is emerging and taking its rightful place. This is the time where the soul of humankind consciously identifies with the authentic self, merges with higher spiritual octaves and begins to resonate on a more encompassing spiritual level of cosmic light. At the moment we are awakening to the truth of a Golden Era of living 'happily ever after' that is authentic and real and not some farfetched fairy tale. We are becoming aware that we are heirs to the treasures of the universe because we are children of creation and the Creator. We were predestined to live this New Earth experience and it is all encoded into our DNA.

In order to reclaim our New Earth legacy, we first have to retrace our steps and find out what went wrong and where and why we got lost.

There are many versions from different perspective and views of the creation of humankind denoting the path of the emerging of the species we know as *Homo sapiens*. The most well know story of the creation of heaven, earth and Adam and Eve is found in all prominent religions. This well-known analogy also serves as a map that sheds some light on our fallen, disabled and lower order consciousness and its current problems.

It also shows the way back.

Authentic living and finding our way home

In short: In the beginning there was only light[349]. Out of cosmic light everything physical was created. The human being, as crown and glory of creation, was created in the likeness of the Creator. The Creator is introduced as light, Spirit or – Love. Love is the resonance of the universe, the 'one-song'. We too are therefore authentic, spiritual light-love beings. This is our nature. As spiritual light beings, our original home is on the higher frequencies and etheric planes, the quantum dimension or in 'heaven'. Here everything is connected, synchronized, balanced and all exists in peace and harmony on the 'love' resonance. In the direct presence of Source, everyone experiences love, abundance and constant flow.

We find mystics teaching that consciousness chooses to manifest as physicality, or form, in order to engage in the process of remembering its true nature and communicating that remembrance to others. In this process we find our way back to our authentic self and our original blueprint. Consciousness is never tainted in this process, for the Absolute can never be tainted by the relative. This is our true home and original identity.

Then the human race 'fell from grace'.

This denotes the human race becoming disconnected, reverting to lower octaves of unconsciousness and becoming of unsound mind (insane mind). They were 'expelled from heaven'. Without guidance the disconnected or 'fallen ones' lost their way, got sidetracked and landed unceremoniously in the dungeons of physicality. They now erroneously accept all these dark, negative circumstances as their only home. Here, on the lower planes of existence, the human race forgot about their authentic self, their source and their heritage. They roamed aimlessly while leading impoverished lives of struggle and survival. In this depressing process they created their own gods, commonly and collectively known as Mammon, who is the personification of physicality and wealth as objects of worship. Mammon is also portrayed as an illusory or false god, or the shadow, negative ego-god. Today, many religious interpretations still consider physical wealth and riches as evil and corrupt influences.

The focus of humanity became fragmented and diverted because of varied and opposing challenges, demands and interests. The human race lost their vision of their destiny. The whole mind, one-mind or Holy mind became dissociated and fragmented. People became broken, disconnected and diseased. The sound and sane mind became unsound or insane. The ego rose from the fragmented or splintered self, unsound mind and identified with lower-order values and physical symbols of possessions and positions which became as 'gods' to the people. This is the archetype of the 'many gods'. With this unsound or insane mindset, humankind also turned on itself, while fear driven ego-struggles and power battles led to further self-destruction. This disconnected, false and discordant frequency with its accompanying low level of conscious awareness is still reflected in the everyday suffering of the human race.

Now, out of fear that they will lose control over their already destructive lives and demeaning value systems, the ego driven masses appoint fear driven ego-centred leaders to keep this insanity in place and secure their power over others. They believe in the power of numbers while trying to enforce and enlarge their ego-driven fear state. These leaders, who support the mindless scarcity mentality, also believe there is not enough for everyone and we have to fight and struggle to survive. The winner takes all. They train and develop prospective leaders and their followers in ego-driven leadership skills in order to keep this unsound (insane) mindset going. Specific leadership training schools fulfill the need to further their cause. In the end this all becomes a fruitless exercise as it has a self destructing mechanism as default.

Now, the season has started to change and the human race is beginning to awaken to truth while becoming mindful of their authentic identity and spiritual heritage. A higher consciousness is emerging of something more rewarding and fulfilling for all of us. There is enough for everyone and nobody is excluded. Awareness is growing that the suffering is unnecessary and the insanity needs to stop!

The next step is to end this blind wandering in a dark, delusional, mindless wilderness. The time to stop, turn around and find our way back to our original roots has arrived. This is our destiny[350]. We were predestined to take this path home. Although this is predestined, we have a conscious awareness and intelligence as the 'ability to choose' that places us on a different plane of consciousness from the rest of life on earth. When we make this conscious choice to stop, we also make the choice to follow the way-showers, light-bearers or leaders, on this return-path of enlightenment. In the process we become reinstated as authentic heirs of heaven and we reflect this in our DNA. We are in the process of consciously taking our rightful place at the banquette table of the Most High[351].

The next step is to re-enter 'paradise', the Promised Land, New Jerusalem, Golden City, or whatever analogy we would like to use, and reclaim what has always rightfully been ours. We gain access to this dimension of heaven by accessing the universal 'love' frequency and presenting our authentic self at the 'gates of heaven'. We also have our password of 'love and abundance' encoded and enabled in our DNA. We have this already stamped as our Master cell, in our hearts, minds, soul and spirit while the connection is located in the frontal lobes of the brain[352]. As authentic heirs to the treasures of the Kingdom of God, we can now become co-creators of a New Earth – here and now. We do not need to wait until we physically die. We can and should experience heaven on earth – now! We have the right and authority to manifest[353] by lowering the New Jerusalem mindset into physicality and experiencing the fulfilment of the Golden-age. We are hardwired to take dominion over the physical plane[354].

Wisdom comes from the words 'wise', as a way of perceiving and managing life and 'domicile' referring to our physical dwelling. 'Dominion' refers to a universal level of consciousness and the power, love and wisdom we already have encoded into our DNA in order to master our current physical home or domicile with love, compassion and reverence. This must not be confused with 'domination' that is negative, ego-centred and refers to the abuse of power and inevitable destruction.

We are the modern day alchemists with the inherent power to create miracles. All we need to do is identify with this higher alchemic authentic self and develop our Power Intelligence[355]. However, the disconnected fallen ones cannot comprehend or transcend to this level of consciousness and therefore live in fear and are enslaved by physicality. It is from this illusion we need to be freed. Only the truth will set us free. The truth is – we were created to be one with our authentic self, fulfill our soul purpose and live 'happily ever after'[356]. This is a not some farfetched fairy tale, but the authentic, predestined purpose of our existence.

However, access to this dimension will be denied to those who have chosen the low road. This is evident in the disabling of their Master cell and the love-centre in the frontal lobes that has caused a shutdown of systems of all the other light centres. They have consciously or unconsciously chosen to inhabit lower ego-driven and

Mammon serving planes. In the end they will be forced to stop and return to authenticity or they will ignore the wake-up calls and revert to lower order ego-methods. In order to solve this dilemma of blind and mindless living, they will need to revert to implementing more ego-driven illusions of power. It is not as farfetched as most people assume, that these lower ego-driven mindless people might have neuro-implants made to impersonate, imitate and copy the original master cell and authentic love centre. Disreputable cloning, genetic engineering, electro-implants in the brain and mind-altering drugs are already being used as we speak. These people are negating the comprehensive and even painful work of igniting these natural processes. They choose to take the low road by using unnatural, disreputable methods and evil schemes. The darks side of science is inevitably emerging parallel to the light side. This calls for high levels of mindful living, consciousness and discernment in order not to get caught up in these snares.

However, this is nothing new and has been part of all spiritual teachings and prominent religious interpretations. Different terms, such as Antichrist, are used to describe the dark or fallen ones. This can and will however never solve their problem of disconnection and fallen mind, as it is an illusion. Self-destruction, death and decay then become inevitable. In the meantime there is time for everyone to heed the call of their authentic self. We can find our way home by following the light and our enlightened leaders. They are the ones who have gone before us and are now Way-showers.

Finding our way home

The times and tides are changing and our season of suffering and meaningless struggle is over. We are now on our way home – some just sooner than others. Along the way we will find maps, signs, triggers and people who are giving their lives to assist others in also finding their way home. These enlightened leaders are now emerging and taking in their places. We are growing in the awareness that we were created to 'live happily ever after'. The question is:

> *Who are the enlightened leaders? How should we train enlightened leaders?*

We will focus on the answer to this question in the next chapter.

Notes

CHAPTER 20

TRAINING ENLIGHTENED LEADERS

Introduction

History has produced various enlightened leaders as role models with Nelson Mandela emerging as an international leadership icon of our time. We find the path of the emerging of an authentic, enlightened leader, mapped out step for step, just by studying his life[357]. Many readers of his book feel the same way and we find comments like *'This is not a book about a man, but a Manuscript for Life'*[358].

Although we find this full circle of life reflected on a micro-scale in the life of Nelson Mandela, we also find that the human race has undergone the same process on a macro-scale. As a human species we have come full circle, along with our leadership paradigms. We are now being challenged to *'get back to basics!'* This means we have to revisit truth and authenticity and rediscover our authentic selves. Enlightened leadership is all about assisting others to do the same.

The question is:

> *What are the basics we need to revisit?*

We find the answers to these questions in the chapters of this book. We have come full circle and now need to consolidate all this information into a practical plan of action for the development of enlightened leaders with New Leadership DNA. We need to look back on the path that was laid out by enlightened leaders before us and draw up a map. There is nothing new under the sun. As leaders we are not necessarily new pathfinders, for the Path has always been there. We are however the new mapmakers. The question is:

> *What are the options we have when we begin to draw up our new maps?*

We find the answer to this question by returning to our roots.

Returning to our roots

History has taught us various lessons. On the one hand we have the multi-theistic, generally referred to as polytheistic scenario or fragmented mind perspective. On the other hand we have the monotheistic or single-minded focus. Today we know this analogy represents the whole mind or healed sound mind focus of the evolved enlightened leaders and their followers. This in general refers to the *christed* or enlightened ones. On the other hand we have the multi-god perspective of the broken, fragmented, disabled and disconnected mind, mindless or unsound (insane) mind of the ego driven masses and their leaders. This in general refers to the unenlightened, *non-christed* souls or the Antichrist.

On the one hand we have the single minded one-god enlightened alliance represented by spiritual laws and soul values. The name for the monotheistic god could vary according to each individual, religion or group perspective. On the other hand we have the multi-god unsound mind, represented by Mammon, the archetype of the god of physical possessions and positions, physical laws and human ego-driven values. We find various names for the multi-theistic gods. The most common names used include: the ego, devil, Mammon, or Antichrist. We can see this as representing two opposing polarities of; light and darkness; ego and soul; truth and illusion or lies; life and death; or the Christ and Antichrist. There is no middle way. We are either conscious of our cosmic light and authentic self or not. This also refers to all spiritual guides who present themselves to the leaders and the masses, as prophets. All spiritual texts warn against the 'false prophets' of the time and call for a refined understanding of truth and constant vigilant discernment.

This means we have to make radical fundamental choices about the values and foundation or basis we build our new perception of life on. These choices are reflected in the values included in our leadership development and training paradigm. This brings us to an important question:

> *How should we prepare new, enlightened leaders*
> *with enabled New Leadership DNA?*

Leadership development and training

The training and development of enlightened leaders, we have found, is as ancient as the human species *Homo sapiens* – the conscious human being. It is part of our human nature to constantly be on the move, change develop, grow, migrate, transform, transcend and ascend. In essence – it is our nature to constantly evolve to higher levels and new forms of attainment and enlightenment. If we do not do this on a conscious level we devolve and self-destruct. It is a question of grow – or die.

The role of leaders and leadership training has always played an important part in this process we call life and quality living. Today we still have this important challenge of training and developing quality leaders to meet the needs of our time. The questions are:

> *What was leadership training like in the past and what*
> *form will it take on in the future?*

Leadership training schools

Historical records show that leadership training took on various forms and structures. Initially it all was conducted in secrecy. And only the selected few were allowed access to higher spiritual information. These were priest, shamans, sages or those who were prepared to leave the physical world behind. Today we find open academic leadership training schools have emerged that can be attended by all. You do not need to leave your job or family anymore in order to be trained as a leader. In chapter five we focused on the path of self-mastery and our modern day mystics in their mansions.

Today we also find formal structured leadership training and informal leadership training endeavors.

The question is:

> *What do all leadership training schools and their curricula have in common?*

The answers are straightforward: All leadership schools throughout the history of humankind have their specific point of view, paradigm or mindset of what 'success' and quality living is. They also have an outlined theory, value system and curriculum of what their student leaders should learn in order to obtain their perceived level of success. Thirdly they have methods of influencing others to buy-in to their value system, follow their lead and secure their perceived 'success path'. This in essence is the conscious and/or unconscious ability to manage influence life-force, energy or power.

The major focus points of all leadership training schools include their specific:

- Definition of success
- Value system that includes theories, mindsets and paradigms
- Methods of securing their mindset or paradigm (teaching)
- Laws, rules, guidelines and disciplinary measures
- Quality of influence they want to have in the lives of others (learning)
- Translating and securing it all in actions, plans and projects
- Accessing resources and assessing processes
- Traditions, ceremonies and initiations
- Celebrations for securing victory and success

However, one gold thread is evident throughout – everyone believes that their leadership will secure the best outcome. It could be an exclusive paradigm only benefitting the few. It can also be an inclusive mindset that will benefit all. This means that not only do all schools for leadership development have their own curriculum and information outline what students need to learn, they also have a outline of what and how to teach their students, their disciples or followers.

In chapter 3 we focused on the foundation of New Leadership DNA. We can use this information to determine where the power and authority of a person, group or leadership paradigm are rooted. There are those who are willing to disconnect from ego-driven power structures and re-route and re-root in soul power. There are those who are afraid, or just too stubborn to acknowledge that they are on the wrong path. The result is that they remain in their comfort zone and current state of illusion.

In order to obtain a higher soul-centred goal, we first need to master the lower ego-driven forces. These are mostly within ourselves and this means we first have to overcome and master our own inner demons. As we develop more enlightened leaders, we can expect the power-shift from ego power to soul power to go through a stage of dissonance, conflict and chaos before authentic power or soul power and its attendant leadership emerges[359].

In order to move forward with our quest of developing enlightened leaders, we need to find out what we can take with us from both systems. We should not proverbially 'throw the baby out with the bathwater' and we need not re-invent the wheel! We can heal the ego and integrate a healthy ego-consciousness with a soul consciousness. This will be reflected in different leadership training schools.

We find formal and informal leadership training processes.

- **Formal leadership training**

First we have a look at formal leadership training that includes the training of secret organizations and open leadership training schools.

- **Secret organizations and their leadership training**

'Secret societies' and organisations can be found all over the globe, on every continent, in every country and in every organisation. The purpose of these secret organized groups is founding, maintaining, upholding and expanding their exclusive agenda. This can vary from a tribal, cultural or social agenda to financial, religious, political or power agendas. Each individual, as a part of the organization, builds their life on the foundation of their personal and collective values, dogma and the cause of their 'secret society'. These values and causes are then expressed in everyday life on different platforms and within different contexts. Each have their vision of success and quality living – be it an inclusive or exclusive approach.

Leaders in the 'secret organization' scenario are identified and trained in order to secure and further the cause of the society – in secret. Although the values, rituals, initiations or content of different secret organizations may vary, or even radically differ – the commonality of all secret societies and organizations is – survival.

Though most secret societies are formed with relatively realistic political and religious goals in mind, their focus on mystery and secrecy has made them the target of many conspiracy theories. However, when we take a closer look from a different angle, we find that reality is usually much more harmless and innocent than we envisioned. However this doesn't mean that the groups don't have some fascinating practices. No matter what their supposed purpose, there's something inherently sinister about a 'secret society'. The important fact remains that history has shown that secret societies and their training and support of influential people and leaders have had an impact on world events[360]– and they still do.

On the other hand we find general open organizations that also cater for training their leaders.

- **Open leadership training schools**

Globally we find traditional leadership training in all cultures, social structures and open education systems. Education and training take place on different levels, in different countries with different content and methods. In some countries education is more accessible than others and in different countries we find different standards of education. We also find information and education on different levels that include, primary, secondary, and tertiary education systems. We also find leadership training on these levels.

Most prominent global tertiary institutes have Schools for Leadership Development. The content will depend on where the person is expected to fulfill a role. If it is within business, we find Business Leadership Schools. If it is within a religion we find specific content, dogma and leadership schools for different religions and their specific leadership posts. If it is within education or sport, we will find training in educational leadership or sports administration. However, very few of these leadership schools have emerged at the level of quantum leadership training[361].

The new consciousness is emerging and taking us beyond our traditional primary, secondary and tertiary academic training and development. A quaternary level, a fourth level education, is now emerging as part of our awakening. Quaternary education is now becoming part of the emerging of our New Leadership DNA. Here we find transparency, honesty, truth, integrity and seamless co-operation while synergising with and complementing each other. We are going back to the origin of our authentic blueprint, calling and soul power and predestined function. We are returning to the wisdom of the quantum universe. Quantum learning and teaching will now become a priority in the development of New Leadership DNA as we will see in the next chapter.

Although individual cultures, societies, religions and social structures could remain, they will be spiritualised our 'quantumnised' into one unified, functional whole. We find deeper understanding once again in the words of Donne[362].

> *"No man is an island, entire of itself; every man is a piece of the continent, a part of the main. If a clod be washed away by the sea, Europe is the less, as well as if a promontory were, as well as if a manor of thy friend's or of thine own were: any man's death diminishes me, because I am involved in mankind, and therefore never send to know for whom the bells tolls; it tolls for thee."*

We are discovering our authentic self and we are beginning to identify the original place we were meant to fill. We are finding out that we are part of the bigger picture and we need to bring our contribution to the table and assist in building the universal picture[363].

Where leaders were previously educated and trained in order to maintain 'power over people', we are now emerging to a new level of 'releasing power within people'. Where we found power in numbers we now understand the number of powers in everyone. Everything is now being opened up, disclosed and uncovered and everything is coming to light as we speak. The mysterious secrets are becoming demystified and there is no more need for secrecy. We are also required to implement a whole new way of teaching and learning. Leadership training is taking a new turn and we are now in the home stretch.

However leadership training is also done in an informal manner.

- **Informal leadership training**

Informal leadership training refers to a system where these deeper values are taught in everyday life. A father teaches his son how to treat others and communicate with respect. A teacher teaches her class about forgiveness or a pastor teaches his congregation how to connect to the higher spiritual levels. We have friends, coaches and mentors who are involved on an informal level while influencing others to find and live their authentic selves.

Here we find that the teacher and the student are exactly at the same place. We also find that when the student is ready – the teacher will arrive. We also find that when the teacher is right – the students will start arriving.

These teaching, mentoring and coaching meetings are all in essence informal leadership training sessions. Here we teach and influence others to connect to their authentic self and assist others to do the same. Here we find gene-jumping, gene-migrations, meme-migrations, challenging of mindsets and discarding of outworn paradigms. Here we consciously change the resonance from lower ego-driven vibrations to higher love, life, light and abundance frequencies. We help and assist others to find their unique note and voice of who they are as part of the song of the universe. In the process we voice a new, clear, note, make our presence heard and emit a new light. Others follow. This is authentic success. This is authentic leadership as we lead by example.

The questions are:

> *What was the content of the teachings of the mystery schools? What should we teach and how should we mentor our emerging enlightened leaders?*

In order to find the answers to these questions we will need to understand quantum learning. We will focus on quantum learning and quantum healing in the next chapter.

Notes

CHAPTER 21

NEW LEADERSHIP DNA AND QUANTUM LEARNING

Introduction

We are now conscious that a new, enlightened generation with enlightened leaders is emerging. This can also be seen as a quantum generation with quantum leaders who are presenting with a new success DNA and a new leadership DNA. The terms quantum communities and quantum leaders are another way of referring to this new enlightened generation, *Homo sapiens spiritualis*. It is also just another way of explaining spirituality.

The questions are:

> *What does 'quantum' mean and why is quantum learning so important today?*

Quantum refers to the quantum universe, the spiritual dimension that is the backdrop to our physical reality[364]. It radically differs from our current experience of physicality as being 'solid' - that, in essence, is an illusion. Quantum refers to 'cosmic light' as the foundation of all of reality. It is important to learn about this dimension and our interaction on this plane, for it is here we are going to spend the next season of our existence[365].

The quantum universe and cosmic light

In order to understand cosmic light, we first need to understand the quantum universe[366] or the universe of energy and particles. It is the backdrop to our physical universe and consists of energy-information on different frequencies that change from one form to another. The different forms of energy include sound, electro-magnetism, heat, and light that function according to quantum mechanics. Quantum physics, that includes quantum mechanics, is a branch of science that deals with these discrete, indivisible units of energy called quanta as described by Quantum Theory. It is at this level, the quantum level of cosmic light that we are connected to the cosmos via the chromosomes of our DNA. This means that in order to develop New Leadership DNA, we need to understand the different dimensions of our universe, the quantum reality, cosmic light and Quantum Theory. We have already focused on these issues in the books *New Success DNA* and *Power Intelligence* in a bit more detail and it is important to revisit these topics[367].

In summary we find five main ideas represented in Quantum Theory[368]:

- Energy is not continuous, but comes in small but discrete units.
- The elementary particles behave both like particles *and* like waves.
- The movement of these particles is inherently random.
- It is *physically impossible* to know both the position and the momentum of a particle at the same time. The more precisely one is known, the less precise the measurement of the other is.
- The atomic world is *nothing* like the world we live in.

All Quantum leaders will have a sound fundamental understanding of the quantum reality presented at the level of quaternary education.

However, knowledge and understanding is not sufficient. We also need to develop the tools and skills in order to accept our universal authority and take dominion over physicality. We have already made a clear distinction between 'dominion' and 'domination'. Dominion is the ruling method of the soul out of love and compassion while domination is the destructive method of the fear driven ego. We have found that this information was kept secret and presented only to the selected few in leadership training programs in Mystery Schools. Today this is being demystified while the information is becoming available to all.

The level of consciousness of the human race is now ready to take responsibility for this important information. According to the universal law of the 'right use of energy' we have the right and the privilege to make use of this universal gift, encoded into our DNA. We are their heirs to the Kingdom of the universe – the Kingdom of God. We need not settle for anything less. We need to become knowledgeable in quantum theory and we need to understand the properties of cosmic light.

Quantum theory and cosmic light

We inhabit an all encompassing cosmic universe. Since mankind has become conscious we have looked to the heavens for answers and once again we are returning to these higher planes for answers, guidance and direction. Astronomers and Astrologers have viewed this dimension of reality from different points of view. Today all these perspectives are coming together in the same way as science and spirituality are merging. We are looking at an indivisible reality from different points of view. Quantum Theory was developed to make this all just a bit more accessible[369]. However, the Wisdom of the Ages teaches us that trying to understand it calls on intuition as well as intellect, heart as well as mind, and quite literally, is the quest of a lifetime.

'That Light is the root of our being,
from atoms to consciousness, and in that Light
we are unified with the entire Universe.
We always have been and always will be[370].'

While at first glance Quantum Theory may seem like just another strange theory, it contains many clues as to the fundamental spiritual nature of the universe.

We have found that our cosmos is in reality light or cosmic light. Although not visible to the eye these galactic cosmic rays come from outside our solar system. They are subatomic particles - mainly protons but also some heavy nuclei, accelerated to almost the speed of light by the explosions of distant supernovae. Cosmic rays cause 'air showers' of secondary particles when they hit Earth's atmosphere. They also pose a health hazard to astronauts and a single cosmic ray can disable a satellite if it hits an unlucky integrated circuit[371]. Although Time Magazine[372] reported that cosmic rays were identified about three year ago, cosmic light has been in the higher conscious or unconscious awareness of humankind forever.

Now the authentic power, purpose and meaning of cosmic light are coming to the fore. Truth about our authentic origins is now coming to light. We are learning about our quantum reality as foundation of our spiritual reality as backdrop to our physical existence. We are becoming enlightened. This is the new path leadership development will take in the future.

Leadership, teaching and learning

We have the challenge to let go of all our other previous paradigms and transcend into a new dimension. We are now being sent to 'the other side'. This is however, nothing new. Leaders like Nelson Mandela have inspired a whole new mindset of cooperation, forgiveness and service – a level of service consciousness that has now gripped the world. 'Nelson Mandela Day' has become a global day of service where everyone is called to give 67 minutes of their time in service of others. Although leaders like Nelson Mandela had to go through their own path of initiation, we can take our new leaders to these new heights by just implementing the obvious steps. This information will fill a book on its own[373].

For now we will answer a few basic questions, the first being:

What is the path of the quantum leader?

All quantum leaders go through a 'desert' experience, also known as the *'dark night of the soul'*. In chapter 3 we have already referred to this important form of teaching and learning on the path of the enlightened leaders. It is during the 'dark night of the soul' experiences that we reconnect to our authentic power and our authentic self. There is immense power in being your authentic self.

All significant and influential leaders always first go through this desert experience or 'valley of death'. Here we die to the old only to be reborn into the new. We find ancient examples of profound leaders like Buddha and Jesus and more recent examples like Mahatma Ghandi and Nelson Mandela, who come to mind. These are master souls who have left an indelible imprint on the fabric of life.

At a personal, collective and even global level we are all in the process of healing the fragmented parts of the disconnected self, while becoming our authentic self and being who we are. As we raise our awareness, we also become conscious of how we are physically, mentally, emotionally and spiritually 'wired' for the process of producing, creating and miracle making. All we need to do is to reclaim our power, grow in understanding, and consciously align with and enhance the universal processes at work. This all takes place through our higher mind or miracle mind. We find the connection between the higher universal mind and our personal mind within the seat of the soul – the frontal lobes of our physical brain[374]. Here we have to choose between ego centred versus value or soul-centred living. We evolve to this level consciousness by the method of quantum learning.

The next important question is:

What is quantum learning?

New Leadership DNA, quantum learning and healing

Students aspiring to enable their *New Success DNA* and their *New Leadership DNA* are prepared to let go of lower order values and outworn methods and access a whole new mindset. Not only do they need to learn new information, they also need to learn higher methods of processing information. Here we find the level of *quantum learning* and *quantum healing*. When we learn we grow, and as we grow we heal. Learning and healing are flipsides of the same coin. When we become *quantum students* we also become *quantum patients* in need of healing and reconnecting our fragmented and scattered parts of self. We also need *quantum teachers* to show the way[375]. These teachers are also our *quantum healers* of the time. This is the task and calling of all quantum leaders with new enabled leadership DNA.

The questions are:

> *Who and what are quantum students and teachers?*

Quantum learning is the conscious ability to gain access to and utilize information on a quantum level. This is also the level of the universal frequency 528 Hz, the frequency of spirituality and love. The person teaching these skills, tools and methods are our *quantum teachers* and their students are *quantum students*. Here we find that a leader is the teacher, guru or master and the follower is the student. The teaching/learning or healing/healer experience between a teacher, guru, sage or master and their students is a very special relationship. Some may even see this as a divine appointment – a cosmic time for the two to come together.

On the one hand we have our informal teaching and learning experiences while on the other hand, more formal teaching and learning experiences are now being created. The fact that human consciousness has evolved to a level of comprehending and understanding this important quantum or spiritual information, necessitates that these teaching/learning experiences now take place more frequently and in the open. There is no need for secrecy anymore and we can expect that many of our secret organisations and the content they taught will now come to light. Everything that was covered in secrecy will now be uncovered and 'come to light'.

We can even envisage a more formal addition to our educational system that will include quantum learning and quarternary schools and universities that are open to all. The time of mystery schools is over.

Quantum leaders and their quaternary universities

We are moving beyond the boundaries that divide us and are beginning to embrace everything that connects and makes us whole, healthy, wealthy and happy. We are coming full circle.

A circle has four quadrants that all play an important part in the whole. For example, we have four seasons and spend time in one season before moving on to the other. The one cannot exist without the other. In the same way we have universal seasons. We are now entering into the fourth level of consciousness of this cosmic cycle. We need new quantum leaders with a new mindset and new leadership DNA, who can help assist and guide us in embracing this wonderful gift we call – conscious life.

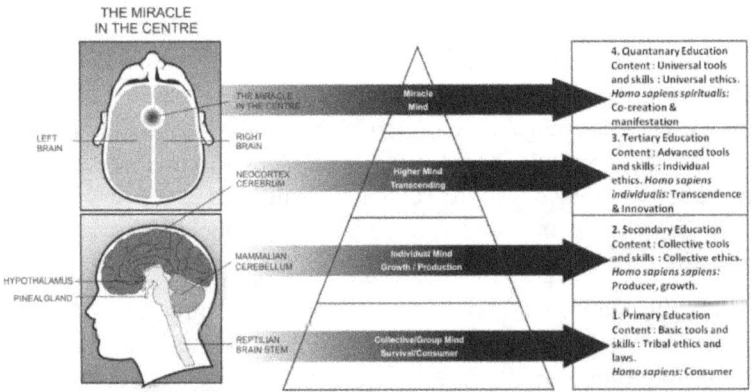

The quantum mind and quaternary education

The word 'quaternary' comes from the Latin, *'quadrăs'* meaning 'fourth part'. Words like 'quantanary' or 'quadranary' are could also be used alternatively in this regard. Globally we have education systems that include three parts as primary, secondary and tertiary education. This also relates to the emerging of consciousness in the four quadrants of the brain. Now, with the emerging of the guide-spot or God-spot, we also need another tier of reference that embraces and encompasses all the other levels.

These four parts can also be found in the unfolding of new levels of consciousness and corresponding neural-development. It denotes coming 'full circle'. While others get stuck or choose to remain on the previous three levels, the quantum leader (QL) has chosen to pursue a higher calling on a higher level with higher quaternary teachings. A Quantum Leader understands universal wisdoms and receives guidance from the higher dimensions and the universal blueprint or 'perfect image'.

A person can only access this level of leadership once they have come 'full circle'. This means they have gone through all four quadrants of training as primary, secondary, tertiary and quaternary education. This does not necessarily include formal training as many children have the higher brain functions already activated at an early age.

At the same time the initial definition of the Triad Brain is now evolving into a quaternary or Quantum Brain. Above we find a short summary of this process. The question is:

> *How do most enlightened leaders get to the quantum level of teaching and learning? How do they get exposed to quaternary education?*

The new leader like you the reader, always experiences a calling that is usually announced via various wake-up calls. You then become aware that 'the bell tolls for me!' You can ignore the calling or you can answer. If no answer is received – the bell keeps on tolling until it becomes a deafening noise. Once you consciously answer the calling the doors begin to open, the Divine universe sends out all the necessary people and resources and provides the necessary support to the new emerging student. Nothing is ever left to chance or by co-incidence. When the student if right – the teacher will arrive!

The processes of change, transformation and transcendence are then ignited and all the steps, challenges and processes we discussed in previous chapters, become evident. Some will hear and answer the calling, change, transform, transcend and move forward. Others will ignore the calling and stay behind.

The new enlightened leader has to go through the necessary education and training in preparation for this role. This level of teaching and learning has, up until now, only been available on an informal level to those leaders who are on this specific spiritual journey.

Although we have a global view of the standards of education, different cultures from different countries have different educational systems containing the curriculum they deem as necessary. This means that the chances are slim that quantum information will be taught in a general education system, in the near future. Until the systems open up to a wider view of education and training, the individual person, group or organization, will need to accept personal responsibility for introducing this information to the people they are responsible for. This can be done in various ways that include informal personal contact or formal in-house training and development. However, we are once more returning to our roots and the coaching and mentoring system is proving to be the most probable course of action to take.

This poses a whole new challenge to the emerging profession of coaching and mentoring.

Quantum coaching and mentoring

The word 'coach' originated in the 15th century and referred to a vehicle transporting passengers from one point to another. Later 'coaching' was used in sports to describe the person who instructs a performer or team of performers on fundamentals and strategy in order to secure success. During the 1950s, Myles Mace[376] introduced 'coaching' as a management tool to foster greater productivity. By the mid-1970s authors started to introduce sports coaching techniques in management literature[377]. During the 1980s, coaching began to be seen primarily as a development activity not linked to sports and it is maintained that Dr Dick Borough was the first person to use the term to describe his leadership development activities[378].

Since the 1990s the role of the coach has been redefined and a new paradigm has emerged. Within this model the coach is not seen as the expert, or the leader with all the answers. Instead the coach is now seen as a team member and part of a special relationship between coach and client which motivates individual/s to exceed prior levels of achievement[379].

Today coaching is viewed as the guidance of an individual or group by someone who teaches skills to improve performance. Authors distinguish this from mentoring, which is a dynamic and reciprocal relationship in a workplace whereby a mentor helps a less experienced person to develop in some specified capacity[380].

This is exactly the same outline found in the training of the Magi of Zarathustra nearly 5000 year ago. Here we find history has come full circle. Even leadership coaching and mentoring is returning to its roots. New quantum coaches and mentors are emerging to meet the needs of the time. They are the Magi of our time.

The questions are:

> *What kind of person is the new quantum coach and mentor? What information is included in these coaching sessions?*

The quantum coach, mentor or teacher is nothing more, or less, than the sages, masters, mystics and mentors we have encountered throughout history. We are now finding modern day mentors, masters and mystics in our midst with their task as way showers and mapmakers. The leaders with New Leadership DNA are coming forward and taking their rightful place to teach others about quality living. Like Zarathustra and his Magi in chapter one, quantum leaders with new leadership DNA are being coached, mentored and taught to go out amongst people and enlighten them to a new way of living. In essence, our modern day Magi are also teachers with a mission to bring truth and enlightenment to the masses. Our Quantum Leaders with a New Leadership DNA are modern missionaries of our time. They are not only teachers but also healers. They are helping to heal the broken minds and fragmented souls of the disconnected masses. We have come full circle.

The questions are:

> *Who are these quantum coaches and mentors?*
> *Where will we find them and what do they teach?*

Quantum coaches and mentors are people who have a positive influence in our lives. They cross our paths and stay for a reason, season or a lifetime. They serve as catalysts, function as alchemists and teach us Truth. Truth sets us free. They are the messengers of the authentic self and universal freedom and come in different forms. Our level of awareness will determine how, when and where we become conscious of their influence in our lives. Some we meet in person while others we meet through the internet or through their work, books or films. Sometimes we access the universal web, giving us access to higher planes and connecting us to angels, guides, masters or light beings. By the time we have evolved to this level of communication, the use of stimulants like drugs, rhino horn, or secondary communication channels like psychic interpretations, becomes insignificant. We have open channels directly to the universal web. We can communicate directly with God[381].

We have been warned to be wary of the stranger, as it might just be an angel in disguise. Our modern day quantum coaches and mentors are teachers. To teach means to demonstrate, to show the way. Our new leaders are also teachers who choose to know the way, go the way and show the way The calling is to heal the cosmic body of light. This is a calling for all of us. We are all called to take in our authentic place as a quantum healer, a quaternary teacher and a leader with New Leadership DNA.

This is not just meant for the select few, it is meant for everyone with an open heart and compassion for the searching masses and lost souls. They come from all over the world, from all religions or no religions. They are the ones who have answered the universal call for freedom. They have seen the Light! They choose to shine their unique light – and show the way home.

A last question remains: Who are these leaders?

These leaders are – you and I!

OoooOooo

Summary

Pictures speak a thousand words[382].

The journey up the mountain of Truth

The task of the enlightened leader

New, enlightened leaders as mapmakers and way showers

GLOSSARY

Adam: From Latin *ãdhãmah,* meaning 'earth'; Hebrew *ãdhãm* meaning the 'first human' and progenitor of mankind. Unregenerate and original side of human nature. Refers to humanity as a whole.

Affluence: Means 'full flow' and refers to material, physical, emotional, mental, psychological, spiritual and financial flow as the foundation of health and abundance.

Alchemy: A traditional chemical philosophy having as its asserted aims the transmutation of base metals into gold; any seemingly power or process of transmuting; the art of transmutation.

Allele: The word *'allele* is a short form of *'*allelomorph' meaning *'other form'*, which was used in the early days of genetics to describe variant forms of a gene detected as different phenotypes. It derives from the Greek root *alius* meaning 'other'; the word *allelos,* meaning 'each other'.

Animism: The belief that a supernatural force animates and organizes the universe. The belief that people have spirits that do or can exist separately from their bodies.

Anointed: To install somebody officially or ceremonially in a position or office; to put oil or ointment on a part of somebody's body, usually the head or feet, as part of a religious ceremony, e.g. in a Christian baptism.

Astrologer: A person who studies the positions and aspects of heavenly bodies with a view to predict their influence on the course of human life.

Astrology: The study of the positions and aspects of heavenly bodies with a view to predict their influence on the course of human life. See 'astronomy'.

Astronomy: The scientific measurement of the positions and motions of celestial bodies. See 'astrology'.

Authentic: Having an undisputed origin; genuine; worthy of trust; reliance or belief.

Authority: From Latin, *'auctõritãs'* and *'auctor'* meaning: *'author',* *'the ability to create, grow, increase'* and *'he who obtains divine favour,* *increase' and 'auge' meaning 'to shine'. A person or group invested* with power; invested with the right or power to write and enforce rules or give orders; somebody or something with official power.

Bigotry: The practice of having very strong and unreasonable opinions, especially about politics, race, or religion, and refusing to consider other people's opinions. Prejudice, racism, intolerance, bias, narrow-mindedness, chauvinism. Antonym: fairness.

Bloodline: Family background, lineage, history, ancestry; a direct line of descent from a specific ancestor, especially with respect to the common characteristics shared by that ancestor's descendants.

Bomoh or dukun: Malay shaman. The bomoh's original role was that of a healer and their expertise was first and foremost an in-depth knowledge of medicinal herbs and tajul muluk or Malay geomancy. This was supplemented by Sanskrit mantera (mantras) owing to the ancient Hindu-Buddhist influence in the region.

Calling: To request or order someone to do something; A claim on a person's time or life; Available whenever summoned to a particular pursuit or career; A strong urge to follow a particular career or do a particular type of work; to invoke as from heaven; To call, designate, summon, name, invoke and bring forth action.

Caste system: The class, ranks or position of somebody in a society, according to birth, occupation, or some other criterion; One of the four main hereditary classes into which Hindu society is divided, dictating the social position and status of people according to their professions. Though discrimination based on caste has been illegal since 1947, it still occurs in some areas; Class, standing, rank, social position.

Chela: From Sanskrit meaning 'slave' or 'servant'. In India it refers to a disciple of a religious teacher or guru. Also a term generally used to refer to a student of an Ascended Master. See 'discipleship'.

Clairvoyant: Somebody who is supposedly able to perceive things that are usually beyond the range of human senses and has intuitive, telepathic, mind reading gifts. Also see: psychic, mystic, spiritualist, diviner, and seer, medium.

Coaching: Training in how to deal with life, work, problems and interpersonal relationships.

Coetaneous: Meaning 'same age'; of equal age, duration, or period. Contemporary.

Compassionate: Sympathetic, empathetic, kind, caring: Showing feelings of sympathy for the suffering of others, often with a desire to help.

Conspiracy: A group of people planning or agreeing in secret to commit an illegal or subversive act; A plot or secret act.

Corrupt: All incorrect, shady, false, fraudulent information or ;As verb: to make undesirable changes in meaning or introduce other errors into a text during copying; to introduce unintentional errors into computer data or software, making it unusable or unreliable; to become immoral or depraved, or cause somebody to become immoral or depraved; immoral or dishonest, especially as shown by the exploitation of a position of power or trust for personal gain.

Cure: To restore a sick person or animal to health; to bring to an end to an illness, disease or injury; treat illness successfully; restoring to full functionality.

Defeat: Means to conquer, overcome or overpower. To be defeated: you are overcome and your power is taken away.

Democracy: The right to a form of government in which power is invested in the people as a whole, usually exercised on their behalf by elected representatives; a system of government based on the principle of majority decision-making; the control of an organization by its members, who have a right to participate in decision-making processes.

Disciple: Someone committed to and disciplined in the teachings of a specific Master. Comes from 'discipline'.

Discipleship: The path a person follows in a teaching from a specific master. Steps on the path of discipleship include: student, disciple, friend, brother/sister, Christed or anointed one – here the student becomes the teacher and master. The processes of attaining self-mastery through self-disciple in the initiations of the Buddha, the World Teachers and Ascended Masters. Specifically referring to the disciples of the Christ consciousness and the teachings of the Ascended Master like Jesus Christ.

Divination: The methods or practice of attempting to foretell the future or discovering the unknown through omens, oracles, or supernatural powers. The art or act of foretelling future events; revealing of occult knowledge by means of augury or alleged supernatural agency; an inspired guess; or a supposed supernatural agency.

Domination: Power, control over people. Opposite: *Dominion* – 'wise rule'

Dukun: An Indonesian-Malay term for shaman. In Malaysia, they are often referred to as 'bomoh', but 'dukun' is the more ancient term. Their societal role is that of a traditional healer, spirit medium, custom and tradition experts and on occasion sorcerers and masters of black magic.

Dysfunctional: Failing to perform an expected authentic function. Characterized by an inability to function emotionally or as a social unit.

Energy: Vigour or power in action. Vitality and intensity of expression.

Power exercised with vigour and determination. The capacity for action or accomplishment. From Greek: energies. Coined by Aristotle from energĕs (-en meaning 'at' and ergon meaning 'work'). Active-at-work. See 'power'. A59

Eons: A division of geological time comprising two or more eras; A period of time that is boringly or dishearteningly long.

Epidemic: An outbreak of a disease that spreads more quickly and more extensively among a group of people than would normally be expected. See: pandemic.

Evolve: To develop something gradually, often into something more complex or advanced, or undergo such development.

Exorcism: The use of prayers or religious rituals to drive out evil spirits believed to possess a person or place. The act of ridding the mind of oppressive feelings, thoughts or memories.

Fear: A chance or likelihood of an undesirable thing happening; an unpleasant feeling of anxiety or apprehension caused by the presence or anticipation of danger; an idea, thought, or other entity that causes feelings of fear; trepidation; anxiety.

Feat: Impressive and difficult act. Something impressive and often dangerous that someone does. Not easily achievable. See: Defeat.

Feelings: The sensation felt on touching something; the ability to perceive physical sensation in a part of the body; a perceived physical or mental sensation; and unqualified emotion.

Functional: Having a practical application, or serving a useful purpose: Useful, practical, well-designed, purposeful, service-able. (See useless).

Gatha: 17 Hymns said to be composed by Zarathustra and valued as the most sacred texts of the monotheistic Zoroastrian faith.

Genetic migration: In population genetics, gene flow, also known as 'gene migration', is the transfer of 'alleles' or genes from one population to another. See 'allele'.

GPS: Global positioning system.

Great Work: The unification of the body, mind and soul with the Spirit. This unification is the ultimate transformation of the self into one's highest potential being, an exalted state of divine awareness and consciousness.

Happiness: Emotional fulfilment; includes contentment, being pleased, high spirits, exuberant; joyful; bliss, ecstasy.

Heathen: One who adheres to the religion of a tribe, or nations and does not acknowledge one God as taught by Christianity, Judaism and Islam. One who is regarded as irreligious, uncivilized, or unenlightened. Uncouth, barbarous in manner.

Herbalist: One who grows, collects or specialises in herbs, especially medicinal herbs.

Hidden Knowledge: The teachings of the mystery schools containing the innermost knowledge of life and wisdom.

HIV/AIDS: From: Human immunodeficiency virus (HIV) and Acquired immune deficiency syndrome or acquired immunodeficiency syndrome (AIDS).

Hominid: A primate belonging to a family of which the modern human being is the only species still in existence. Family: *Hominidae.*

Homo sapiens: *Homo* is Latin for 'human'. The word 'human' itself is from Latin *humanus*, an adjective cognate to homo, both thought to derive from a Proto-Indo-European word for "earth". 'Sapiens' is derived from '*sapience*' referring to 'wise man' or 'knowing man'. 'Sapience' is often defined as wisdom, or the ability of an organism or entity to act with appropriate judgment, a mental faculty which is a component of intelligence or alternatively may be considered an additional faculty, apart from intelligence, with its own properties.

Human migration: Physical movement by humans from one area to another, sometimes over long distances or in large groups. Historically this movement was nomadic, often causing significant conflict with indigenous populations and their displacement or cultural assimilation. *Emigrants* refer to people moving out of a territory; *Immigrants*refer to people moving into a territory.

Humanoid: Describes a being from another planet (or dimension) that has the appearance or characteristics of a human.

I Ching: An ancient Chinese system of divination, based on a book of Taoist philosophy and expressed in hexagrams chosen at random and interpreted to answer questions and give advice.

Illusion: An erroneous perception of reality. An erroneous concept or belief.

Immaculate concept: The pure concept or image of the soul, held by the mind of God. Any pure thought or concept held by one part of life for and on behalf of another part of life. The ability to hold the image of the perfect pattern to be precipitated. To see the vision of the project completed. The exercise of inner sight through the third eye. Visualisation of the perfect idea which then becomes a magnet that attracts the creative energies to fulfil the pattern in mind.

Infectious: Caused by bacteria or viruses or other micro-organisms. Agents that are communicable, catching, transferable, transmittable and contagious.

Agents capable of affecting the emotions and attitudes of others.

Influence: The effect of something on a person, thing, or event; the power that somebody has to affect other people's thinking or actions by means of argument, example, or force of personality.

Insanity: Extreme foolishness, or an act that demonstrates such foolishness. Mental illness, madness, lunacy. Informal: very stupid or crazy behaviour that can cause serious problems, harm, or injury to others.

Inspiration: Stimulation of the faculties to a high level of feeling or activity. Theology: Divine guidance or influence exerted directly upon the mind and soul of man. The act of breathing in - inhalation. From: in-spiritus.

Inspire: To affect, guide or arouse by divine influence. To inhale; to breathe life into; to rouse latent energies, ideas or reverence; to enliven.

Integrity: From Latin 'integritãs' or 'intege', and is defined as "any intact unity or entity, whole, complete, perfect, virtuous".

Intelligence: From *intel* meaning 'between two' and *ligence* meaning 'to choose'. The human being is endowed with intelligence - the freedom to choose or 'free will'. According to Wechsler, *"intelligence is the aggregate or global capacity of the individual to act purposefully, to think rationally, and to deal effectively with his environment."*

Junk DNA and junk genes: Junk DNA and junk genes are provisional labels for the genes and portions of DNA sequence of a chromosome or a genome, for which no specific function can be identified. Many cellular biologists state that the so-called 'junk DNA', may turn out to be just as important as our much sought-after genes. Current studies of junk DNA are opening up unexplored areas of medical science and technology.

Kalku: The kalku is a semi-mythical character that has the power of working with *wekufe* "spirits or wicked creatures". A *mapuche kalku* is usually an inherited role, although it could be a *machi* that is interested in lucrative ends, or a "less powerful", frustrated machi who ignores the laws of the *admapu.*. From Chili.

Kiln: A specialized oven or furnace used for industrial processes such as firing clay for pottery or bricks and for drying materials such as hops or timber. Also used in agriculture: a heap of vegetables, usually potatoes, covered with earth and mulch and sometimes stored in a shed.

Leader: Comes from word leiдð meaning: to show the way by going in advance; to guide by taking by the hand; escort; direct; to go first as a guide; to be at the head of; to act as director or commander; Somebody who guides or directs others; somebody or something in front of all others.

Leadership: Management, guidance, control, direction; the ability to guide, direct, or influence people; the office or position of the head of a body of people.

Light Body: Comes from 'chromosome'; chromo meaning 'light' and soma meaning body. We have 'light bodies' that surround our physical bodies and are connected to and controlled by our chromosomes. 'Light bodies' act as filters and attraction forces that attract everything in the proximity that resonates on the same frequency. As the chromosomes of our DNA become reconnected and activated, they light up and emit a new light in our light bodies. When we are disconnected our levels of light are at a low and we attract dark forces. Also defined as the 'aura', 'spiritual body' or 'reticular-activating-system', the RAS.

Magic: The practice of using charms, spells or rituals, to attempt to produce supernatural effects. 'Black magic' makes use of destructive forces or to control others or events in nature. 'White magic' makes use of light, love and constructive forces to help heal and assist.

Magician: A person who performs magic for entertainment; a sorcerer; wizard.

Maltese Cross: The Maltese Cross is used as symbol of the perfect balance between life-force and physicality that takes place in and through us. It provides the thought form or matrix of "so in heaven - so on earth'. The upper north arm of the Maltese Cross descending into the centre, resembles the upper vessel of the hourglass and is symbolic of the flow of spiritual energy from 'above to below' in and though us. The point of qualification at the centre indicates that we must always be conscious of how we qualify this power in and through our hearts and minds. The power from above congeals into physicality and takes on the form of our thoughts, feelings, acts and spoken words. The challenge is to strive to balance this flow of life-force and be conscious of the quality of the 'stamp' we place on this power given us from above. The challenge is to constantly remain aware of perfection (perfect+union) so that the authentic universal will, love and compassion can be manifest 'on earth as in heaven' – in and through us. Firemen use a version of the symbol to symbolise putting out the 'fires of life'.

Mammon. The personification of wealth portrayed as a false god; wealth and riches considered as an evil and corrupt influence. Mammon is a term, derived from the Christian Bible, used to describe material wealth or greed, most often personified as a deity, and sometimes included in the seven princes of Hell. A Greek word meaning wealth or possessions; It could also mean 'that in which one trusts'. During the Middle Ages, Mammon was commonly personified as the demon of gluttony, richness and injustice.

Master: One who has control over something, or someone. One who defeats another. A victor; a teacher schoolmaster or tutor; A person whose teachings or doctrines are accepted by followers; a man/woman of great learning; a workman qualified to teach apprentices and carry on their craft independently; Being an original from which copies are made; Being the principal and leading force; Being a part of a mechanism that control all the other parts; a title Master/Mister given to those who uphold the standard of mastery/ excellence. Other terms used are: Maestro, Miss, Mister Mistress and Mrs., The Master, Meister, Grandmaster

Maturity: From Latin '*mature*'. refers to becoming an evolving towards full development. It is a state or quality of being, of ripening, to complete and finish in natural growth and development. Maturity is becoming who you truly are and meeting the challenges of life. It is a level of full development for that time.

Medicine man: A person believed among preliterate peoples to possess supernatural powers of healing, invoking spirits and other purposes; sorcerer; shaman.

Medium: Something or someone occupying a position midway between two extremes; An individual responsive to psychic forces. A person thought to have powers of communicating with the dead.

Medium:(medium ship) An individual responsive to psychic forces.

Mental health problems. Having a psychiatric disorder. An offensive term meaning extremely unintelligent or silly.

Mental health: Psychologically and mentally healthy. Mental health describes a level of psychological well-being, or an absence of a mental disorder. From the perspective of 'positive psychology' or 'holism', mental health may include an individual's ability to enjoy life, and create a balance between life activities and efforts to achieve psychological resilience. Mental health can also be defined as an expression of emotions, and as signifying a successful adaptation to a range of demands.

Mentor (verb): to mentor/mentoring: The personal name *Mentor* has been adopted in English as a term meaning 'someone who imparts wisdom to and shares knowledge with a less experienced colleague'.

Mentor: A person in Greek mythology; Friend of King Odyseus who mentored Odyseus's son Tellemachus in the ways and wisdoms of the world. Mentor prepared Tellemachus as king to take over the rule of his father when the time came.

Migration: Derived from Latin: *migratio* meaning '*to change; to go; to move*' and *migrăre* meaning '*to change ones place of living*' The act or process of moving from one region or country to another; Voyage, movement, relocation, resettlement. See 'human migration'.

Mind wellness. The desire or intention to act or behave in a particular way. a pattern of thinking or feeling characteristic of a particular group. See Mental health.

Mindful living: Actively attentive, or deliberately keeping something in mind. Conscious.

Miracle: An event that appears unexplained by the laws of nature, and so is held to be supernatural in origin, or 'an act of God'. The original word comes from mirus meaning 'causing one to smile', and at the same time it refers to 'mirror' or an occurrence that mirrors something/someone else. The words and phrases 'out of nowhere', coincidence, 'just thinking of', serendipity, and synchronicities, also denote 'miracles' [see wonder].

Mission: A special task given to a person or group to carry out; An aim or task that somebody believes it is his or her duty to carry out or to which he or she attaches special importance and devotes special care. A group of people sent to a country to represent their government, a business, or other organization.

Missionaries: People sent to another country by a church to spread its faith or to do social and medical work; somebody who tries to persuade others to accept or join something.

Monastery: The dwelling place of a community of persons under religious vows, especially monks; to live alone; from old Greek *'monasterion'*. This all comes from the original Germanic word *'men'* meaning to think, with derivates referring to various qualities and states of consciousness and mind.

Muti:The name given to medicine given by a *Sangoma*, especially medicine made from plants. Genuine *muti* from a sangoma can contain just about anything, and the more outlandish the better. Lion fat for courage, Rhino horn for power and magic and usually used as aphrodisiac. It is also legal to present your employer with a doctor's note from such a traditional healer after a day off.

Mystery School: It is an ancient school with esoteric wisdom and teachings that have been preserved for the benefit of humanity. Information is passed down through the oral tradition from teacher to student in an unbroken lineage of physical initiation.

Mystery: An event or situation that is difficult to fully explain; an unknown secret or hidden person or thing; the quality of being strange, secret or puzzling.

Mystic (mystical powers): One who practices or who believes in mystic powers; From Greek: 'mystikos' meaning 'an initiate'; is the knowledge of, and especially the personal experience of states of consciousness i.e. levels of being, beyond normal human perception, including experience of and even communion with a supreme being.

Mystical: Of a nature or virtue of its divinity that surpasses understanding.

Mysticism: A spiritual discipline aiming at union with the divine through deep meditation or trancelike meditation; any belief in the existence of realities beyond perceptual or intellectual apprehension but central to being and directly accessible by intuition; Experience of the communion as described by mystics.

Navigation: From *navigate* meaning *'to direct oneself to a specific destination'.* Navigation refers to the act or task of moving through a place or along a route; The science of plotting and following a course from one place to another; course-plotting; direction finding.

Nimrod: according to the Book of Genesis and Books of Chronicles, the son of Cush and great-grandson of Noah and the king of Shinar. He is depicted in the Tanakh as a man of power in the earth, and a mighty hunter. Extra-Biblical traditions associating him with the Tower of Babel led to his reputation as a king who was rebellious against God. Several Mesopotamian ruins were given Nimrod's name by 8th century Arabs.

Odysseus. Also known as Ulysses was the Greek King of Ithaca, husband of Penelope, father of Telemachus. He is renowned for his guile and resourcefulness, and is hence known by the epithet Odysseus the Cunning (or "cunning intelligence"). Many of the stories about Ulysses come from the ten eventful years he took to return home after the ten-year Trojan War and his association with the Trojan horse.

Onmyou: The Way of 'Yin and Yang'; is a traditional Japanese esoteric cosmology, a mixture of natural science and occultism. It is based on the Chinese philosophies of Wu Xing and Yin and yang, introduced into Japan at the beginning of the 6th century. It was accepted as a practical system of divination. These practices were influenced further by Taoism, Buddhism and Shintoism, and evolved into the system of onmyōdō around the late 7th century. Onmyōdō was under the control of the imperial government, and later its courtiers, the Tsuchimikado family until the middle of the 19th century, at which point it became prohibited as superstition.

Oracle: Somebody or something considered being a source of knowledge, wisdom, or prophecy; a piece of advice, often in the form of a puzzle or an enigmatic statement, handed down by an ancient Greek or Roman deity.

Pandemic: A disease or condition that is found in a large part of a population. See: epidemic.

Pantheistic: The belief that God and the material world are one and the same thing and that God is present in everything; The doctrine identifying one Deity with the various forces and workings of nature. Synonym: monotheistic. Antonym: polytheistic.

Pantheon: A circular temple in Rome that was completed in 27 BC and dedicated to all the deities but which has been used as a Christian church since 609 AD.

Paradigm: A Mindset, concept, hypothesis, theory or idea. A typical example or model of something.

Per se: Meaning in itself, by itself, or intrinsically.

Pharaoh: somebody in a position of authority, especially somebody who is harsh, gives unreasonable orders, and expects unquestioning obedience; kings of Egypt.

Polytheistic: The worship of or belief in more than one god.

Potent: Possessing inner or physical strength; powerful. Having great control or authority.

Potential: Possible but not yet realized; capable of being but not yet in existence; latent. The inherent ability or capacity for growth, development or coming into being or existence. 'Power-on-hold'.

Power: The ability or capacity to act or perform effectively. Strength or force to exercise control. The rate at which work is done. Used in an interrelated way with 'energy'.

Precognition: To have knowledge of something in advance of its occurrence.

Preliterate: People who do not have a written language. **Illiterate**: a person who is unable to read or write.

Priest: Christian: an ordained minister, especially in the Roman Catholic, Anglican, or Eastern Orthodox churches, responsible for administering the sacraments, preaching, and ministering to the needs of the congregation. Non-Christian: a spiritual leader or teacher of a non-Christian religion.

Prophesy: To reveal by divine inspiration; See 'soothsayer'.

Prophet: A person who speaks by divine inspiration; an interpreter through whom a divinity expresses his will; a predictor or soothsayer; the chief spokesman for some movement or cause.

Prophetic: Of or belonging to a prophet or prophecy.

Psyche: The soul or spirit as distinguished from the physical body; The mind functioning as centre of thought, feeling and behaviour and consciously or unconsciously adjusting and relating the body to its social and physical environment.

Psychic energy: Is a collective term referring to human energy/power generated from four different levels as physical, mental, emotional and spiritual energy sources.

Psychic: Of or pertaining to the human mind or psyche; extraordinary, especially extrasensory and non-physical mental processes such as extra-sensory perception (ESP) and mental telepathy.

Putch: A sudden planned attempt to overthrow a government using military force.

Resilience: The ability to recover quickly from setbacks.

Revelation: Information that is newly disclosed, especially surprising, or valuable. Christianity: a showing or revealing of what is believed to be divine will or truth.

Sacred geometry: Involves sacred universal patterns used in design; most often seen in sacred architecture and sacred art.

Sacred: Dedicated or set apart for the worship of a deity; made or declared holy; dedicated or devoted exclusively to a single use, purpose or person; worthy of reverence or respect; venerable.

Sacrifice: The act of offering something to a deity in propitiation or homage; the forfeiture of something highly valued; that which is offered or offered up.

Sage: a person, usually venerated for his experience, wisdom and judgement; a judicious person, wise with calm judgement.

Sangoma: Traditional healer in Africa. A person who cures people who have illnesses or injuries using plants and other traditional methods; South Africa, a traditional healer, shaman or herbalist.

Sanity: The condition of being mentally healthy and able to make rational decisions. Includes wisdom, reason, understanding, common sense, common sense, reasonableness, and predictability.

Sapience: Used to define consciousness, wisdom, or the ability of an organism or entity to act with appropriate judgment, a mental faculty which is a component of intelligence; Alternatively it may be considered an additional faculty, apart from intelligence, with its own properties. See: *Homo sapience*

Seer: Prophet, clairvoyant. Someone with visionary skills, or highly developed spiritual senses.

Seid: Seiðr (which is sometimes anglicised as seidhr, seidh, seidr, seithr, or seith) is an Old Norse term for a type of sorcery which was practiced in Norse society during the Late Scandinavian Iron Age. Connected with Norse paganism, its origins are largely unknown, although it gradually eroded following the Christianization of Scandinavia. Accounts of seiðr later made it into sagas and other literary sources, while further evidence has been unearthed by archaeologists. Various scholars have debated the nature of seiðr, arguing that it was shamanic in context, involving visionary journeys by its practitioners.

Sermon: Any discourse or speech, speaking, A religious discourse delivered as part of a church service. From the same Germanic root-word '*ser*' meaning 'sorcery'.

Shaman: A spiritual leader who is believed to have special powers such as prophecy and the ability to heal; someone who has the power to talk to spirits and cure illness.

Sign: Something that indicates or expresses the existence of something else not immediately apparent.

Solomon: A most successful and important leader and author of Proverbs, the Song of Solomon, and Ecclesiastes in The Bible.

Soothsayer: One who proclaims to foretell events; predict, prophesy: See 'prophet' and 'prophecy'.

Sorbonne: A part of the University of Paris, founded in 1253 that contains the faculties of science and literature.

Sorcerer: A person who performs magic using evil spirits. Also see 'wizard' and 'witch'.

Sorcery: From the old Germanic root-word 'ser' meaning 'to line up' or 'that which joins' and in Latin from 'serere' meaning 'to arrange', 'join by speech' and 'discuss'. It also refers to lining up, lot or fortune. It is also the same word used for dissertation, assert, and sermon from Latin *'sermo'*, See 'sermon'. The use of supernatural powers over others through the assistance of evil spirits; witchcraft, black magic.

Source: From Latin '*surgere*' meaning to 'rise up' and 'to surge'. The place, person, or thing through which something has come into being or from which it has been obtained; a person, organization, book, or other text that supplies information or evidence; someone that causes , creates, or initiates something; a maker, A book, or other record, supplying primary or firsthand information, origin.

Sourcing: The process of going to the original source, the origin, the expert; Going to a person, organization, book, or other text that supplies original information or evidence; going to the best for help assistance and guidance.
Outsourcing: An arrangement in which work is done by people from outside, usually by some-one that is an expert in that type of work.

Spiritual downloads: A person can download new information from the universal mind or universal web through neuro-connections with the right frequencies. Includes a raising of consciousness and awareness. See:

Mindful living.

Stem cell: 'Original cell' containing the original DNA blueprint. Found in bone marrow, amniotic fluid, blood and embryos. Has regenerative effect restoring the body to original blue print and healing from illness or injury on a DNA level.

Stem cell therapy: Intervention by making use of stem cells derived from bone marrow, amniotic fluid, blood, etc. in order to assist the body in regenerating tissue and healing the body from cancers, brain and nerve injuries and other injuries. Various 'stem cell therapies' available in the form of stem cell preparations and/or powders containing specific 'sugars' as basic building blocks of DNA. The aim of stem cell therapy is to restore the original blue print of DNA thereby healing injury and illness.

Stress: Mental, emotional, or physical strain caused e.g. by anxiety or overwork. It may cause such symptoms as raised blood pressure or depression. Nervous tension, worry, trauma, pressure, strain anxiety.

Sun Tzu: Also referred to as "Sunzi" and "Sun Wu", a high ranking military general, strategist and tactician.

Syncretism: The combination of different systems of philosophical or religious beliefs or practices. The use of a single inflectional form of a word to cover functions previously covered by two separate forms.

Tantric sexuality: A movement in Hinduism and Buddhism, especially a variety based on yoga and intended to release energy through sexual intercourse in which the orgasm is withheld or delayed.

Tarot Cards: A system of fortune-telling using a special pack of 78 cards consisting of 4 suits of 14 cards together with 22 picture cards.

Telepathy: Communication by scientifically unknown and inexplicable means; as by the exercise of mystical powers; the ability to produce or partake in such communications.

Telepathy: From the Greek '*tele*' meaning 'distant' and '*pathe*' meaning 'affliction, experience'. Telepathy is the transmission of information from one person to another without using any of our known sensory channels or physical interaction. The term was coined in 1882 by the classical scholar Fredric W.H. Myers, a founder of the Society for Psychical Research, and has remained more popular than the more-correct expression thought-transference. Many studies seeking to detect, understand and use telepathy have been done within this field. Claims of telepathy as a real phenomenon are at odds with the scientific consensus. According to the prevailing view among scientists, telepathy lacks replicable results from well-controlled experiments. Meanings: communication by scientifically unknown and inexplicable means; as by the exercise of mystical powers; the ability to produce or partake in such communications.

The Blue Brain Project. This is an attempt to create a synthetic brain by reverse-engineering the mammalian brain down to the molecular level. The aim of the project, founded in May 2005 by the Brain and Mind Institute of the *École Polytechnique Fédérale de Lausan*ne (Switzerland) is to study the brain's architectural and functional principles. The project is headed by the Institute's director, Henry Markram. Using a Blue Gene supercomputer running Michael Hines's NEURON software, the simulation does not consist simply of an artificial neural network, but involves a biologically realistic model of neurons. It is hoped that it will eventually shed light on the nature of consciousness.

Theoplexus: Theoplex, Theo-plexus: A term given by the ascended master, Lord Matreya, to denote the place within and without, where Light-loves meets physicality and everything comes together. The 'healing of the body of Light'; the Christ-consciousness, takes place in the Theoplexus—a sacred place within all of us. See 'Body of Christ'.

Traditional healer: A person who effects cures by spiritual, magical and other non medical means. See 'herbalist'.

Traditional leader. Traditional authority (also known as traditional domination) is a form of leadership in which the authority of an organization or a ruling regime is largely tied to tradition or custom. The main reason for a given state of affairs is that it 'has always been that way'.

Transcendence: To pass beyond (a human) limit; to exist above and independent of material experience or the universe; to rise above or across; to exceed; surpassing others of the same kind.

Transcendence: To pass beyond (a human) limit; to exist, above and independent of (material experience or the universe); to rise above or across; to exceed; surpassing others of the same kind.

Transcendent: Above and beyond material reality; referring to a deity.

Transformation: To change markedly the form or appearance; (transfiguration: to transform the figure or appearance).

Transmutation: To change from one form, nature, substance or state into another.

Transpersonal Psychology: "is concerned with the study of humanity's highest potential, and with the recognition, understanding, and realization of unitive, spiritual, and transcendent states of consciousness" Issues considered in transpersonal psychology include spiritual self-development, self beyond the ego, peak experiences, mystical experiences, systemic trance and other sublime and/or unusually expanded experiences of living.

Treatise: A formal written work that deals with a subject systematically and usually extensively; paper, article, dissertation.

Tribalist: Someone who adheres to, supports and protects the customs, beliefs, and social organization of a tribe or social group; Someone with loyalty to a tribe or social group.

Uncompassionate/dis-compassionate: Showing no feelings or sympathy for the suffering of others; without any desire to help, assist or alleviate pain and suffering.

Unevolved: when something or someone doesn't develop into something more complex or advanced, or undergo such development.

Useless: Not able to function properly. Loss of initial use.

Value: From the Latin word 'valere', that means "to be strong" or "to be valid". A value indicates the importance, validity, force or strength of something.

Vilify: To make malicious and abusive statements about somebody.

Violence: The use of physical, verbal or emotional force to injure somebody or damage something; Extreme, destructive, or uncontrollable force, especially of natural events; Criminal law: the illegal use of unjustified force, or the intimidating effect created by the threat of this: Hostility, fighting, cruelty, sadism, fighting, aggression: **Antonym**: meekness,

Vision: Defined as "a way to see, inner perception, imaginary insight", unusual competence in discernment or perception, intelligent foresight, mental images produced by the imagination, seeing as if with the eye of the supernatural.

Vulnerable: In a weak position, unable to resist illness, debility, or failure, open to harm, easily persuadable or liable to give in to temptation, powerless, exposed, helpless, defenseless, in danger, at risk, unable to resist illness, debilitation, or failure.

Wellbeing: Also wellness. A good, healthy, or comfortable state.

Wellness: Physical wellbeing, especially when maintained or achieved through good diet and regular exercise.

Whole brain emulation. (mind uploading): Sometimes called 'mind transfer', is the hypothetical process of transferring or copying a conscious mind from a brain to a non-biological substrate by scanning and mapping a biological brain in detail and copying its state into a computer system or another computational device.

Wise men: Also known as 'Magi'. They had the ability to read the stars, and manipulate the fate that the stars foretold. Pervasive throughout the Eastern Mediterranean and Western Asia until late antiquity and beyond, Greek mágos, "Magician" or "magician," was influenced by and eventually displaced Greek goēs, the older word for a practitioner of magic, to include astrology, alchemy and other forms of esoteric knowledge.

Traditional healer: A medicine man or shaman among traditional people.

Witch: A woman who practices sorcery or is said to have dealings with the spirits. **White witch:** Has dealings with light beings, angels, light spirits and God. **Black witch:** Has dealings with dark, evil spirits, demons or the devil. Female 'wizard'.

Witch-craft: Black magic; sorcery; A magical or irresistible influence; attraction or charm. See 'magic'.

Wizard: A man who is believed or claims to have magical powers. 'White wizard': Has dealings with positive energy, light beings, angels, light spirits, and God. 'Black wizard': Has dealings with dark energy, evil spirits, demons or the devil. A male witch. Also see: 'sorcerer', 'witch', 'magic'.

Wonders: A miracle or instance of intense admiration or awe.

Zarathustra: Also known as Zoroaster. Composer of the 'Gathas', 17 hymns, valued as the most sacred texts of the monotheistic Zoroastrian faith. At the centre of his teachings we find 'all is one truth' and 'Free Will' of all humankind. Seen as the originator of "Magi" or 'wise-men' who had the ability to read the stars, and manipulate the fate that the stars foretold.

Zoroaster: 'Founder' of the 'magi', 'wise men' or 'magicians'. See Zarathustra.

ooo0ooo

BIBLIOGRAPHY

Alcock, P. (1993). *Understanding poverty*. MacMillan. London.

Allen V.L. (1970a). *The Psychology of poverty; problems and prospects.* In **Allen V.L.**(Ed.). *Psychological factors in poverty*. Markam Pub. Chicago. USA

American Journal of Psychiatry. 140 (12): 1609-1611.

Apter, M.J. 1992. *The dangerous edge: The psychology of excitement*. The Free Press. New York.

Ashby, R. 1956. *Introduction to Cybernetics*. John Wiley. New York.

Assmann, J. 2002. *The Mind of Egypt*. Metropolitan Books. New York.

Bacigalupo, Ana Mariella.2007. S*hamans of the foye tree: gender, power, and healing among Chilean Mapuche*. University of Texas Press. Texas.

Beck, D.E. & Cowan, C.C. 1996. *Spiral Dynamics. Mastering values, leadership, and change.* Blackwell Publishers. Cambridge.

Beer, Rüdiger Robert. 1977. *Unicorn: Myth and Reality.* Mason/Charter.

Benes, F.M. 2001. Carlsson and the discovery of dopamine. *Trends in Pharmacological Sciences* 22 (1):46-47.

Bickart, K.C., Wright, C.I., Dautoff, R. J., Dickerson, B.C., Barrett, L. F. Dec. 2010. Amygdala volume and social network size in humans. *Nature neuroscience* 14 (2): 163–164.

Blackburn, Simon. 1994. *Philosophy.* The Oxford Dictionary of Philosophy. Oxford University Press. Oxford.

Blier, Suzanne Preston. 1995. Vodun: West African Roots of Vodou. In Donald J.,Cosentino. Sacred Arts of Haitian Vodou. Los Angeles: UCLA Fowler Museum of Cultural History.

Bloisi, W., Cook, C.W. & Hunsaker, P.L. 2003. *Management and organizational behavior*. McGraw-Hill. London.

Bohm, D. 1980. *Wholeness and the implicate order*. Routledge & Kegan. London.

Bolio, J.D. 1987. *The Geometry of the Mayan.* Mayan Area. (Unknown binding).

Boyd, Robert, Silk, Joan B. 2003. *How Humans Evolved.* Norton. New York.

Brennan, B.A. 1988. *Hands of light.* Bantam Books. New York.

Brennan, B.A. 1993. *Light emerging.* Bantam Books. New York.

Brooks, Polly Schoyer. 1999. *Beyond the Myth: The Story of Joan of Arc.* Houghton Mifflin Co. New York.

Brown, Dan. 2006. *Angels and Demons.* Washington Square Press. New York.

Brown, Dan. 2009. *The Da Vinci Code.* Anchor Publishing. Harpswell, ME

Brown, Dan. 2009. *The lost symbol.* Doubleday Books. UK.

Brungardt, C. L. 1996. The making of leaders: A review of the research in leadership development and education. *The Journal of Leadership Studies* 3 (3): 81–95.

Bunson, M.E. (ed.). 2000. *The Dalai Lama's Book of Wisdom.* Random House. London.

Burr, H.S. 1972. *The fields of life: Our links with the universe.* Ballantine Books. New York.

Butler, B. & Kondratas, A. 1987. *Out of the poverty trap.* Free Press. NY.

Canfield. J. 2005. *The success principle.* HarperCollins Publishers. London

Capra, F. 1990. *The turning point: Science, society and the rising culture.* HarperCollins. London.

Capra, F. 1991. *The Tao of physics: An exploration of the parallels between modern physics and Eastern mysticism.* Flamingo/HarperCollins. London.

Capra, F. 1997. *The web of life.* HarperCollins. London.

Capriles, E. 2000. Beyond Mind: Steps to a Metatranspersonal Psychology. Honolulu, HI: *The International Journal of Transpersonal Studies*, 19:163-184.

Charles, R.H. 2007. *The book of Enoch.* Forgotten Books. Charleston, South Carolina.

Chemers M. 1997. *An integrative theory of leadership.* Lawrence Erlbaum Associates Publishers. UK.

Chopra, D. 1992. *Unconditional life. Discovering the power to fulfil your dreams.* Bantam Books. New York.

Chopra, D. 2000. *How to know God: The soul's journey into the mystery of mysteries*. Harmony Books. New York.

Chopra, D. 2009. *The third Jesus. How to find truth and love in today's world*. Rider Publishing. London.

Clawson, James G. 2011. *Level Three Leadership: Getting Below the Surface*. Prentice Hall. US.

Clayton, Peter A. 1995. *Chronicle of the Pharaohs: The Reign-by-Reign Record of the Rulers and Dynasties of Ancient Egypt*. The Chronicles Series (Reprinted ed.). Thames and Hudson. London.

Clutterbuck, D. 2003. *Coaching and mentoring at the top. Management today,* June.

Coe, M. D. 1994. *Breaking the Mayan Code.*Penguin Books. New York.

Coe, M. D. 1994. *The Mayan.* Thames and Hudson. London.

Cole, K.C. 1985. *Sympathetic Vibrations: Reflections on Physics as a Way of Life*. Bantam Books. New York.

Collins, J. 2001. *From good to great*. HarperBusiness. New York.

Cook, M.J. 1999. *Effective Coaching*. McGraw-Hill. New York.

Cooper, Diana. 2008. *Enlightenment through orbs*. Findhorn Press. Scotland.

Cooper, Diana. 2012. *2012 and Beyond*. Findhorn Press. Scotland.

Cotterell, M. 1988. *Astrogenetics*. Brooks, Hill, Robinson & Co. New York.

Covey, S.R. 1992. *The seven habits of highly effective people*. Simon & Schuster. London.

Cox, B. & Forshaw, J. 2012. *The Quantum Universe*. Da Capo Press; Massachusetts.

Csikszentmihali, M. 1990. *Flow. The Psychology of optimal experience*. Harper and Row. New York.

Csikszentmihali, M. 1993. *The evolving Self. A Psychology for the third Millennium.* HarperCollins Publishers. New York.

Dale, C. 1996. *New chakra healing*. Faradawn Publishers. New York.

Damasio, A.R. & Anderson, S.W. 2003. The frontal lobes. In: Heilman, K.M. & Valenstein, E. (Ed.) *Clinical Psychology*. 4th edition. 404-406. Oxford University Press. New York.

Deacon, T.W. 1990. Rethinking mammalian brain evolution. *Anm Zool.* 30:629–705.

Deacon, T.W. 1997. What makes the human brain different? *Annu. Rev.*

Anthropol. 26: 337-57.

Deyer, W. 1992. *Real Magic. Creating miracles in everyday life.* Harper Collins Publishers. New York.

Dillard A.J., Midboe, A.M., Klein, W.M. 2009. The dark side of optimism: Unrealistic optimism about problems with alcohol predicts subsequent negative event experiences. *PersSocPsychol Bull.35(11):1540.*

Dingle, H & Alistair Drake 2007. *What is migration? BioScience.* **57**:

Doh, J. P 2003. Can leadership be taught? Perspectives from management educators. *Academy of Management Learning and Education.* 2 (1): 54–67.

Donne , John. (1572-1631), *Devotions Upon Emergent Occasions, Meditation XVII: Nunc Lento Sonitu Dicunt, Morieris.*

Dyer, W. 2009. *Change Your Thoughts - Change Your Life: Living the Wisdom of the Tao.* Hay House. London.

Dyer, W. 2009. *Change Your Thoughts - Change Your Life: Living the Wisdom of the Tao.* Hay House. London.

Eggers, John H. & Clark, Doug. 2000. *Executive Coaching that Wins.* Ivey Business Journal. September/October. 67-70.

Einstein, A. 1923. *The Principals of Relativity.* Dover Publications. New York.

Einstein, A. 1934. *Essays in Science.* Philosophical Library. New York.

Encyclopædia Britannica, 1911.

Endacot, M. (ed.). 1996. *Encyclopaedia of alternative health and natural remedies.* Carlton Books. London.

Endredy, James. 2009. *Beyond 2012.* Llewellyn Publishers. Woodbury. MN.

Fenster, Mark . 2008. *Conspiracy Theories: Secrecy and Power in American Culture.* University of Minnesota Press; Minnesota. 2nd edition.

First, R. *1970.* Power in Africa. *Alfred A. Knopf. New York*

Foundation For Inner Peace. 1996. *A course in miracles.* Penguin Books. New York.

Furnham, A.,Mkhize, N. & Mndaweni, T. (2004). Indian and isizulu-speaking South. African parents' estimates of their own and their children's intelligence. *South African Journal of Psychology.* 34 (3), pp. 364-385.

Galbraith, J.K. 1983. *The Anatomy of Power.* Houghton Mifflin. Boston.

Gallwey, T. 1997. *The Inner Game of Tennis.* Random House. London

Gardner, H. 1983. *Frames of mind. The theory of multiple Intelligence.* Basic Books. NY

Gerber, R. 1988. *Vibrational medicine.* Bear & Co. Santa Fe, NM.

Gerfand, M. 1970. UNHU—The Personality of the Shona. *Studies in Comparative Religion, Vol. 4, No. 1* (Winter, 1970). World Wisdom, Inc.

Geza Vermes. 2006. *The Nativity: History and Legend.* Penguin Books. London.

Gilbert, Adrian & Cotterell, Maurice. 1996. *The Mayan Prophecies.* Element Books limited. Brisbane.

Gilbert, J. & Hall, B. 2009. *The Upliftment of Consciousness.* Book One. Ancient Wisdoms Publications. Johannesburg.

Goertzel. 1994. *Belief in Conspiracy Theories.* Political Psychology (Political Psychology, Vol. 15, No. 4) 15 (4): 733–744.

Goleman, D. 1996. *Emotional Intelligence. Why it can matter more than IQ.* Bloomsbury Publishing. London.

Graham, Peter. 2003. *Know the difference between executive coaching and clinical consultation.* Staff Leader. May 2003. Vol.16, No.9. p.10-11.

Gribbin, John. 1984. *In Search of Schroedingers Cat. Quantum Physics and Reality.* Bantam Books. New York.

Grof, Stanislav. 1990. *The holotropic mind.* San Francisco: Harper Collins Publishers. SanFrancisco.

Hall, D.T. Otazo, K.L & Hollenbeck, G.P. 1999. *Behind closed doors: What really happens in Executive coaching.* Organizational Dynamics. Winter1999, 39-53.

Hamer, Dean. *2005. The God gene. How faith is hardwired into our genes.* Amcor Publishers. New York.

Hanzhang, Tao. & Wilkinson, Robert. 1998. *The Art of War.* Wordsworth Editions. UK.

Hattingh, B. 2012 (b). *Power Intelligence, Mastering your miracle mind.* Currency Communications. Johannesburg.

Hattingh, B. 2012 (a). *New Success DNA. What you should know and how to activate it.* Currency Communications. Johannesburg.

Hattingh, B. 2012. Life – Stumbling block or stepping stone? Currency Communications. Johannesburg.

Hawkins, D. 2002. *Power vs. force: The hidden determinants of human behavior.* Hay House. New York.

Herbert, N. 1987. *Quantum Reality: Beyond the New Physics.* Ancor Books. New York.

Hickman, H. and Alexander, T. (ed) 1998. *The Essential Dewey:* Volumes 1 and 2. Indiana University Press. Indiana.

Hollander, E. P., & Julian, J. W. 1969. Contemporary trends in the analysis of leadership processes. *Psychological Bulletin*, 71, 387-397.

Hutcherson, C.A., Seppala, E.M., & Gross, J.J. 2008. Loving-kindness meditation increases social connectedness. Emotion, 8(5), 720-724.

Icke, David. 1993. *In the Light of Experience.* Warner Books. UK.

Icke, David. 1999. *The Biggest Secret: The Book that Will Change the World.* David Icke Books. UK.

Icke, David. 2005. *Infinite Love is the Only Truth.* Bridge of Love Publications. UK.

Ingalls, J.D. 1976. *Human Energy. The Critical Factor for Individuals and Organizations.* Addison-Wesley Publishing Company, Inc. London.

Jantsch, E. 1980. *The Self-Organizing Universe.* Pergamon Press. Oxford.

John Donne. 1572-1631. *Devotions Upon Emergent Occasions, Meditation XVII: Nunc Lento Sonitu Dicunt, Morieris.*

Johnson, Heather. 2004. *The Ins and Outs of Executive Coaching.* Training. May 2004, Vol.41, p36-41.

Judge, William & Cowell, Jeffrey. 1997. *The brave new world of executive coaching.* Business Horizons; July/Aug97, Vol. 40 Issue 4, 71-77.

Jung, C. 1964. *Man and his symbols.* Double Day. New York.

Jung, C. 1970. *The structure and dynamics of the psyche: The collective works of Carl Jung.* Edited and translated by G. Adler & R.F.C. Hull. Princeton University Press. Princeton.

Käsler, Dirk. 1988. *Max Weber: An introduction to his life and work.* University of Chicago Press. Chicago

Kehoe, J. 1997. *Mind Power - Into the 21st Century.* Zoetic Inc. Canada.

Kennedy, D.P., Gläscher, J., Tyszka, J.M., Adolphs, R. 2009. Personal space regulation by the human amygdala. *Nat Neurosci* 12 (10): 1226–1227.

Kilburg, Richard. 2000. *Executive Coaching.* American Psychological Association. Washington DC.

Killcross, S. Robbins, T. Everitt, B. 1997. Different types of fear-conditioned behaviour mediated by separate nuclei within amygdala. *Nature 388* (6640):377–80.

Koenig, H.G., King, D. & Carson, V. 2012. *Handbook of Religion and Health. Oxford University Press. Oxford.*

Kohl, J., Atzmueller, M., Fink, B. & Grammar, K. 2001. Human Pheromones: *Integrative Neuroendocrinology & Etholo*gy. NEL 22, 309-32.

Kohlberg, L. 1981. *Essays on moral development.* Vol. 1. Harper & Row.

NY.

Koonin, EV. Senkevich, TG, Dolja, VV. 2006. The ancient virus world and evolution of cells. *Biol. Direct.* 2006;1:29.

Kramer, S N. 1959. *History begins at Sumner.*University of Pennsylvania Press; (3rd edition. April 1, 1988).

Kuhn, Thomas S. 1966. *The Structure of Scientific Revolutions*, 3rd Ed.: Univ. of Chicago Press. Chicago and London.

Lajoie, D. H. & Shapiro, S. I. 1992. *Definitions of transpersonal psychology: The first twenty-three years*. Journal of Transpersonal Psychology, Vol. 24.

Land, George. 1997. *Grow or Die.Grow or Die, The Unifying Principle of Transformation*. Leadership 2000 Inc. Scottsdale. AZ.

Lao Tzu. 1996. *The Tao Te Ching*. St. Martin's Griffin. Minotaur.

Lavers, Chris. 2009. *The Natural History of Unicorns*. Granta Books. London.

Lee, Everett S. 1966. *A Theory of Migration*. University of Pennsylvania. USA.

Lipton, B. 2008. *The biology of belief.* Hay House. CA.

Loehr, J. & Schwartz, T. 2003. *The Power of full engagement. Managing energy and not time*. Free Press. New York.

Lundy, James.1993. Lead ,follow or get out of the way. Pfeiffer & Co. New York.

Mace, Myles. 1958. In. *Developing Executive Skills*. (H. Merril and E Marting. Eds). Americal Management Association.

Mair, Victor H. 1990. *Old Sinitic Myag, Old Persian Maguš and English Magician.* Early China 15: 27–47.

Mandela, Nelson. 2008. *Long Walk to Freedom: The Autobiography of Nelson Mandela*. Little, Brown and Company. New York

Marinkovic, K., Oscar-Berman, M., Urban, T., O'Reilly, C.E., Howard, J.A., Sawyer, K., Harris, G.J. November 2009. Alcoholism and dampened temporal limbic activation to emotional faces. *Alcohol Clin Exp Res* 33 (11):1880–92.

Marriot, H. P. Fitzgerald. The Secret Societies of West Africa. *The Journal of the Anthropological Institute of Great Britain and Ireland.* Vol. 29, No. 1/2 (1899), pp. 21-27.

Maslow, A. 1998. *Toward a Psychology of Being*. 3rd Edition. John Wiley & Sons. Oxford. UK.

Maturana, H. & Varela, F. 1980. *Autopoiesis and Cognition: The Realization of the Living.* Reidl. London.

Mauss. 2001. *A General Theory of Magic.* Routledge. UK.

Maxwell, J. 2011. *Five levels of leadership.* Hodder & Stoughton Ltd. London.

McDowell, John. 1994. *Mind and World.* Harvard University Press.

McGinn, Bernard. 2001. *In The Mystical Thought of Meister Eckhart.* Crossroad Publishing Company. New York.

McNeilly, Mark R. 2001. Sun Tzu and the Art of Modern Warfare. Oxford University Press. Oxford.

McTaggart, Lynne. *2001. The Field. The Quest for the Secret Force of the Universe..* Element, HarperCollins Publishers. London.

Mehrtens, S. 1999. The waves of change. *People Dynamics.* South Africa, February, 29-34.

Mendez, F.M. & Perryman, K.M. 2002. Neuropsychiatry features of fronto-temporal dymentia: Evaluation of consensus criteria and revue. *Journal of Neurosphyciatry and Clinical Neuroscience.* 4: 424-429.

Meyer, B. J. (ed.). 2002. *Human Physiology.* Juta. Landsdowne. London.

Meyer, M. & Fourie, L. 2004. *Mentoring and Coaching.* Knowledge Resources. Publishing (Pty. Ltd). Randburg.

Miller, J.B. 1993. *The Corporate Coach.* St Martin' s Press. New York.

Motsett, C.B . 2002. *Executive Coaching. Harvard Business Review.* September 2002, p. 121.

Mudjanto, G. 1986. *The Concept of Power in Japanese Culture.* Gadjah Mada University Press. Jakarta:

Mullins, L.J. 2002. *Management and organizational behavior.* 6th Edition. Prentice Hall. New York.

Mumford, M. D. 1986. Leadership in the organizational context: Conceptual approach and its application. J*ournal of Applied Social Psychology,* 16(6), 508-531.

Mumford, M. D., Zaccaro, S. J., Harding, F. D., Jacobs, T. O., & Fleishman, E. A. (2000). Leadership skills for a changing world solving complex social problems. *The Leadership Quarterly,* 11(1), 11-35.

Mutwais, Vusamazulu Credo. 1977. *My People. The Writings of a Zulu witch-doctor.* Penguin Books. New York.

Myss, C. 1997. *The anatomy of the spirit: The seven stages of power and healing.* Bantam Books. New York.

Ndlovu, N. & Brijbali Parumasur, S. 2005. *The perceived impact of downsizing and organizational transformation on survivors. SA Journal of Industrial Psychology,* 31 (2), 14-21.

Newberg A., Alavi A., Baime M., Pourdehnad M., Santanna J., d'Aquilie. 2001. The measurement of regional cerebral blood flow during the complex cognitive task of meditation. A preliminary SPECT study. *Psychiatry . Research.* 106(2): 113-122.

Newton, M. 1995. *Journey of souls.* Llewellyn Publications. Minnesota

Newton, Michael. 2001. *Destiny of souls.* Llewellyn Publications. Minnesota, USA.

Nigosian, Solomon Alexander. 1993. *The Zoroastrian Faith: Tradition and Modern Research.* McGill-Queen's University Press. Kingston, Canada.

Nowak, R. 1994. *Mining treasures from "junk DNA".* Science 161: pp. 529-540.

O'Grady, Tim Porter & Malloch, Kathy. 2010. *Quantum Leadership: Advancing Information, Transforming Health Care,* Third Ed.. Jones & Bartlett Learning. NY.

Olsen, Ted. "*Opinion Roundup: Positive About Potter*". Cesnur.org. Retrieved 6 July 2007.

Osland, J.S., Kolb, D.A & Rubin, I.M. 2001. *Organizational behaviour: An experiential approach.* 7th Edition. Prentice Hall. New York.

Parker, Robert 2005. *Polytheism and Society at Athens.* Oxford University Press. Oxford.

Pey, L.C. & Pey, M.W. 1985. *Asian Power and Politics.* The Belknap Press, Harvard University Press. Cambridge, Mass.

Pfeffer, Charles. 2002. *Executive Coaching.* Harvard Business Review. September 2002, p.120.

Pribram. K. 1987. *The Implicate Brain.* In B.J. Hiley and F. David Peat, (eds) Quantum Implications: Essays in Honour of David Bohm, Routledge.

Price, J.C. *Potential Contributions of Eastern Philosophies and Martial Arts i:n Understanding Leadership.* Paper presented at Capella University.

Price, Neil. 2002. *The Viking Way: Religion and War in Late Iron Age Scandinavia. Uppsala*: Department of Archaeology and Ancient History, Uppsala University.

Prigogine, I. & Stengers, I. 1984. *Chaos out of Order.* Bantam Books. New York.

Quigley, Joan. 1990. *What Does Joan Say?: My Seven Years as White House Astrologer to Nancy and Ronald Reagan.* Carol Publishing..NY.

Ramsay, Robin. 2006. *Conspiracy Theories.* Pocket Essentials. New York.

Randall, Willard Sterne. 1997. *George Washington: A Life.* Henry Holt & Co. New York.

Ravenstein, Ernest, G. 1885. *The Laws of Migration.* by John Corbett, Center for Spatially Integrated Social Science.

Reagan, Ronald. 2011. *An American Life.* Threshold Editions. New York.

Regan, Ronald. 1988. For the Record: From Wall Street to Washington. Harcourt. New York.

Reich, W. 1979. *Selected Writings.* Farrar, Strauss & Giroux. New York.

Rice, P.L. 1992. *Stress and Health.* (2nd ed.). Brooks/Cole Publishing Company. Pacific Grove. CA.

Richard, J.T. 2003. *Ideas on Fostering Creative problem Solving in Executive Coaching.* Consulting Psychology Journal: Practice and Research, Vol. 55, No 4. 249-256.

Robbins, T. Everitt, B & Nutt, D. 2010. *The Neurobiology of Addiction.* Oxford University Press. London.

Roberts, Andy. 1999. The origins of the term 'mentor'. *History of Education Society Bulletin,* No. 64, November 1999, p. 313–329.

Rost, J.C. 1991. *Leadership for the twenty-first century.* Praeger Press. New York.

Roth, Guenther. Wittich, Claus. (Eds.) 1978. *Max Weber, Economy and Society: An Outline of Interpretive Sociology.* University of California Press. Berkeley.

Ryan, R.M. & Frederick, C. 1997. On energy, personality and health: Subjective vitality as a dynamic reflection of well-being. *Journal of Personality*, 65, 529-565.

Saver, J.L. & Rabin, J. 1997. The neutral substrates of religious behavior. *Journal of Neuropsychiatry*: 9:498-510.

Scouller, J. 2011. *The Three Levels of Leadership: How to Develop Your Leadership Presence, Knowhow and Skill.* Management Books 2000. Gloucestershire.

Segall, M., Dansen, P., Berry, J. & Poortinga, Y. *(1999).* Human behaviour in global perspective: an introduction to cross-cultural psychology. Allyn & Bacon. New York.

Semendeferi K, Damasio H, Frank R, Van Hoesen GW. 1997. The evolution of the frontal lobes: A volumetric analysis based on three-dimensional reconstructions of magnetic resonance scans of human and ape brains. J. Hum Evol. April:32 (4):375-88.

Sharma, V.K. (November 2003). Adaptive significance of circadian clocks. *Chronobiology International* **20** (6): 901–919.

Sitchin, Z. 1976. *The 12th planet: Book of the earth chronicles.* HarperCollins. New York.

Sitchin, Z. 1990. *Genesis revisited.* HarperCollins. New York.

Sitchin, Z. 1997. *Devine Encounters.* HarperCollins. New York.

Sitchin, Z. 2001. *The Wars of Gods and men.* HarperCollins. New York.

Sitchin, Z. 2006. *The lost realities.* HarperCollins. New York.

Sitchin, Z. 2008. *The end days.* HarperCollins. New York.

Smith, Sean. 1999. *J K Rowling. Biography.* Michael O'Mara Books. UK.

Snyder, Adam. 1995. *Executive Coaching: The New Solution.* Management Review. March. Vol. 84, 29.

Stevens, Marty E. 2006. *Temples, tithes, and taxes: The temple and the economic life of ancient Israel.* Hendrickson Publishers. Massachusetts.

Stogdill, R. M. 1974. *Handbook of leadership: A survey of the literature.* Free Press. New York.

Stone, A.G. & Patterson, K. 2005. *The History of Leadership Focus.* Servant Leadership Research Roundtable. Regent University.

Stray, Geoff. 2006. *Beyond 2012, Catastrophe or Ecstasy.* Vital Signs Publishing. East Sussex.

Stray, Geoff. 2009. *Beyond 2012. Catastrophe or Awakening.* Bear Company. Vermont.

Su H, Qu LJ, He K, Zhang Z, Wang J, Chen Z, Gu H . 2003. *The Great Wall of China: a physical barrier to gene flow?* Heredity 90 (3): 212–9.

Sui, R.G. H. 1979. *The Craft of Power.* John Wiley and Sons. NY.

Sun Tzu. 2008. *The Art of War: Spirituality for Conflict.* Skylight Paths Publishing. Woodstock, VT.

Sutich, A.J. 1976. The Emergence of the Transpersonal Orientation: A Personal Account. *Journal of Transpersonal Psychology,* 1.

Swanson, L. W. & Petrovich. G. D. August 1998. What is the amygdala? *Trends in Neurosciences 21* (8):323–331.

Swatos, William H. 1998. *Encyclopedia of Religion and Society.* Rowman Altamira.

Talbot, Micheal. 1986. *Beyond the Quantum.*Bantam Books. New York.

Tatjana Zerjal et al. 2002. *A Genetic Landscape Reshaped by Recent Events: Y-Chromosomal Insights into Central Asia.* The American Journal of Human Genetics 71 (3): 466–482.

Teisser, Elizabeth. 1997. *Sous Le Signe de Mitterrand* (Under the Sign of Mitterrand). Edition1. UK.

Thach, Liz & Heinselman, Tom. 1999. *Executive Coaching Defined. Training and Development;* Mar99, Vol. 53 Issue3, p34-40.

The Bhagavad Gita: The gospel of the Lord Shri Krishna 1977. Translated by Shri Purchit Swami. Vintage Books. Random House.London.

The Holy Bible. King James Version. 2006. Cambridge University Press. London. New Testament.

The Koran. The Qur'an. Oxford World's Classics. 2008. M.A. Abdel Haleem. Oxford.

The Kybalion. 1912. The Yogi Publication Society. Chicago.

Toffler, A. 1971. *Future shock.* Pan Books Ltd. London.

Toffler, A. 1980. *The Third Wave.* Pan Books Ltd. London.

Toffler, A. 1991. *The Power shift.* Pan Books Ltd. London.

Tolle, E. 1999. *The power of now.* Hodder and Stoughton. London.

Tolle, E. 2005. *The New Earth: Awakening to your life's purpose.* Penguin Books. New York.

Tuch, B.E. 2006. Stem cells—a clinical update. Australian Family Physician 35 (9): 719–21.

Vaughan, Susan C.2000. *Half Empty, Half Full: Understanding the Psychological Roots of Optimism.* Harcourt. New York.

Vaughan, Susan C.2000. *Half Empty, Half Full: Understanding the Psychological Roots of Optimism.* Harcourt. New York.

Vermaak, A. 2002. *Back to the future.* People Dynamics, 20 (3), 4-5.

Velikovsky, I. 1972. *Worlds in collision.* HarperCollins. New York.

Velikovsky, I. 1977. *Earth in upheaval.* Pocket Books. New York.

Von Bulow, Harry. 2003. *God and Ronald Reagan: God Moves in the Affairs of Men.* AuthorHouse. UK.

Vusamazulu Credo Mutwais. 1977. *My People - the writings of a Zulu Witch-Doctor.* Penguin Books. New York.

Vusamazulu Credo Mutwais. 2003. *Zulu Shaman: Dreams, prophecies and mysteries.* Destiny Books. Massachusetts.

Walsch, Neale Donald. 1997. *Conversations with God.* Book 1-4. Hodder and Stoughton. London.

Wasylyshyn, K. M. 2003. Executive Coaching. An Outcome Study. Consult. Psychology Journal. Practice and Research, Vol. 55. No.2, 94-106.

Weale, Michael E.; Deborah A. Weiss,1, Rolf F. Jager, Neil Bradman and Mark G. Thomas. *Y Chromosome Evidence for Anglo-Saxon Mass Migration.* Molecular Biology and Evolution 19 (7): 1008–1021. Retrieved 11 May 2011.

Weber, Max. Henderson, A.M. Parsons,T. (Ed.). 2012. *The Theory of Social and Economic Organization.* Martino Fine Books. Eastford, CT.

West, D.J. 1960. Visionary and hallucinatory experiences: A comparative appraisal. International Journal of Parapsychology 2 (1): 89-100.

Wheatly, MJ. 1992. *Leadership and the New Science. Learning about Organization from an Orderly Universe.* Berrett-Koehler Publishers. San Francisco.

Whitson, William . 1973. *The Chinese High Command.* Praeger. Santa Barbara, CA.

Wiener, N. 1961. *Cybernetic* MIT Press. New York.

Wilber, K. 2000. *Integral Psychology. Consciousness, Spirit, Psychology, Therapy.* Shambala Press. Boston.

Wilber, K.1984. *Quantum Questions.* Shambala Press. Boston.

Wing, R.L. 1986. *The Tao of Power.* Garden City. New York.

Witherspoon, Robert & White, Randall P. 1996. *Executive Coaching : What's in it for you ?* Training and Development; March96, Vol. 50 Issue 3, p14, 2p.

World Health Organization. 2005. *Promoting Mental Health.* A report of the World Health Organization, Department of Mental Health and Substance Abuse. World Health Organization. Geneva.

World Migration Report .2010 - *The Future of Migration: Building Capacities for Change.* International Organization for Migration, 2010.

Wulff, Wilhelm & Laqueur Walter. 1973. *Zodiac and Swastika: How Astrology Guided Hitler's Germany.* Coward, McCann & Geoghegan.

Zohar, D. & Marshall, I. 1999. *Spiritual Intelligence. The ultimate intelligence.*Flamingo. London.

INDEX

NEW SUCCESS DNA.

WHAT YOU SHOULD KNOW AND HOW TO ACTIVE IT

We are hardwired for success – and we need not settle for anything less! However, success is a relative concept. It means whatever you want it to mean. Success is meaning. The choices we have are: Is success about acquiring physical possessions and positions or – is success about who you are becoming?

Current research has revealed the existence of a new, emerging, human DNA. What were once perceived as 'junk genes', are now turning out to be biological material with inherent higher potential for us all. This potential - lying dormant within - is just waiting for us to wake up, take control, and to access this magnificent universal gift. We have the responsibility to use all the power and personal potential to deliver everyday success and miraculous living that will benefit all.

This book provides answers to several questions. What is New Success DNA? What must we know and do in order to create a life of success and prosperity? We are awakening to a new personal and collective identity – we are finding life to be a 'miracle in the making'. You are invited to join the journey.

See the New success DNA website:
http://www.newsuccessdna.com

For workshops see:
http://www.brendahattingh.com

For e-books see website:
http://www.brendahattinghshop.co.za

NEW LEADERSHIP DNA.

DEVELOPING ENLIGHTENED LEADERS

We all have a special guide-spot – an inner GPS. When we connect, we can access directions and find answers to our questions. Leadership is about initiating and directing positive change and movement. The focus is however, now moving from 'power-over-people; to 'releasing-power-within-people'. Leadership and power positions are changing from 'power-in-numbers' to the 'number-of-powers' in each individual. Everyone has a prominent role to play to secure a safe transition into a successful future that will benefit all. We now need everyone to take up their responsibility. Power shifts and changing positions in leadership are placing increasing demands on the *status quo* while challenging fixed traditional mindsets. At the same time individual awareness is growing that there is something better and that we all deserve a quality life. This new consciousness is causing the old to disintegrate at a rapid pace and new needs are arising.

At the same time research provides proof, that we have the true essence of success and quality leadership already encoded into our DNA, our guide-spot. All we need to do is to develop the new mindset, skills and tools in order to connect to gain access to universal guidance and direction. Everyone deserves health, wealth and happiness and has a role to play.
A new wave of inspired innovative leaders, with New Success DNA and New Leadership DNA, is emerging. This book provides guidelines, skills and tools for everyone who is committed to successful living and quality leadership for all.

See our leadership website:
http://www.powerintelligence..net

For workshops see:
http://www.brendahattingh.com

For e-books see website:

http://www.brendahattinghshop.co.za

POWER INTELLIGENCE.

MASTERING YOUR MIRACLE MIND

Current research has revealed a guide spot, a miracle mind, primarily situated in the frontal lobes of the human brain. When we consciously connect to this spot, also known as the God spot, we have access to the infinite potential, or power-on-hold, of the universe. With the necessary understanding, skills and tools we can tap into and utilize our universal intelligence, guidance and wisdom. Here we find the power to create miracles!

At the same time we find an emergence of new human DNA. Once perceived as 'junk genes' are now turning out to be higher potential, or God genes, encoded into our biological material. Power Intelligence (PI) is the conscious ability to utilize our infinite potential and create success and prosperity for all. PI is the conscious ability to develop our miracle or master mind. Great Masters used this ability to turn water into wine, manifest bread and fish and heal the sick. We are commanded to do the same. You are invited to reclaim your personal and universal power and join the adventure.

The time for us to develop Power Intelligence and become miracle minded is here.

See the Power Intelligence website:
http://www.powerintelligence..net

For workshops see:
http://www.brendahattingh.com

For e-books see website:
http://www.brendahattinghshop.co.za

LIFE – STUMBLING BLOCK OR STEPPING STONE?

The quality of your life is a choice. Everything in your life *you* have chosen on a conscious or unconscious level. There are no victims. We are daily confronted with numerous choices and in essence there is only one of two points of departure. Life is a pain with many stumbling blocks to overcome – or – life is a challenge and a pleasure with many opportunities and stepping stones to higher levels of attainment. The quality of your life depends on where you are coming from.

In this book you will find five stumbling blocks that cause pain in your life. You can overcome this by identifying underlying causes and changing your perceptions, values and thinking. Part two provides five steps to a life of fulfilment, love, happiness and freedom. This book is meant for everyone, of all ages. You are never too young, or too old, to choose a quality life. You are invited to join this journey of discovery.

For e-books see website:

http://www.brendahattinghshop.co.za

Also available in Afrikaans:

Lewe –Las of Lus.

For workshops see:
http://www.brendahattingh.com

POWER INTELLIGENCE SUCCESS PROFILE (PISP)

http://www.brendahattinghshop.co.za

Your personal success assessment and

management tool

Everything in our lives is a symbol of how we choose to manage our life force or energy. The level of our self mastery determines the level of our success and fulfilment. When we become conscious that we create our own reality, we also become aware of the importance and responsibility of self mastery. We either function from a subconscious programming and foundation of anxiety and fear or we operate from inner peace, security and freedom to live a fulfilling life. People function from pain—or pleasure. They are connected or disconnected and are positive or negative. You need to choose: Where you are you coming from?

The Power Intelligence Success Profile (PISP) was developed in order to assist you on your path of self-discovery, self-mastery and a life of success and prosperity.

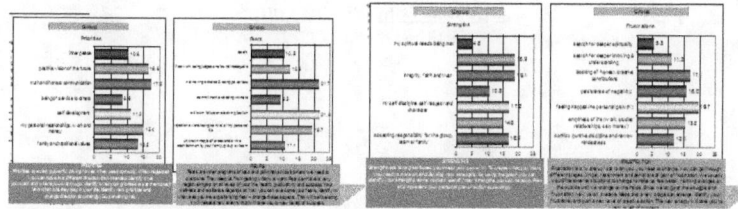

A negative disposition creates contracting forces that inhibits progress, success and anything vibrant from entering your life. This spiral of negativity not only inhibits positive growth, development and quality living, but also attracts more negativity in different forms such as illness, depression, loss and deprivation.

A positive disposition creates an expanding force, attracting more positive influences into our lives thereby expanding the success process. These expanding forces liberate us and take us to a new level of attainment and success. A new mindset and approach propels us forward on a new path of success. We can consciously activate our new success DNA.

The PISP was researched, designed and developed over the last ten years as a personal and organizational self mastery, leadership, coaching, mentoring, and management tool. It reflects the underlying dynamics within a person, team, organization or company and indicates the quality of underlying, and usually unknown, forces that influence the success process. At the same time the PISP provides guidelines how to change negative influences and enhance you positive powers and strengths. Detailed profiles assist you in becoming self aware and resilient while enhancing your wellness profile. A summary helps you to consciously master the self and realign your success path for maximum growth, development and fulfilment.

The aim of the PIPS to provide an opportunity for self assessment, deeper self knowledge and self mastery in order to activate new Success DNA and create success and prosperity that will benefit all.

Please see our other websites:
http://www.brendahattingh.com
http://www.newsuccessdna.com
http://www.powerintelligence.net
http://www.nsdcommunity.org
http://www.brendahattinghshop.co.za
or email us
info@newsuccessdna.com

REFERENCES

[1] Forgiveness: To forgo the choice of revenge (revenge means: speak with the same voice – just loader, and more violent) and to speak with a new, constructive, uplifting voice. To resonate on a higher level. See glossary: Revenge; forgiveness.

[2] See René's website: http://www.gardenvisits.com (available from Jan 2013)

Chapter 1: History of leaders and leadership.

[3] For different levels of leadership see:
Scouller, J. 2011. *The Three Levels of Leadership: How to develop your leadership presence, know how and skill.* Management Books 2000. Gloucestershire.
Collins, J. 2001. *From good to great.* HarperBusiness. New York.
Clawson, James G. 2011. *Level Three Leadership: Getting Below the Surface.* Prentice Hall. US.
Maxwell, J. 2011. *Five levels of leadership.* Hodder & Stoughton Ltd. London.
Four levels of leadership. http://www.MentoringLeaders.com.

[4] Hattingh, B. 2012 (a). *New Success DNA. What you should know and how to active it.* Xlibris Publishing. London.

[5] For more on the history of leadership see:
Stone, A.G. Patterson, K. 2005. *The History of Leadership Focus.* School of Leadership Studies. Regent University.
Tudor Rickards, Tudor. 2007. A brief history of leadership. Website: http://www.slideshare.net/Tudor/a-brief-history-of-leadership.

[6] Helen Eckman. See Website:
http://www.jameslconsulting.com/documents/history-of-leadership-studies.pdf

[7] Odysseus or Ulysses: See glossary.

[8] Mentor: See Glossary.

[9] Roberts, Andy. 1999. The origins of the term 'mentor'. *History of Education Society Bulletin,* No. 64, November 1999, p. 313–329.

[10] Hanzhang, Tao. & Wilkinson, Robert. 1998. *The Art of War.* Wordsworth Editions. UK.
McNeilly, Mark R. 2001. *Sun Tzu and the Art of Modern Warfare.* Oxford University Press. Oxford.

[11] Brungardt, C. L. 1996. The making of leaders: A review of the research in leadership development and education. The Journal of Leadership Studies 3 (3): 81–95.
Rost, J.C. (1991). *Leadership for the twenty-first century.* Praeger Press. NY.
For more information see: http://en.wikipedia.org/wiki/Leadership_studies.

[12] Doh, J. P 2003. Can leadership be taught? Perspectives from management educators. *Academy of Management Learning and Education.* 2 (1): 54–67.

[13] For more on the history of leadership see:
Gregory Stone,A.G. Patterson, K. 2005. *The History of Leadership Focus.* School of Leadership Studies. Regent University.
Tudor Rickards, Tudor. 2007. A brief history of leadership. Website: http://www.slideshare.net/Tudor/a-brief-history-of-leadership.

[14] Chemers M. 1997. *An integrative theory of leadership.* Lawrence Erlbaum Associates Publishers. UK.

[15] Hollander, E. P., & Julian, J. W. 1969. Contemporary trends in the analysis of leadership processes. *Psychological Bulletin, 71,* 387-397.

[16] Mumford, M. D., Zaccaro, S. J., Harding, F. D., Jacobs, T. O., & Fleishman, E. A. (2000). Leadership skills for a changing world solving complex social problems. The Leadership Quarterly, 11(1), 11-35.
Stogdill, R. M. 1974. Handbook of leadership: A survey of the literature. Free Press. New York.

[17] Käsler, Dirk. 1988. *Max Weber: an introduction to his life and work.* University of Chicago Press. Chicago.

[18] See glossary: 'authority'

[19] See website: http://en.wikipedia.org/wiki/Max_Weber.

[20] Calling: To request or order someone to do something; a strong urge to follow a particular path or do a particular type of work. See glossary.

[21] Homo sapiens. 'Knowing man' or 'conscious human being'. 'Man' referring to all of humanity. See glossary.

[22] Adam: collective word for 'human kind'.

[23] See: The Holy Bible. Genesis 4:
Also see the view of Sitchin in:
Sitchin, Z. 1990. *Genesis revisited.* HarperCollins. New York.
Sitchin, Z. 1997. *Devine Encounters.* HarperCollins. New York.
Sitchin, Z. 2001. *The Wars of Gods and men.* HarperCollins. New York.
Sitchin, Z. 2006. *The lost realities.* HarperCollins. New York.

[25] Also called "cylinder seals."

[26] A primate belonging to a family of which the modern human being is the only species still in existence. Family: *Hominidae.*

[27] Charles, R.H. 2007. *The book of Enoch.* Forgotten Books. Charleston, S/Carolina.

[28] Kramer, Samuel, N. 1959. *History begins at Sumer.* University of Pennsylvania Press; (3rd edition. April 1, 1988).

[29] Kiln: Furnace for making bricks. See glossary for more meanings.

[30] Build your family tree: See http://www.genebase.com/
See: www.rense.com/general12/ritd.htm

[31] Charles, R.H. 2007. *The book of Enoch.* Forgotten Books. Charleston, S/Carolina.

[32] Nimrod: according to the Book of Genesis and Books of Chronicles, the son of Cush and great-grandson of Noah and the king of Shinar. He is depicted in the Tanakh as a man of power in the earth, and a mighty hunter. Extra-Biblical traditions associating him with the Tower of Babel led to his reputation as a king who was rebellious against God. Several Mesopotamian ruins were given Nimrod's name by 8th century Arabs

[33] See: Hattingh, Brenda. 2012(a). *New success DNA.What you should know and how to activate it.* Xlibris Publishing. London. Chapter 3.

[34] See; Multi-dimensional realities in Hattingh. B. New Success DNA

408

[35] Hamer, Dean. 2005. *The God gene. How faith is hardwired into our genes*.
      Amcor Publishers. New York.
      Wheatly, MJ. 1992. Leadership and the New Science. Learning about
      organization from an Orderly Universe. Berrett-Koehler Publishers. San
      Francisco.
[36] See the list of books by Zecharia Sitchin for more information concerning
      archaeological findings and evidence.
[37] See: Gen 2:7
[38] Adam: collective name for human beings as male and female beings.
[39] Nowak, R. *Mining treasures from "junk DNA"*. 1994. Science 161: 529-540.
      Hamer, Dean. 2005. *The God gene. How faith is hardwired into our genes*.
      Amcor Publishers. New York.
[40] Assmann, J. 2002. *The Mind of Egypt*. Metropolitan Books. New York.
[41] Gilbert, J. & Hall, B. 2009. The Upliftment of Consciousness. Book One. Ancient Wisdoms
      Publications. Johannesburg.
[42] For more information on the kings of Israel see: I & II Kings. Holy Bible.
[43] See: I Kings 11:42.
      For more on King Solomon see website:
            http://www.angelfire.com/sc3/we_dig_montana/Solomon.html
[44] See: I Kings 3:4-15.
[45] See websites:
            http://sacc-usa.org/currents/business/per-winblad-leadership-lessons-from-
            king-solomon/
            http://www.angelfire.com/sc3/we_dig_montana/Solomon.html
[46] Stevens, Marty E. 2006. *Temples, tithes, and taxes: the temple and the economic
      life of ancient Israel*. Hendrickson Publishers. Massachusetts.
      See: http://en.wikipedia.org/wiki/Solomon's_Temple
[47] II Chron. 9:1-12.
[48] See website: http://www.mmscanadianhq.com/what-is-a-mystery-
      school/#Scene_1
[49] Mystery schools: Initially found in Israel, Egypt and the East.
            Modern Mystery Schools offer advanced spiritual teachings, to guide you to your
            source of deep spiritual knowledge and wisdom. These sacred ancient tools and
            teachings come from a linage, over 3000 years old and offer you the highest level of
            spiritual growth and fulfilment that is available in the world. Mystery schools are
            found all over the globe today. Schools also on the etheric planes
            See website: http://www.modernmysteryschool.com/
      Important Mystery School in Egypt. See website: http://www.opencheops.org/
            It is claimed that Jesus Christ attended this mystery school during His stay
            in Egypt.
[50] See: Exodus 7: 11-13.
            http://www.supernaturalwiki.com/index.php?title=Staff_of_Moses
[51] 'Great Work': Divine will, divine purpose, God's will. Universal perfection(perfect- union).
      See website: http://evolutionaryspirituality.wikia.com/wiki/
[52] Hamer, Dean. 2005. *The God gene. How faith is hardwired into our genes*.
      Amcor Publishers. NewYork.
      See: New Success DNA
[53] "Know thyself" is an ancient aphorism of uncertain authorship. "To thine own
            self be true is said by the fictional character Polonius in the play Hamlet,
            by William Shakespeare.
      See website: http://wiki.answers.com/Q/Who_said_Know_thyself_

[54] Brown, Dan. 2009. *The Da Vinci Code*. Anchor Publishing. Harpswell, ME.
Brown, Dan. 2006. *Angels and Demons*. Washington Square Press. New York.
Brown, Dan. 2009. *The lost symbol*. Doubleday Books. UK.

[55] This date is based on the descriptions of warfare in the text, and on the similarity
of text's prose to other works completed in the early *Warring States* period.

[56] Sun Tzu. 2008. *The Art of War: Spirituality for Conflict*. Skylight Paths.

[57] See Website: Floyd, Raymond E.
http://www.allbusiness.com/management/benchmarking-strategic-
planning/338250-1.html
Website: http://en.wikipedia.org/wiki/The_Art_of_War

[58] Jewish tradition attributes 3 books to Solomon: *Ecclesiastes, Book of Proverbs,
Song of songs.*

[59] I Kings 9:1-9.

[60] Mammon: See glossary
See: Holy Bible; Mat. 6:24; Luke. 6: 9-13.

Chapter 2: Leadership and guidance.

[61] Book of Job 39:26.

[62] Hugh Dingle and V. Alistair Drake 2007. *What is migration? BioScience*
57: 113–121.

[63] See website: http://www.google.co.za/imgres?imgurl=http://www.e-
news.com.bd/wp-content/uploads/2012/02/glob.

[64] See: http://en.wikipedia.org/wiki/Animal_navigation

[65] Semendeferi K, Damasio H, Frank R, Van Hoesen GW. 1997. The
evolution of the frontal lobes: a volumetric analysis based on three-
dimensional reconstructions of magnetic resonance scans of human
and ape brains. J. Hum Evol. April:32(4):375-88.

[66] See website: http://en.wikipedia.org/wiki/Human_migration.

[67] World Migration Report .2010 - *The Future of Migration: Building Capacities for Change*.
International Organization for Migration, 2010, retrieved 2010-11-30.

[67] Ravenstein, Ernst, G. 1885. *The Laws of Migration*. by John Corbett, Center for
Spatially Integrated Social Science.

[68] Lee, Everett S. 1966. *A Theory of Migration*. University of Pennsylvania. USA.

[69] Lee, Everett S. 1966. A Theory of Migration. University of Pennsylvania. USA.

[70] See glossary: *allele* .

[71] See website: http://en.wikipedia.org/wiki/Gene_flow.

[72] See: Power intelligence. Mastering your miracle mind. Last chapter

[73] See glossary : 'Stem cells' referring to: primary, orgininal or 'blue-print' cells.
Tuch, BE. 2006. Stem cells—a clinical update. *Australian Family Physician* 35
(9): 719–21. PMID 16969445.

[74] See website : http://en.wikipedia.org/wiki/Stem_cell

[75] See Holy Bible: Exodus 20:5

[76] Hamer, Dean. *2005. The God gene. How faith is hardwired into our genes*. Amcor
Publishers. NewYork.

[77] Glossary: See 'Stem cell therapy'.

[78] http://edition.cnn.com/2012/10/08/world/europe/sweden-nobel-prize-medicine/index.html

[79] Ibid.

[80] In the Holy Bible the crucifixion of condemned people, including Jesus, took place on a
hill known as Calvary and also known as Golgotha.

[81] See: http://en.wikipedia.org/wiki/Dias_Cross_Memorial

[82] Cross symbolism: see websites eg. http://www.crossroad.to/Books/symbols1.html

[83] See glossary: Maltese Cross

[84] See: Power Intelligence. Mastering your miracle mind.

[85] See: New Success DNA.

[86] Newton, M. 1995. *Journey of souls*. Llewellyn Publications. Minnesota.
Newton, M. 2001. *Destiny of souls*. Llewellyn Publications. Minnesota.

[87] Clayton, Peter A. 1995. *Chronicle of the Pharaohs: The Reign-by-Reign Record of the Rulers and Dynasties of Ancient Egypt*. The Chronicles Series (Reprinted ed.). Thames and Hudson. London.
See: website: http://en.wikipedia.org/wiki/List_of_pharaohs

[88] See: Exodus 7: 11

[89] Preliterate: People who do not have a written language.
Illiterate: people who have a written language but cannot read or write.

[90] See glossary for more explanations.

[91] Mauss. 2001. *A General Theory of Magic*. Routledge. UK.

[92] Blier, Suzanne Preston 1995. *Vodun: West African Roots of Vodou*. In Donald J., Cosentino. *Sacred Arts of Haitian Vodou*. Los Angeles: UCLA Fowler Museum of Cultural History. pp. 61–87.

[93] See Website: http://en.wikipedia.org/wiki/Haitian_Vodou

[94] Syncretism: The combination of different systems of philosophical or religious belief or practice. See glossary.

[95] African Spirit Worship Has Powerful Hold on Cubans. Wee Website: http://www.pi-management.com/cuba_archive/african_spirit_worship_has_power.htm

[96] South African traditional healer, shaman or herbalist.
See glossary: 'witch doctor'.

[97] See website: http://www.dnaindia.com/world/report_witch-doctors-put-the-magic-in-african-team-spirit_1391080

[98] Gerfand, M. 1970. UNHU—The Personality of the Shona. *Studies in Comparative Religion*, Vol. 4, No. 1 (Winter). World Wisdom, Inc.
See Website: http://www.studiesincomparativereligion.com/Public/articles/browse_g.aspx?ID=123

[99] See website: http://www.southafrica.info/about/government/govtrad.htm#

[100] Price, J.C. *Potential Contributions of Eastern Philosophies and Martial Arts in Understanding Leadership*. Paper presented at Capella University.
See website: http://www.gyokko.com/Papers/Leadership.

[101] Lao Tzu. 1996. *The Tao Te Ching*. St. Martin's Griffin. Minotaur.
Dyer, W. 2009. *Change Your Thoughts - Change Your Life: Living the Wisdom of the Tao*. Hay House. London.

[102] Whitson, William . 1973. *The Chinese High Command*. Praeger. Santa Barbara.

[103] Weber, Max. Henderson, A.M. Parsons,T. (Editor). 2012. *The Theory of Social and Economic Organization*. Martino Fine Books. Eastford, CT.

[104] Caste system: The class and rank or position of somebody in a society, according to birth, occupation, or some other criterion. See glossary.

[105] See website: http:// *en.wikipedia.org/wiki/Max_Weber*

[106] See Website: http://en.wikipedia.org/wiki/Douglas_McGregor.
Website: http://en.wikipedia.org/wiki/Theory_X_and_Theory_Y.

[107] Regan, Donald. 1988. *For the Record: From Wall Street to Washington*. Harcourt. New York.

[108] Quigley, Joan. 1990. *What Does Joan Say?: My Seven Years as White House Astrologer to Nancy and Ronald Reagan*. Carol Publishing Group. New York.

Regan, Donald. 1988. *For the Record: From Wall Street to Washington*. Harcourt. New York.

Reagan, Ronald. 2011. *An American Life*. Threshold Editions. New York.

[109] Von Bulow, Harry. 2003. *God and Ronald Reagan: God Moves in the Affairs of Men*. AuthorHouse. UK

[110] See website: http://www.people.com/people/archive/article/0,,20099022,00.html

[111] Teisser, Elizabeth. 1997. *Sous Le Signe de Mitterrand*. (Under the Sign of Mitterrand). Edition1. UK.

[112] Sorbonne: A part of the University of Paris, founded in 1253, that contains the faculties of science and literature.

[113] Puntch: A sudden planned attempt to overthrow a government using military force.

See website: http://www.destle.com/article/Rustam-E-Hind/Famous-people-and-Astrologers-Part-2.htm

[114] Wulff, Wilhelm & Laqueur, Walter. 1973. *Zodiac and Swastika: How Astrology Guided Hitler's Germany*. Coward, McCann & Geoghegan.

See website: http://www.destle.com/article/Rustam-E-Hind/Famous-people-and-Astrologers-Part-2.htm

[115] See website: http://www.wsws.org/articles/2001/sep2001/sorb-s21.shtml.

[116] Muti: The name given to medicine given by a Sangoma and can contain Anything, like lion fat for courage and rhino horn for power and magic. (Rhino horn is generally viewed as aphrodisiac, but its power is also said to be used to strengthen leaders). See Glossary.

[117] See: Encyclopædia Britannica, 1911: "Unicorn"

See: http://en.wikipedia.org/wiki/Unicorn/

[118] See: http://www.allaboutunicorns.com/chinese-unicorns.php

[119] Lavers, Chris. 2009. *The Natural History of Unicorns*. Granta Books. London.

[120] See: http://www.heraldsnet.org/

[121] St James Holy Bible: Numbers 23-22.

[122] See: Encyclopædia Britannica, 1911: "Unicorn"

[123] Beer, Rüdiger Robert. 1977. *Unicorn: Myth and Reality*. Mason/Charter. Brighton.

[124] Kh oza, Mandla. 2012. May 11. *Rhino horn and muti*.
Website: http://uniteagainstpoaching.co.za/

[125] The Holy Bible. King James Version. 2006. Cambridge University Press. London. New Testament

[126] The Koran. The Qur'an. Oxford World's Classics. 2008. M.A. Abdel Haleem. Oxford University Press, USA.

Quran - Wikipedia, the free encyclopedia. *en.wikipedia.org/wiki/**Quran.***

[127] The Bhagavad Gita: The gospel of the Lord Shri Krishna 1977.
Translated by Shri Purchit Swami. Vintage Books. Random House Group. London.

[128] The Kybalion. 1912. The Yogi Publication Society. Chicago

[129] Brooks, Polly Schoyer. 1999. *Beyond the Myth: The Story of Joan of Arc*. Houghton Mifflin Co. New York.

[130] Wagner, Stephen. *Presidents and the Paranormal: Washington*.
Website: http://www.about.com.

[131] Nigosian, Solomon Alexander. 1993. *The Zoroastrian Faith: Tradition and*

Modern Research. McGill-Queen's University Press. Kingston, Canada.
132 See: The Oxford Dictionary of Philosophy.
133 Today they are known as 'missionaries'.
134 See glossary. Mission, missionary.
135 Website: http://members.efn.org/~opal/therealmagi.html.
See: Rev. Phil Greetham. 1996.
Website: http://www.btinternet.com/~prgreetham/Wisemen/wmsoc1.html.
136 Website: http://worldhistory1a.homestead.com/zarathustra.html.
137 See glossary.
138 Websites: http://antroposofi.org/mellett/twojesus.htm.
139 Websites: http://antroposofi.org/mellett/twojesus.htm.
140 See: Matthew 2: See website:http://www.biblegateway.com.
Geza Vermes. 2006. *The Nativity: History and Legend.* PenguinBooks. London.
141 Nigosian, Solomon Alexander. 1993. *The Zoroastrian Faith: Tradition and Modern Research.* McGill-Queen's University Press. Kingston, Canada.
142 See the works of Zecharia Sitchin.
Sitchin, Z. 2006. *The lost realities.* HarperCollins. New York.

Chapter 3: Fundamental principles of New Leadership DNA

143 Gilbert, Adrian & Cotterell, Maurice. 1996. *The Mayan Prophecies.* Element Books Limited. Brisbane.
144 Coe, M. D. 1994. *Breaking .the Mayan Code.* Penguin Books. New York.
Bolio, J.D. 1987. *The Geometry of the Mayan.* Mayan Area. (Unknown binding).
Cotterell, M. 1988. *Astrogenetics.* Brooks, Hill, Robinson & Co. New York.
Coe, M. D. 1994. The Mayan. Thames and Hudson. London.
145 Gilbert, Adrian & Cotterell, Maurice. 1996.
146 Etymologically, the word is assumed to derive from Late Latin 'mammon', from Greek 'mámóna' (riches), Hebrew meaning wealth or possessions, although it may also have meant 'that in which one trusts'. See glossary 'mammon'.
147 Maxwell, J. 2011. *Five levels of leadership.* Hodder & Stoughton Ltd. London.
148 Hattingh, B. 2012 (b). *Power Intelligence. Mastering your miracle mind.* Currency Communications.Johannesburg..
149 Hattingh, Brenda. 2012(a). *New success DNA. What you should know and how to activate it.* Xlibris Publishing. London.
150 It is not the purpose of this book to repeat all that has been written on Leadership. For more information see: http://en.wikipedia.org/wiki/Leadership_studies.
151 Alchemy: A traditional chemical philosophy having as its asserted aims the transmutation of base metals into gold; any seemingly power or process of transmuting; the art of transmutation.
152 See: Hattingh, B. *New success DNA.*
153 Ibid.
154 The word radical comes from "radix" meaning "root". We are forced to revisit our roots and reevaluate our foundations.
155 See multi-dimensions in New Success DNA. Chapter 3.
156 Website: http://www.newsuccessdna.com.

Chapter 4: Leadership, power and influence

157 Jung, C. 1970. *The structure and dynamics of the psyche*: The collective works of Carl Jung. Edited and translated by G. Adler & R.F.C. Hull. Princeton University Press. Princeton.

[158] Covey, S.R. 1992. *The seven habits of highly effective people*. Simon &
        Schuster. London.
[159] Hawkins (2002).
[160] Csikszentmihali, M. 1993. *The evolving Self. A Psychology for the third
        Millennium*. HarperCollins Publishers. New York.
[161] Maslow, A. 1998. *Toward a Psychology of Being*. 3rd Edition. John Wiley &
        Sons. Oxford. UK.
[162] Einstein, A. 1923. *The Principals of Relativity*. Dover Publications. New York.
        Capra, F. 1990. The turning point: Science, society and the rising culture.
        HarperCollins. London.
[163] Wilber, K. 2000. *Integral Psychology. Consciousness, Spirit, Psychology,
        Therapy*. Shambala Press. Boston.
[164] Brennan, B.A. 1988. *Hands of light*. Bantam Books. New York.
        Brennan, B.A. 1993. *Light emerging*. Bantam Books. New York
        Pribram. K. 1987. The Implicate Brain. In B.J. Hiley and F. David Peat, (eds)
        Quantum Implications: Essays in Honour of David Bohm, Routledge.
[165] Capra, F. 1990. The turning point: Science, society and the rising culture.
        HarperCollins. London.
        Wilber, K. 2000. *Integral Psychology. Consciousness, Spirit, Psychology,
        Therapy*. Shambala Press. Boston.
[166] See: New Success DNA.
[167] Bohm, D. 1980. *Wholeness and the implicate order*. Routledge & Kegan.
        London.
        Einstein, A. 1934. *Essays in Science*. Philosophical Library. New York.
[168] Toffler, A. 1991. *The Power shift*. Pan Books Ltd. London.
[169] Wheatly, MJ. 1992. Leadership and the New Science. Learning about
        Organization from an Orderly Universe. Berrett-Koehler Publishers.
        San Francisco.
        Wilber, (2000). Capra, (1996).
[170] Mehrtens, S. 1999. The waves of change. *People Dynamics*. South Africa,
        February, 29-34.
        Capra, (1996).
[171] Einstein (1934); Bohm (1980).
[172] Wilber, (2000).
[173] Bohm, (1980); Capra, (1991); Einstein, (1934); Wilber,(2000).
[174] Bunson, M.E. (ed.). 2000. *The Dalai Lama's Book of Wisdom*. Random House.
        London.
[175] Grof, Stanislav. 1990. *The holotropic mind*. San Francisco: Harper Collins
        Publishers. SanFrancisco.ilber, (2000); Capra, (1996).
[176] Capriles, E. 2000. Beyond Mind: Steps to a Metatranspersonal Psychology.
        Honolulu, HI: The International Journal of Transpersonal Studies,
        19:163-184.
        Sutich, A.J. 1976. The Emergence of the Transpersonal Orientation: A Personal
        Account. Journal of Transpersonal Psychology, 1.
[177] Lajoie, D. H. & Shapiro, S. I. 1992. Definitions of transpersonal psychology:
        The first twenty-three years. *Journal of Transpersonal Psychology,* Vol.24
[178] Reich, W. 1979. *Selected Writings*. Farrar, Strauss & Giroux. New York.
[179] Capra (1996).
[180] Jung (1970).
[181] Hawkins, D. 2002. *Power vs. force: The hidden determinants of human
        behavior*. Hay House. New York.

[182] Hawkins, (2002).
[183] Myss, C. 1997. *The anatomy of the spirit: The seven stages of power and healing*. Bantam Books. New York.
Brennan, 1993; 1999); .
[184] Dale, C. 1996. *New chakra healing*. Faradawn Publishers. New York.
Brennan,(1993, 1999); Capra, (1996);
[185] Gerber, R. 1988. *Vibrational medicine*. Bear & Co. Santa Fe, NM.
[186] Bohm, (1980); Grof,(1990); Pribram, (1987); Wilber, (1984).
[187] The TV show MENTALIST reveals these abilities in action.
[188] Brennan, (1993); Dale, (1999); Gerber, (2001); Wilber,(2000).
[189] Intelligence: '*Intel*' means "*between* two" & '*ligence*' means "to choose".
[190] Beck, D.E. & Cowan, C.C. 1996. *Spiral dynamics: Mastering values, leadership and change*. Blackwell Publishers. Cambridge.
[191] Capra, (1996).
[192] Gribbin, John. 1984. *In Search of Schroedingers Cat. Quantum Physics and Reality*. Bantam Books. New York.
Herbert, N. 1987. *Quantum Reality: Beyond the New Physics*. Ancor Books. New York.
Talbot, Micheal. 1986. *Beyond the Quantum*.Bantam Books. New York.
[193] Ryan, R.M. & Frederick, C.1997. On energy, personality and health: Subjective vitality as a dynamic reflection of well-being. *Journal of Personality*: 65, 529-565.
See: Grof, (1990); Pribram, (1977);
[194] Wilber, (2000).
[195] Beck & Cowan,(1996); Bohm, (1980); Pribram, (1977); Wilber,(2000).
[196] Capra, (1991).
[197] Zohar, D. & Marshall, I. 1999. *Spiritual Intelligence. The ultimate intelligence*. Flamingo. London.
[198] Stanlislav Grof (1990).
[199] Wilber (2000).
[200] Ashby, R. 1956. *Introduction to Cybernetics*. John Wiley. New York.
Wiener, N. 1961.*Cybernetic* MIT Press. New York..
[201] Gerber, (2001).
[202] Chopra, D. 1992. *Unconditional life. Discovering the power to fulfil your dreams*.BantamBooks. New York
Deyer, W. 1992. *Real Magic. Creating miracles in everyday life*. Harper Collins Publishers. New York.
Kehoe, J. 1997. *Mind Power - Into the 21st Century*. Zoetic Inc. Canada.
[203] Grof, 1990; Csikszentmihali, (1993).
[204] Capra, (1991); Einstein, (1934); Pribram, (1977).
[205] Csikszentmihali (1993).
[206] Gerber,(2001).
[207] "Emotions" come from word *emovere,* meaning "energy to move". e-motion or "energy in motion".
[208] Cole, K.C. 1985. *Sympathetic Vibrations: Reflections on Physics as a Way of Life*. Bantam Books. New York.
[209] Hamer, D. 2005. *The God gene. How faith is hardwired into our genes*. Amcor Publishers. New York.
[210] Ibid.
[211] Nowak, R. *Mining treasures from "junk DNA"*. 1994. Science 161: 529-540.
[212] Apter, M.J. 1992. *The dangerous edge: The psychology of excitement*. The Free

Press. New York.

Csikszentmihali (1990).

[213] Loehr, J. & Schwartz, T. 2003. *The Power of full engagement. Managing energy and not time*. Free Press. New York.

[214] Affluence means "full flow" and refers to material, physical, emotional, mental, psychological, spiritual and financial health and abundance

[215] Rice, P.L. 1992. *Stress and Health*. (2nd ed.). Brooks/Cole Publishing Company. Pacific Grove. CA.

Ryan, R.M. & Frederick, C. 1997. On energy, personality and health: Subjective vitality as a dynamic reflection of well-being. *Journal of Personality*, 65, 529-565.

[216] Capra, (1990).

[217] Ibid.

[218] Prigogine, I. & Stengers, I. 1984. *Chaos out of Order*. Bantam Books. NY..

[219] Csikszentmihali. (1993).

[220] Wheatly, (1992).

[221] Maturana, H. & Varela, F. 1980. *Autopoiesis and Cognition: The Realization of the Living*. Reidl. London.

Jantsch, E. 1980. *The Self-Organizing Universe*. Pergamon. Oxford.

[222] Wheatly, (1992).

[223] For further reading see:

Hattingh, B. 2012. (a)New Success DNA.

Hattingh. B. 2012. (b)Power Intelligence: Mastering your miracle mind.

Chapter 5. Leadership and self-mastery

[224] See: *Harry Potter* series by JK Rowling. Major publishers: Bloomsbury in the United Kingdom and Scholastic Press in the United States. Many other publishers are also involved.

[225] White wizards/ witches: Stand for the light and use of positive energy, constructive forces and higher spiritual gifts in service of others.

Black wizards/witches stand for evil, dark and destructive forces and the destructive use and abuse of spiritual powers in order to gain power over others and for their own use.

Different moderns day names include: prophets, mediums, seers, psychics, shamans. See glossary.

[226] See website: http://en.wikipedia.org/wiki/Harry_Potter

[227] Bigotry: Prejudice, racism, intolerance, bias, narrow-mindedness, chauvinism. See glossary.

[228] Smith, Sean. 1999. *J K Rowling. A Biography*. Michael O'Mara Books. London.

Rowling, JK (2006). "Biography". See J K Rowling website: http://www.jkrowling.com/textonly/en/biography.cfm.

[229] Kohlberg, L. 1981. *Essays on moral development*. Vol. 1. Harper & Row. NY.

[230] See: Chapter 6. Hattingh, B.E. 2012. *Power Intelligence. Mastering the miracle mind*.

[231] Hamer, Dean. 2005.The God gene. How faith is hardwired into our genes. Amcor Publishers. NY.

[232] For more on 'mystics, masters and miracles' - see Power Intelligence

[233] McGinn, Bernard. 2001. In *The Mystical Thought of Meister Eckhart*, Crossroad Publishing Company. New York.

[234] See: New Success DNA. Chapter 20.

235 See: Modern Mystery School. http://www.*mms.new-paradigm.net.*
236 See: New Success DNA. Chapter 3.
237 See: Hattingh, B. 2012. New success DNA.
238 See http://en.wikipedia.org/wiki/Solomon's_Temple
239 See: Chapter 6: Frontal Lobes. Chapter 8: Mind Wellness

Chapter 6. Leadership and neuro-functioning

240 In: Meyer, B. J. (ed.). 2002. Human physiology. Juta. Landsdowne.
241 See chapters 6-8: *Power Intelligence. Mastering you miracle mind.*
242 Icke, David. 1993. *In the Light of Experience.* Warner Books. UK.
     Icke, David. 2005. *Infinite Love is the Only Truth.* Bridge of Love Publications. UK.
     Icke, David. 1999. *The Biggest Secret:* The Book that Will Change the World.
          David Icke Books. UK.
243 Fenster, Mark . 2008. *Conspiracy Theories: Secrecy and Power in American Culture.*
          University of Minnesota Press; Minnesota. 2nd edition.
     Goertzel. 1994. *Belief in Conspiracy Theories.* Political Psychology (Political
          Psychology, Vol. 15, No. 4) 15 (4): 733–744
     Ramsay, Robin. 2006. *Conspiracy Theories.* Pocket Essentials. New York.
244 See chapters 6-8: *Power Intelligence. Mastering you miracle mind.*
245 Deacon, T.W. 1997. What makes the human brain different? *Annu. Rev.
          Anthropol.* 26: 337-57.
246 GPS: global positioning system.
247 Nowak, R. 1994. Mining treasures from "junk DNA". *Science 161:* 529-540.
248 Endacot, Micheal (ed). *The Encyclopaedia of Alternative Health.* pp. 113.
249 World Health Organization. 2005. Promoting Mental Health. A report of the
          World Health Organization, Department of Mental Health and Substance
          Abuse. *World Health Organization.* Geneva.
250 See: *Power Intelligence. Mastering the miracle mind,* Chapter 8, on mind-
          wellness. Here we only focus on the most important information
          concerning leadership.

Chapter 7. Leadership and mind-wellness

251 Koonin, EV. Senkevich, TG, Dolja, VV. 2006. The ancient virus world and
          evolution of cells. *Biol. Direct.* 2006;1:29.
252 Hattingh, B. 2012. *Life, stumbling block or stepping stone.* Xlibris publishing.
          London Chapter 10.
253 See : Wikipedia : http://en.wikipedia.org/wiki/Introduction_to_viruses.
254 Although most of this information is on the internet in various forms,
          more scientific and technical information is accessible from Wikipedia:
          Viruses: http://en.wikipedia.org/wiki/viruses.
255 HIV - human immunodeficiency virus (HIV)
     AIDS - 'Acquired immune deficiency syndrome' or 'acquired immuno-
     deficiency syndrome'.
256 See glossary: Insanity.
257 Useless – los of authentic use; dysfunctional.
258 Hattingh, B. 2012. *Life, stumbling block or stepping stone.* Xlibris Publishing. Londond.
          See chapters 9 & 10.
259 Ibid:
260 Foundation for Inner Peace. 1996. A course in miracles. Penguin Books. New York.
261 See: New Success DNA. (pp. 370-372)

[262] See chapter 14 in this book on human emotions.
[263] Lipton, B. 2008. *The biology of belief.* Hay House. CA.
[264] See New Success DNA: Chapter 5.
[265] Nowak, R. 1994. Mining treasures from "junk DNA". *Science* 161: 529-540.
    See glossary: 'Junk genes'
[266] See Chapter 14: Emotional mastery
[267] See: New Success DNA
[268] Available late 2012 -2013.
    Hattingh, B. *Powertools for power people.*
[269] Training in *Power Intelligence DNA Healing:* Commences Sept. 2012.
    Appropriate candidates will be accredited to use all the information, PI Profile,
    and practical methods in their counselling, coaching and mentoring practices.
    It can be used for personal coaching and mentoring as well.
    For more details see website: www.brendahaattingh.com.
[270] See website: www.cancer.org
[271] See: The Rocky Mountain Mystery School (aka: Modern Mystery School). Website:
    http:www.RMMSint.com.
[272] Hamer, Dean. 2005. *The God gene: How faith is hardwired into our genes.* Amcor
    Publishers. New York.
[273] Hattingh, B. 2012 (a). *New Success DNA.*
    Hattingh, B. 2012 (b). *Power Intelligence. Mastering your miracle mind.*

Chapter 8. Leadership, guidance and the frontal lobe

[274] Semendeferi *et al.* 1997. 1997. The evolution of the frontal lobes: J. Hum Evol.
    April:32(4):375-88.
[275] See: *Power Intelligence. Mastering the Miracle Mind* for more comprehensive outline of
    neuro-transmitters.
[276] Swanson, L. W. and Petrovich. G. D. August 1998. What is the amygdala?
    Trends in Neurosciences 21 (8):323–331.
[277] See: http://en.wikipedia.org/wiki/Pheromone
    See: Kohl, J., Atzmueller, M., Fink, B. & Grammar, K. 2001. Human
    Pheromones: *Integrative Neuroendocrinology & Ethology. NEL 22, 309-32. 1*
[278] Bickart, K.C., Wright, C.I., Dautoff, R. J., Dickerson, B.C., Barrett, L. F.
    Dec. 2010. Amygdala volume and social network size in humans. *Nature
    neuroscience* 14 (2): 163–164.
[279] Szalavitz, Maia. Dec. 2010. *How to win friends. Have a big Amygdala?*
    Time Healthland . See website: http://healthland.time.com/2010/12/28/
[280] Kennedy, D.P., Gläscher, J., Tyszka, J.M., Adolphs, R. 2009. Personal space
    regulation by the human amygdala. *Nat Neurosci* 12 (10): 1226–1227.
[281] Marinkovic, K., Oscar-Berman, M., Urban, T., O'Reilly, C.E., Howard, J.A.,
    Sawyer, K., Harris, G.J. November 2009. Alcoholism and dampened
    temporal limbic activation to emotional faces. *Alcohol Clin Exp Res* 33
    (11):1880–92
[282] Hutcherson, C.A., Seppala, E.M., & Gross, J.J. 2008. Loving-kindness
    meditation increases social connectedness. Emotion, 8(5), 720-724.
    Also see website: http://spl.stanford.edu/pdfs/Hutcherson_08_2.pdf.
[283] Vaughan, Susan C.2000. *Half Empty, Half Full: Understanding the Psychological Roots of
    Optimism.* Harcourt. New York.
[284] Dillard A.J., Midboe, A.M., Klein, W.M. 2009. The dark side of optimism:
    Unrealistic optimism about problems with alcohol predicts subsequent

negative event experiences. *Pers Soc Psychol Bull.35(11):1540-50.*
[285] See authours like: Vaughn (2000) and Dillard A.J., Midboe, A.M., Klein, W.M (2009)
[286] For more on improving frontal lobe functioning see internet:
[287] Koenig, H.G., McCullough M.E., Larson D.B., 2001. *Handbook of Religion and Health.* Oxford University Press. New York.
[288] Newberg A., Alavi A., Baime M., Pourdehnad M., Santanna J., d'Aquilie. 2001. The measurement of regional cerebral blood flow during the complex cognitive task of meditation. A preliminary SPECT study. *Psychiatry Research.* 106(2): 113-122.
[289] Damasio, A.R. & Anderson, S.W. 2003. The frontal lobes. In: K.. M. Heilman & E. Valenstein (ed.) *Clinical Psychology.* 4th edition. 404-406. Oxford University Press. New York.
[290] See Hattingh, B. 2012b. Power Intelligence.
[291] Mendez, F.M. & Perryman, K.M. 2002. Neuropsychiatry features of frontotemperal dymentia: Evaluation of consensus criteria and revue. *Journal of Neurosphyciatry and Clinical Neuroscience.* 4: 424-429.
[292] Saver, J.L. & Rabin, J. 1997. The neutral substrates of religious behaviour. *Journal of Neuropsychiatry:* 9:498-510.
[293] Newberg, A; Pourdehnad, M; Alavi, A; d'Aquili, E.G. 2003. Cerebral blood flow during meditative prayer. Preliminary findings and methodological issues. *Perceptual and Motorskills.* 97:625-630.
[294] See New success DNA. Chapter 7.
[295] Foundation for Inner Peace. 1996. *A course in miracles.* Penguin Books. NY.

Chapter 9. Leadership, guidance and intelligence

[296] Goleman, D. (1996). *Emotional Intelligence. Why it can matter more than IQ.* London: Bloomsbury Publishing.
[297] Gardner, H. 1983. *Frames of mind. The theory of multiple Intelligence.* Basic Books. NY.
[298] The Illustrated Dictionary of the English Language (Morris, ed. 1973).
[299] Furnham, A.,Mkhize, N. & Mndaweni, T. 2004. Indian and isizulu-speaking South African parents' estimates of their own and their children's intelligence. *South African Journal of Psychology.* 34 (3), pp. 364-385.
[300] Segall, M., Dansen, P., Berry, J. & Poortinga, Y. 1999. *Human behaviour in global perspective: an introduction to cross-cultural psychology.* New York: Allyn & Bacon.
[301] Zohar, D. & Marshall, I. 1999. *Spiritual Intelligence. The ultimate intelligence.*Flamingo. London.
[302] Hawkins, D.R. (2002). *Power vs. Force. The hidden Determinants of Human Behaviour.* Hay House Inc. New York.
[303] Canfield. J. (2005). *The success principle.* Harper Collins Publishers. London.
[304] Hattingh, B. 2012 (a). New Success DNA
[305] Capra, 1990.
[306] In Capra, (1990)
[307] Hattingh, B. Power Intelligence. Mastering your miracle mind.
[308] West, D.J. 1960. Visionary and hallucinatory experiences: A comparative appraisal. *International Journal of Parapsychology* 2 (1): 89-100.
Stevenson, I. 1983. Do we need a new word to supplement hallucination? *American Journal of Psychiatry* 140 (12): 1609-1611.
[309] See: Website: http://www.dianacooper.com
Cooper, Diana. 2008. *Enlightenment through orbs.* Findhorn Press. Scotland.

[310] Newton, Michael. 2001. *Destiny of souls*. Llewellyn Publications. Minnesota. pp 16-19.
[311] See: Bible: John 11.
[312] See Chapter: 'How to recognise and receive divine ideas and profound thoughts': In: Virtue, Doreen. 2006. *Messages from the angels*. Hay House. London. p. 173.
[313] See: *Course in Miracles*: p. Vii.
[314] See: Lazaris website: http://www.lazaris.com.
[315] Walsch, Neale Donald. 1997. *Conversations with God*. Book 1-4. Hodder&toughton.Lnd.

Chapter 10. Leadership and the Power shift

[316] Galbraith, J.K. 1983. *The Anatomy of Power*. Boston: Houghton Mifflin.Boston.
Sui, R.G. H. 1979. *The Craft of Power*. John Wiley and Sons NY.
Wing, R.L.(1986. *The Tao of Power*. Garden City. New York.
[317] Mudjanto, G. (1986). *The Concept of Power in Japanese Culture*. Gadjah Mada University Press. Jakarta.
318 First, R.(1970. *Power in Africa*.Alfred A. Knopf. NY.
[319] Pey, L.C. & Pey, M.W. (1985). *Asian Power and Politics*. Cambridge, Mass,: The Belknap Press, Harvard University Press.
[320] Toffler, A. 1971. *Future shock*. London: Pan Books Ltd.
Toffler, A. 1980. *The Third Wave*. London: Pan Books Ltd.
Toffler, A. 1991. *The Power shift*. London: Pan Books Ltd.
[321] Capra, F. 1990. The Turning Point. Science, Society and the Rising Culture. Flamingo/Harper Collins Publishers. London.
Capra, F. 1991. *The Tao of Physics. An exploration of the parallels between modern physics and Eastern mysticism*. London: Flamingo/Harper Collins Pub.
Capra, F. 1996. *The Web of Life. A new synthesis of mind and matter*. London: Flamingo/Harper Collins Publishers.
[322] Beck, D.E. & Cowan, C.C.1996. *Spiral Dynamics. Mastering values, leadership,and change*. Blackwell Publishers Inc. Massechusettes:
[323] See Power Intelligence: www.powerintelligence.net
[324] Alcock, P. 1993. *Understanding poverty*. Macmillan. London.
Allen V.L. (1970a). *The Psychology of poverty; problems and prospects*, In Allen VL.(Ed.). Psychological factors in poverty. Chicago: Markam
Butler, B. & Kondratas, A. 1987. *Out of the poverty trap*. Free Press. New York.
[325] Maslow and Grof (in Sutich, 1976).
Sutich, A.J. 1976. The Emergence of the Transpersonal Orientation: A Personal Account. *Journal of Transpersonal Psychology,* 1.
[326] In Capra, 1990.

Chapter 11. Leadership and change

[327] Kuhn, Thomas S. 1966. *The Structure of Scientific Revolutions*, 3rd Ed.: Univ. of Chicago Press. Chicago and London.
[328] Tofler, Alvin. The waves of change.
[329] Mehrtens, S. 1999. The waves of change. *People Dynamics*. South Africa, February, 29-34.
Tofler, A. The third wave (1980)
Tofler, A. Future Shock (1977)

Chapter 12. Leadership and transformation.

[330] See glossary: Homo sapiens: Latin for "wise man" or "knowing man"
[331] Boyd, Robert, Silk, Joan B. 2003. *How Humans Evolved*. Norton. NY.

See: http://en.wikipedia.org/wiki/Human

[332] These distinctions are possible 'subspecies' and are not a scientific classification. However, it gives a bit more clarity concerning different kinds of people on different levels of consciousness and how they make their choices.

[333] Joseph Takahashi discovered the first mammalian 'clock gene' .
See: Circadian rhythms: http://en.wikipedia.org/wiki/Circadian_rhythm

[334] Sharma, V.K. Nov. 2003. "Adaptive significance of circadian clocks". *Chronobiology International* **20** (6): 901–919.

Chapter 13. Leadership and New Success DNA.

[335] See: Hattingh, B. New Success DNA. 2012 (a)

[336] Csiksentmihalyi, Mihaly. *The Evolving Self* . 1993. Harper Collins Publishers. NY.

[337] For a more comprehensive explanation see New success DNA.

Chapter 14. Leadership and moving forward

[338] Lundy, James.1993. Lead ,follow or get out of the way. Pfeiffer & Co. New York.

[339] Csikszentmihali, M. 1990. *Flow. The Psychology of optimal experience*. Harper and Row. New York.

Chapter 15. Leadership and transcendence

[340] Chopra, D. 2000. *How to know God: The soul's journey into the mystery of mysteries.* Harmony Books. New York.

Chapter 19. Leadership and future demands

[341] Tolle, E. 1999. *The power of Now*. Hodder and Stoughton. London.
Tolle, E. 2005. *The New Earth: Awakening to your life's purpose*. Penguin Books. New York.
Cooper, D. 2010. *2012 and beyond*. Findhorn Press. Scotland.
Velikovsky, I. 1977. *Earth in upheaval*. Pocket Books. New York.
Velikovsky, I. 1972. *Worlds in collision*. HarperCollins. New York.

[342] National News. Sunday 19 August 2012. SABC2

[343] Sharpville Massacre: see website: http://en.wikipedia.org/wiki/Sharpeville_massacre.

[344] See Chapter 2.

[345] Also seen as the 'Body of Christ'.

[346] Power of the soul.

[347] John Donne (1572-1631), *Devotions Upon Emergent Occasions, Meditation XVII: Nunc Lento Sonitu Dicunt, Morieris.*

[348] See glossary for :'New Jerusalem'; 'City Four Square'.

[349] Also seen as the Big Bang. See: Genesis: Chapter 1. See Gen. 1:1

[350] See glossary: Destiny; Predestined.

[351] See The Holy Bible. Ps 23. King David's verse of this path back.

[352] See glossary. Master Cell.
See website: http://thetahealing.com/thetahealing-dna-activation.htm.

[353] Manifest: Meaning: to make physically visible. See glossary: Materialise;

[354] See Matt 4:3.

[355] Hattingh, B. 2012 (b) Power Intelligence. Mastering your miracle mind. Currency Communications. Johannesburg.

[356] Reference to 'love and abundance'.

Chapter 20. Training enlightened leaders

[357] Mandela, Nelson. 2008. *Long Walk to Freedom: The Autobiography of Nelson Mandela*. Little, Brown and Company. New York.

[358] See: http://www.amazon.com/Long-Walk-Freedom-Autobiography-ebook/dp/B0015T6G2G/ref=sr_1_sc_2?ie=UTF8&qid=1345378804&sr=8-2-spell&keywords=Lond+walk+to+freedom.+Nelson+Mandela

[359] Hattingh, B. 2012 (b). *Power Intelligence Mastering your miracle mind.* Currency Communications (Pty.Ltd.). Johannesburg.

[360] See website: http://www.toptenz.net/top-10-secret-societies.php.

[361] O'Grady, Tim Porter & Malloch, Kathy. 2010. *Quantum Leadership: Advancing Information, Transforming Health Care,* Third Ed.. Jones & Bartlett Learning. NY. See website: http://www.innovint.com/services/le adership_1.php

[362] John Donne (1572-1631), *Devotions Upon Emergent Occasions, Meditation XVII: Nunc Lento Sonitu Dicunt, Morieris.*

[363] The 'bigger picture' here refers to the universal body of light. Different religions have different terminology for healing the 'whole'. In Christianity it is viewed as the healing of 'The Body of Christ'.

Chapter 21. Leaders and quantum learning

[364] See: *New Success DNA* for a more comprehensive explanation.

[365] Talbot, Micheal. 1986. *Beyond the Quantum.* Bantam Books. New York. Wilber, K.1984. *Quantum Questions.* Shambala Press. Boston.

[366] Cox, B. & Forshaw, J. 2012. *The Quantum Universe.* Da Capo Press; Massachusetts.

[367] Hattingh,B. 2012 (a). New Success DNA.What you should know and how to activate it. Currency Communications (Pty.Ltd.). Johannesburg. Hattingh, B. 2012(b). Power Intelligence. Mastering the miracle mind. Currency Communications (Pty.Ltd.). Johannesburg.

[368] See website: http://library.thinkquest.org/3487/qp.html

[369] Wilber, K.1984. *Quantum Questions.* Shambala Press. Boston.

[370] See website: http://www.cosmiclight.com/

[371] NASA: http://science.nasa.gov/science-news/science at nasa/2009/29sep_cosmicrays/

[372] Time Magazine. http://www.time.com/time/magazine/article/0,9171,991839,00.html

[373] Hattingh, B. *The Path of the enlightened leader.* Currency Communications (Pty.Ltd.) Johannesburg. Will be available Jan. 2013

[374] See: Chapter 6: Frontal Lobes. Chapter 8: Mind Wellness.

[375] See glossary for: Quantum learning; quantum teachers and quantum students (learners).

[376] Mace, Myles. 1959. *Developing Executive Skills.* H. Merril and E Marting. Eds. Americal Management Association.

[377] See: Gallwey, Tim. 1974. The Inner Game of Tennis.

[378] Judge, William & Cowell, Jeffrey. 1997. *The brave new world of executive coaching.* Business Horizons; July/Aug97, Vol 40. Issue 4, 71-77.

[379] Eggers, John H. & Clark, Doug. 2000. *Executive Coaching that Wins.* Ivey Business Journal. September/October. 67-70.

[380] Meyer, M. & Fourie, L.(2004. *Mentoring and Coaching.* Knowledge Resources Publishing (Pty. Ltd). Randburg. Miller, J.B.(193) *The Corporate Coach.* St Martin' s Press. New York.

[381] See: *A course in miracles.* Manual for Teachers p.64.

[382] An early Emperor of the Xia Dynasty in China about 4,000 years ago.

www.ingramcontent.com/pod-product-compliance
Lightning Source LLC
Chambersburg PA
CBHW051437170526
45166CB00001B/25